That Time I Got Reincarnated as a Slime volume 1 is a work of fiction. Names, characters, places, and incidents are the products of the author's imagination or are used fictitiously. Any resemblance to actual events, locales, or persons, living or dead, is entirely coincidental.

A Kodansha Comics Trade Paperback Original.

Published in the United States by Kodansha Comics,
an imprint of Kodansha USA Publishing, LLC, New York.

Publication rights for this English edition arranged through Kodansha Ltd., Tokyo.

First published in Japan in 2015 by Kodansha Ltd., Tokyo, as *Tensei Shitara Suraimu Datta Ken*.

ISBN 978-1-63236-506-4

Printed in the United States of America.

www.kodanshacomics.com

9 8 7 6 5 4 3 2 1

Translation: Stephen Paul
Lettering: Evan Hayden
Editing: Ajani Oloye
Kodansha Comics edition cover design: Phil Balsman

"An emotional and artistic tour de force! We see incredible triumph, and crushing defeat... each panel [is] a thrill!"
—Anitay

"A journey that's instantly compelling."
—Anime News Network

WELCOME TO THE BALLROOM

By Tomo Takeuchi

Feckless high school student Tatara Fujita wants to be good at something—anything. Unfortunately, he's about as average as a slouchy teen can be. The local bullies know this, and make it a habit to hit him up for cash, but all that changes when the debonair Kaname Sengoku sends them packing. Sengoku's not the neighborhood watch, though. He's a professional ballroom dancer. And once Tatara Fujita gets pulled into the world of ballroom, his life will never be the same.

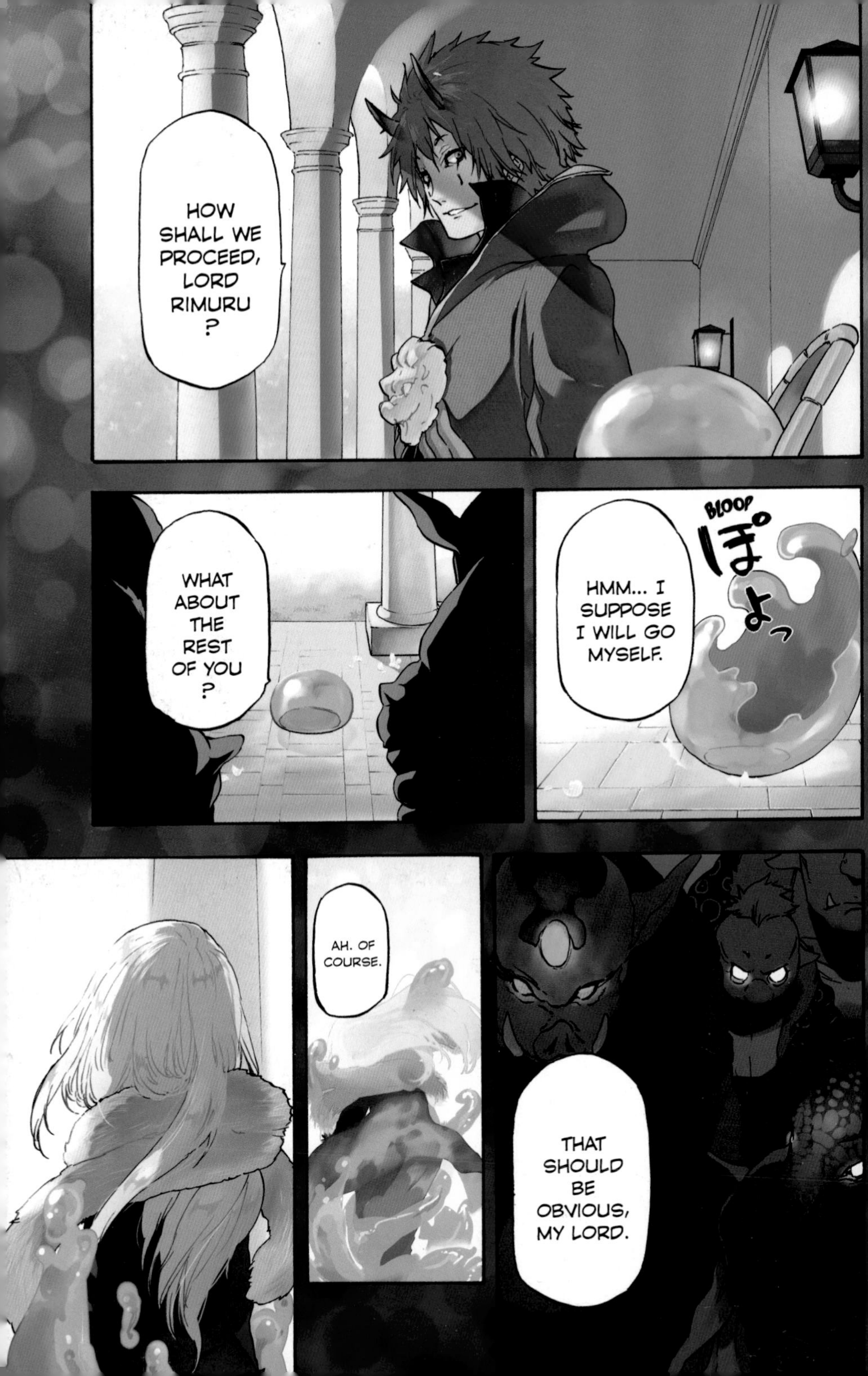
HOW SHALL WE PROCEED, LORD RIMURU?
BLOOP
ぽよっ
HMM... I SUPPOSE I WILL GO MYSELF.
WHAT ABOUT THE REST OF YOU?
THAT SHOULD BE OBVIOUS, MY LORD.
AH. OF COURSE.

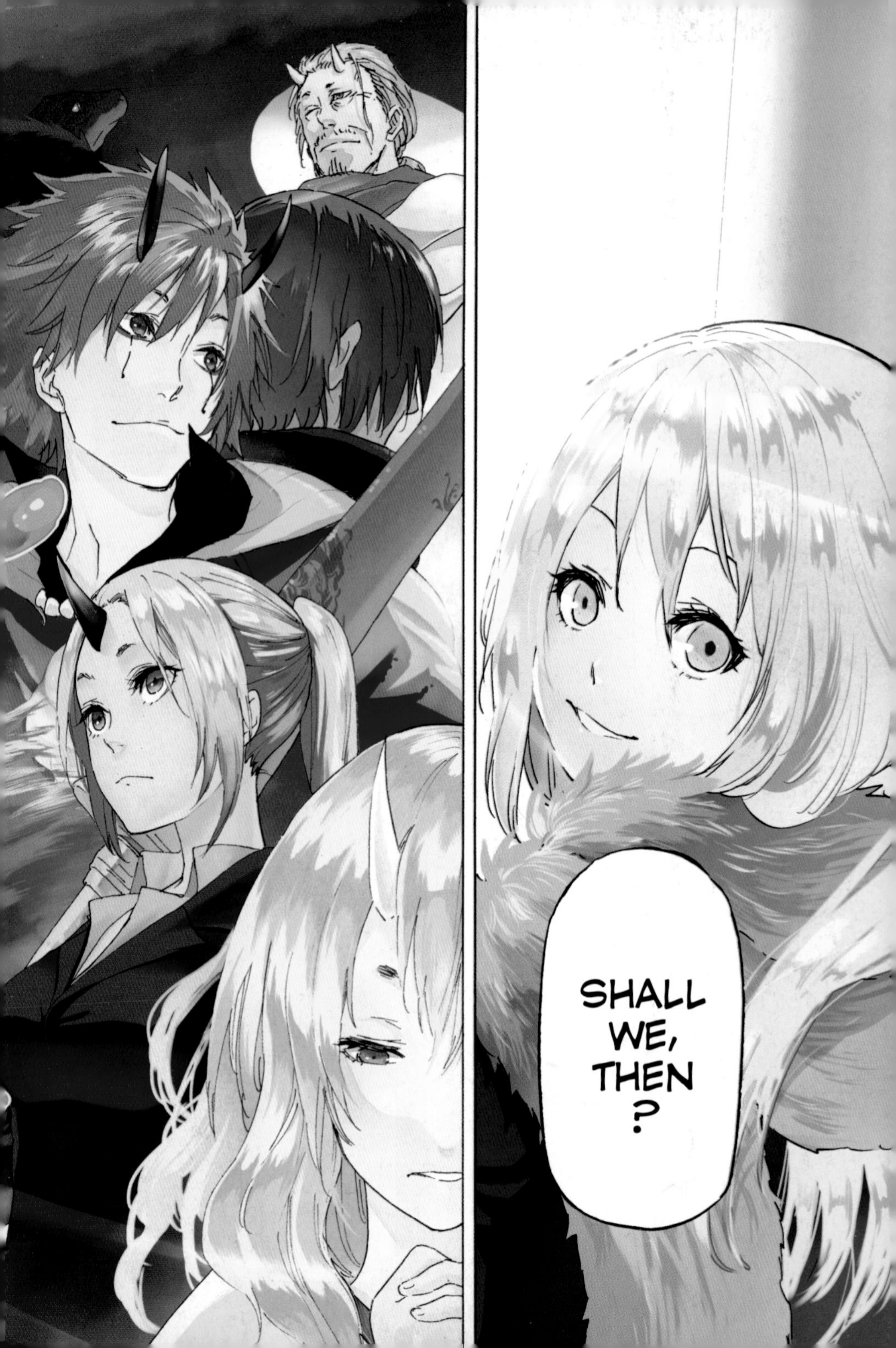
SHALL WE, THEN?

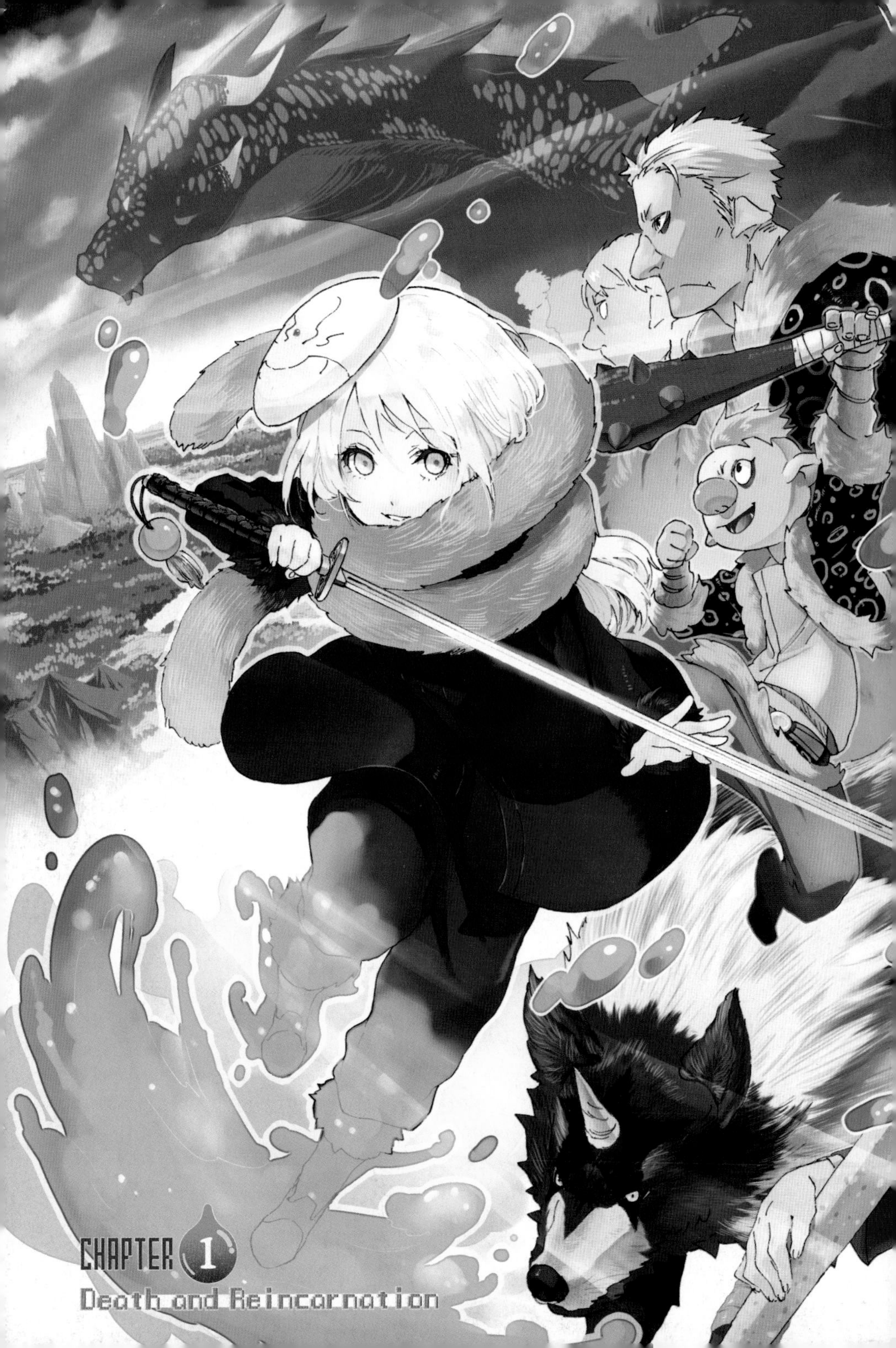
CHAPTER 1
Death and Reincarnation

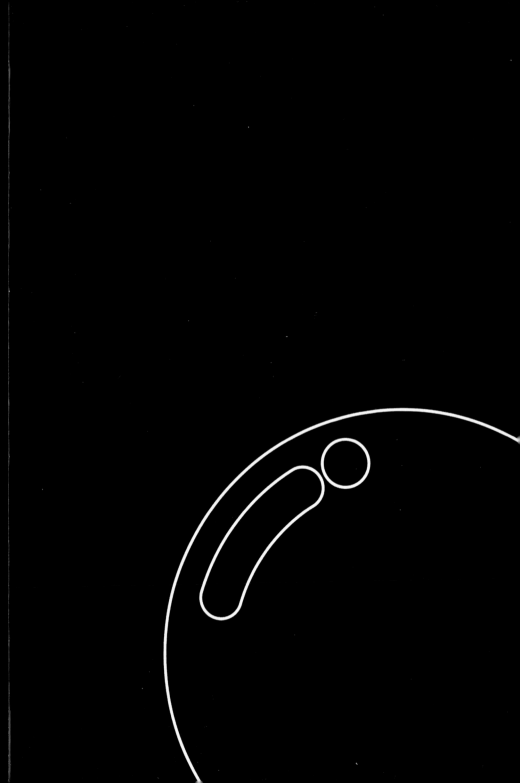

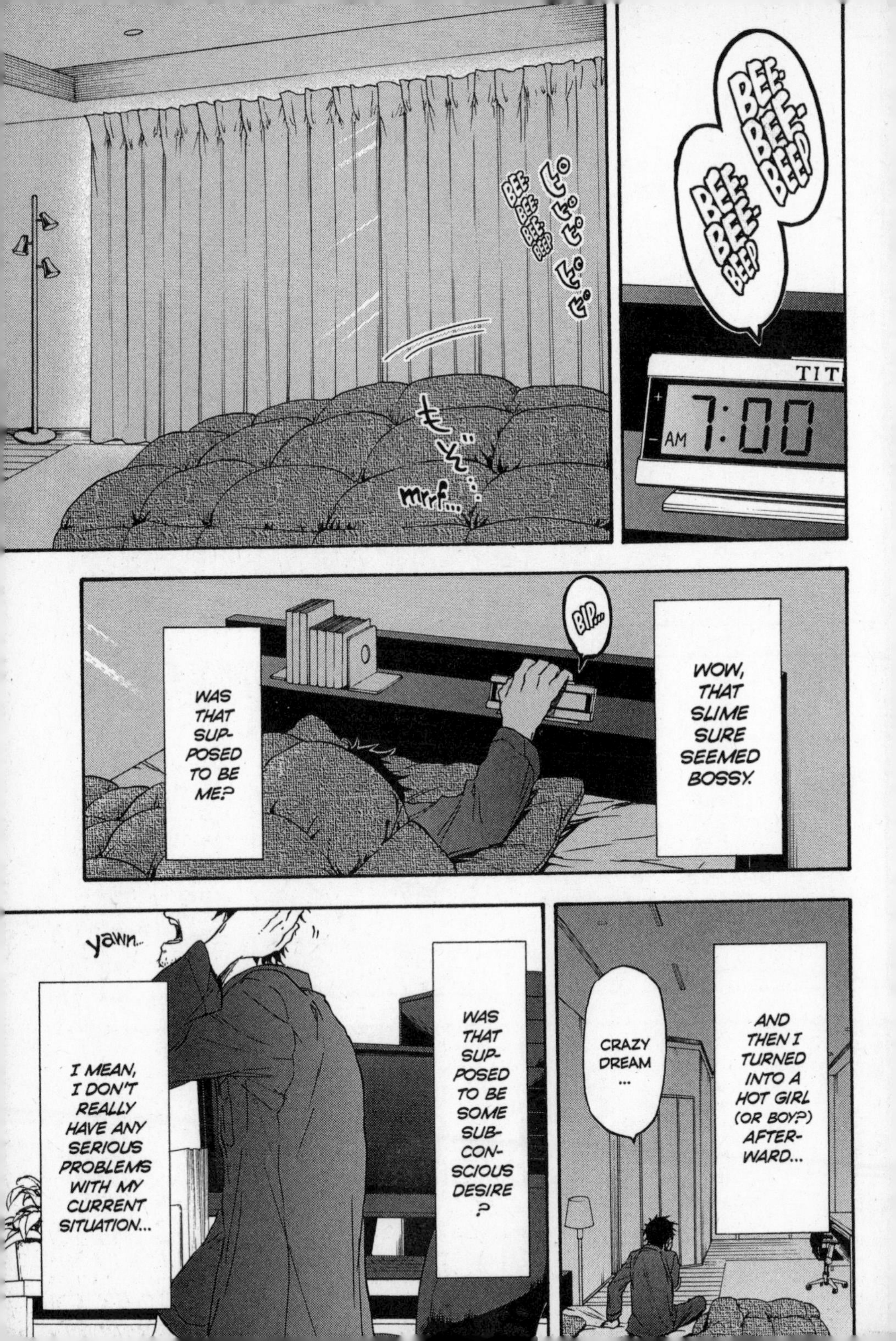
BEE-BEE-BEEP
BEE-BEE-BEEP
TIT
AM 7:00
BEE-BEE-BEE-BEEP
もぞ‥
mrrf...
WOW, THAT SLIME SURE SEEMED BOSSY.
BIP...
WAS THAT SUP-POSED TO BE ME?
AND THEN I TURNED INTO A HOT GIRL (OR BOY?) AFTER-WARD...
CRAZY DREAM ...
WAS THAT SUP-POSED TO BE SOME SUB-CONSCIOUS DESIRE?
yawn...
I MEAN, I DON'T REALLY HAVE ANY SERIOUS PROBLEMS WITH MY CURRENT SITUATION...

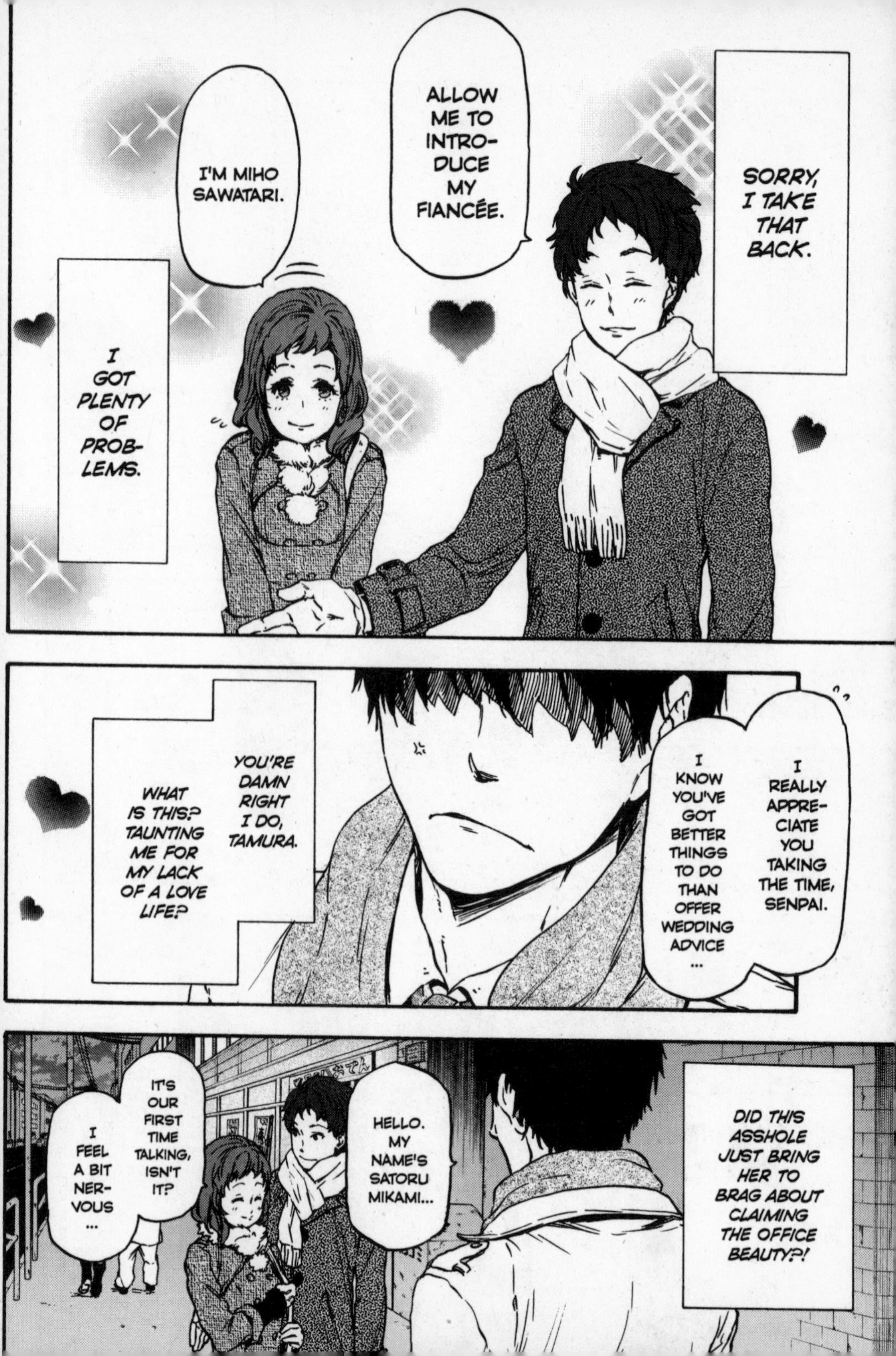
SORRY, I TAKE THAT BACK.
ALLOW ME TO INTRO-DUCE MY FIANCÉE.
I'M MIHO SAWATARI.
I GOT PLENTY OF PROB-LEMS.
I REALLY APPRE-CIATE YOU TAKING THE TIME, SENPAI.
I KNOW YOU'VE GOT BETTER THINGS TO DO THAN OFFER WEDDING ADVICE ...
YOU'RE DAMN RIGHT I DO, TAMURA.
WHAT IS THIS? TAUNTING ME FOR MY LACK OF A LOVE LIFE?
DID THIS ASSHOLE JUST BRING HER TO BRAG ABOUT CLAIMING THE OFFICE BEAUTY?!
HELLO. MY NAME'S SATORU MIKAMI...
IT'S OUR FIRST TIME TALKING, ISN'T IT?
I FEEL A BIT NER-VOUS ...

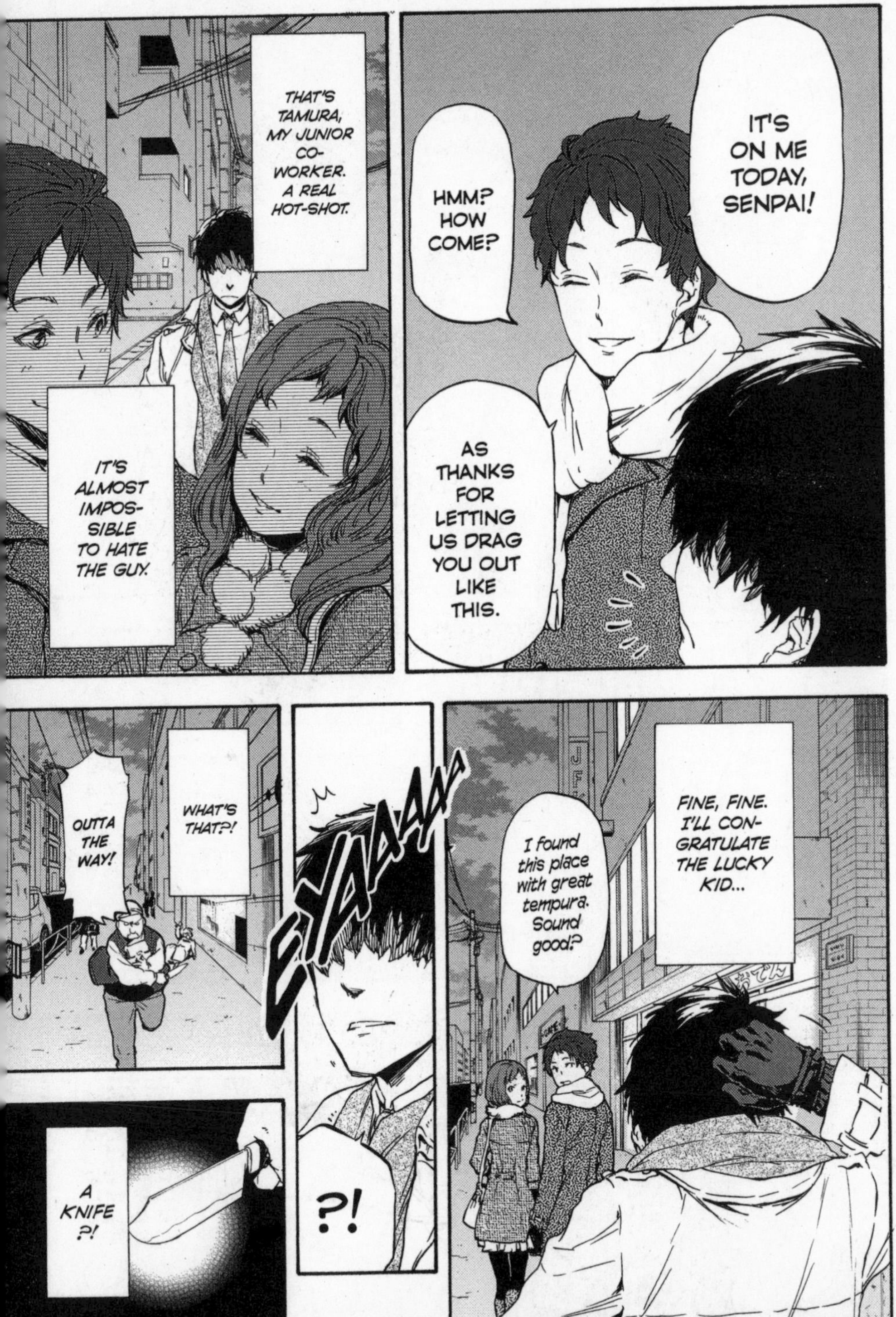
IT'S ON ME TODAY, SENPAI!
HMM? HOW COME?
AS THANKS FOR LETTING US DRAG YOU OUT LIKE THIS.
THAT'S TAMURA, MY JUNIOR CO-WORKER. A REAL HOT-SHOT.
IT'S ALMOST IMPOSSIBLE TO HATE THE GUY.
FINE, FINE. I'LL CONGRATULATE THE LUCKY KID...
I found this place with great tempura. Sound good?
EYAAAA
?!
WHAT'S THAT?!
OUTTA THE WAY!
A KNIFE ?!

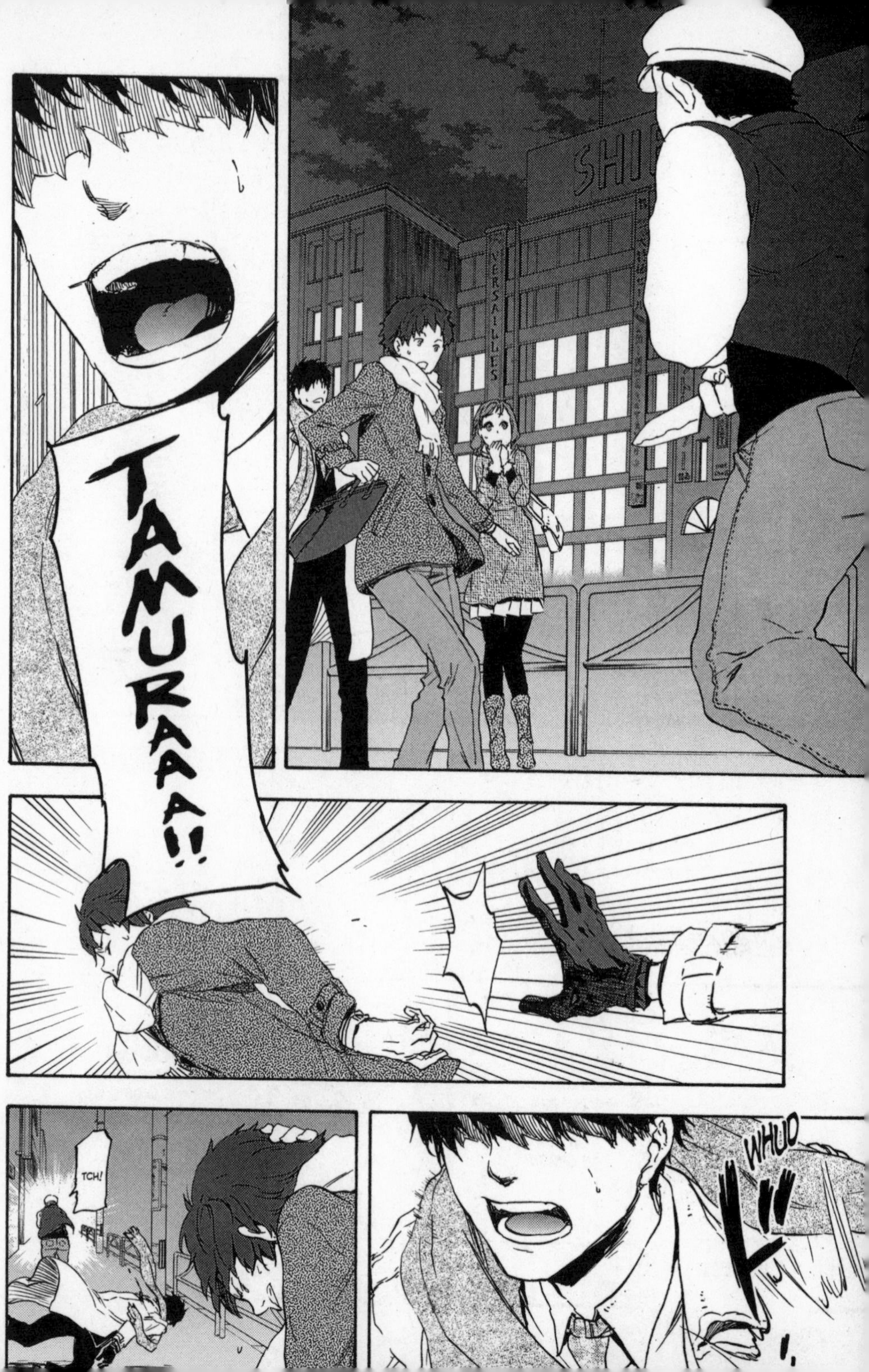
VERSAILLES
TAMURAAA!!
WHUD
TCH!

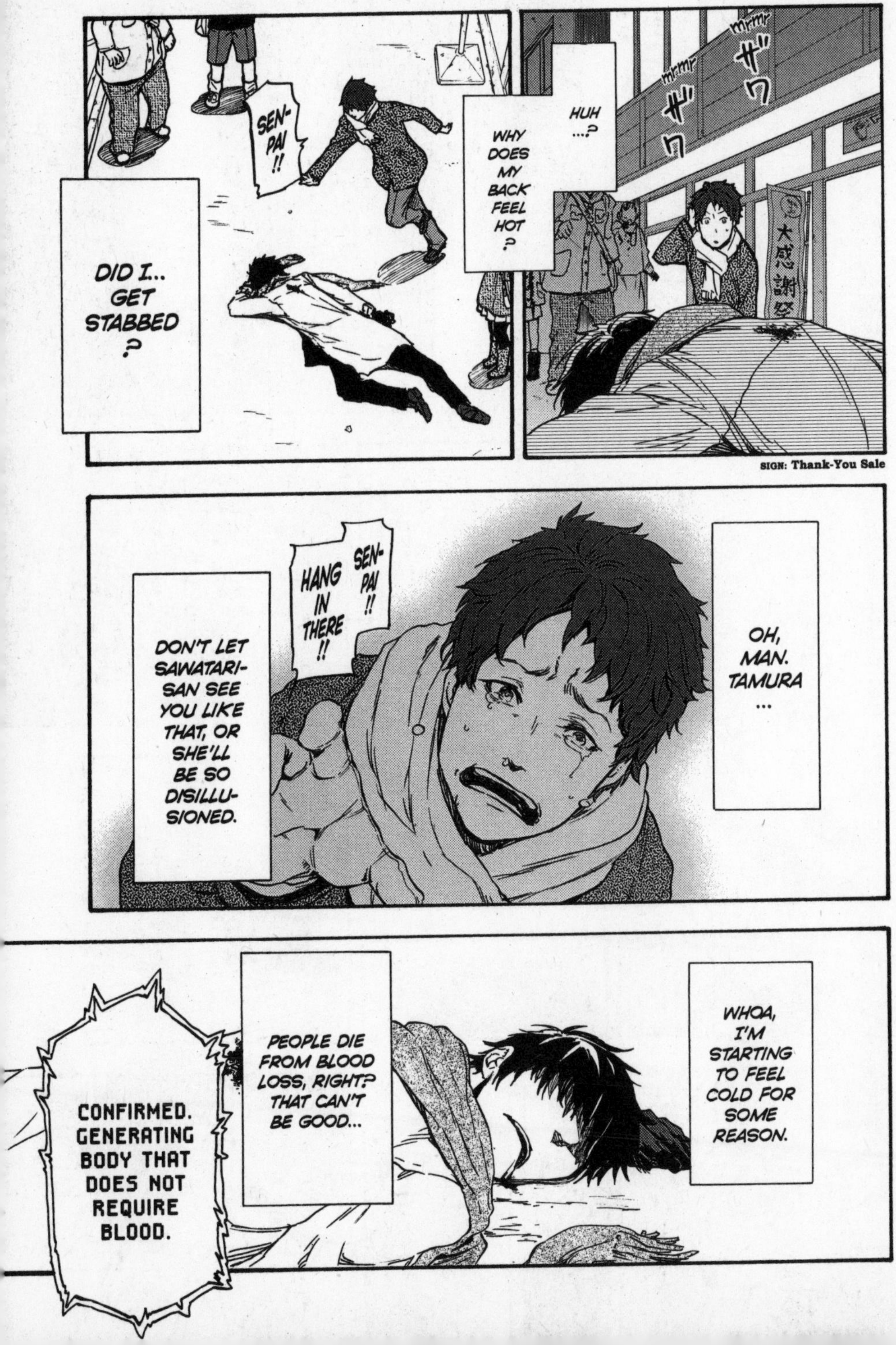
mrmr
ザワ
mrmr
ザワ
HUH ...?
WHY DOES MY BACK FEEL HOT?
SEN-PAI!!
DID I... GET STABBED?
SIGN: Thank-You Sale
OH, MAN. TAMURA ...
SEN-PAI!!
HANG IN THERE!!
DON'T LET SAWATARI-SAN SEE YOU LIKE THAT, OR SHE'LL BE SO DISILLUSIONED.
WHOA, I'M STARTING TO FEEL COLD FOR SOME REASON.
PEOPLE DIE FROM BLOOD LOSS, RIGHT? THAT CAN'T BE GOOD...
CONFIRMED. GENERATING BODY THAT DOES NOT REQUIRE BLOOD.

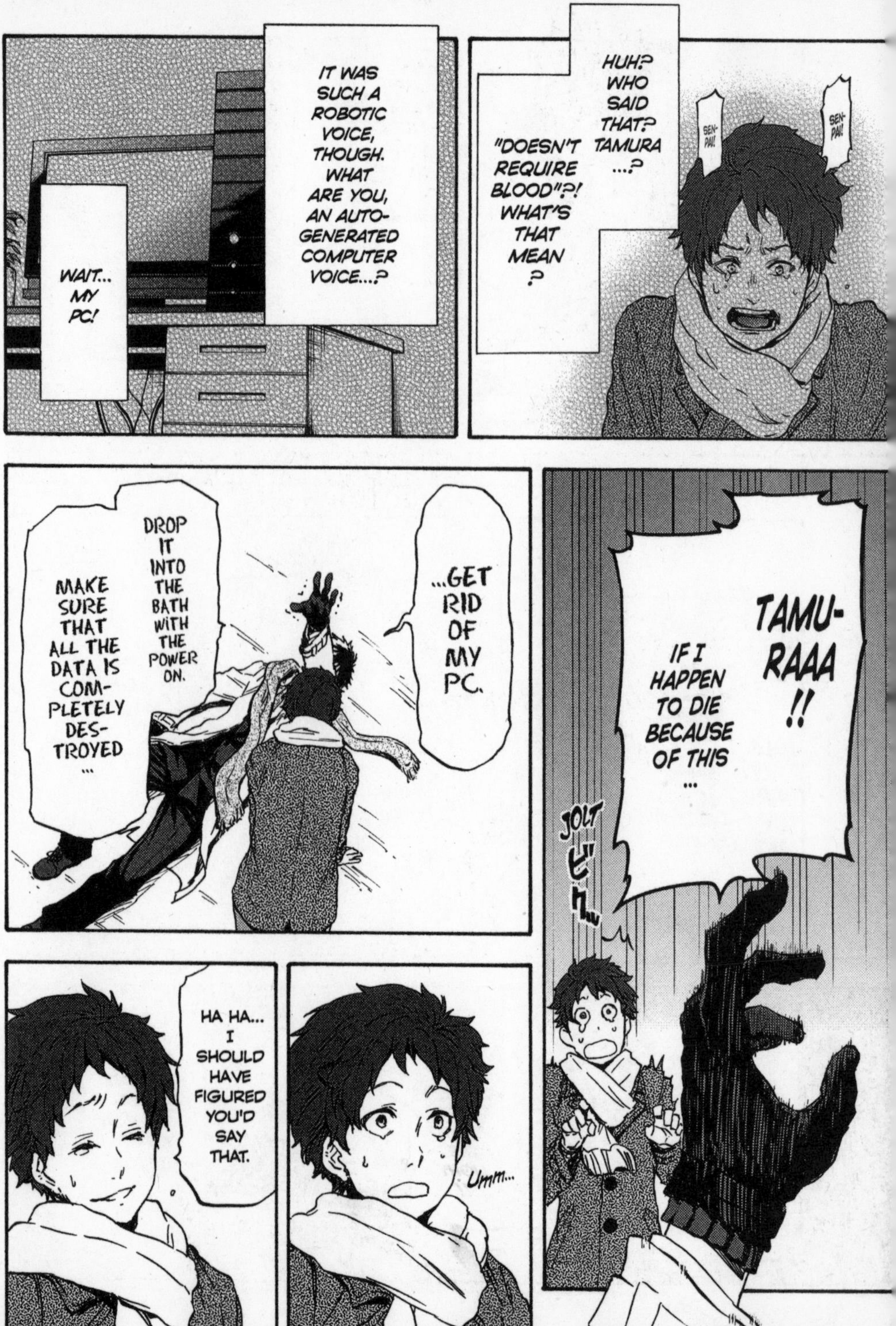
SEN-PAI!
SEN-PAI!
HUH? WHO SAID THAT? TAMURA ...?
"DOESN'T REQUIRE BLOOD"?! WHAT'S THAT MEAN ?
IT WAS SUCH A ROBOTIC VOICE, THOUGH. WHAT ARE YOU, AN AUTO-GENERATED COMPUTER VOICE...?
WAIT... MY PC!
TAMU-RAAA !!
IF I HAPPEN TO DIE BECAUSE OF THIS ...
JOLT
...GET RID OF MY PC.
DROP IT INTO THE BATH WITH THE POWER ON.
MAKE SURE THAT ALL THE DATA IS COM-PLETELY DES-TROYED ...
Umm...
HA HA... I SHOULD HAVE FIGURED YOU'D SAY THAT.

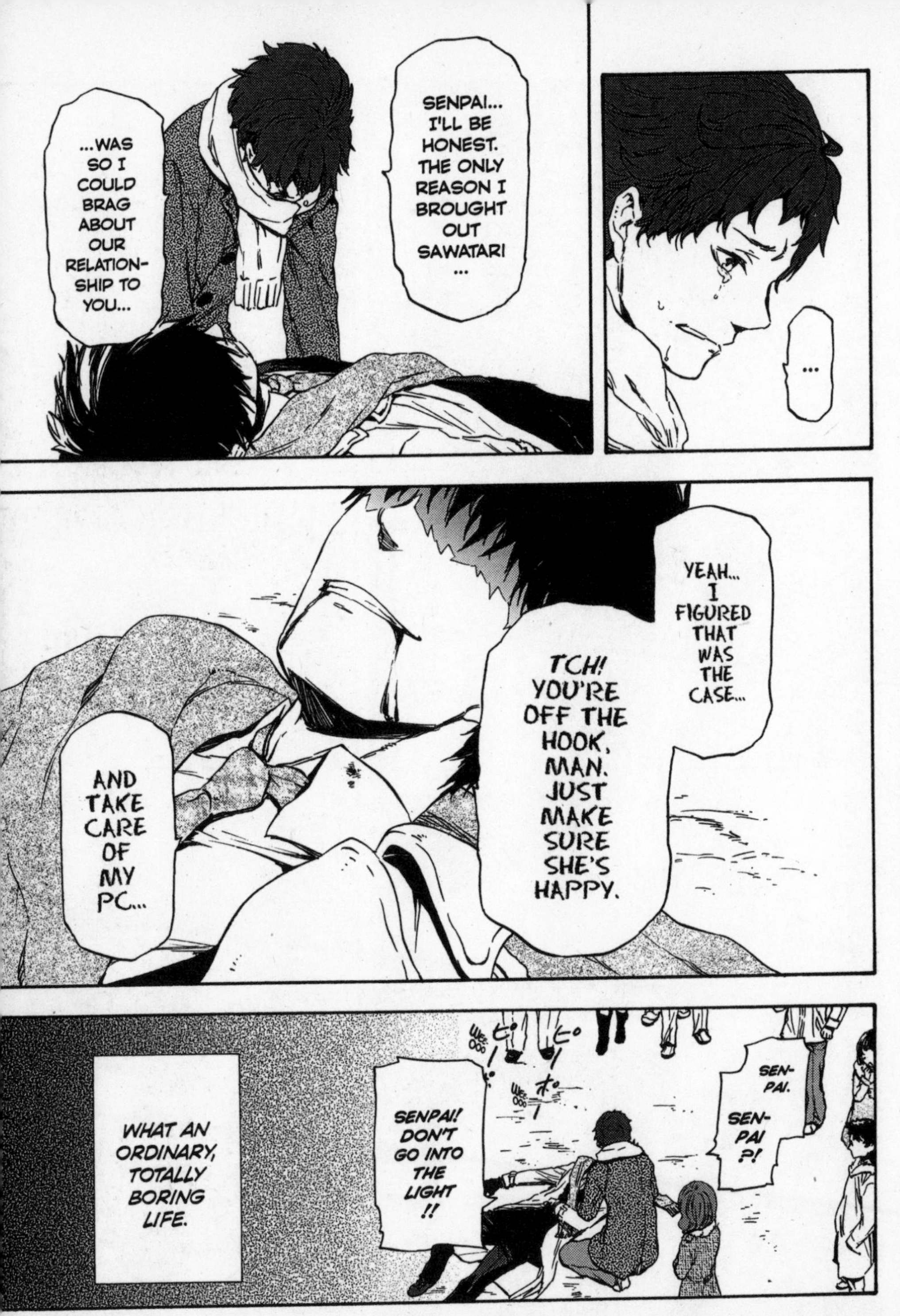
...
SENPAI... I'LL BE HONEST. THE ONLY REASON I BROUGHT OUT SAWATARI ...
...WAS SO I COULD BRAG ABOUT OUR RELATIONSHIP TO YOU...
YEAH... I FIGURED THAT WAS THE CASE...
TCH! YOU'RE OFF THE HOOK, MAN. JUST MAKE SURE SHE'S HAPPY.
AND TAKE CARE OF MY PC...
SEN-PAI.
SEN-PAI?!
WEE-OOO
WEE-OOO
SENPAI! DON'T GO INTO THE LIGHT!!
WHAT AN ORDINARY, TOTALLY BORING LIFE.

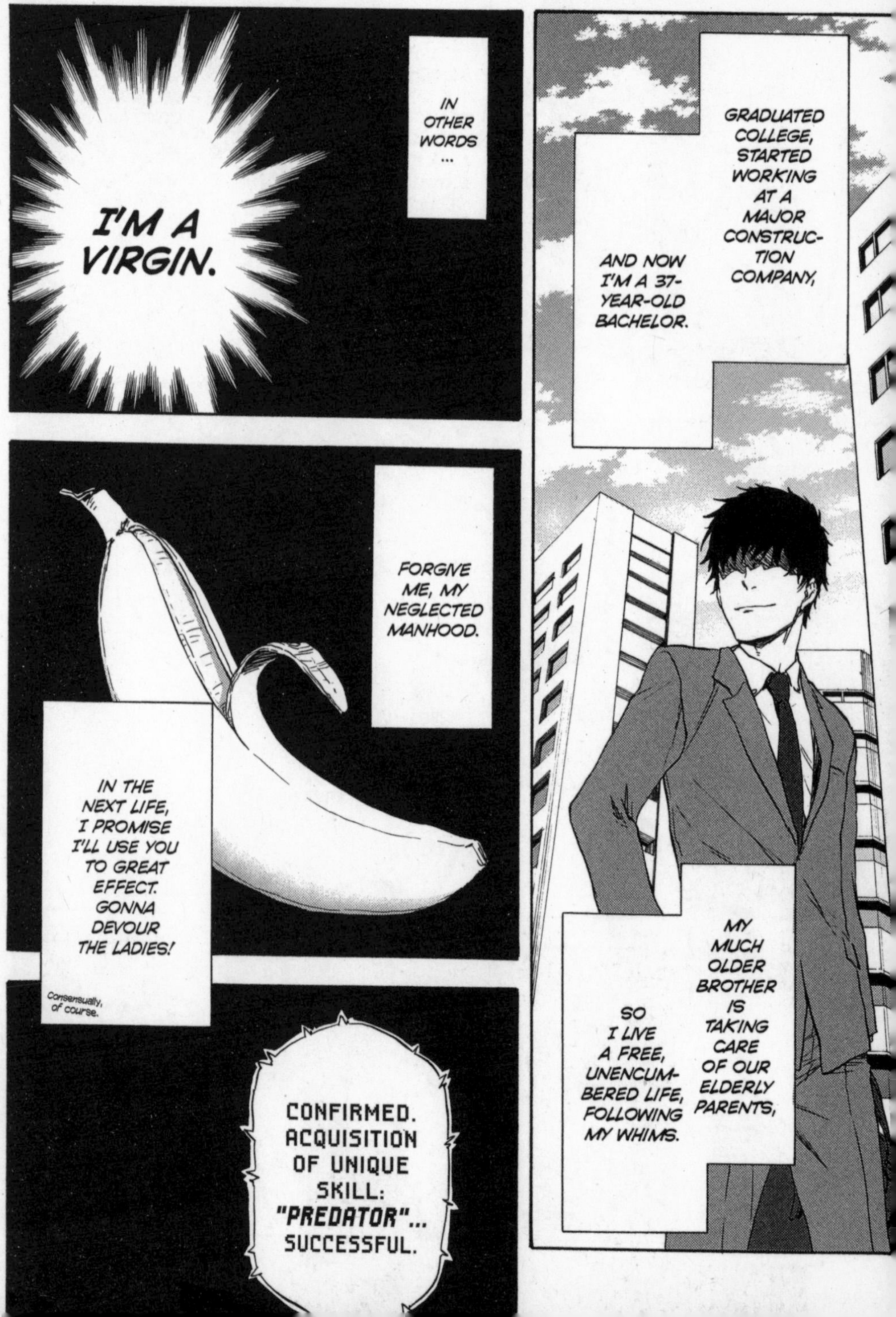
GRADUATED COLLEGE, STARTED WORKING AT A MAJOR CONSTRUCTION COMPANY,
AND NOW I'M A 37-YEAR-OLD BACHELOR.
MY MUCH OLDER BROTHER IS TAKING CARE OF OUR ELDERLY PARENTS,
SO I LIVE A FREE, UNENCUMBERED LIFE, FOLLOWING MY WHIMS.
IN OTHER WORDS ...
I'M A VIRGIN.
FORGIVE ME, MY NEGLECTED MANHOOD.
IN THE NEXT LIFE, I PROMISE I'LL USE YOU TO GREAT EFFECT. GONNA DEVOUR THE LADIES!
Consensually, of course.
CONFIRMED. ACQUISITION OF UNIQUE SKILL: "PREDATOR"... SUCCESSFUL.

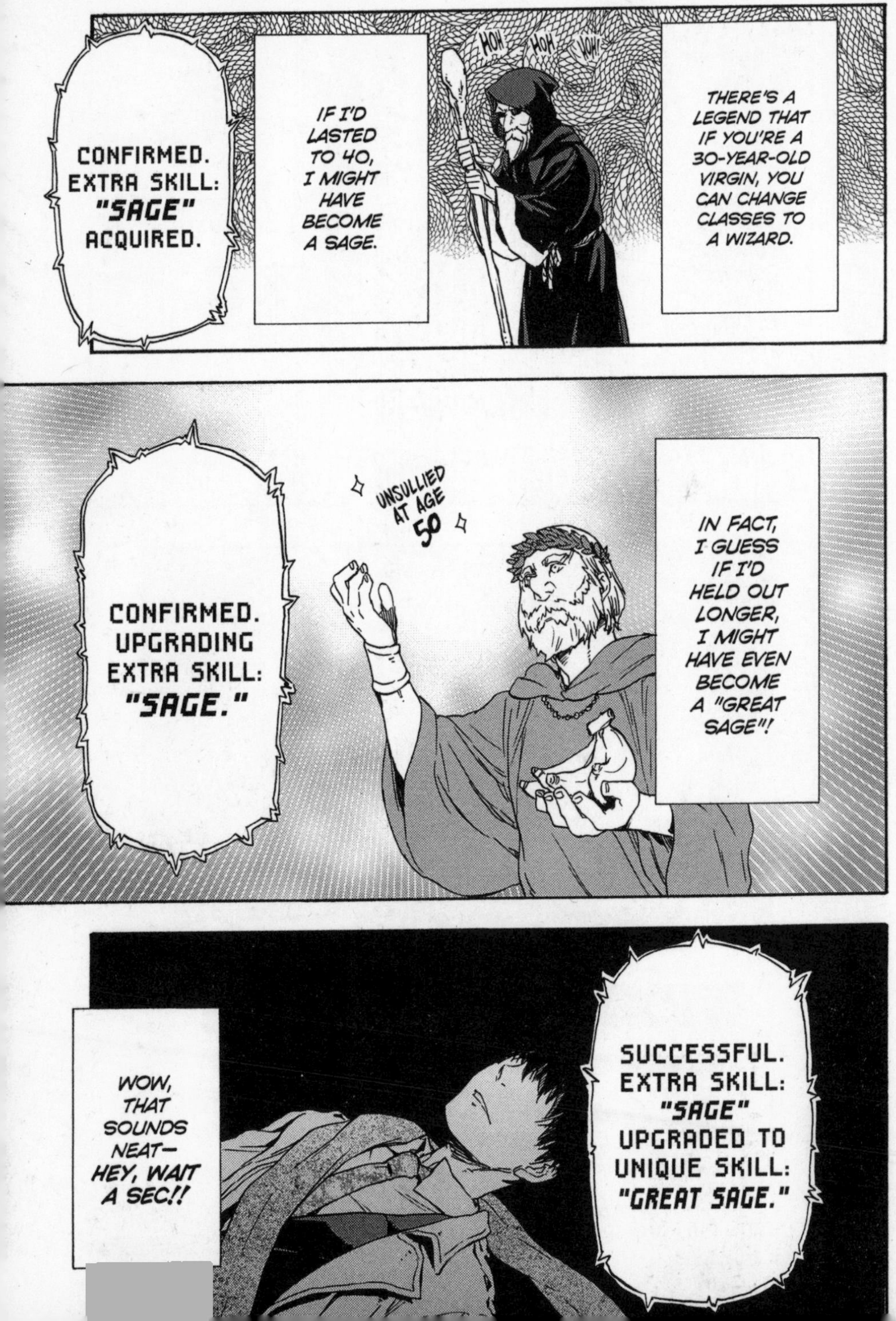
THERE'S A LEGEND THAT IF YOU'RE A 30-YEAR-OLD VIRGIN, YOU CAN CHANGE CLASSES TO A WIZARD.
HOH HOH HOH
IF I'D LASTED TO 40, I MIGHT HAVE BECOME A SAGE.
CONFIRMED. EXTRA SKILL: "SAGE" ACQUIRED.
IN FACT, I GUESS IF I'D HELD OUT LONGER, I MIGHT HAVE EVEN BECOME A "GREAT SAGE"!
UNSULLIED AT AGE 50
CONFIRMED. UPGRADING EXTRA SKILL: "SAGE."
SUCCESSFUL. EXTRA SKILL: "SAGE" UPGRADED TO UNIQUE SKILL: "GREAT SAGE."
WOW, THAT SOUNDS NEAT— HEY, WAIT A SEC!!

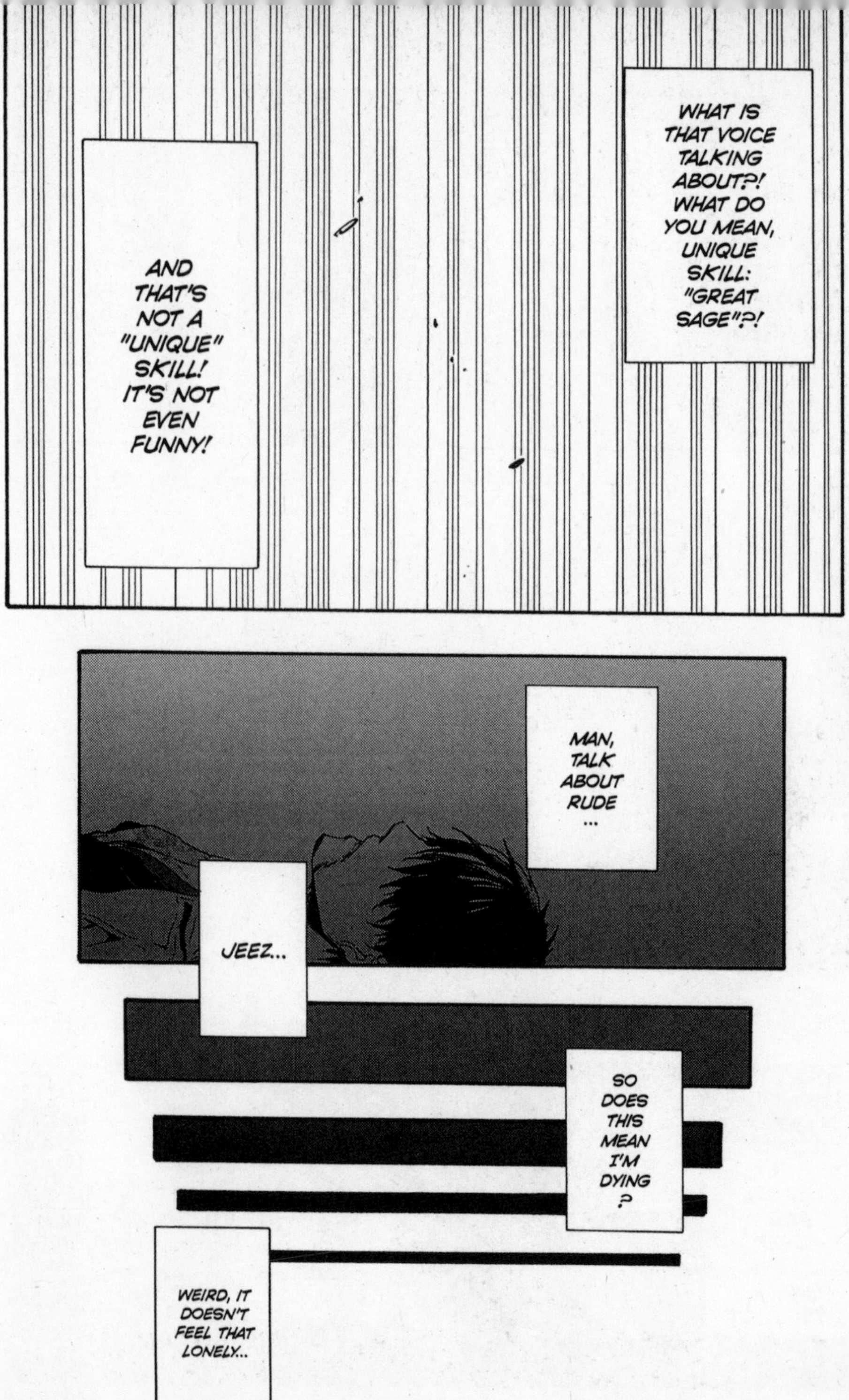
WHAT IS THAT VOICE TALKING ABOUT?! WHAT DO YOU MEAN, UNIQUE SKILL: "GREAT SAGE"?!
AND THAT'S NOT A "UNIQUE" SKILL! IT'S NOT EVEN FUNNY!
MAN, TALK ABOUT RUDE...
JEEZ...
SO DOES THIS MEAN I'M DYING?
WEIRD, IT DOESN'T FEEL THAT LONELY...

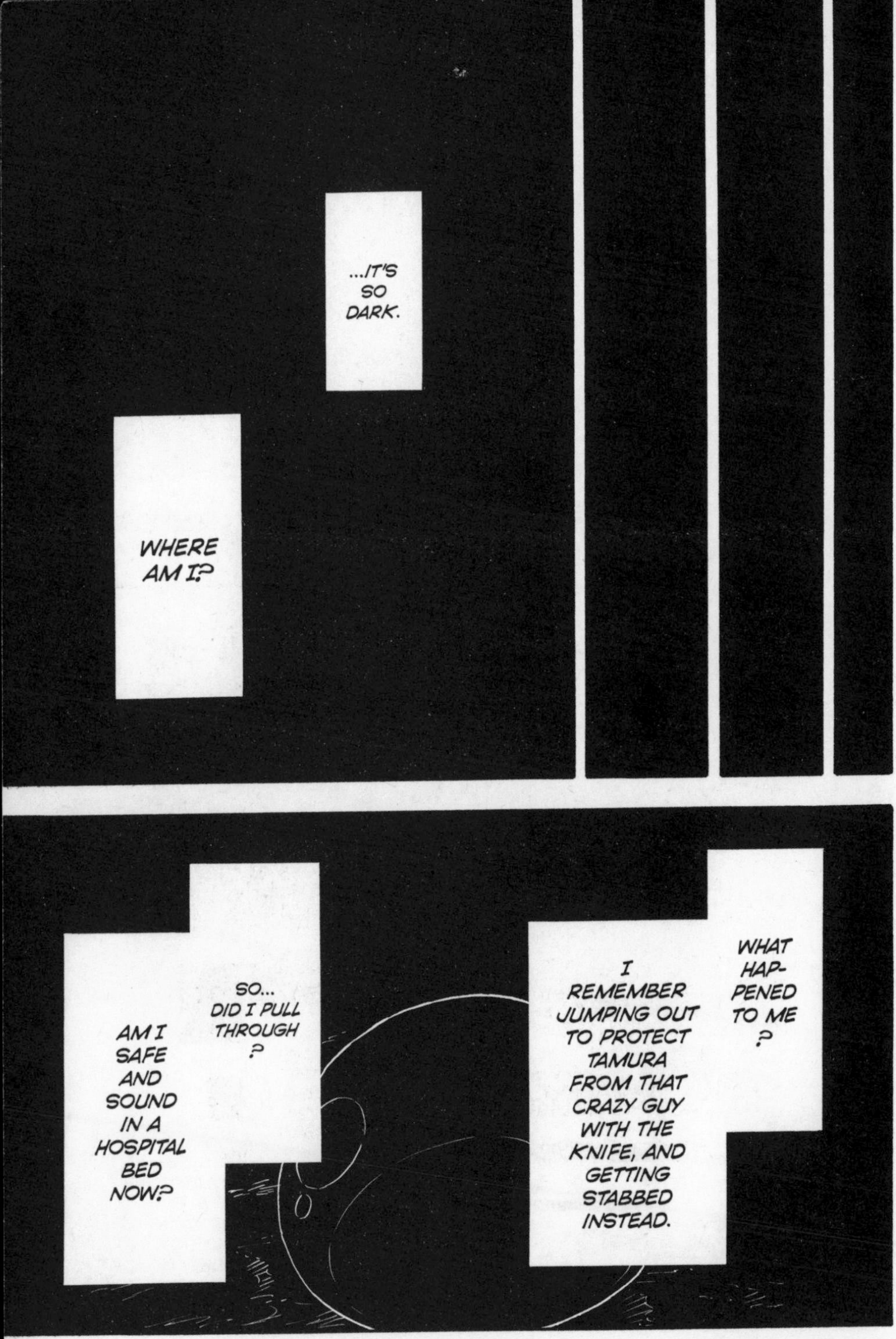
...IT'S SO DARK.
WHERE AM I?
WHAT HAP-PENED TO ME?
I REMEMBER JUMPING OUT TO PROTECT TAMURA FROM THAT CRAZY GUY WITH THE KNIFE, AND GETTING STABBED INSTEAD.
SO... DID I PULL THROUGH?
AM I SAFE AND SOUND IN A HOSPITAL BED NOW?

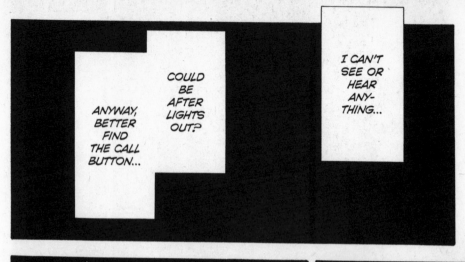

I CAN'T SEE OR HEAR ANYTHING...
COULD BE AFTER LIGHTS OUT?
ANYWAY, BETTER FIND THE CALL BUTTON...
HUH? WHY WON'T MY LIMBS RESPOND ?!
THAT'S CRAZY. MY ARMS AND LEGS COULDN'T HAVE BEEN AMPUTATED! I ONLY GOT STABBED IN THE BACK...
COULD IT BE THAT...HE SEVERED MY SPINAL CORD AND PARALYZED ME?
NO, NO, NO... ANYTHING BUT THAT!
OH ?!
ズルリ
ZLURP

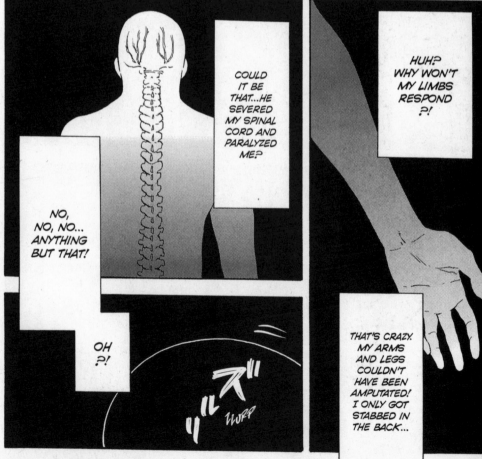

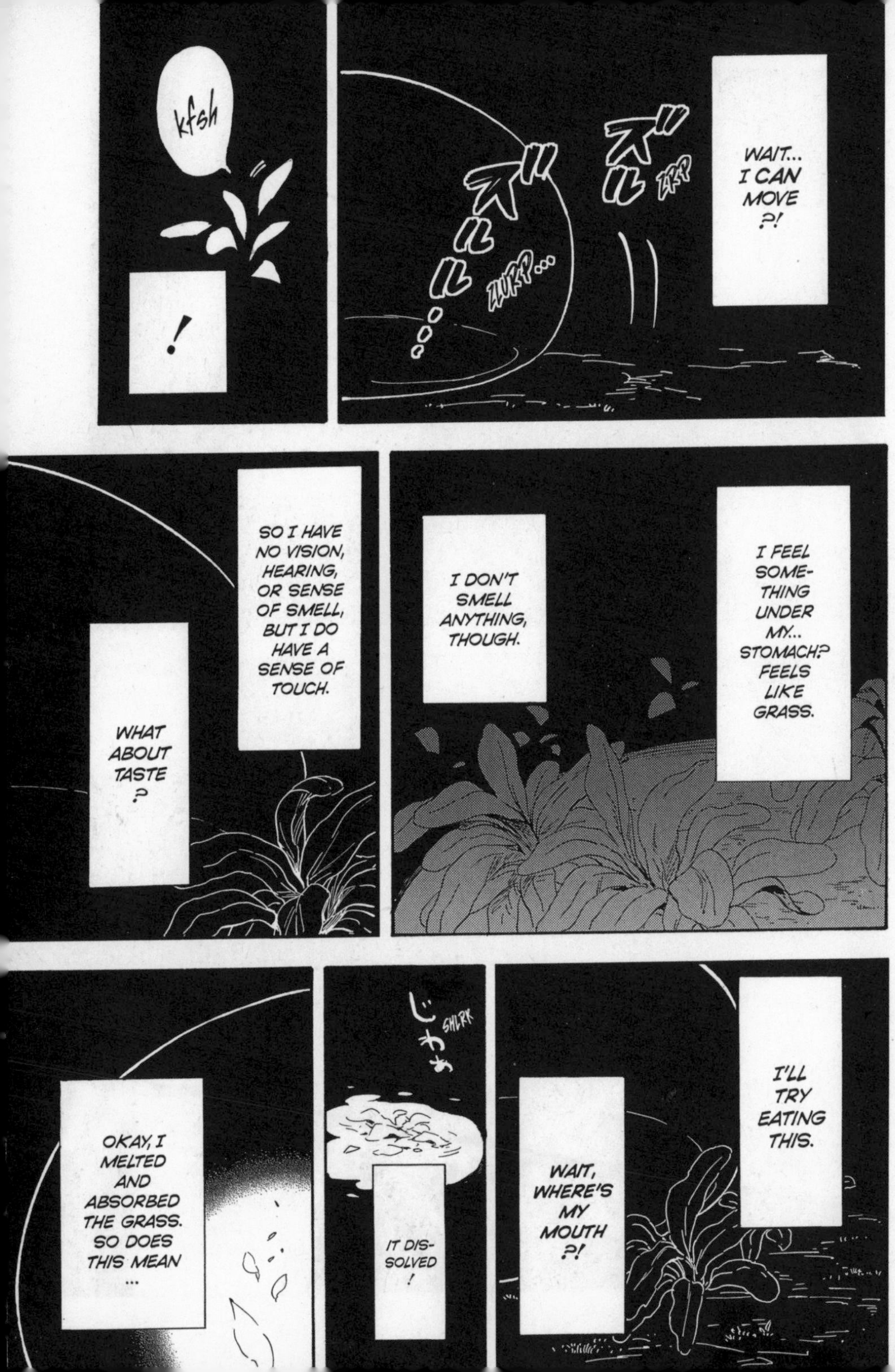
WAIT... I CAN MOVE ?!
ズル
ZRP
ズルル
ZURP...
kfsh
!
I FEEL SOMETHING UNDER MY... STOMACH? FEELS LIKE GRASS.
I DON'T SMELL ANYTHING, THOUGH.
SO I HAVE NO VISION, HEARING, OR SENSE OF SMELL, BUT I DO HAVE A SENSE OF TOUCH.
WHAT ABOUT TASTE ?
I'LL TRY EATING THIS.
WAIT, WHERE'S MY MOUTH ?!
じわぁ
SHLRK
IT DISSOLVED !
OKAY, I MELTED AND ABSORBED THE GRASS. SO DOES THIS MEAN ...

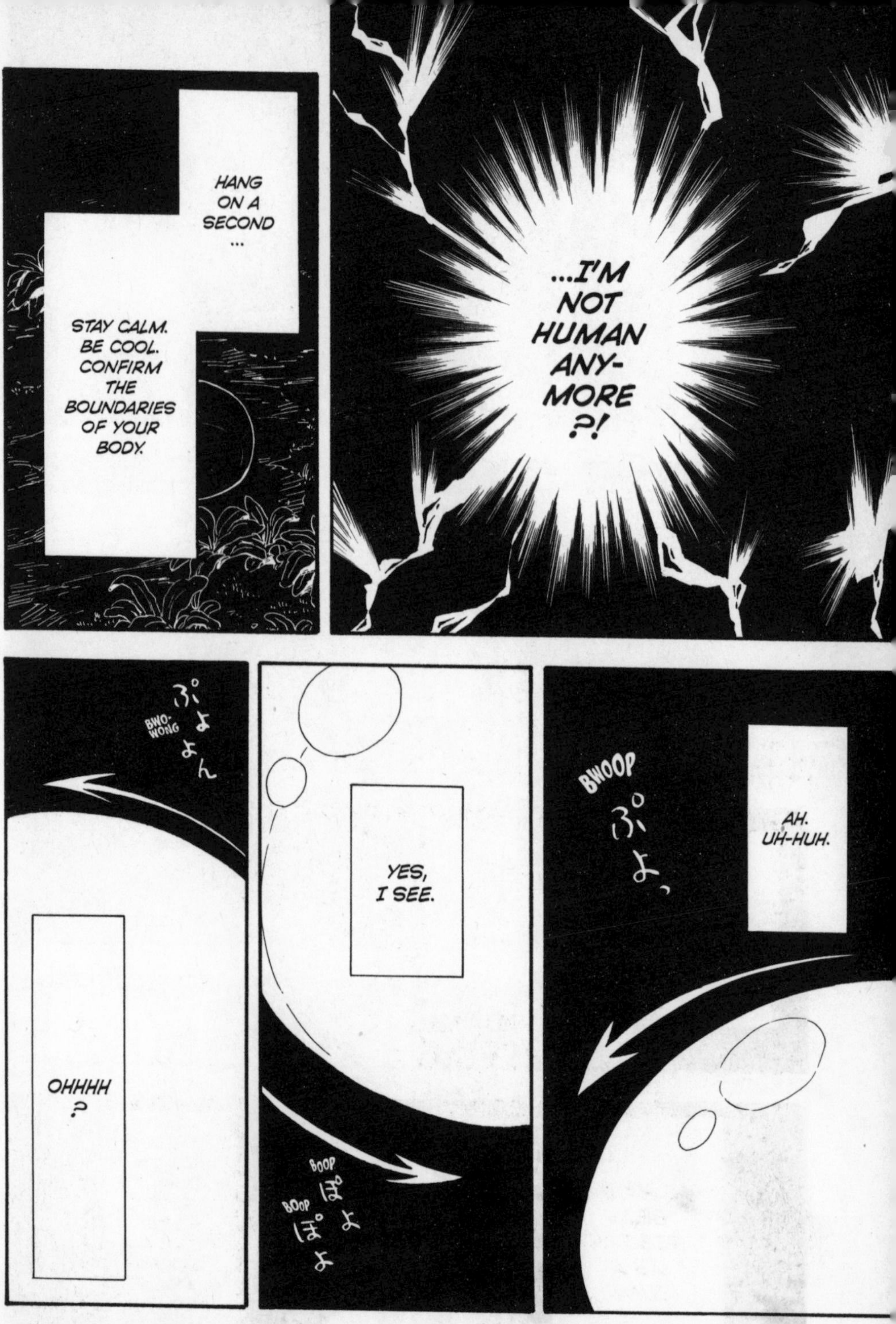
...I'M NOT HUMAN ANYMORE?!
HANG ON A SECOND...
STAY CALM. BE COOL. CONFIRM THE BOUNDARIES OF YOUR BODY.
AH. UH-HUH.
BWOOP
ぷよ、
YES, I SEE.
BOOP
ぽよ
BOOP
ぽよ
BWO-WONG
ぷよよん
OHHHH?

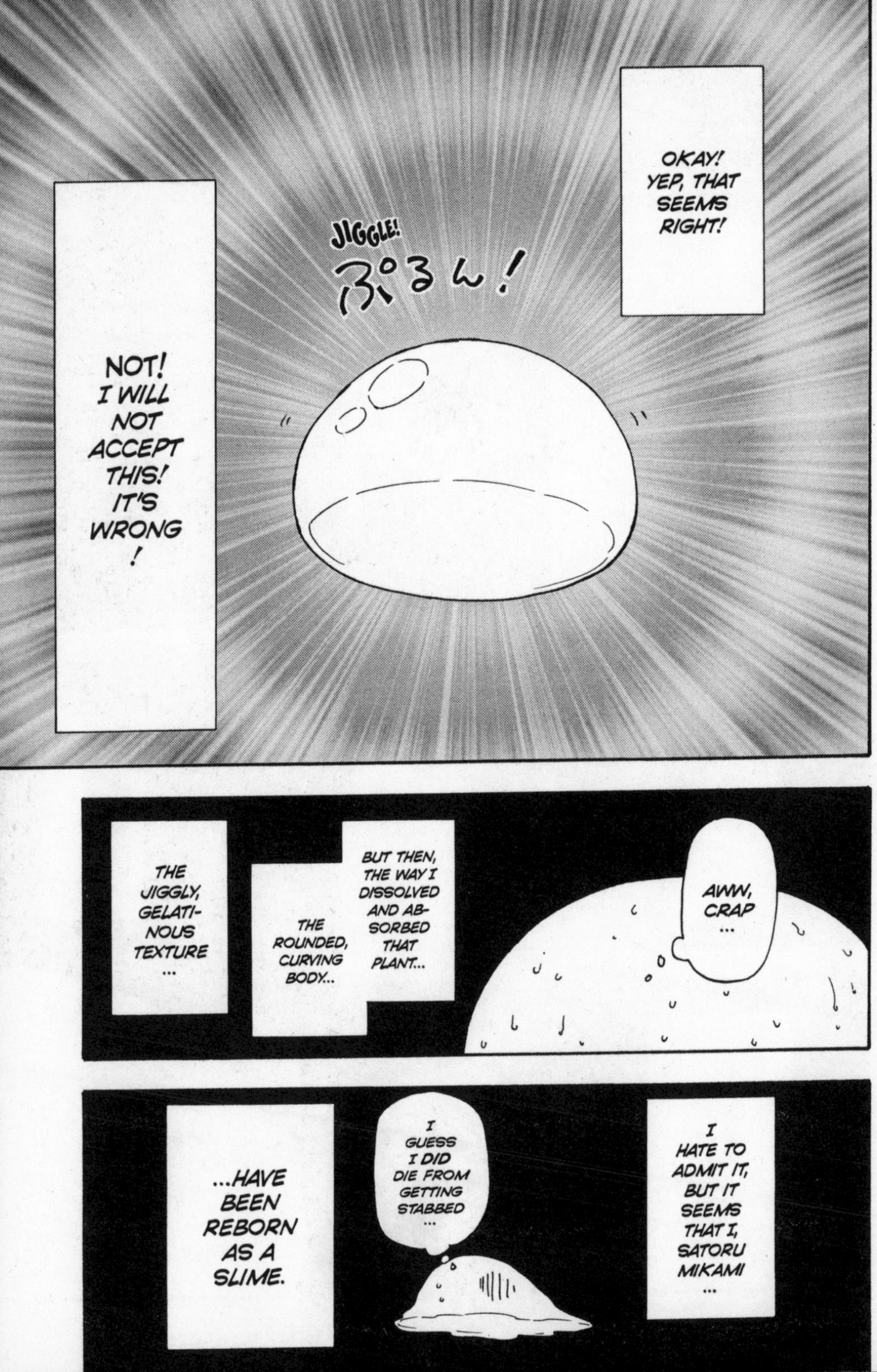
OKAY! YEP, THAT SEEMS RIGHT!
JIGGLE!
ぷるん！
NOT! I WILL NOT ACCEPT THIS! IT'S WRONG!
AWW, CRAP...
BUT THEN, THE WAY I DISSOLVED AND ABSORBED THAT PLANT...
THE ROUNDED, CURVING BODY...
THE JIGGLY, GELATINOUS TEXTURE...
I HATE TO ADMIT IT, BUT IT SEEMS THAT I, SATORU MIKAMI...
I GUESS I DID DIE FROM GETTING STABBED...
...HAVE BEEN REBORN AS A SLIME.

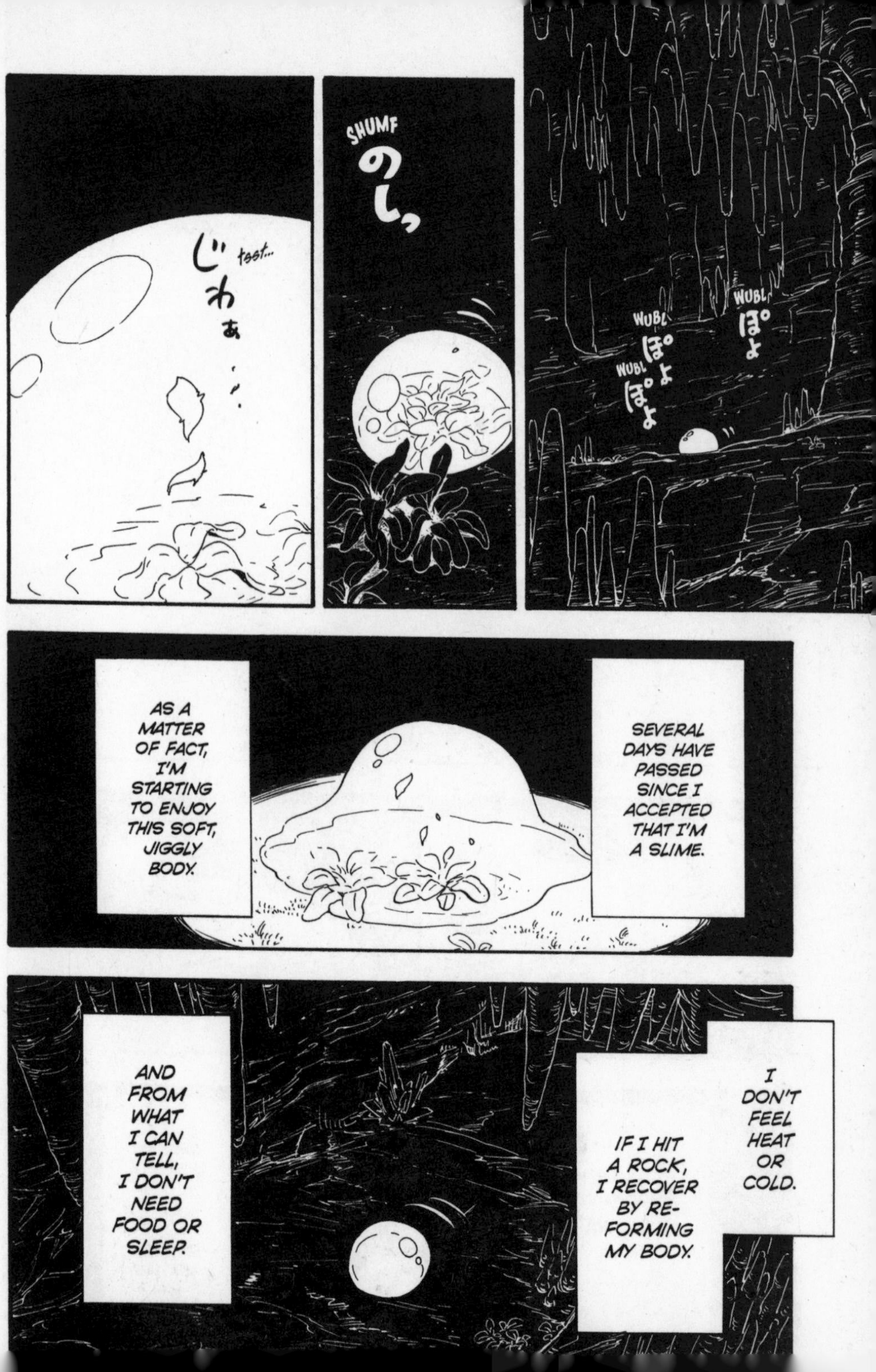
WUBL
ぽよ
WUBL
ぽよ
WUBL
ぽよ
SHUMF
のしっ
tsst...
じわぁ...
SEVERAL DAYS HAVE PASSED SINCE I ACCEPTED THAT I'M A SLIME.
AS A MATTER OF FACT, I'M STARTING TO ENJOY THIS SOFT, JIGGLY BODY.
I DON'T FEEL HEAT OR COLD.
IF I HIT A ROCK, I RECOVER BY RE-FORMING MY BODY.
AND FROM WHAT I CAN TELL, I DON'T NEED FOOD OR SLEEP.

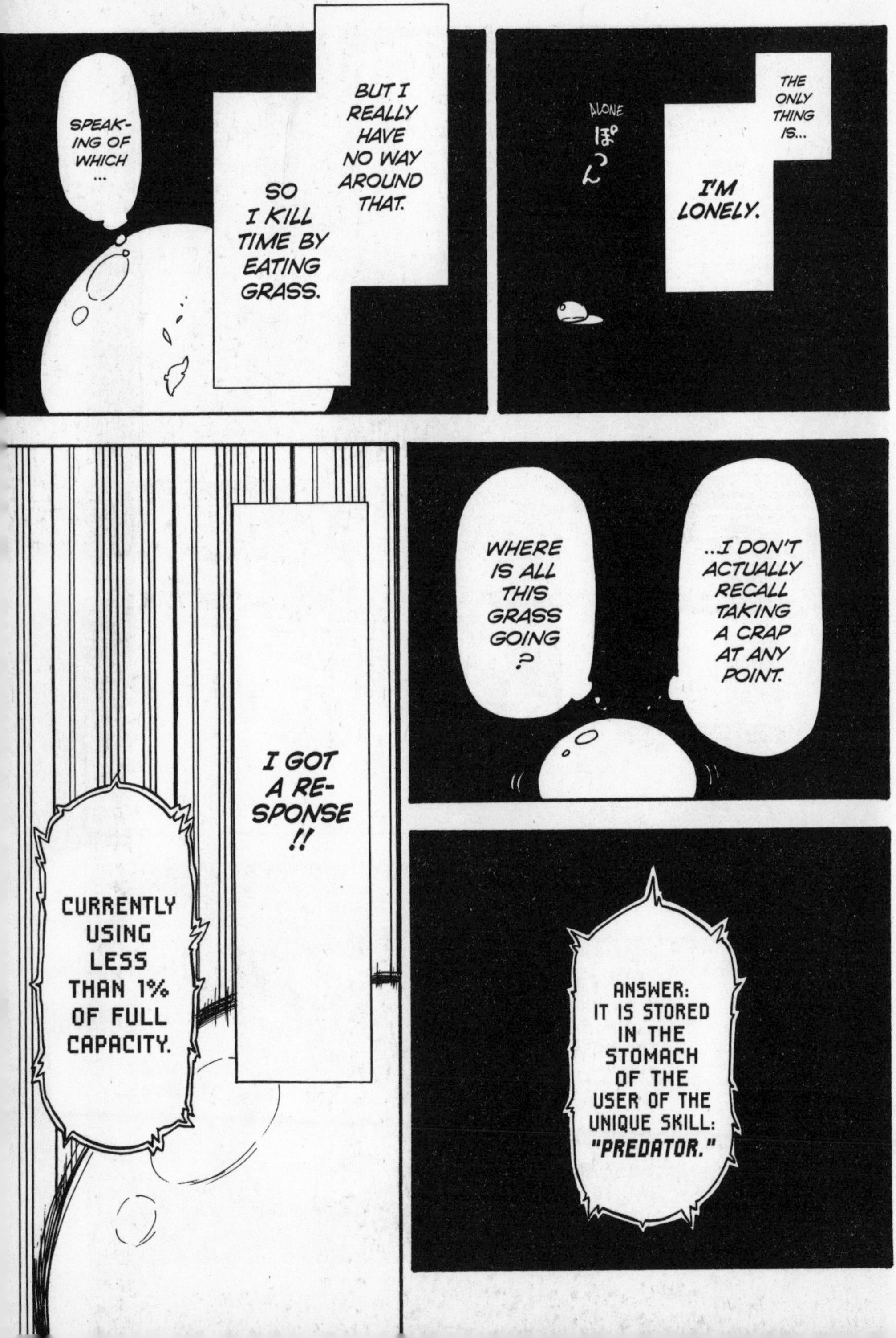
THE ONLY THING IS...
ALONE
ぽつん
I'M LONELY.
BUT I REALLY HAVE NO WAY AROUND THAT.
SO I KILL TIME BY EATING GRASS.
SPEAKING OF WHICH...
...I DON'T ACTUALLY RECALL TAKING A CRAP AT ANY POINT.
WHERE IS ALL THIS GRASS GOING?
ANSWER: IT IS STORED IN THE STOMACH OF THE USER OF THE UNIQUE SKILL: "PREDATOR."
I GOT A RESPONSE!!
CURRENTLY USING LESS THAN 1% OF FULL CAPACITY.

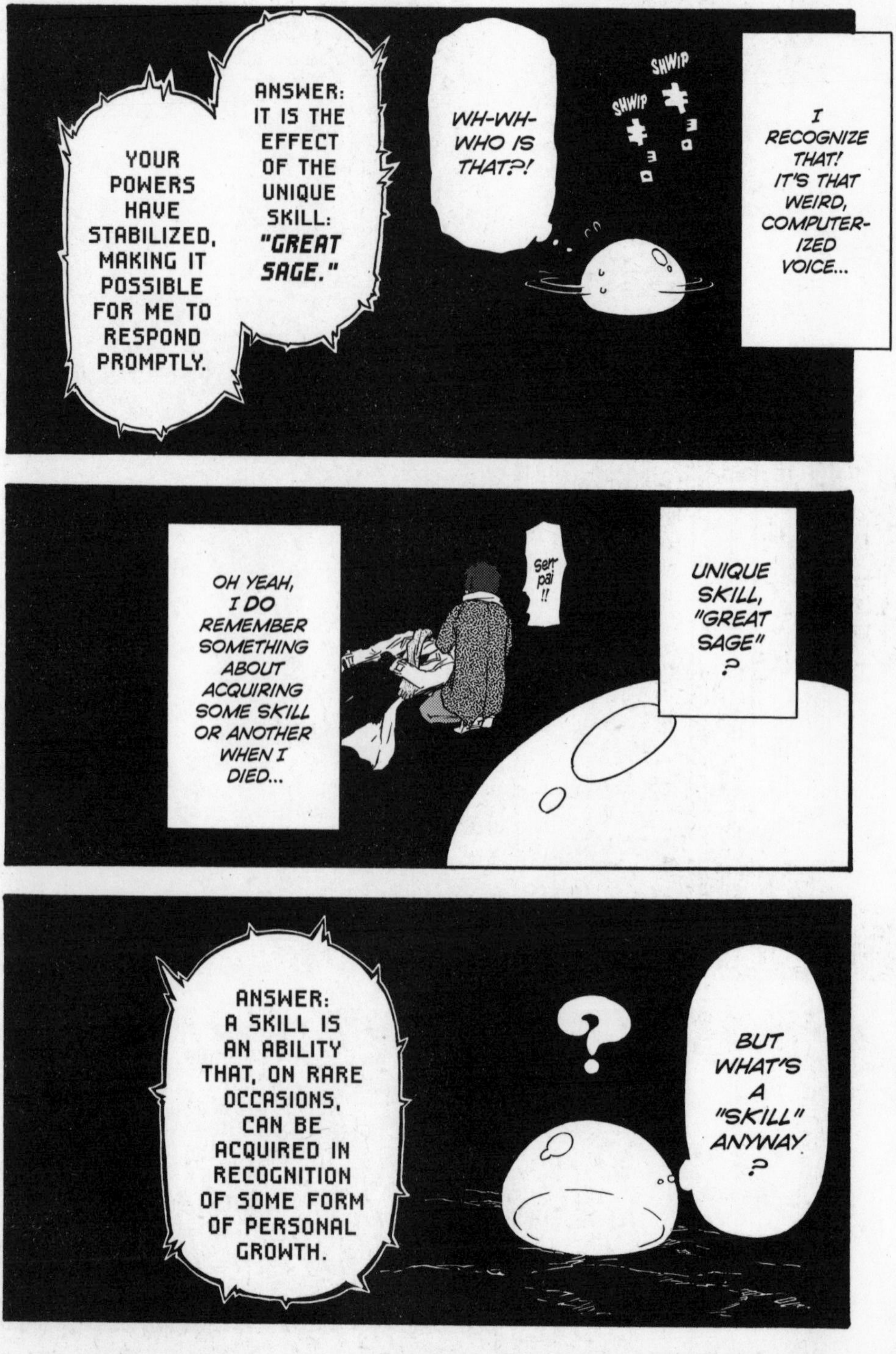
I RECOGNIZE THAT! IT'S THAT WEIRD, COMPUTERIZED VOICE...
SHWIP
SHWIP
WH-WH-WHO IS THAT?!
ANSWER: IT IS THE EFFECT OF THE UNIQUE SKILL: "GREAT SAGE."
YOUR POWERS HAVE STABILIZED, MAKING IT POSSIBLE FOR ME TO RESPOND PROMPTLY.
UNIQUE SKILL, "GREAT SAGE"?
Senpai!!
OH YEAH, I DO REMEMBER SOMETHING ABOUT ACQUIRING SOME SKILL OR ANOTHER WHEN I DIED...
BUT WHAT'S A "SKILL" ANYWAY?
?
ANSWER: A SKILL IS AN ABILITY THAT, ON RARE OCCASIONS, CAN BE ACQUIRED IN RECOGNITION OF SOME FORM OF PERSONAL GROWTH.

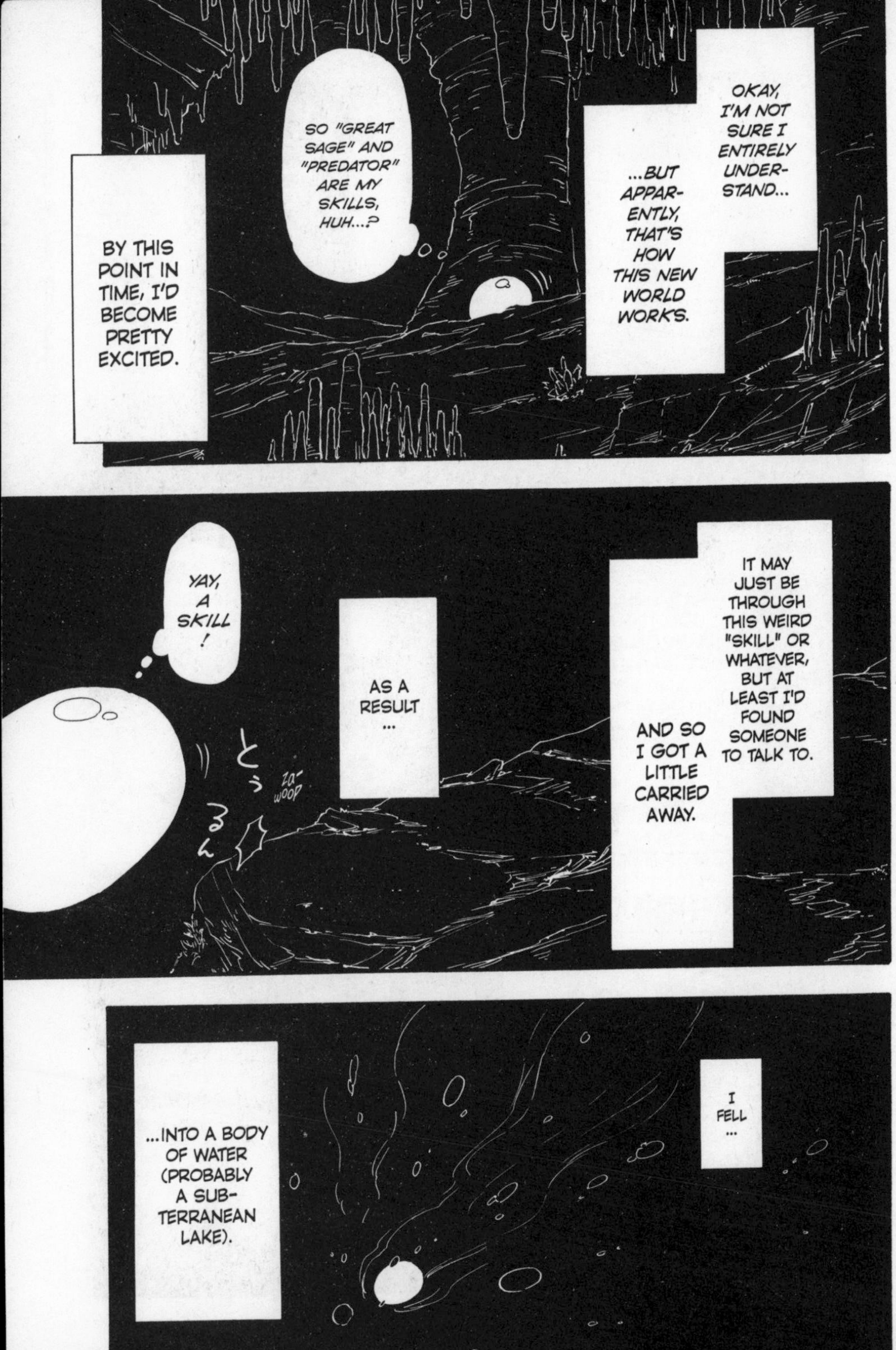
OKAY, I'M NOT SURE I ENTIRELY UNDER-STAND...
...BUT APPAR-ENTLY, THAT'S HOW THIS NEW WORLD WORKS.
SO "GREAT SAGE" AND "PREDATOR" ARE MY SKILLS, HUH...?
BY THIS POINT IN TIME, I'D BECOME PRETTY EXCITED.
IT MAY JUST BE THROUGH THIS WEIRD "SKILL" OR WHATEVER, BUT AT LEAST I'D FOUND SOMEONE TO TALK TO.
AND SO I GOT A LITTLE CARRIED AWAY.
AS A RESULT ...
YAY, A SKILL!
とぅるん
ZA-WOOP
I FELL ...
...INTO A BODY OF WATER (PROBABLY A SUB-TERRANEAN LAKE).

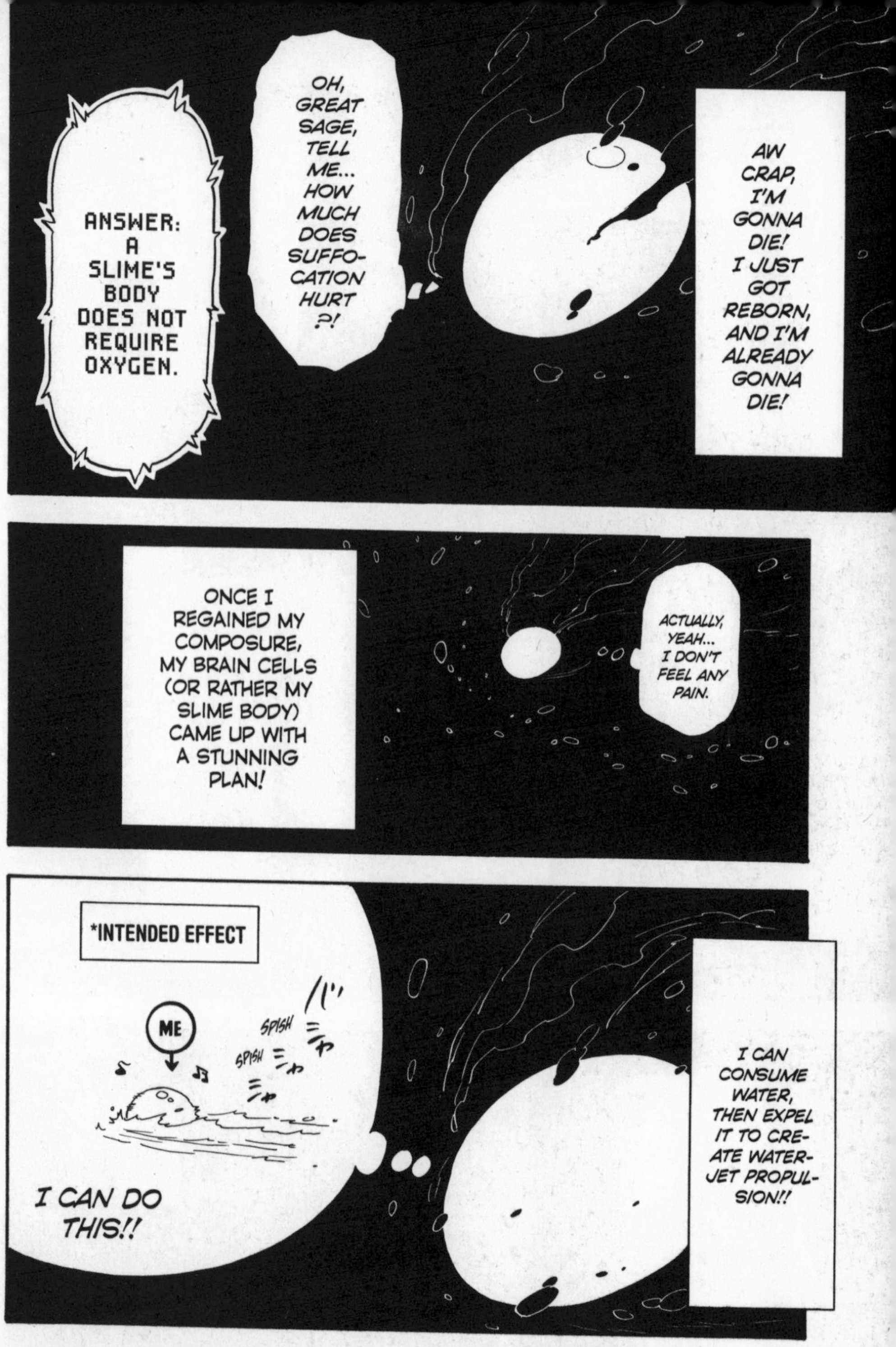
AW CRAP, I'M GONNA DIE! I JUST GOT REBORN, AND I'M ALREADY GONNA DIE!
OH, GREAT SAGE, TELL ME... HOW MUCH DOES SUFFOCATION HURT?!
ANSWER: A SLIME'S BODY DOES NOT REQUIRE OXYGEN.
ACTUALLY, YEAH... I DON'T FEEL ANY PAIN.
ONCE I REGAINED MY COMPOSURE, MY BRAIN CELLS (OR RATHER MY SLIME BODY) CAME UP WITH A STUNNING PLAN!
I CAN CONSUME WATER, THEN EXPEL IT TO CREATE WATER-JET PROPULSION!!
*INTENDED EFFECT
ME
SPISH
SPISH
I CAN DO THIS!!

BA-ZOOM

ZRLP...

SPLAT

SKILL:
"WATER-
PRESSURE
PROPULSION"
ACQUIRED.

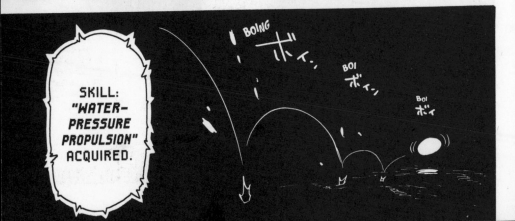

BOING

BOI

BOI

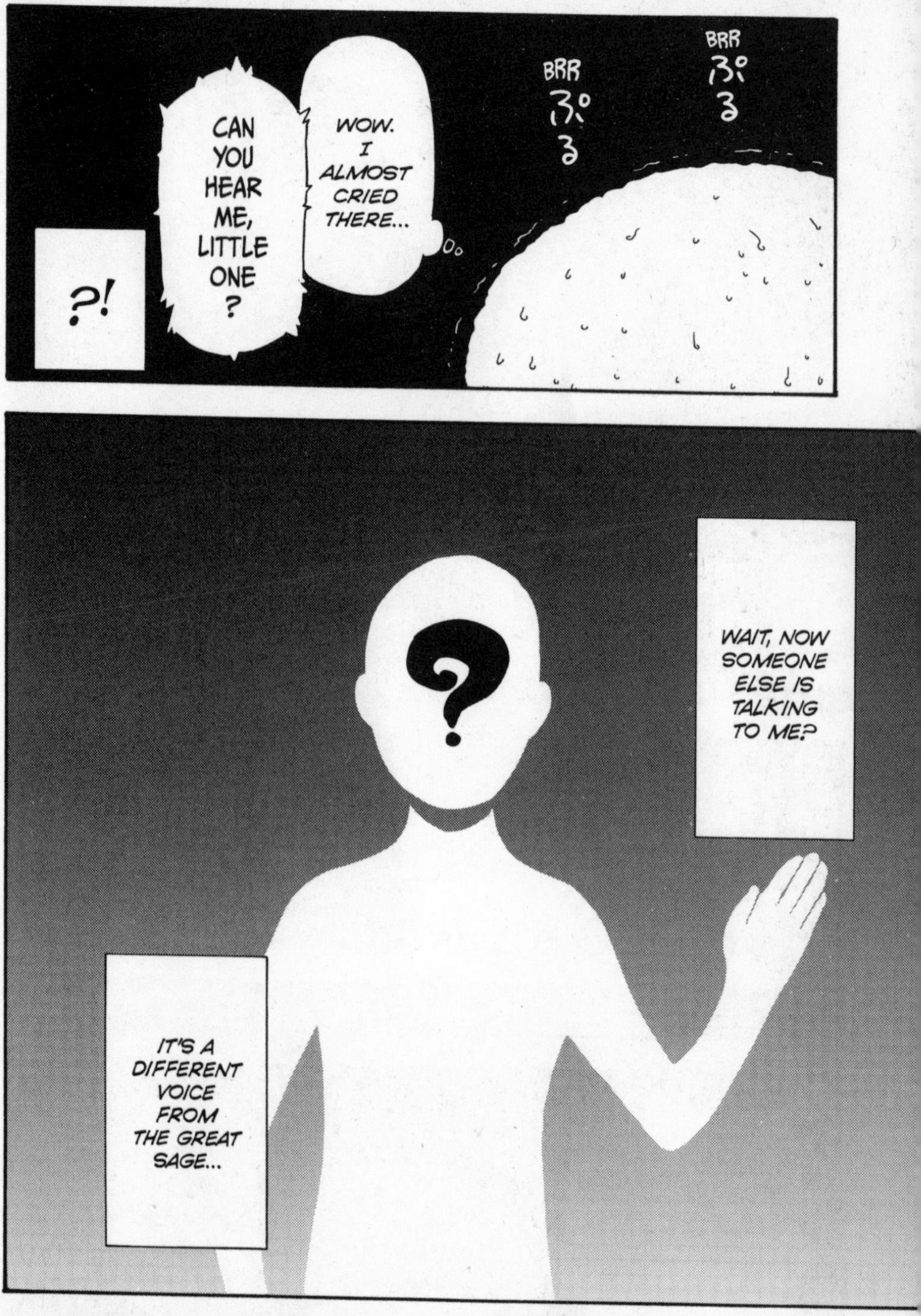
BRR ぷる
BRR ぷる
WOW. I ALMOST CRIED THERE...
CAN YOU HEAR ME, LITTLE ONE?
?!
WAIT, NOW SOMEONE ELSE IS TALKING TO ME?
IT'S A DIFFERENT VOICE FROM THE GREAT SAGE...

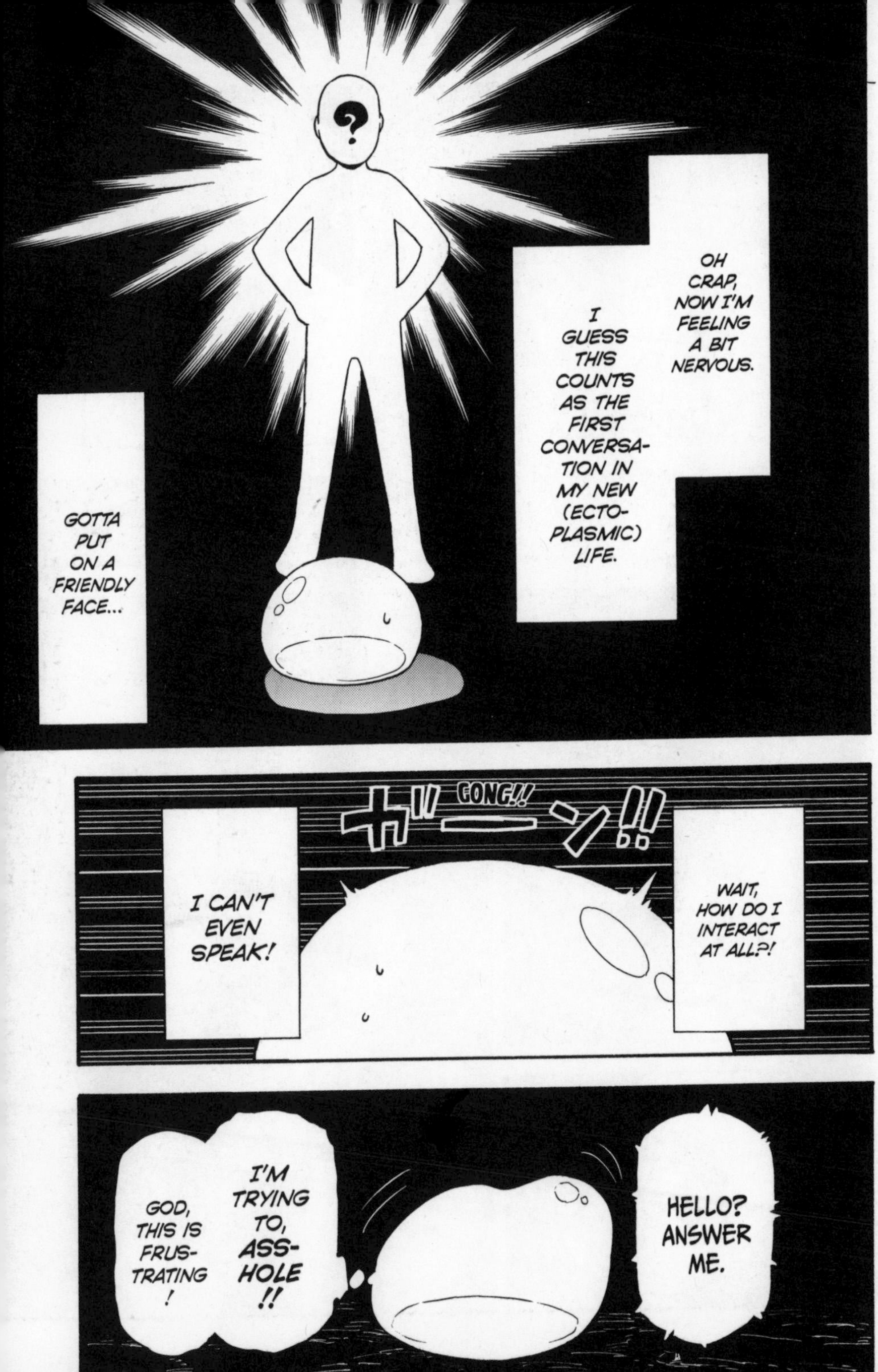
OH CRAP, NOW I'M FEELING A BIT NERVOUS.
I GUESS THIS COUNTS AS THE FIRST CONVERSATION IN MY NEW (ECTOPLASMIC) LIFE.
GOTTA PUT ON A FRIENDLY FACE...
GONG!!
WAIT, HOW DO I INTERACT AT ALL?!
I CAN'T EVEN SPEAK!
HELLO? ANSWER ME.
I'M TRYING TO, ASSHOLE!!
GOD, THIS IS FRUSTRATING!

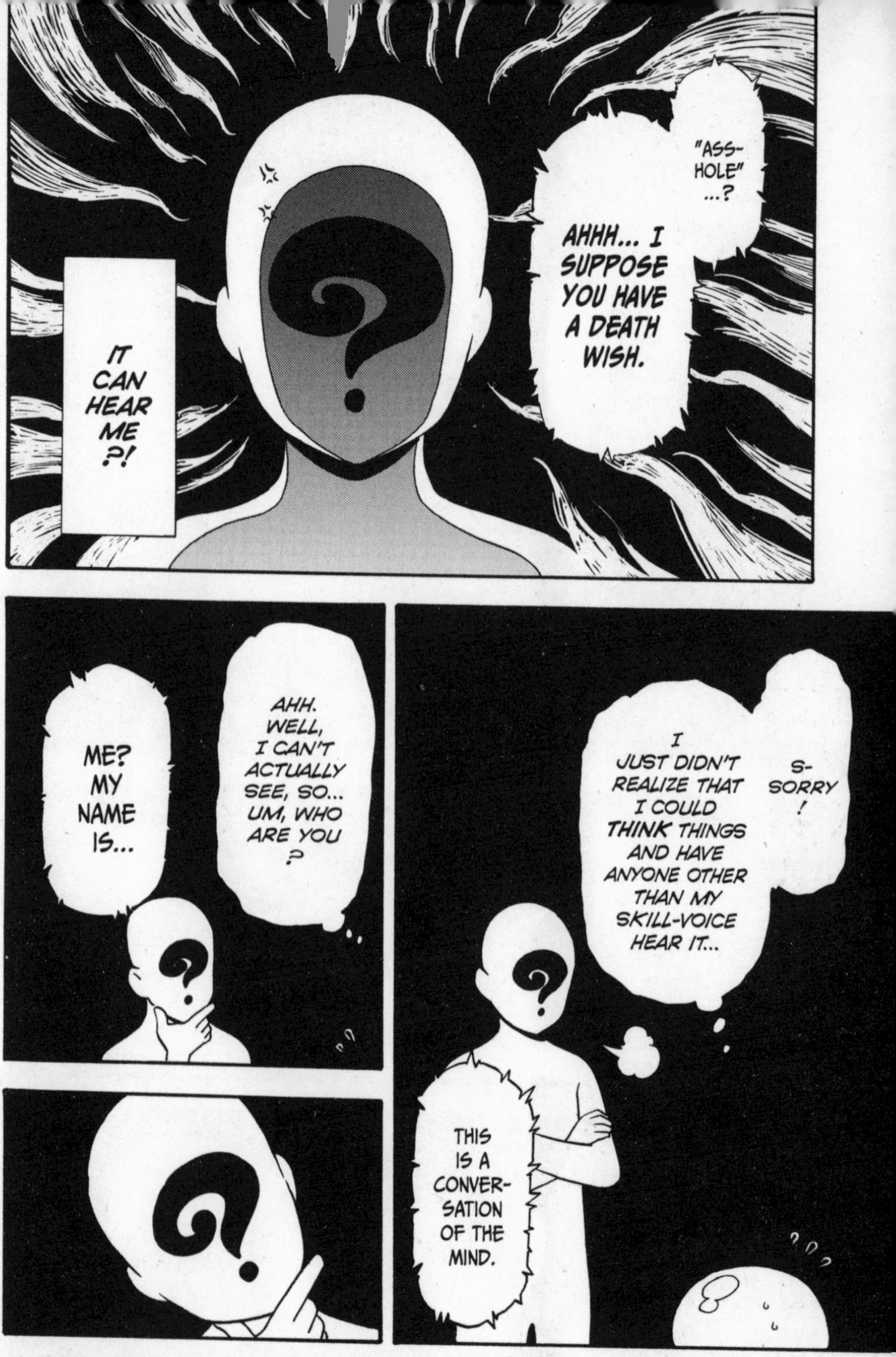
"ASS-HOLE" ...?
AHHH... I SUPPOSE YOU HAVE A DEATH WISH.
IT CAN HEAR ME ?!
S-SORRY !
I JUST DIDN'T REALIZE THAT I COULD THINK THINGS AND HAVE ANYONE OTHER THAN MY SKILL-VOICE HEAR IT...
THIS IS A CONVER-SATION OF THE MIND.
AHH. WELL, I CAN'T ACTUALLY SEE, SO... UM, WHO ARE YOU ?
ME? MY NAME IS...

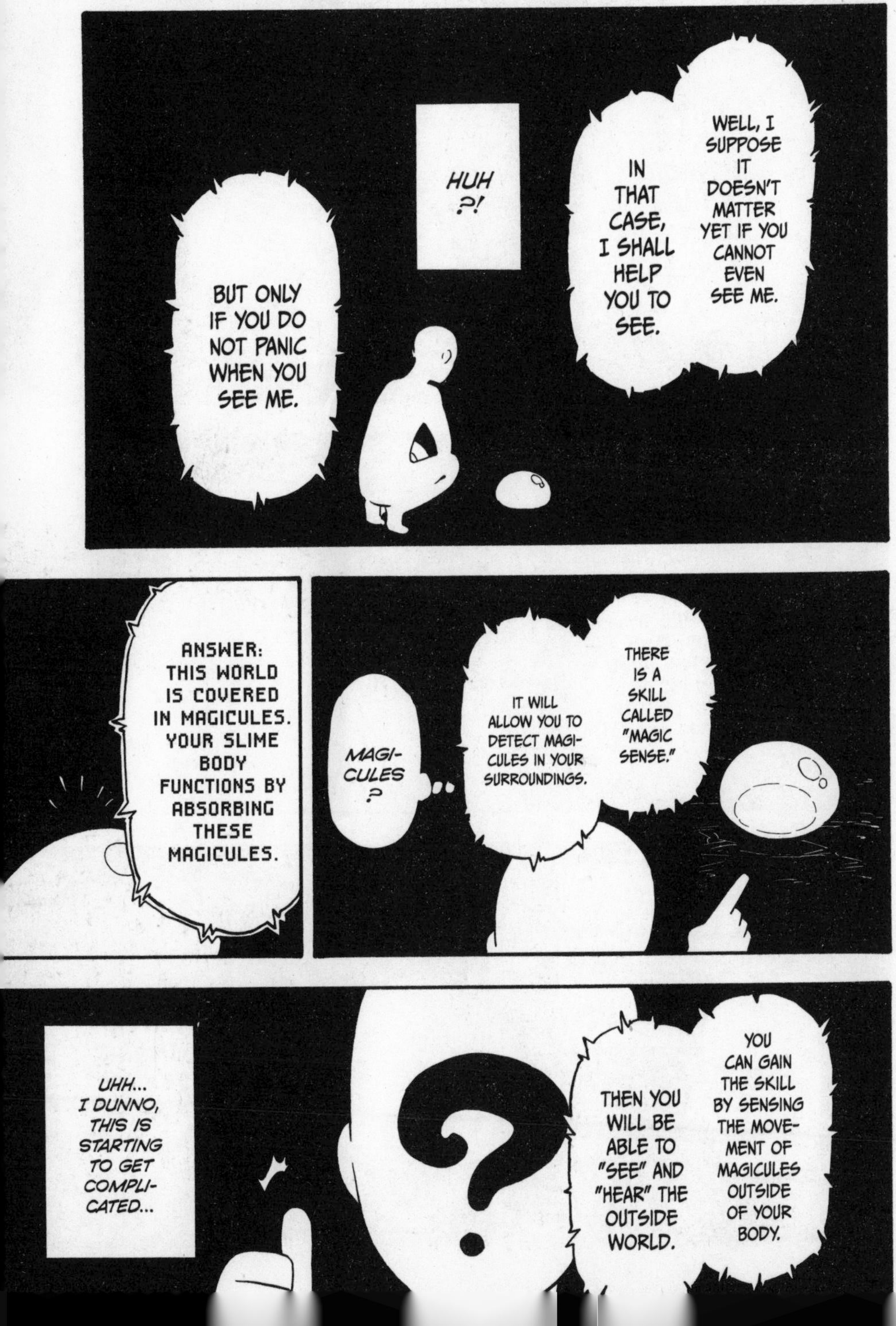
WELL, I SUPPOSE IT DOESN'T MATTER YET IF YOU CANNOT EVEN SEE ME.
IN THAT CASE, I SHALL HELP YOU TO SEE.
HUH?!
BUT ONLY IF YOU DO NOT PANIC WHEN YOU SEE ME.
THERE IS A SKILL CALLED "MAGIC SENSE."
IT WILL ALLOW YOU TO DETECT MAGICULES IN YOUR SURROUNDINGS.
MAGICULES?
ANSWER: THIS WORLD IS COVERED IN MAGICULES. YOUR SLIME BODY FUNCTIONS BY ABSORBING THESE MAGICULES.
YOU CAN GAIN THE SKILL BY SENSING THE MOVEMENT OF MAGICULES OUTSIDE OF YOUR BODY.
THEN YOU WILL BE ABLE TO "SEE" AND "HEAR" THE OUTSIDE WORLD.
UHH... I DUNNO, THIS IS STARTING TO GET COMPLICATED...

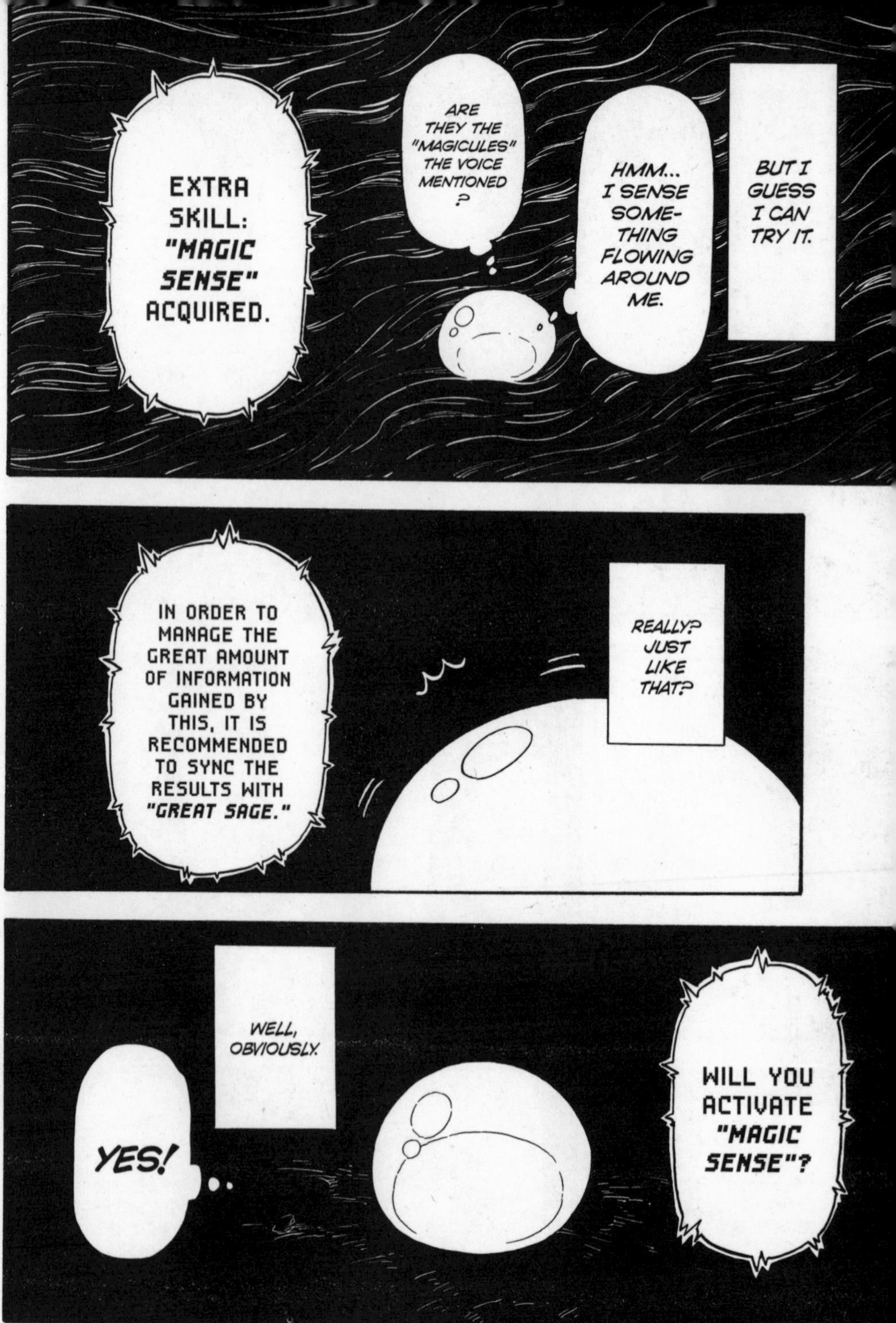

BUT I GUESS I CAN TRY IT.
HMM... I SENSE SOMETHING FLOWING AROUND ME.
ARE THEY THE "MAGICULES" THE VOICE MENTIONED?
EXTRA SKILL: "MAGIC SENSE" ACQUIRED.
IN ORDER TO MANAGE THE GREAT AMOUNT OF INFORMATION GAINED BY THIS, IT IS RECOMMENDED TO SYNC THE RESULTS WITH "GREAT SAGE."
REALLY? JUST LIKE THAT?
WILL YOU ACTIVATE "MAGIC SENSE"?
WELL, OBVIOUSLY.
YES!

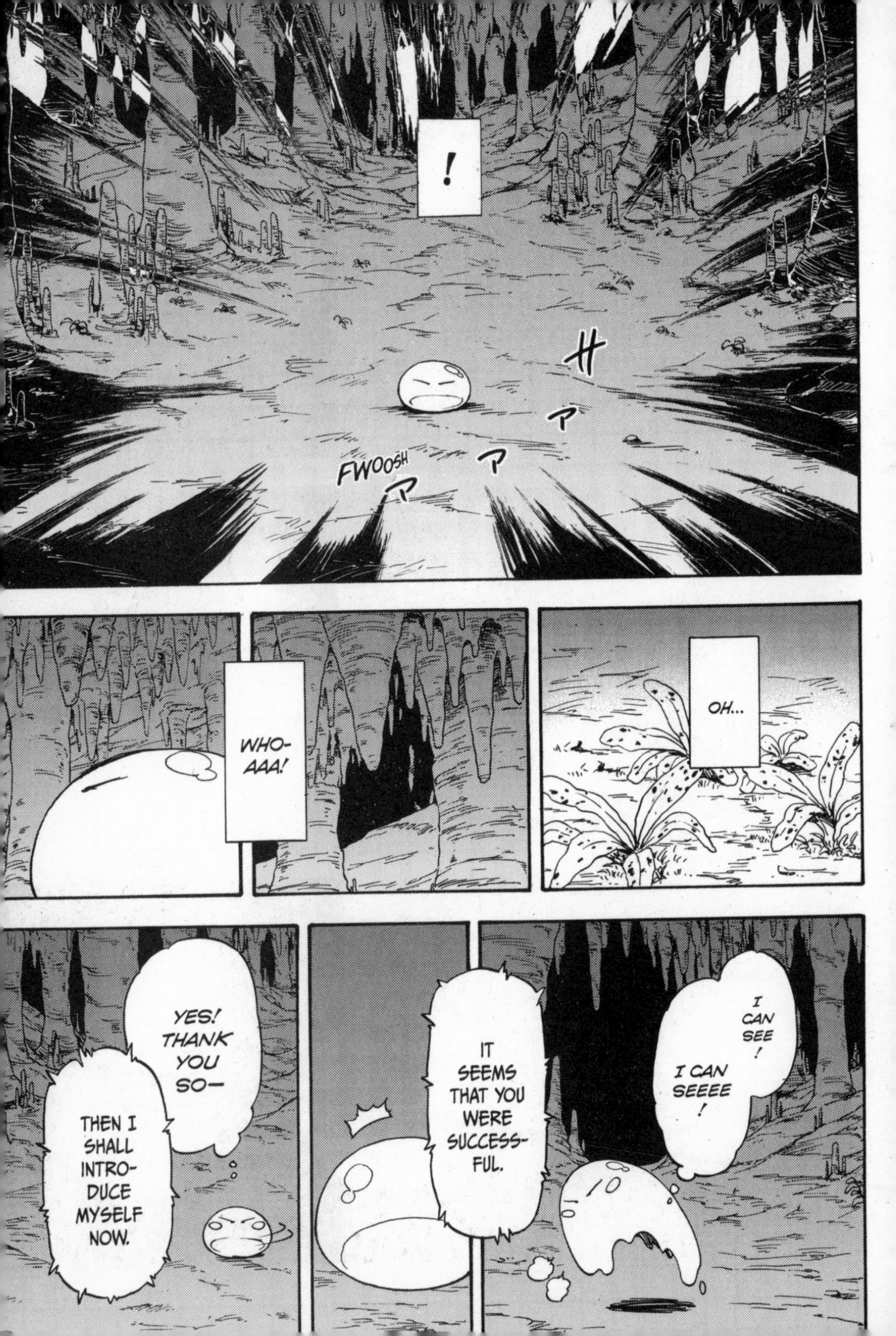
!
FWOOSH
OH...
WHO-AAA!
I CAN SEE!
I CAN SEEEE!
IT SEEMS THAT YOU WERE SUCCESSFUL.
YES! THANK YOU SO—
THEN I SHALL INTRODUCE MYSELF NOW.

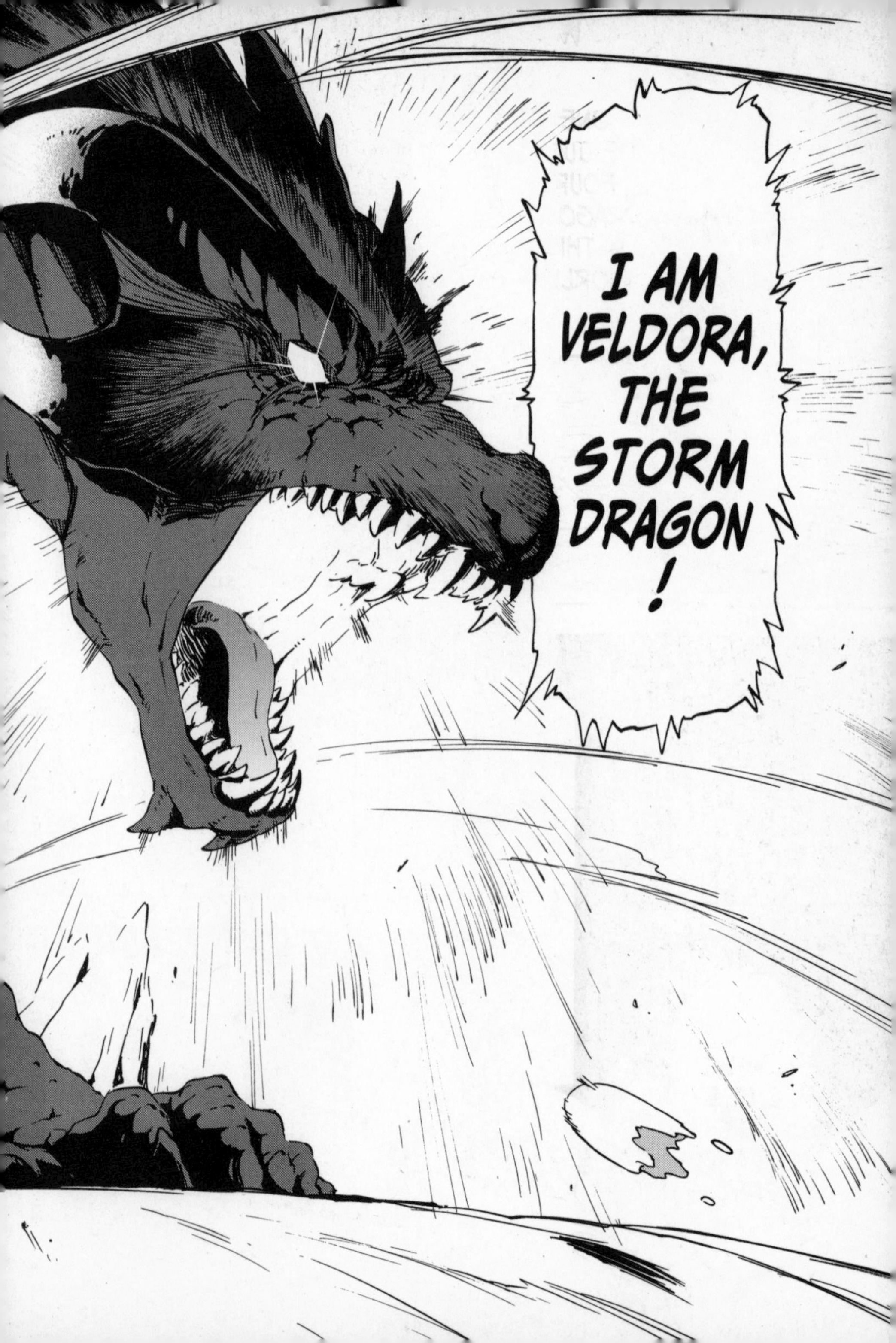
I AM VELDORA, THE STORM DRAGON!

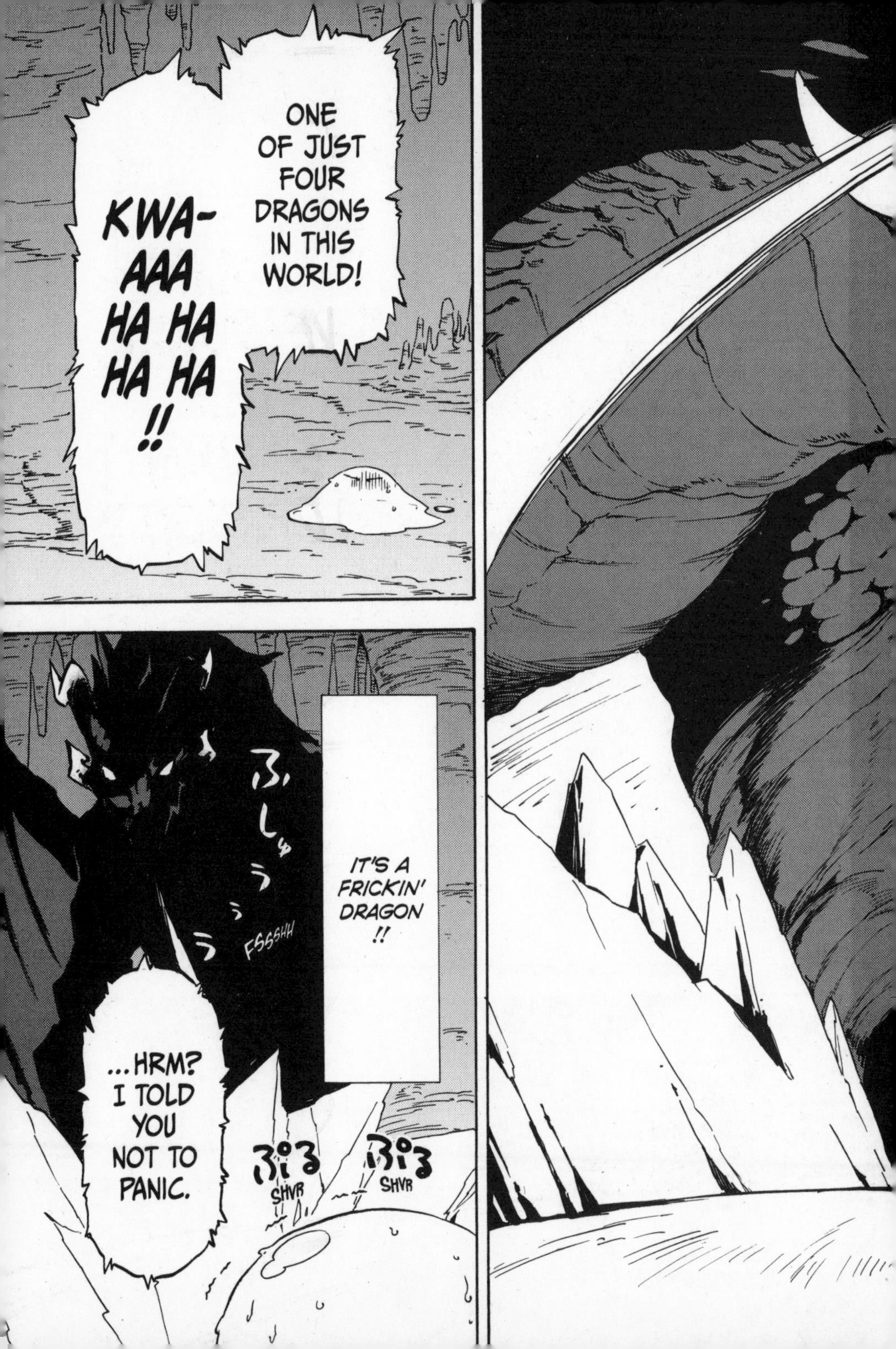
ONE OF JUST FOUR DRAGONS IN THIS WORLD!
KWA-AAA HA HA HA HA!!
IT'S A FRICKIN' DRAGON!!
ふしゅららら
FSSSHH
...HRM? I TOLD YOU NOT TO PANIC.
ぷる SHVR
ぷる SHVR

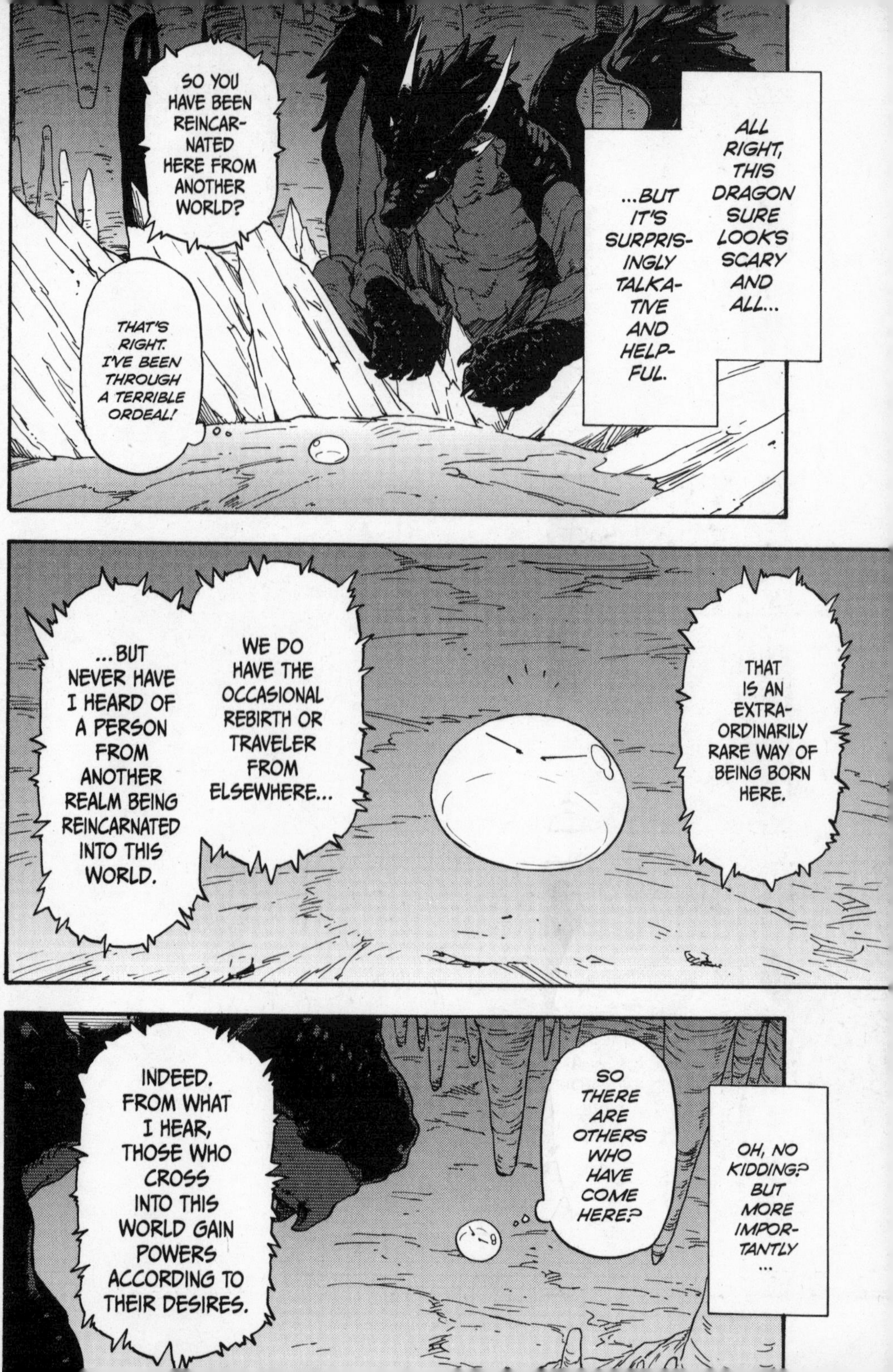
ALL RIGHT, THIS DRAGON SURE LOOKS SCARY AND ALL...
...BUT IT'S SURPRISINGLY TALKATIVE AND HELPFUL.
SO YOU HAVE BEEN REINCARNATED HERE FROM ANOTHER WORLD?
THAT'S RIGHT. I'VE BEEN THROUGH A TERRIBLE ORDEAL!
THAT IS AN EXTRAORDINARILY RARE WAY OF BEING BORN HERE.
WE DO HAVE THE OCCASIONAL REBIRTH OR TRAVELER FROM ELSEWHERE...
...BUT NEVER HAVE I HEARD OF A PERSON FROM ANOTHER REALM BEING REINCARNATED INTO THIS WORLD.
OH, NO KIDDING? BUT MORE IMPORTANTLY...
SO THERE ARE OTHERS WHO HAVE COME HERE?
INDEED. FROM WHAT I HEAR, THOSE WHO CROSS INTO THIS WORLD GAIN POWERS ACCORDING TO THEIR DESIRES.

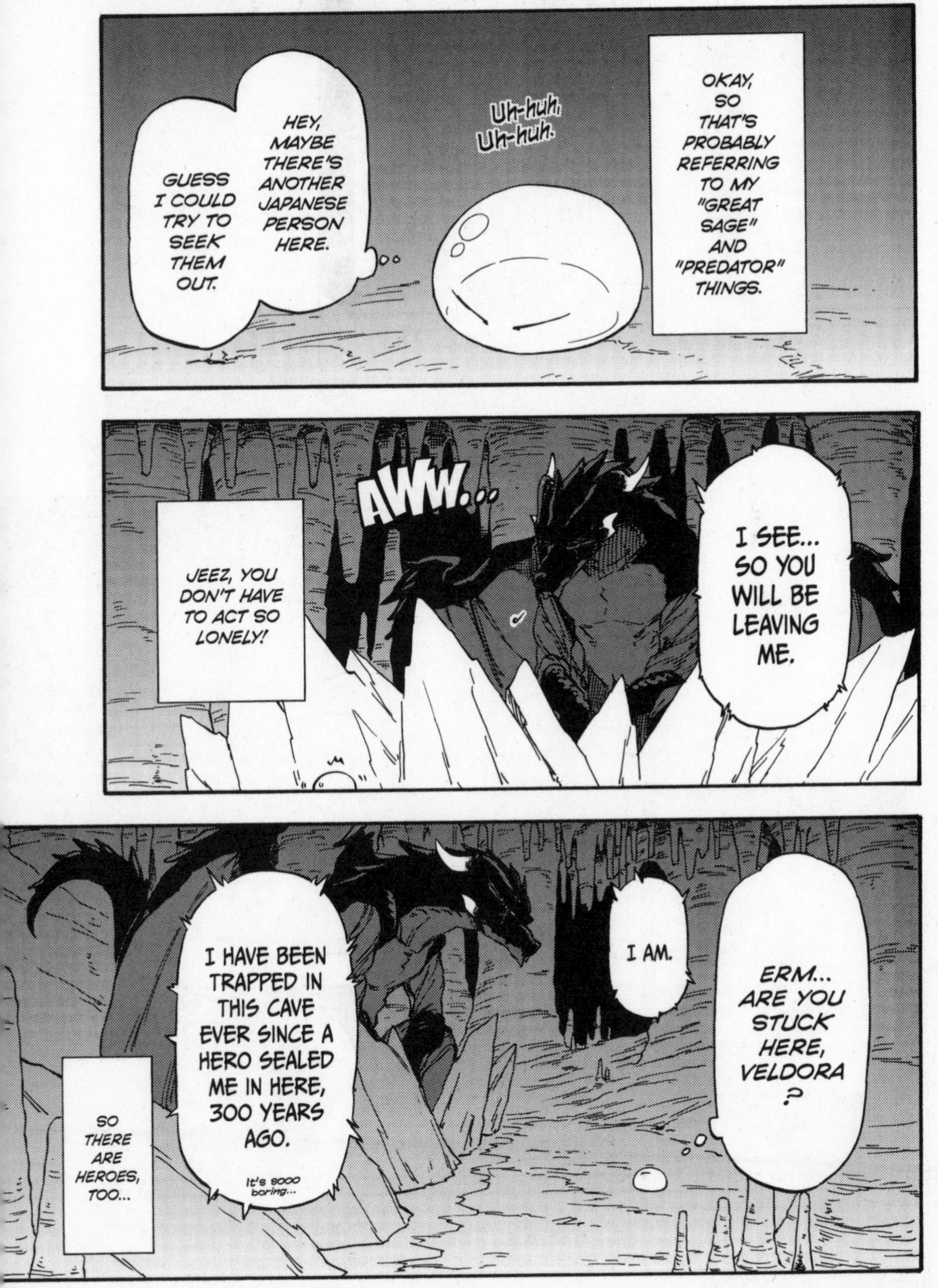

OKAY, SO THAT'S PROBABLY REFERRING TO MY "GREAT SAGE" AND "PREDATOR" THINGS.
Uh-huh. Uh-huh.
HEY, MAYBE THERE'S ANOTHER JAPANESE PERSON HERE.
GUESS I COULD TRY TO SEEK THEM OUT.
I SEE... SO YOU WILL BE LEAVING ME.
AWW...
JEEZ, YOU DON'T HAVE TO ACT SO LONELY!
ERM... ARE YOU STUCK HERE, VELDORA?
I AM.
I HAVE BEEN TRAPPED IN THIS CAVE EVER SINCE A HERO SEALED ME IN HERE, 300 YEARS AGO.
It's sooo boring...
SO THERE ARE HEROES, TOO...

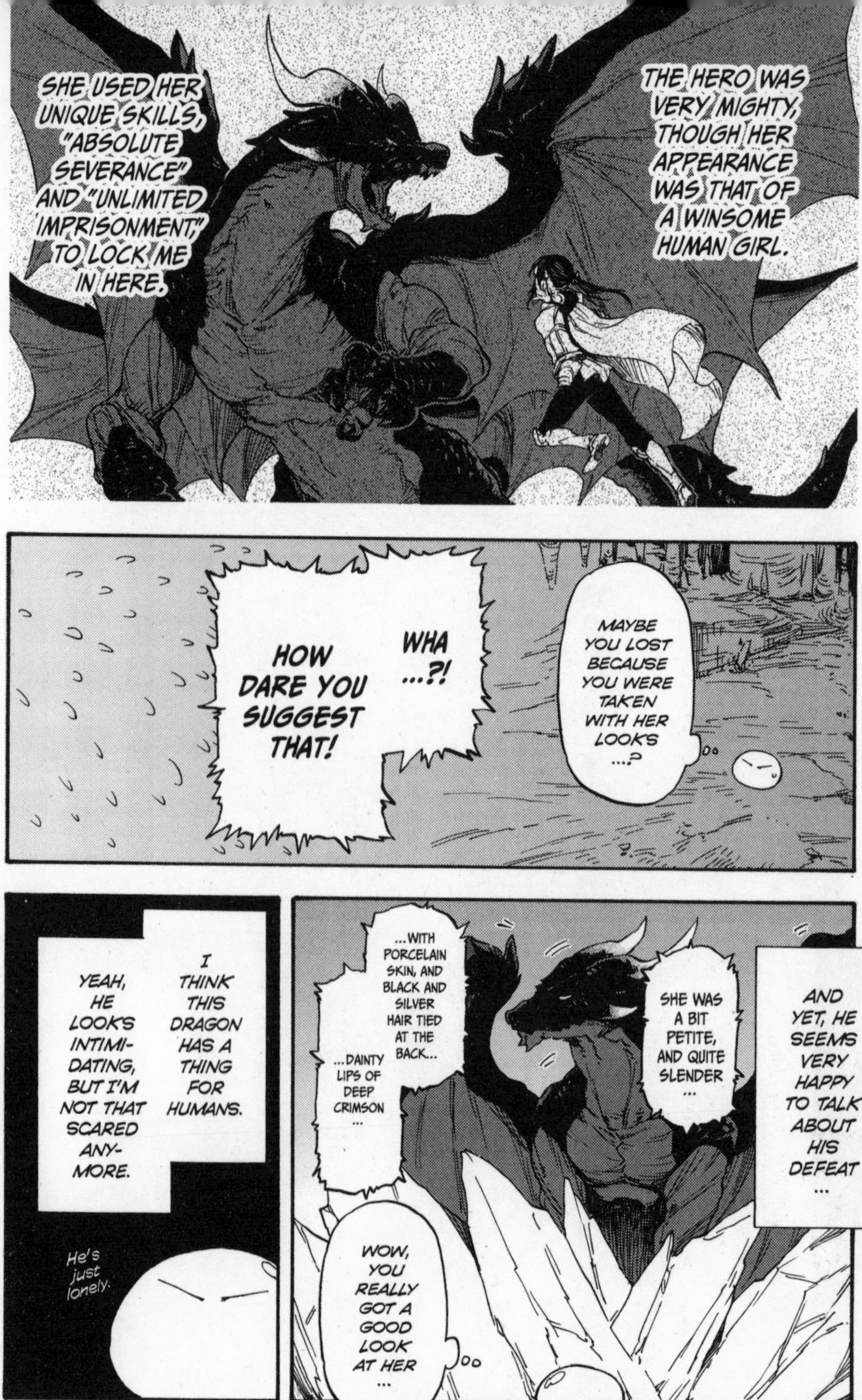
THE HERO WAS VERY MIGHTY, THOUGH HER APPEARANCE WAS THAT OF A WINSOME HUMAN GIRL.
SHE USED HER UNIQUE SKILLS, "ABSOLUTE SEVERANCE" AND "UNLIMITED IMPRISONMENT," TO LOCK ME IN HERE.
MAYBE YOU LOST BECAUSE YOU WERE TAKEN WITH HER LOOKS ...?
WHA ...?!
HOW DARE YOU SUGGEST THAT!
AND YET, HE SEEMS VERY HAPPY TO TALK ABOUT HIS DEFEAT ...
SHE WAS A BIT PETITE, AND QUITE SLENDER ...
...WITH PORCELAIN SKIN, AND BLACK AND SILVER HAIR TIED AT THE BACK...
...DAINTY LIPS OF DEEP CRIMSON ...
WOW, YOU REALLY GOT A GOOD LOOK AT HER ...
I THINK THIS DRAGON HAS A THING FOR HUMANS.
YEAH, HE LOOKS INTIMIDATING, BUT I'M NOT THAT SCARED ANYMORE.
He's just lonely.

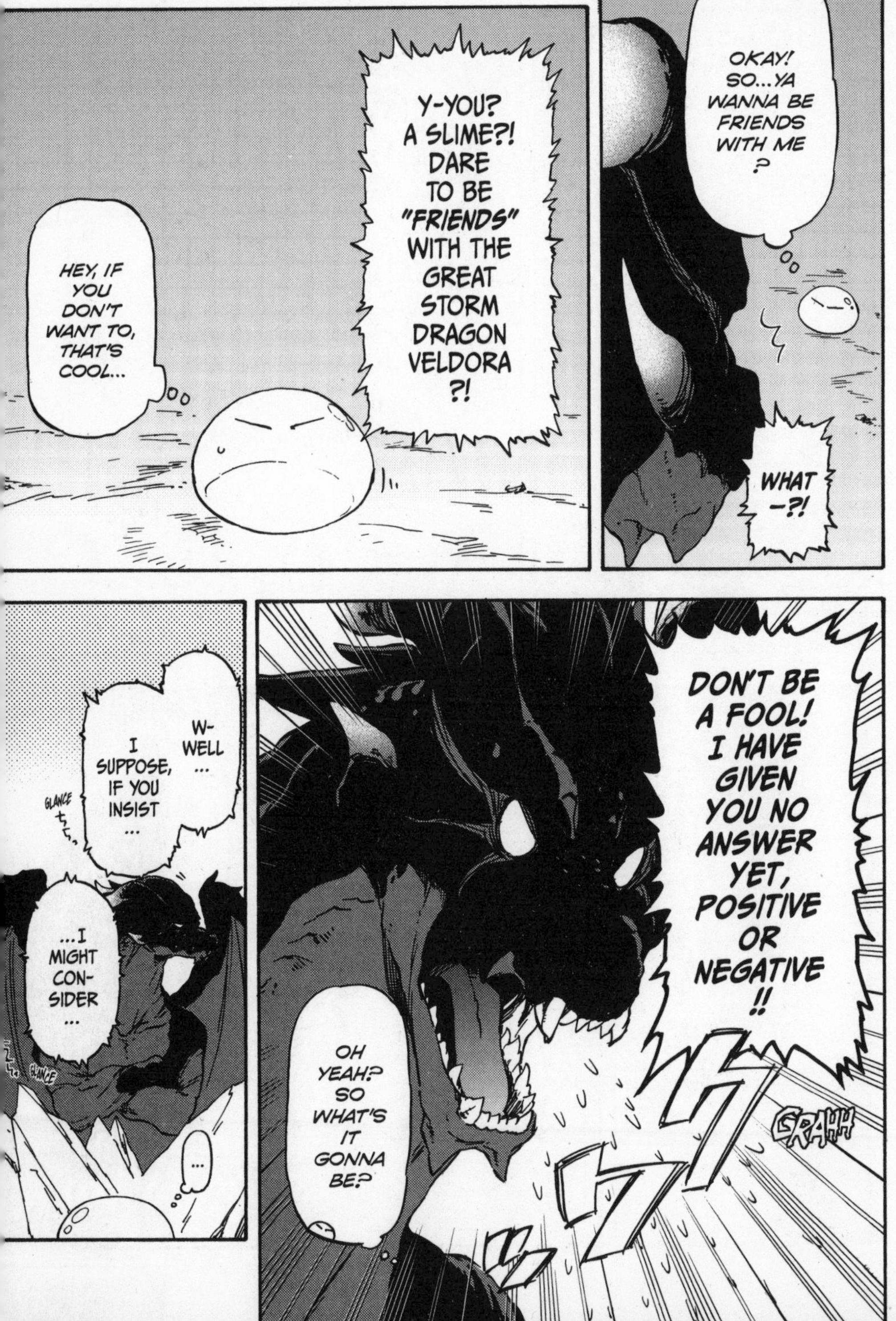
OKAY! SO...YA WANNA BE FRIENDS WITH ME?
WHAT—?!
Y-YOU? A SLIME?! DARE TO BE "FRIENDS" WITH THE GREAT STORM DRAGON VELDORA?!
HEY, IF YOU DON'T WANT TO, THAT'S COOL...
DON'T BE A FOOL! I HAVE GIVEN YOU NO ANSWER YET, POSITIVE OR NEGATIVE!!
GRAHH
OH YEAH? SO WHAT'S IT GONNA BE?
W-WELL...
I SUPPOSE, IF YOU INSIST...
GLANCE
...I MIGHT CONSIDER...
GLANCE
...

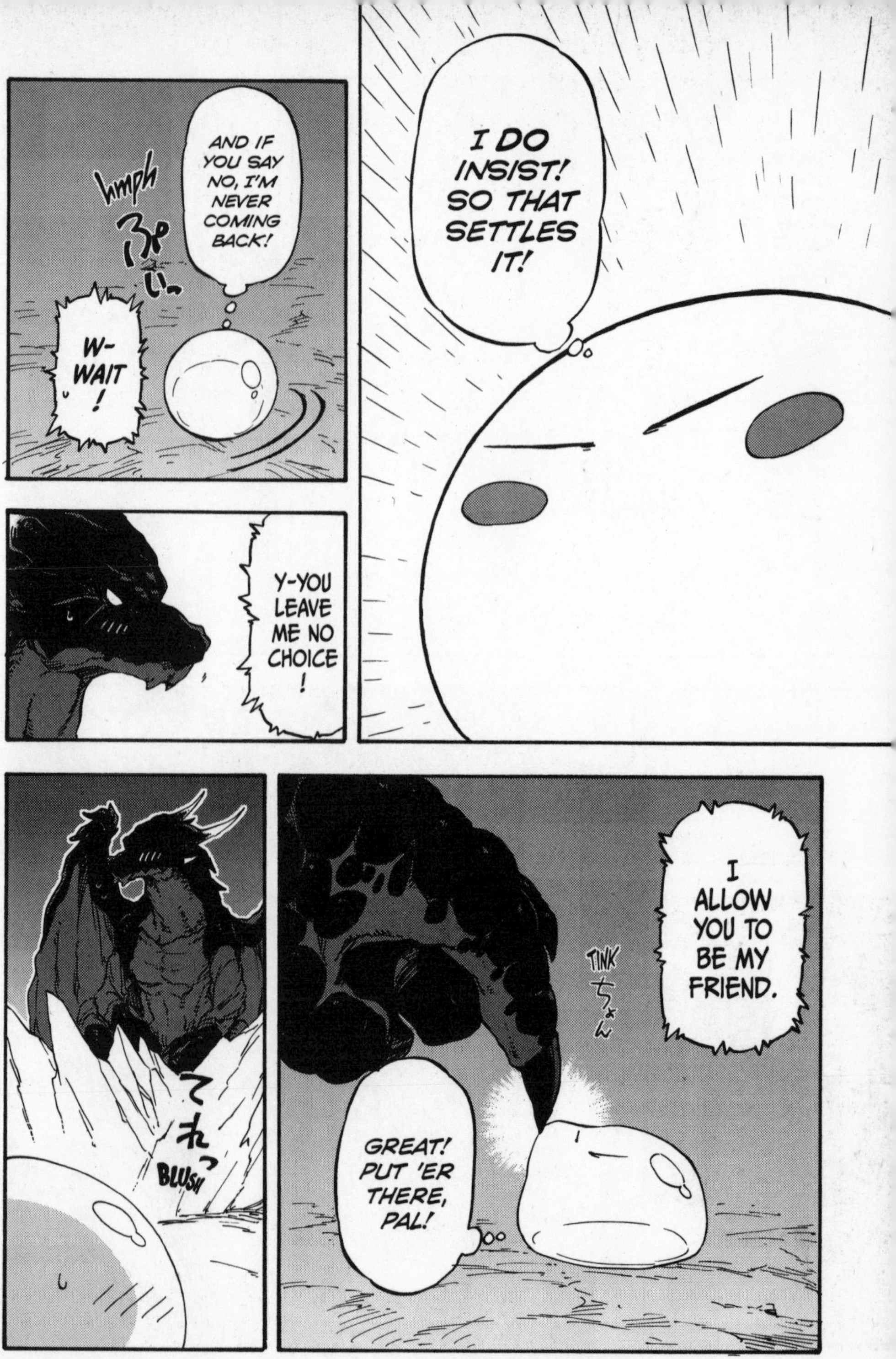
I DO INSIST! SO THAT SETTLES IT!
AND IF YOU SAY NO, I'M NEVER COMING BACK!
hmph
W-WAIT!
Y-YOU LEAVE ME NO CHOICE!
I ALLOW YOU TO BE MY FRIEND.
TINK
GREAT! PUT 'ER THERE, PAL!
BLUSH

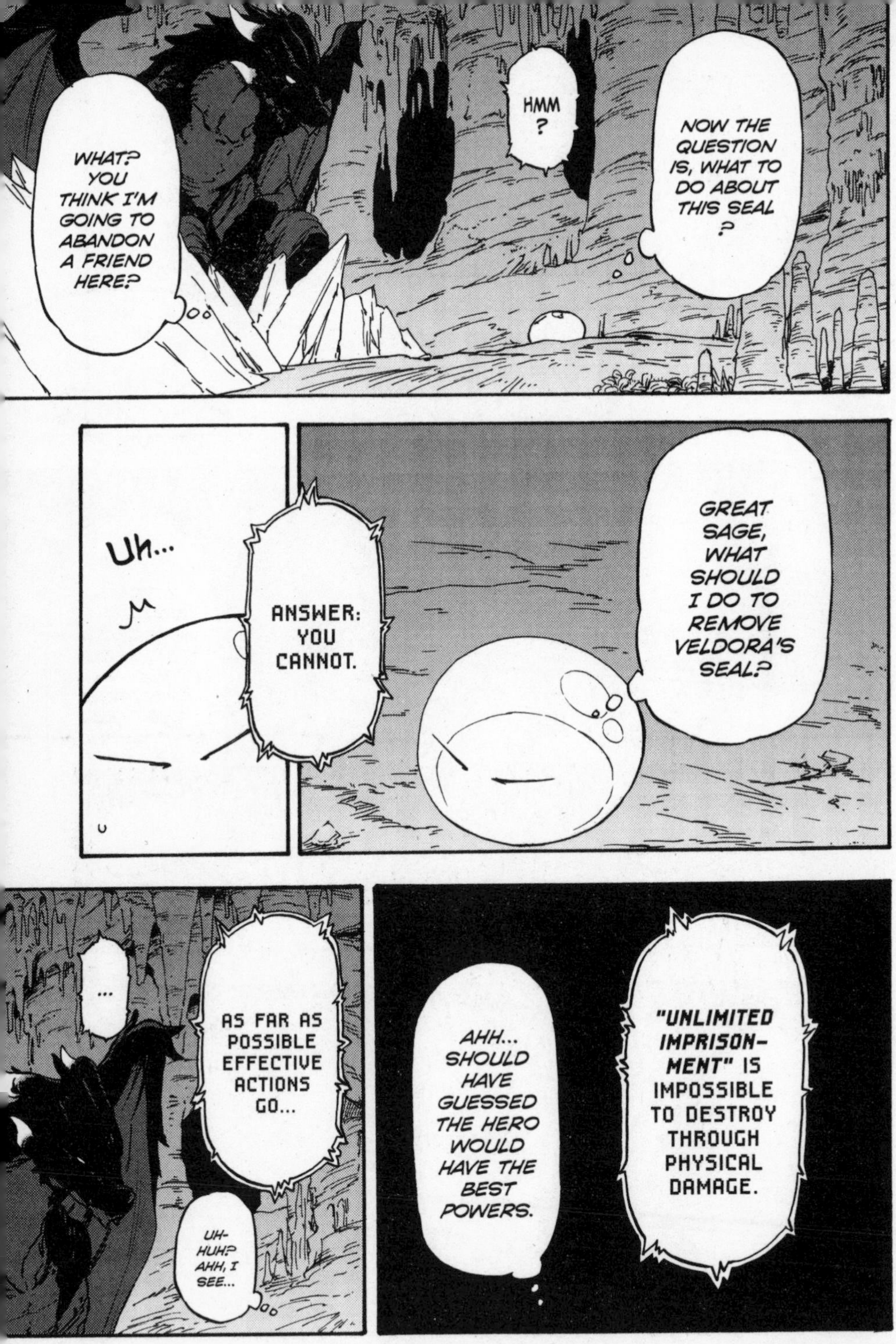
NOW THE QUESTION IS, WHAT TO DO ABOUT THIS SEAL?
HMM?
WHAT? YOU THINK I'M GOING TO ABANDON A FRIEND HERE?
GREAT SAGE, WHAT SHOULD I DO TO REMOVE VELDORA'S SEAL?
ANSWER: YOU CANNOT.
Uh...
"UNLIMITED IMPRISONMENT" IS IMPOSSIBLE TO DESTROY THROUGH PHYSICAL DAMAGE.
AHH... SHOULD HAVE GUESSED THE HERO WOULD HAVE THE BEST POWERS.
AS FAR AS POSSIBLE EFFECTIVE ACTIONS GO...
...
UH-HUH? AHH, I SEE...

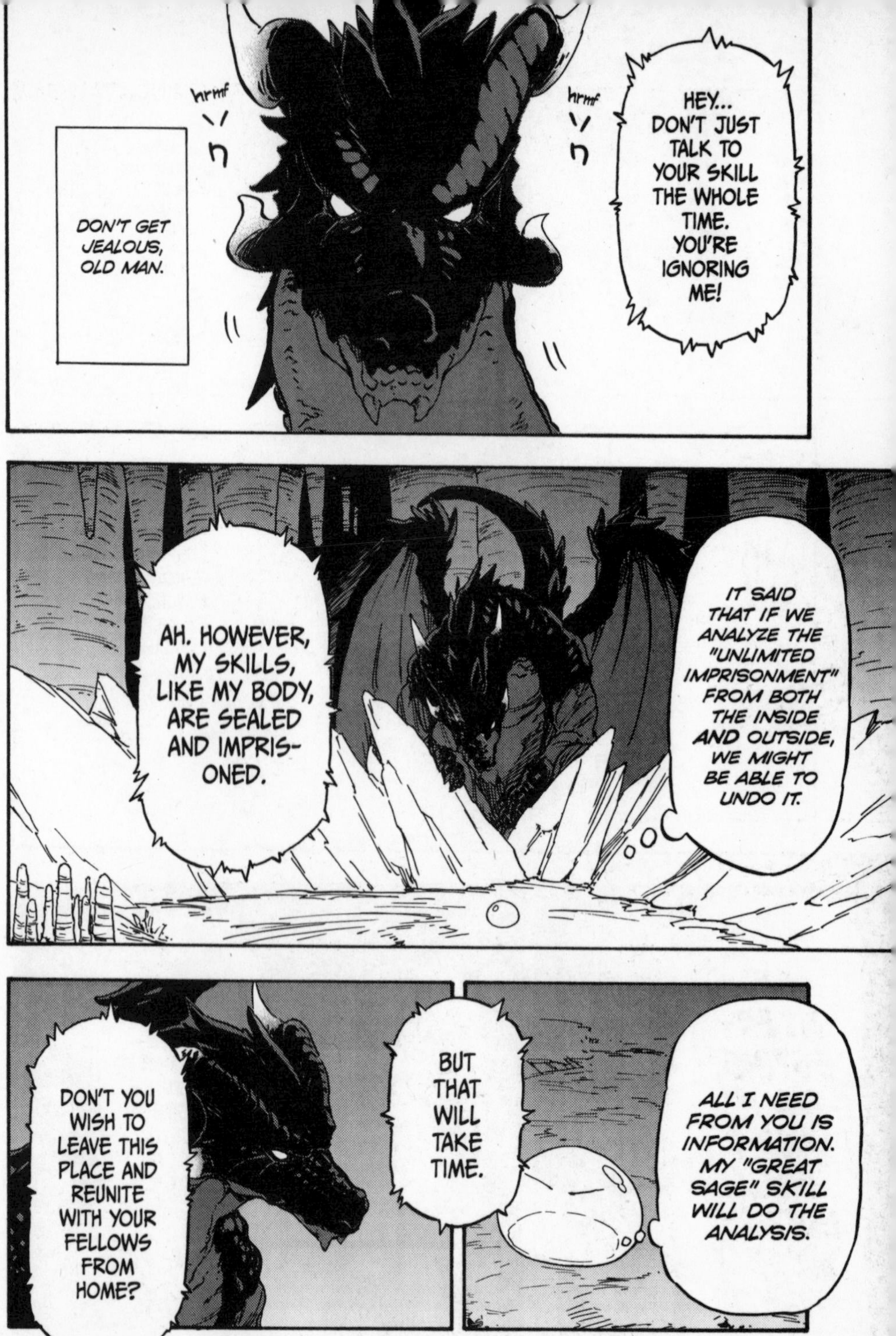
HEY... DON'T JUST TALK TO YOUR SKILL THE WHOLE TIME. YOU'RE IGNORING ME!
hrmf
hrmf
DON'T GET JEALOUS, OLD MAN.
IT SAID THAT IF WE ANALYZE THE "UNLIMITED IMPRISONMENT" FROM BOTH THE INSIDE AND OUTSIDE, WE MIGHT BE ABLE TO UNDO IT.
AH. HOWEVER, MY SKILLS, LIKE MY BODY, ARE SEALED AND IMPRIS-ONED.
ALL I NEED FROM YOU IS INFORMATION. MY "GREAT SAGE" SKILL WILL DO THE ANALYSIS.
BUT THAT WILL TAKE TIME.
DON'T YOU WISH TO LEAVE THIS PLACE AND REUNITE WITH YOUR FELLOWS FROM HOME?

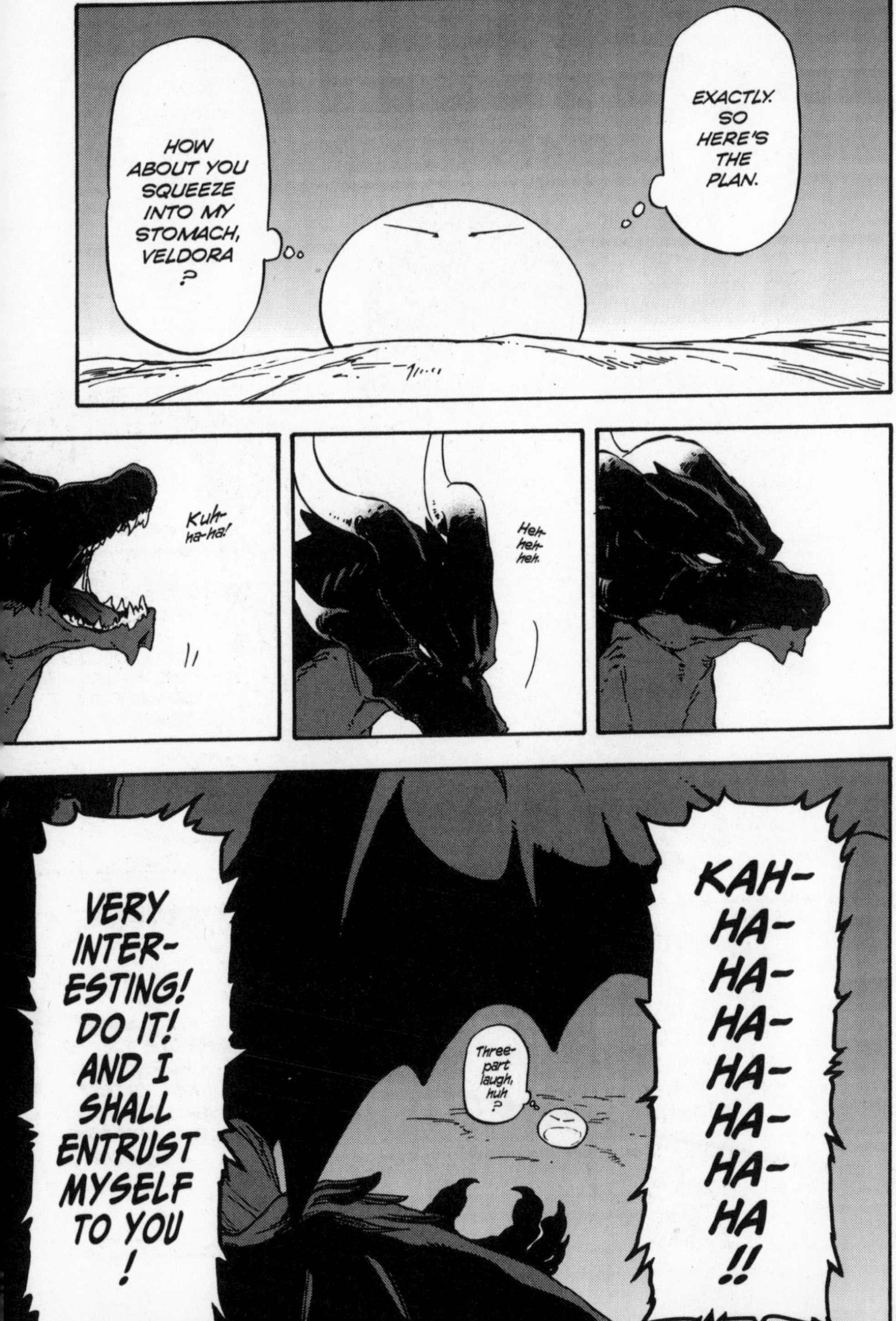
EXACTLY. SO HERE'S THE PLAN.
HOW ABOUT YOU SQUEEZE INTO MY STOMACH, VELDORA ?
Heh-heh-heh.
Kuh-ha-ha!
KAH-HA-HA-HA-HA-HA-HA-HA-HA !!
Three-part laugh, huh ?
VERY INTER-ESTING! DO IT! AND I SHALL ENTRUST MYSELF TO YOU !

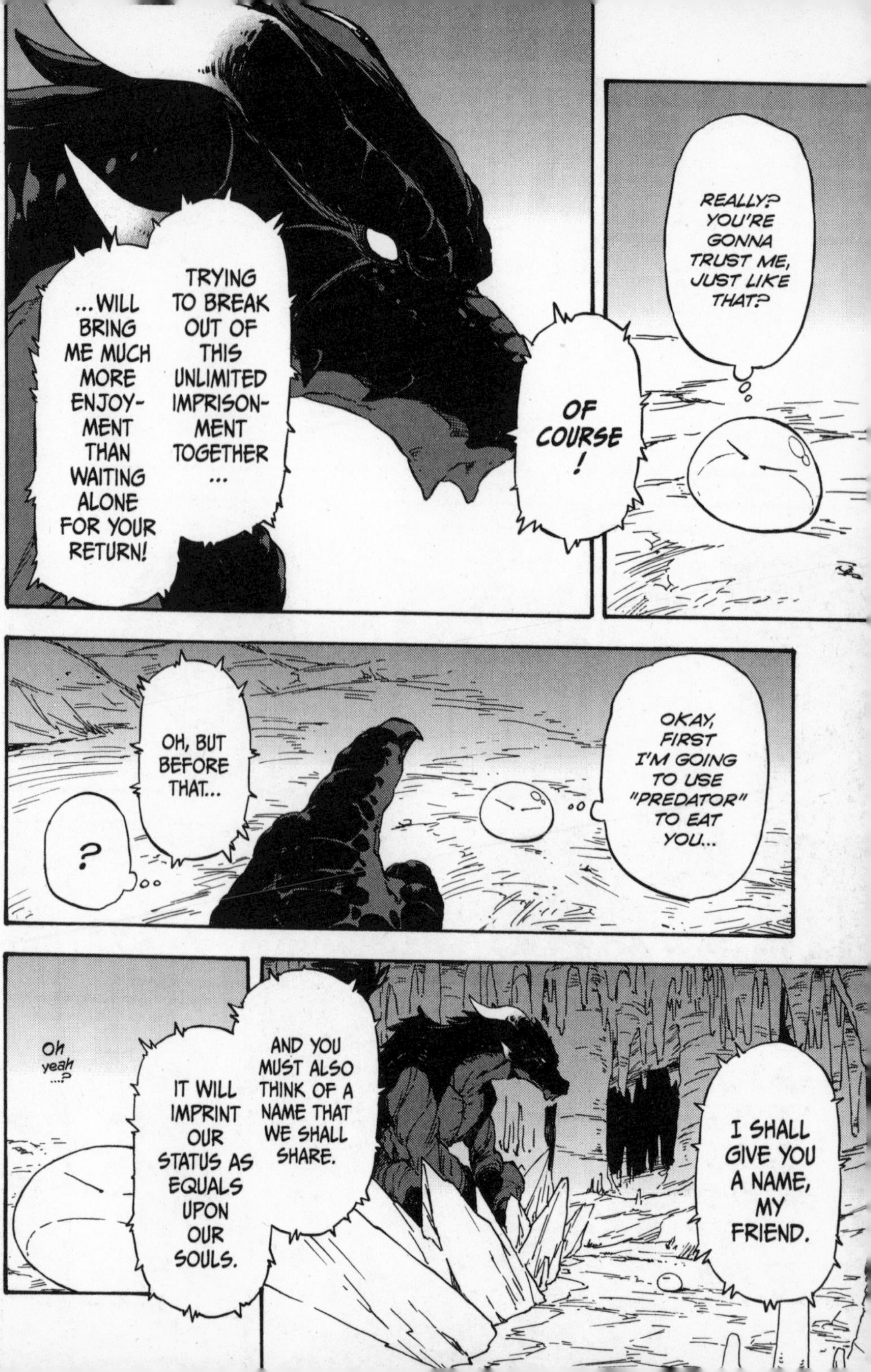
REALLY? YOU'RE GONNA TRUST ME, JUST LIKE THAT?
OF COURSE!
TRYING TO BREAK OUT OF THIS UNLIMITED IMPRISONMENT TOGETHER...
...WILL BRING ME MUCH MORE ENJOYMENT THAN WAITING ALONE FOR YOUR RETURN!
OKAY, FIRST I'M GOING TO USE "PREDATOR" TO EAT YOU...
OH, BUT BEFORE THAT...
?
I SHALL GIVE YOU A NAME, MY FRIEND.
AND YOU MUST ALSO THINK OF A NAME THAT WE SHALL SHARE.
IT WILL IMPRINT OUR STATUS AS EQUALS UPON OUR SOULS.
Oh yeah...?

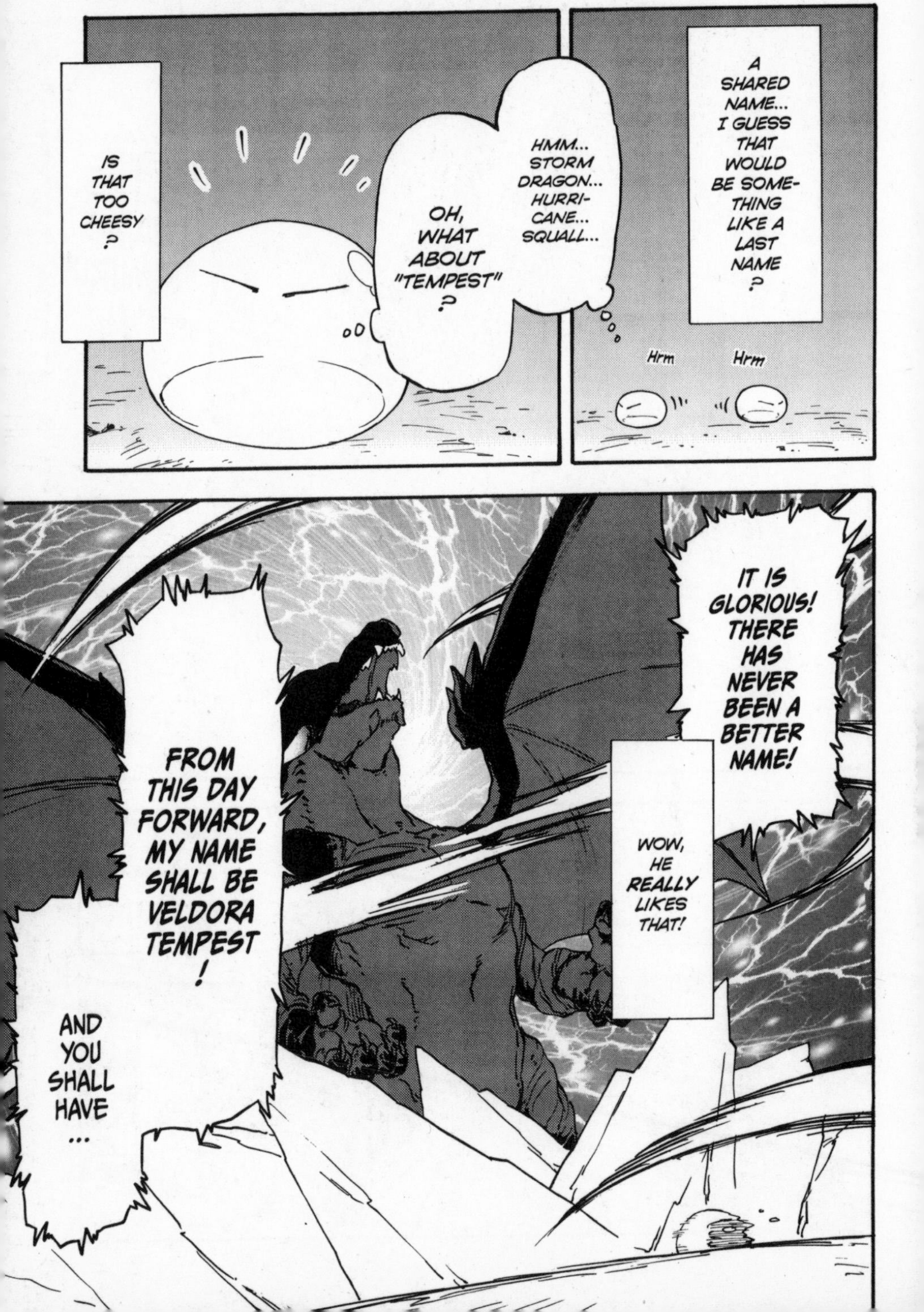
A SHARED NAME... I GUESS THAT WOULD BE SOME-THING LIKE A LAST NAME?
Hrm
Hrm
HMM... STORM DRAGON... HURRI-CANE... SQUALL...
OH, WHAT ABOUT "TEMPEST"?
IS THAT TOO CHEESY?
IT IS GLORIOUS! THERE HAS NEVER BEEN A BETTER NAME!
WOW, HE REALLY LIKES THAT!
FROM THIS DAY FORWARD, MY NAME SHALL BE VELDORA TEMPEST!
AND YOU SHALL HAVE...

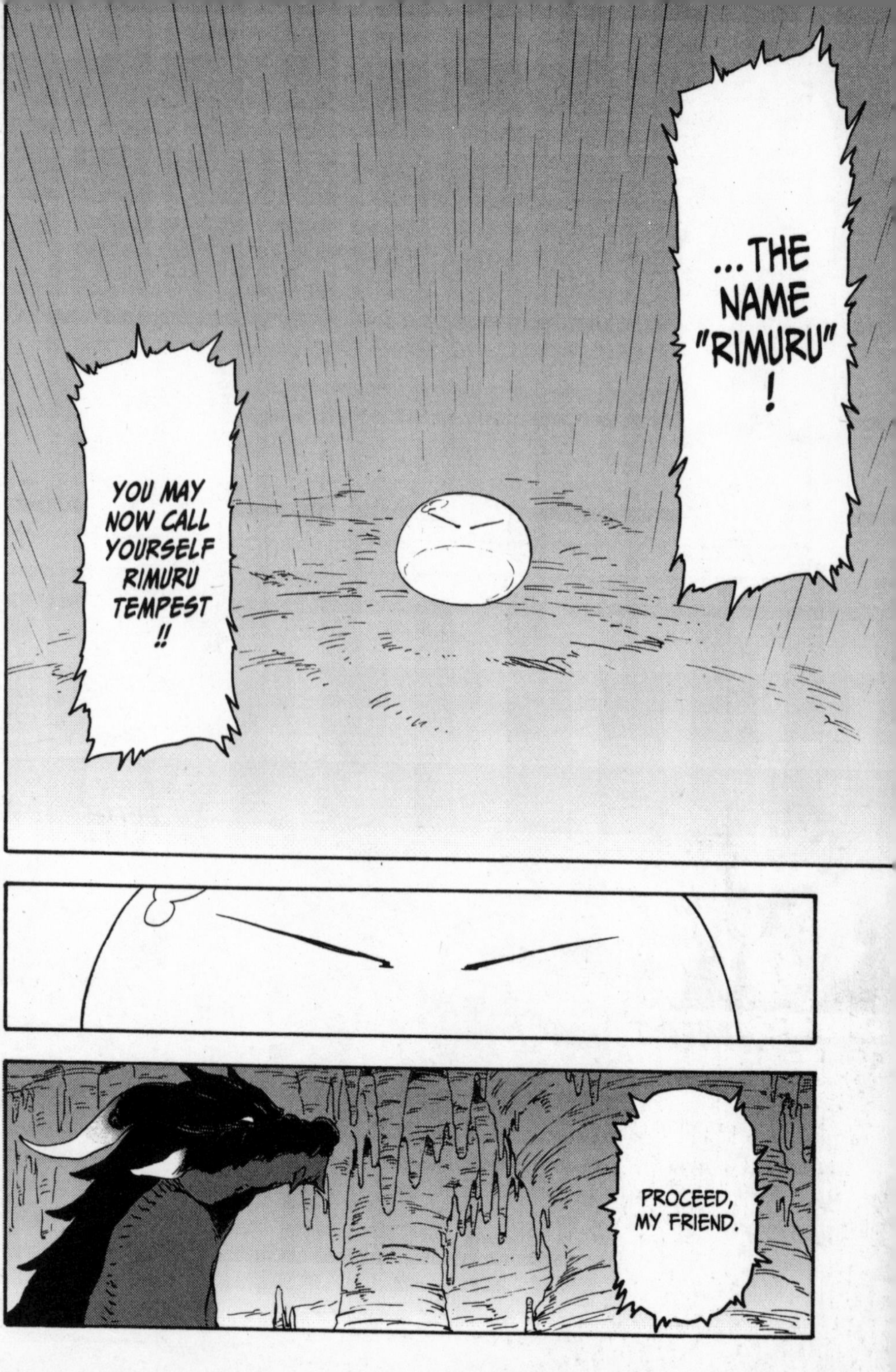
...THE NAME "RIMURU" !
YOU MAY NOW CALL YOURSELF RIMURU TEMPEST !!
PROCEED, MY FRIEND.

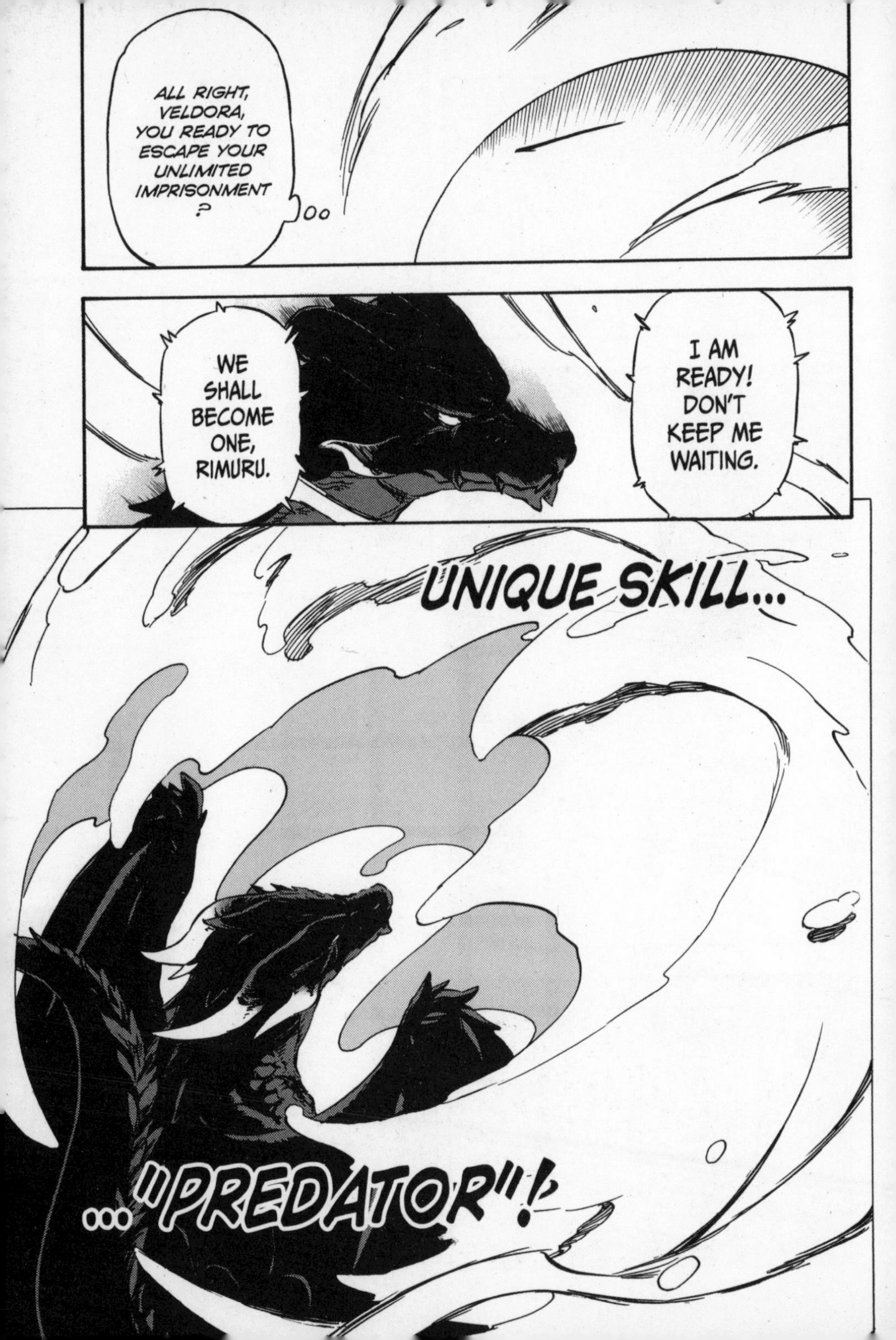
ALL RIGHT, VELDORA, YOU READY TO ESCAPE YOUR UNLIMITED IMPRISONMENT?
I AM READY! DON'T KEEP ME WAITING.
WE SHALL BECOME ONE, RIMURU.
UNIQUE SKILL...
..."PREDATOR"!

しん…
SHHM...

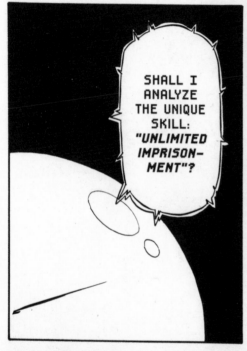

SHALL I ANALYZE THE UNIQUE SKILL: *"UNLIMITED IMPRISON-MENT"*?

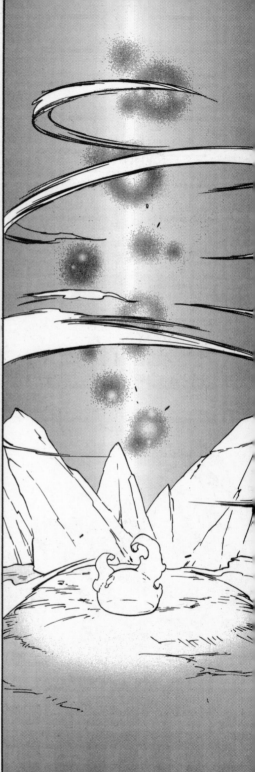

TAKE IT AWAY, GREAT SAGE!

YES, OF COURSE!

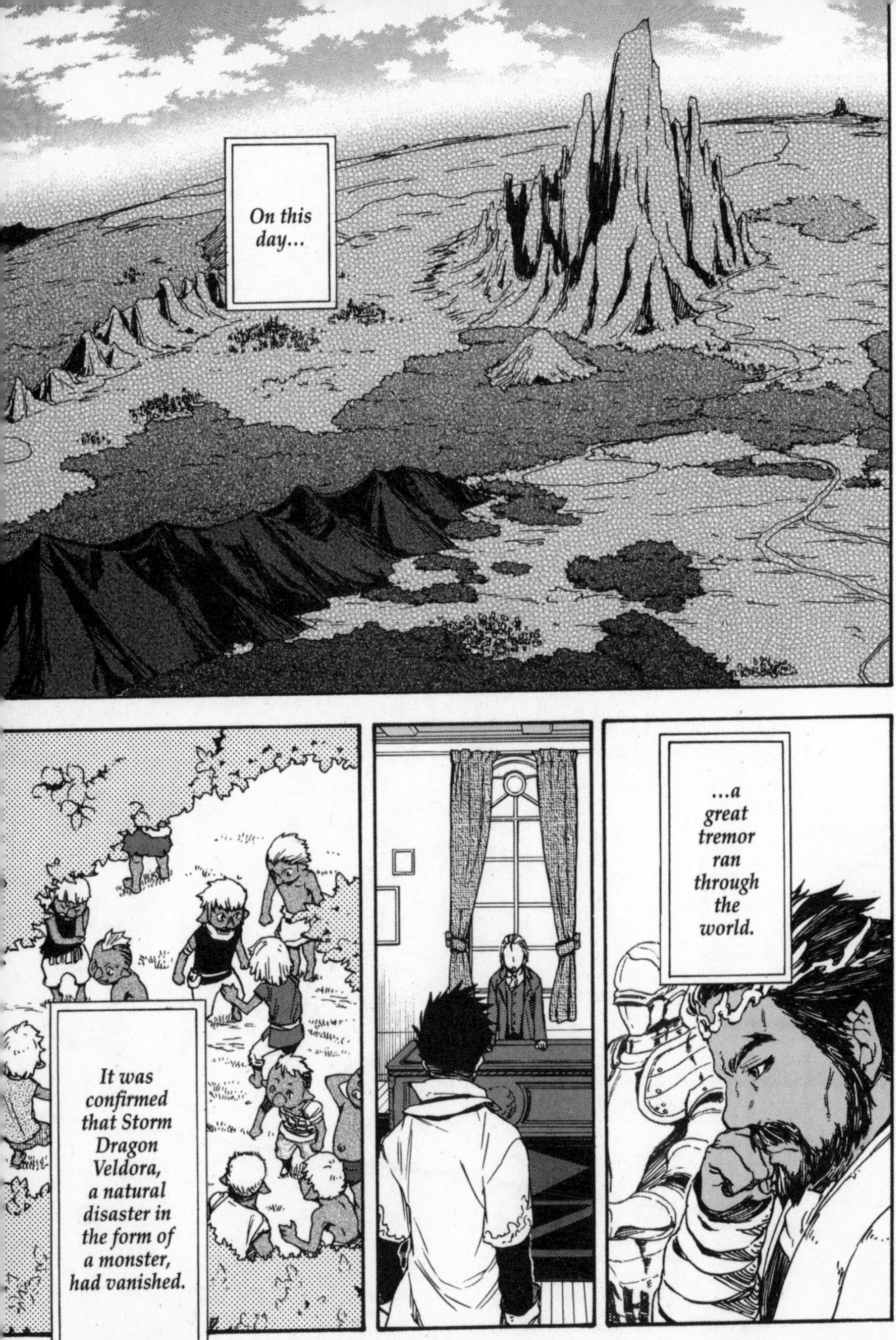
On this day...
...a great tremor ran through the world.
It was confirmed that Storm Dragon Veldora, a natural disaster in the form of a monster, had vanished.

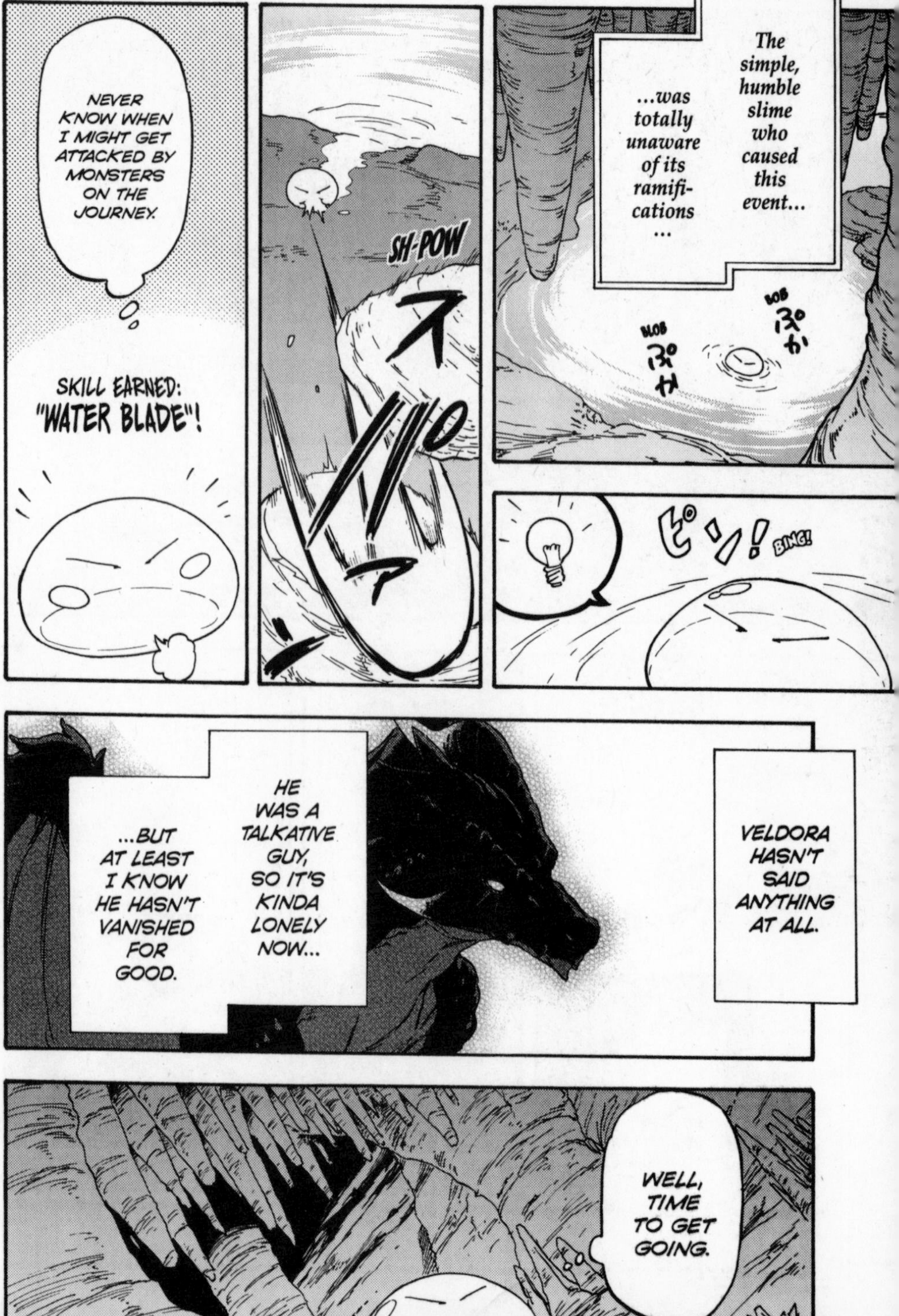
The simple, humble slime who caused this event...
...was totally unaware of its ramifications ...
BLOB
BLOB
BING!
SH-POW
NEVER KNOW WHEN I MIGHT GET ATTACKED BY MONSTERS ON THE JOURNEY.
SKILL EARNED: "WATER BLADE"!
VELDORA HASN'T SAID ANYTHING AT ALL.
HE WAS A TALKATIVE GUY, SO IT'S KINDA LONELY NOW...
...BUT AT LEAST I KNOW HE HASN'T VANISHED FOR GOOD.
WELL, TIME TO GET GOING.

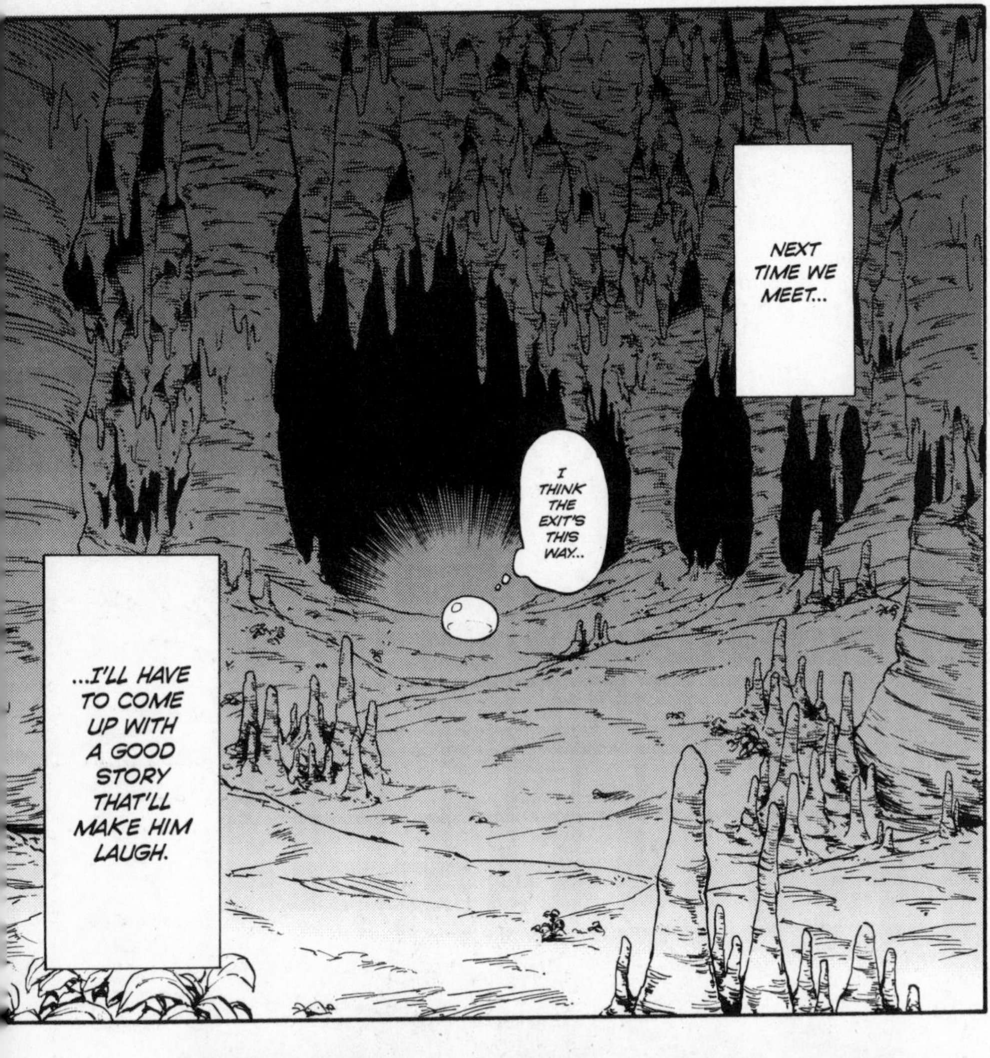
NEXT TIME WE MEET...
I THINK THE EXIT'S THIS WAY...
...I'LL HAVE TO COME UP WITH A GOOD STORY THAT'LL MAKE HIM LAUGH.

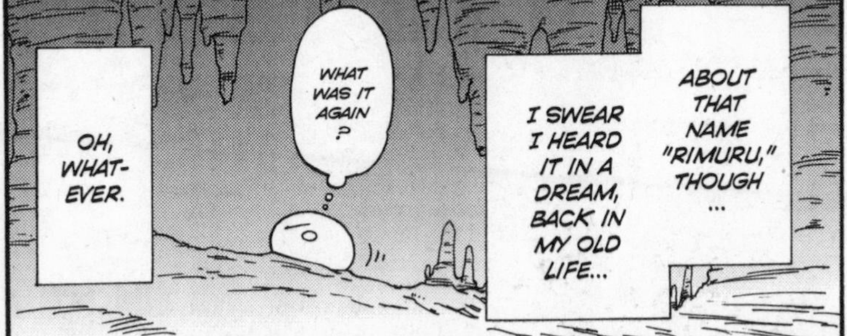
ABOUT THAT NAME "RIMURU," THOUGH ...
I SWEAR I HEARD IT IN A DREAM, BACK IN MY OLD LIFE...
WHAT WAS IT AGAIN ?
OH, WHAT-EVER.

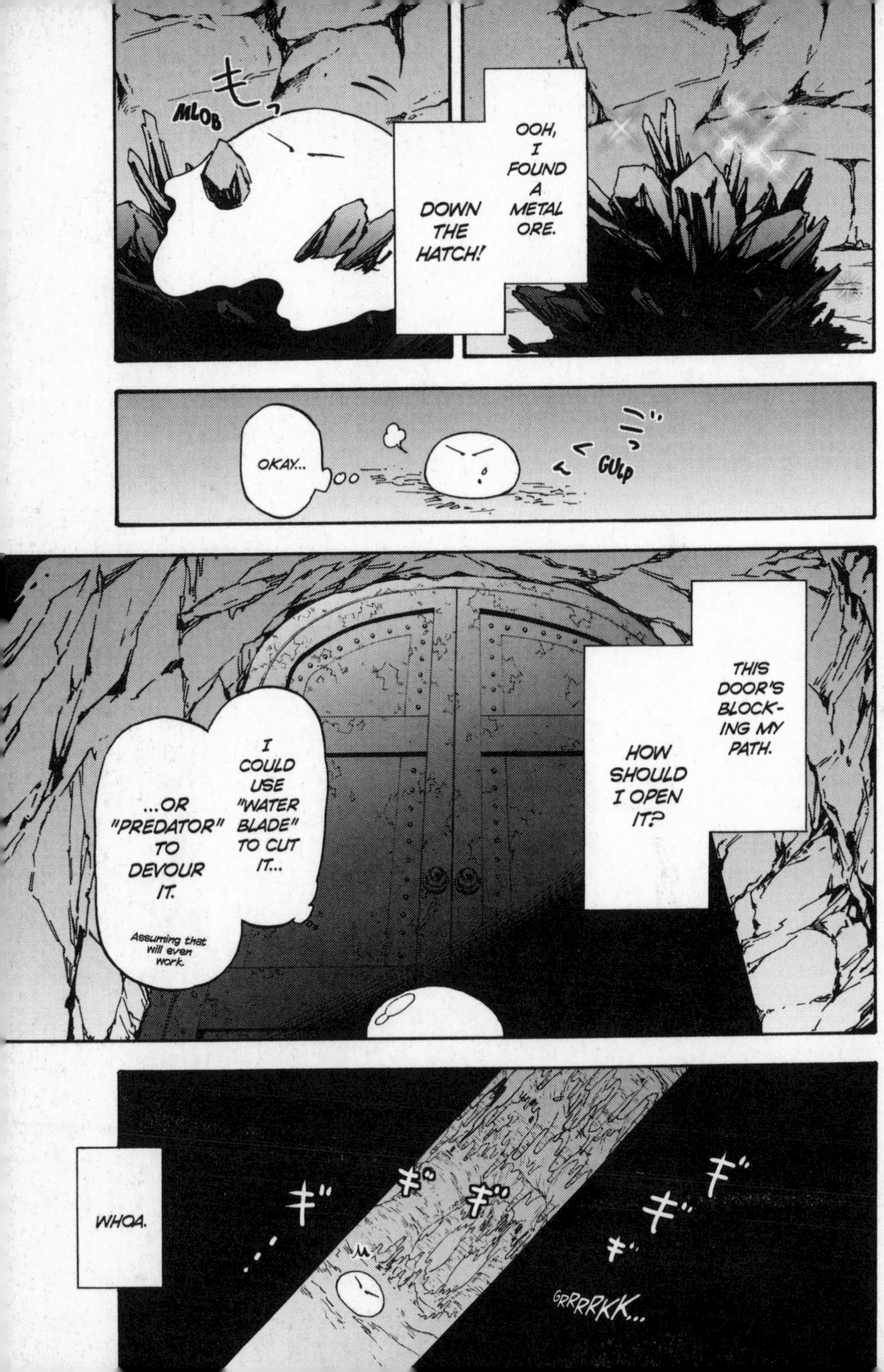
OOH, I FOUND A METAL ORE.
DOWN THE HATCH!
MLOB
GULP
OKAY...
THIS DOOR'S BLOCK-ING MY PATH.
HOW SHOULD I OPEN IT?
I COULD USE "WATER BLADE" TO CUT IT...
...OR "PREDATOR" TO DEVOUR IT.
Assuming that will even work.
GRRRRKK...
WHOA.

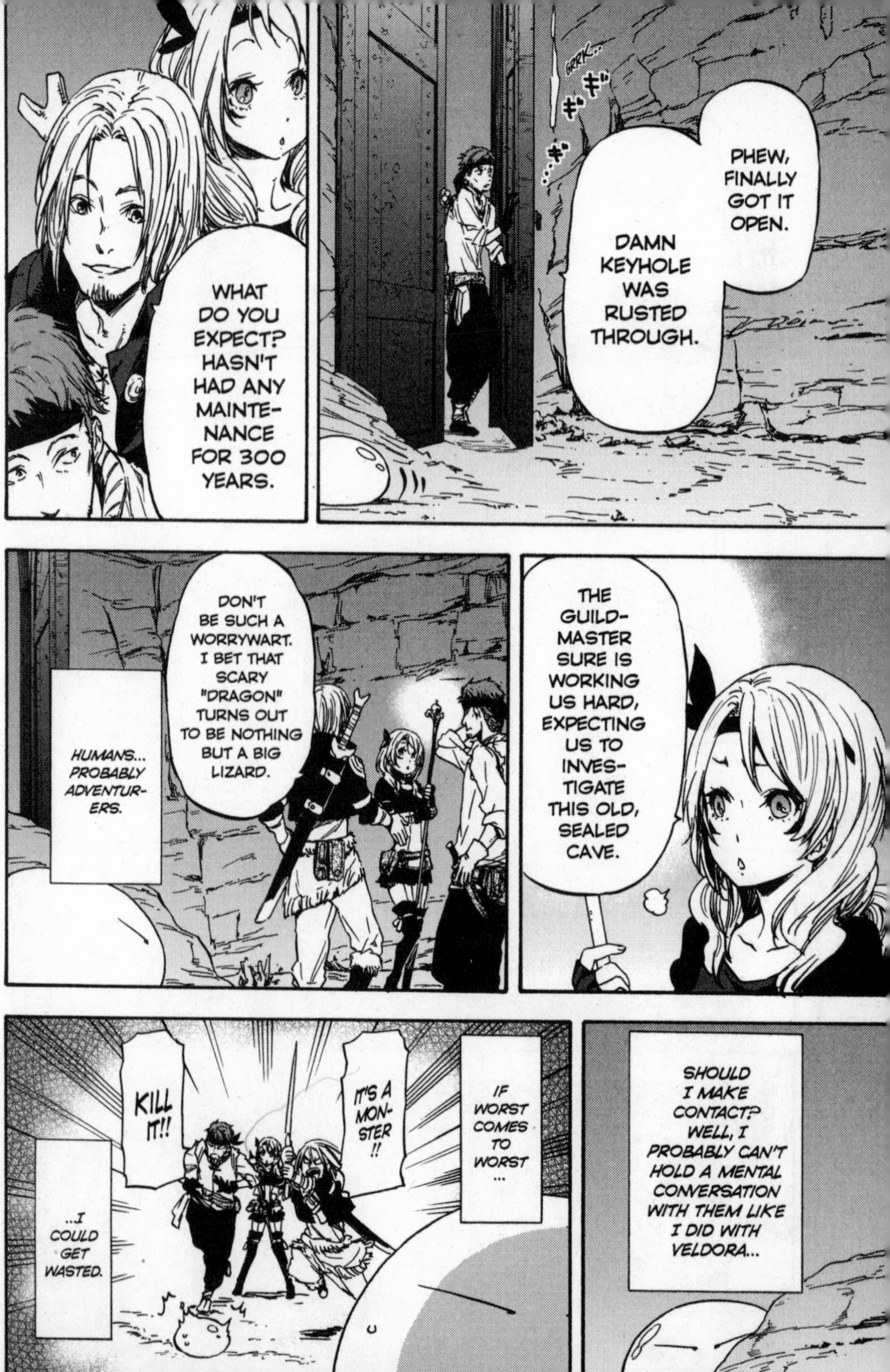
GRRK...
ギギ
ギ...
PHEW, FINALLY GOT IT OPEN.
DAMN KEYHOLE WAS RUSTED THROUGH.
WHAT DO YOU EXPECT? HASN'T HAD ANY MAINTE-NANCE FOR 300 YEARS.
THE GUILD-MASTER SURE IS WORKING US HARD, EXPECTING US TO INVES-TIGATE THIS OLD, SEALED CAVE.
DON'T BE SUCH A WORRYWART. I BET THAT SCARY "DRAGON" TURNS OUT TO BE NOTHING BUT A BIG LIZARD.
HUMANS... PROBABLY ADVENTUR-ERS.
SHOULD I MAKE CONTACT? WELL, I PROBABLY CAN'T HOLD A MENTAL CONVERSATION WITH THEM LIKE I DID WITH VELDORA...
IF WORST COMES TO WORST...
IT'S A MON-STER!!
KILL IT!!
...I COULD GET WASTED.

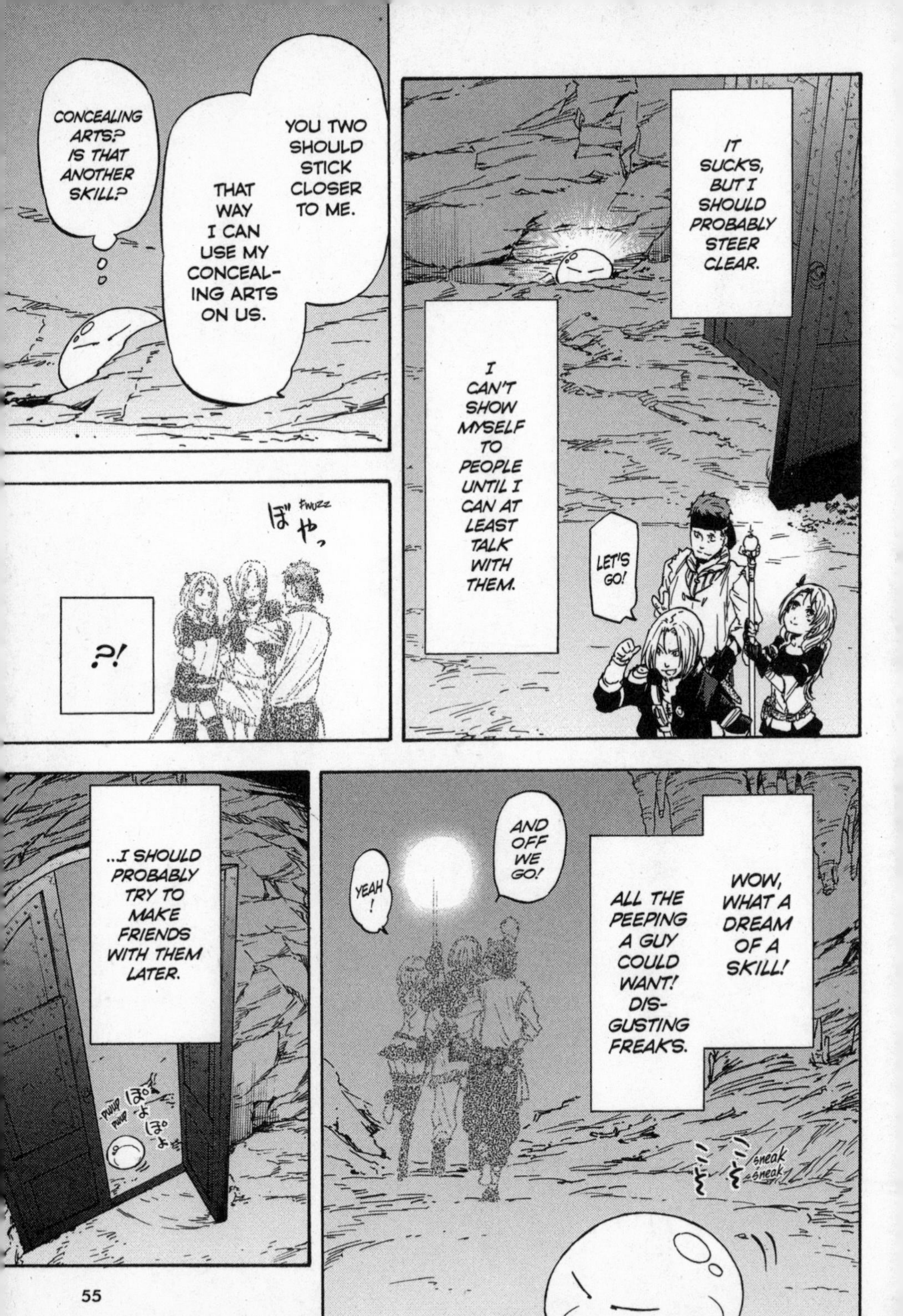
IT SUCKS, BUT I SHOULD PROBABLY STEER CLEAR.
I CAN'T SHOW MYSELF TO PEOPLE UNTIL I CAN AT LEAST TALK WITH THEM.
LET'S GO!
YOU TWO SHOULD STICK CLOSER TO ME.
THAT WAY I CAN USE MY CONCEAL-ING ARTS ON US.
CONCEALING ARTS? IS THAT ANOTHER SKILL?
ぼやっ
FWUZZ
?!
WOW, WHAT A DREAM OF A SKILL!
ALL THE PEEPING A GUY COULD WANT! DIS-GUSTING FREAKS.
AND OFF WE GO!
YEAH!
sneak sneak
...I SHOULD PROBABLY TRY TO MAKE FRIENDS WITH THEM LATER.
ぽよぽよ
PWUP PWUP

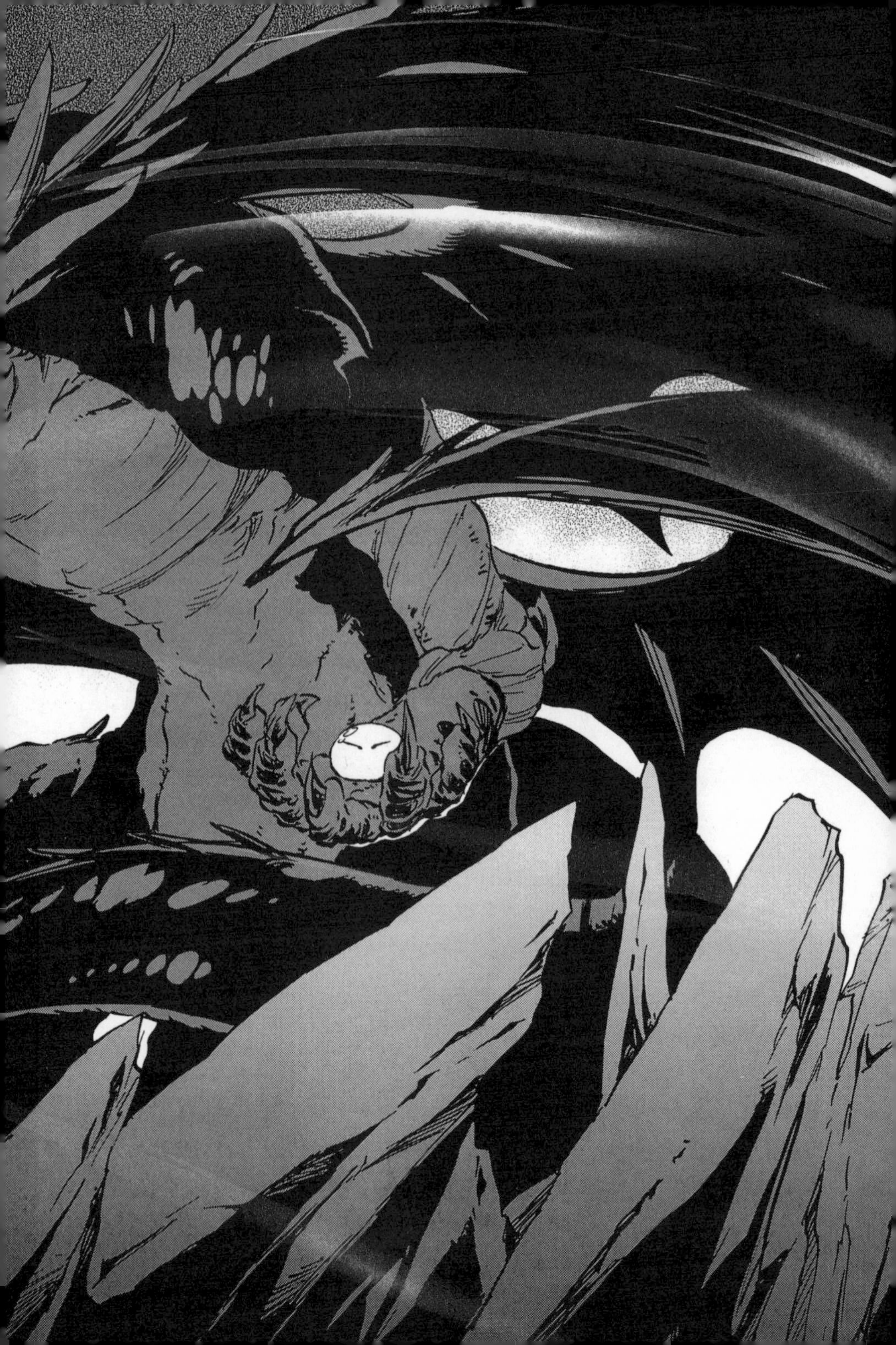

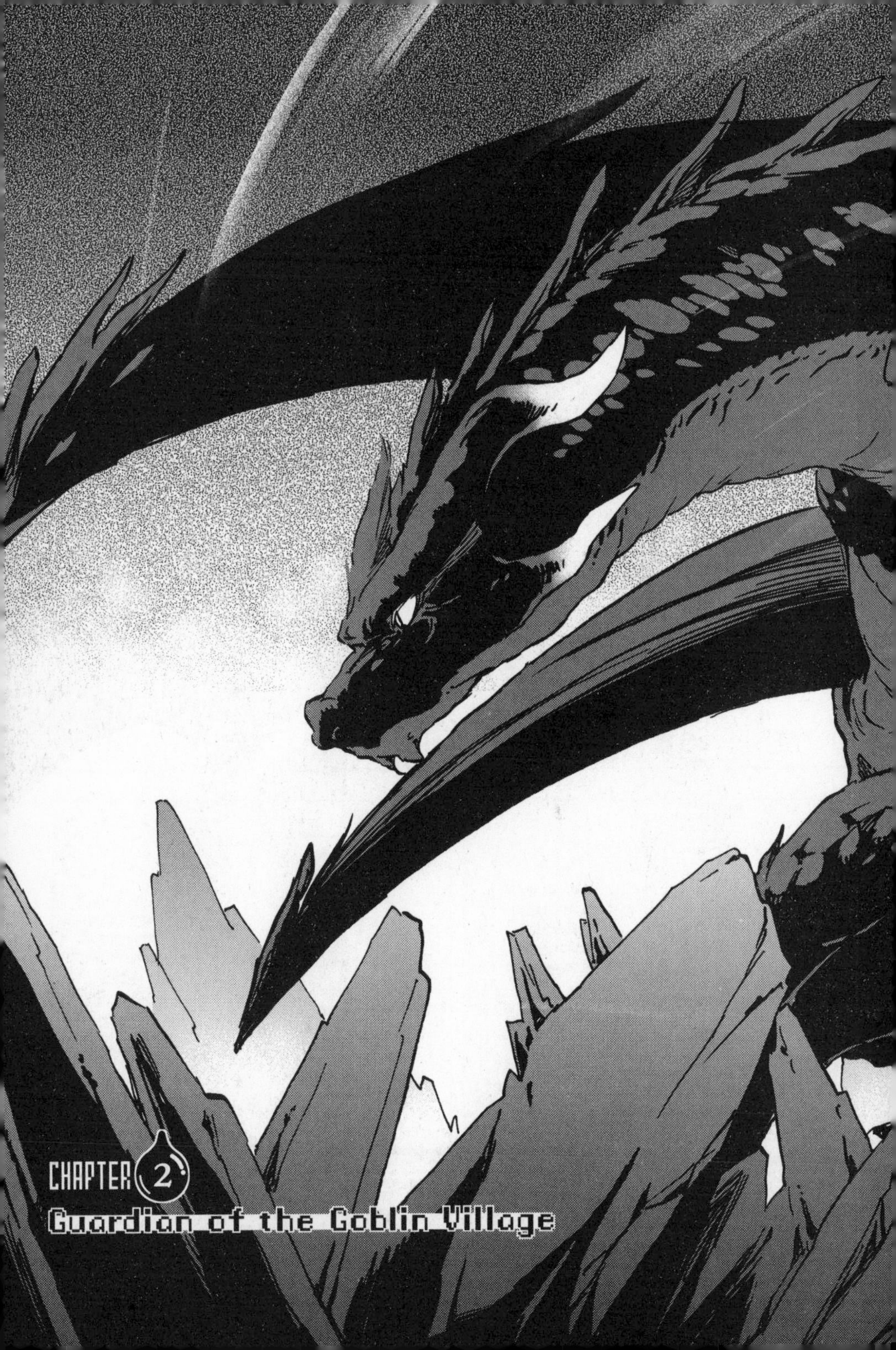
CHAPTER 2
Guardian of the Goblin Village

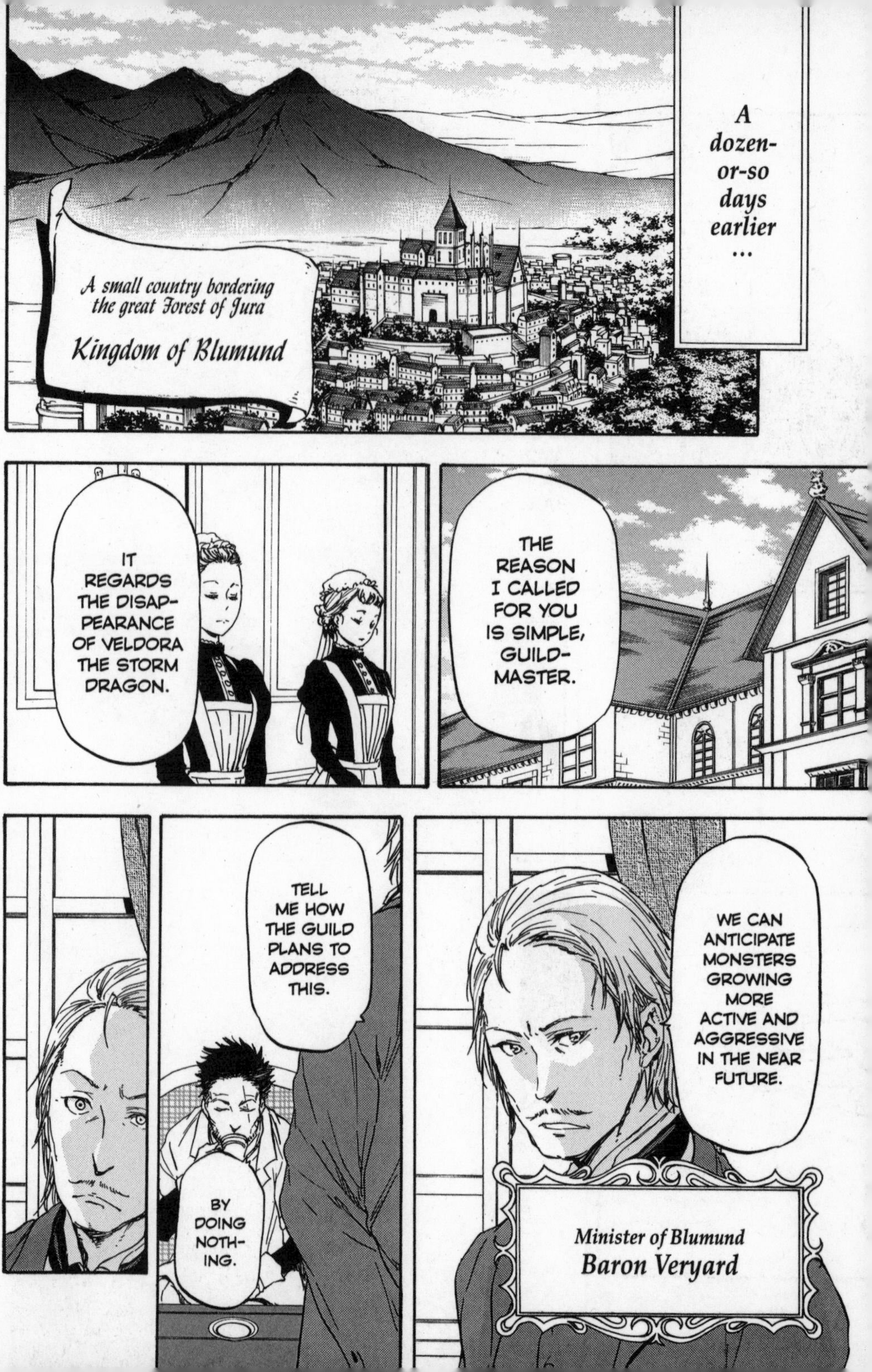
A dozen-or-so days earlier...
A small country bordering the great Forest of Jura
Kingdom of Blumund
THE REASON I CALLED FOR YOU IS SIMPLE, GUILD-MASTER.
IT REGARDS THE DISAP-PEARANCE OF VELDORA THE STORM DRAGON.
WE CAN ANTICIPATE MONSTERS GROWING MORE ACTIVE AND AGGRESSIVE IN THE NEAR FUTURE.
Minister of Blumund
Baron Veryard
TELL ME HOW THE GUILD PLANS TO ADDRESS THIS.
BY DOING NOTH-ING.

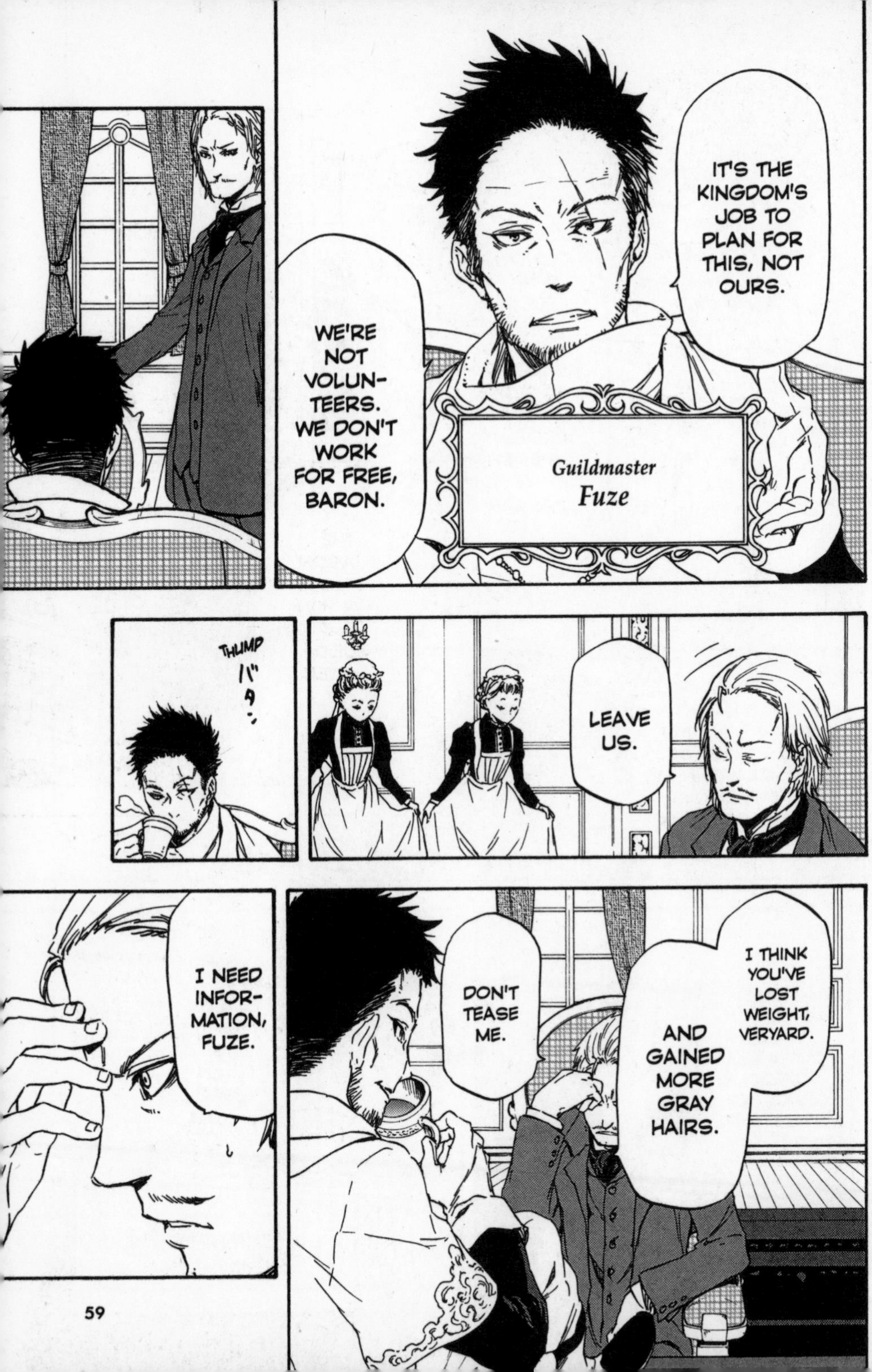

IT'S THE KINGDOM'S JOB TO PLAN FOR THIS, NOT OURS.
WE'RE NOT VOLUNTEERS. WE DON'T WORK FOR FREE, BARON.
Guildmaster
Fuze
LEAVE US.
THUMP
バタン
I THINK YOU'VE LOST WEIGHT, VERYARD.
AND GAINED MORE GRAY HAIRS.
DON'T TEASE ME.
I NEED INFORMATION, FUZE.

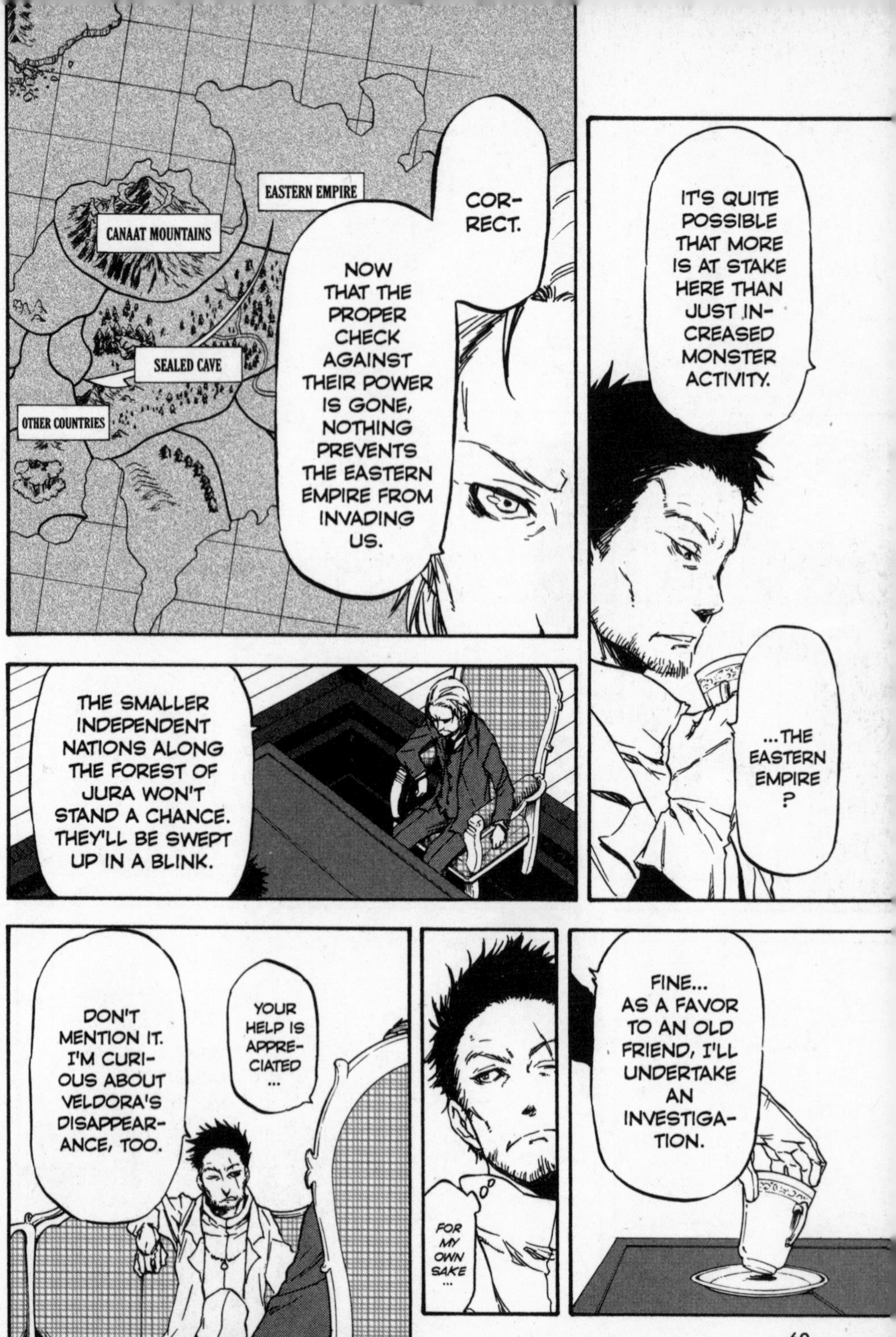
IT'S QUITE POSSIBLE THAT MORE IS AT STAKE HERE THAN JUST INCREASED MONSTER ACTIVITY.
...THE EASTERN EMPIRE?
EASTERN EMPIRE
CANAAT MOUNTAINS
SEALED CAVE
OTHER COUNTRIES
CORRECT.
NOW THAT THE PROPER CHECK AGAINST THEIR POWER IS GONE, NOTHING PREVENTS THE EASTERN EMPIRE FROM INVADING US.
THE SMALLER INDEPENDENT NATIONS ALONG THE FOREST OF JURA WON'T STAND A CHANCE. THEY'LL BE SWEPT UP IN A BLINK.
FINE... AS A FAVOR TO AN OLD FRIEND, I'LL UNDERTAKE AN INVESTIGATION.
FOR MY OWN SAKE...
YOUR HELP IS APPRECIATED...
DON'T MENTION IT. I'M CURIOUS ABOUT VELDORA'S DISAPPEARANCE, TOO.

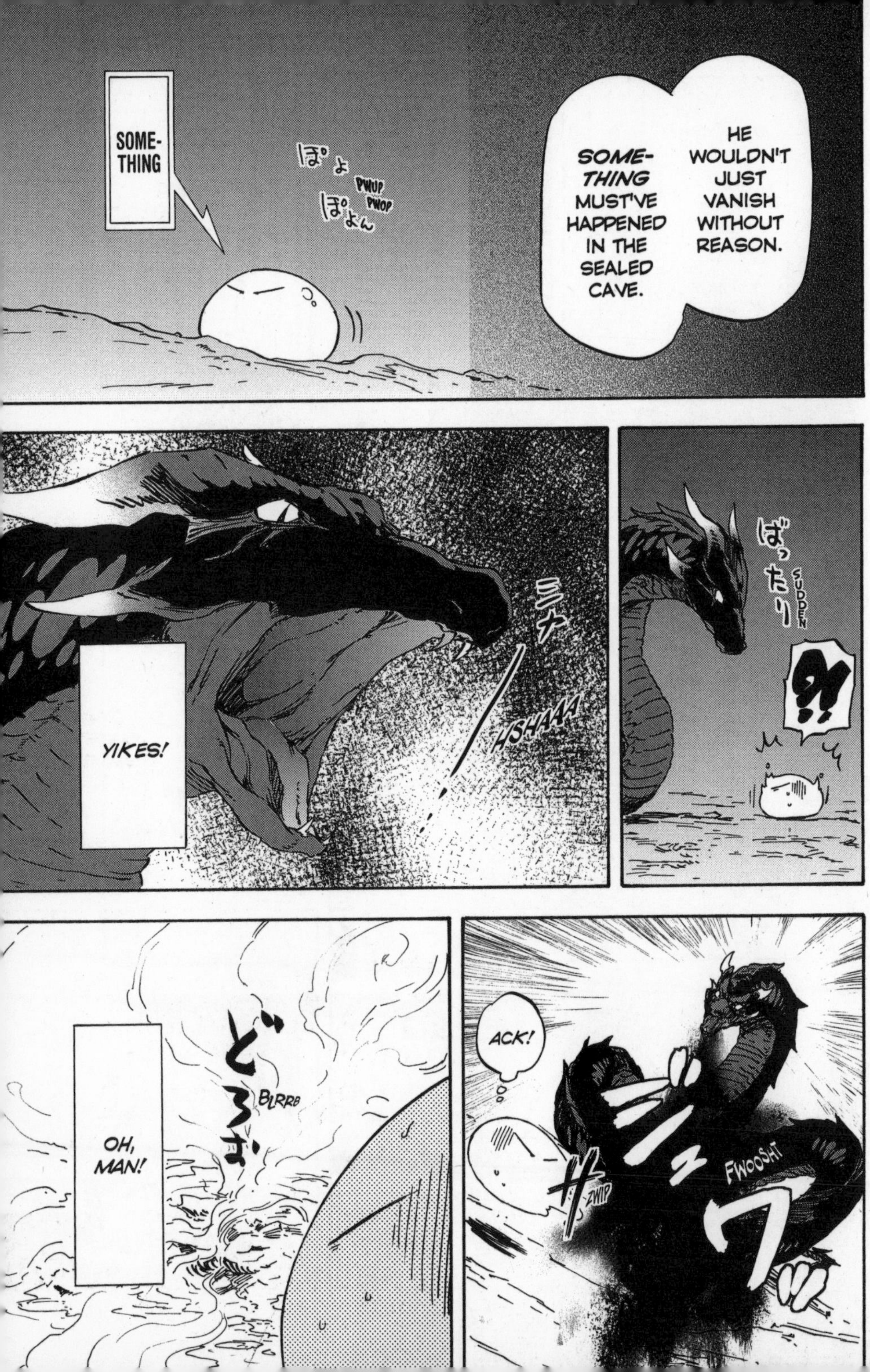
HE WOULDN'T JUST VANISH WITHOUT REASON.
SOMETHING MUST'VE HAPPENED IN THE SEALED CAVE.
ぽよ PWUP
ぽよん PWOP
SOME-THING
ばったり SUDDEN
HSHAAA
YIKES!
ACK!
ZWIP
FWOOSH
BLRRB
OH, MAN!

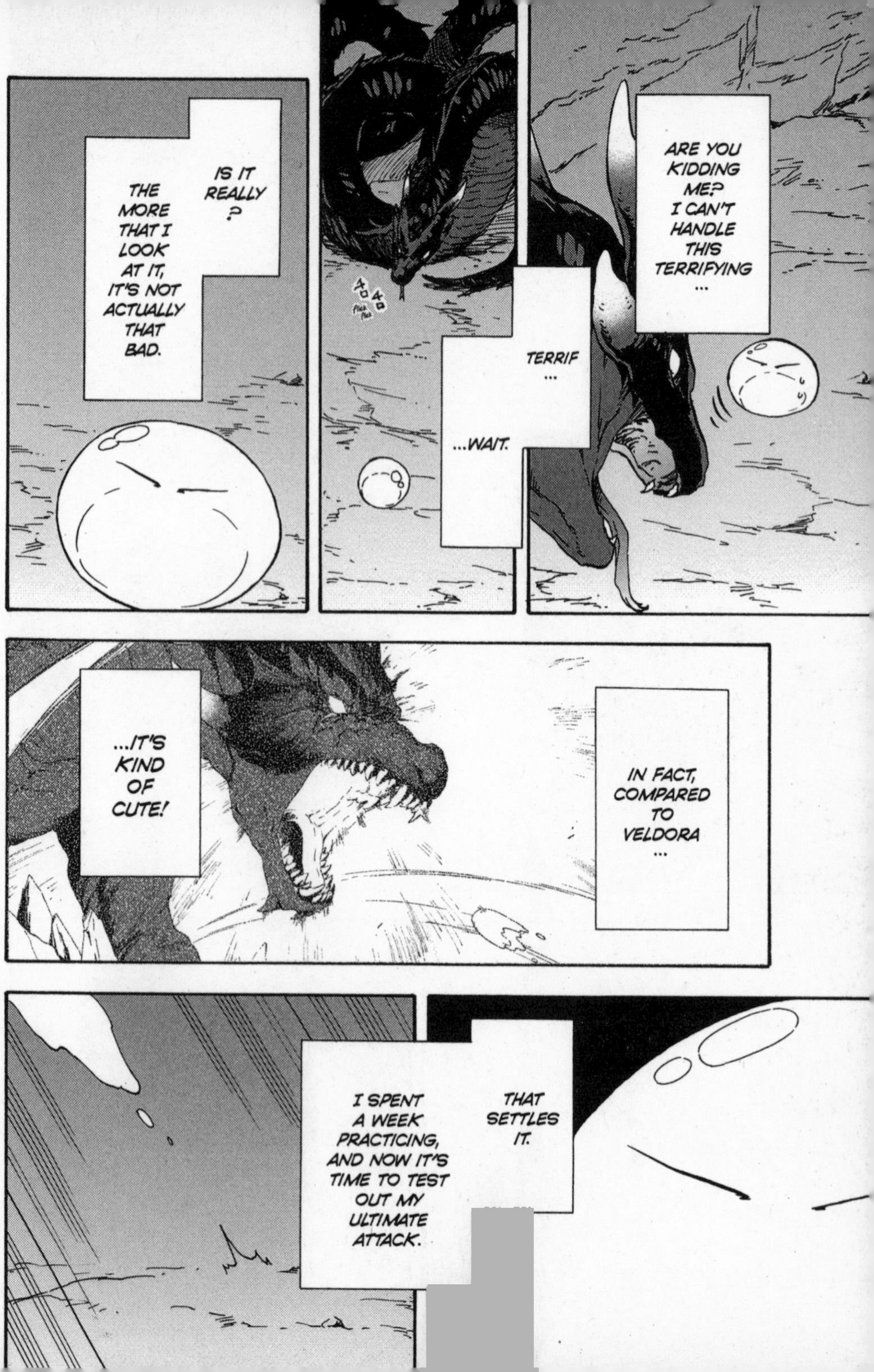
ARE YOU KIDDING ME? I CAN'T HANDLE THIS TERRIFYING ...
TERRIF ...
...WAIT.
IS IT REALLY ?
THE MORE THAT I LOOK AT IT, IT'S NOT ACTUALLY THAT BAD.
IN FACT, COMPARED TO VELDORA ...
...IT'S KIND OF CUTE!
THAT SETTLES IT.
I SPENT A WEEK PRACTICING, AND NOW IT'S TIME TO TEST OUT MY ULTIMATE ATTACK.

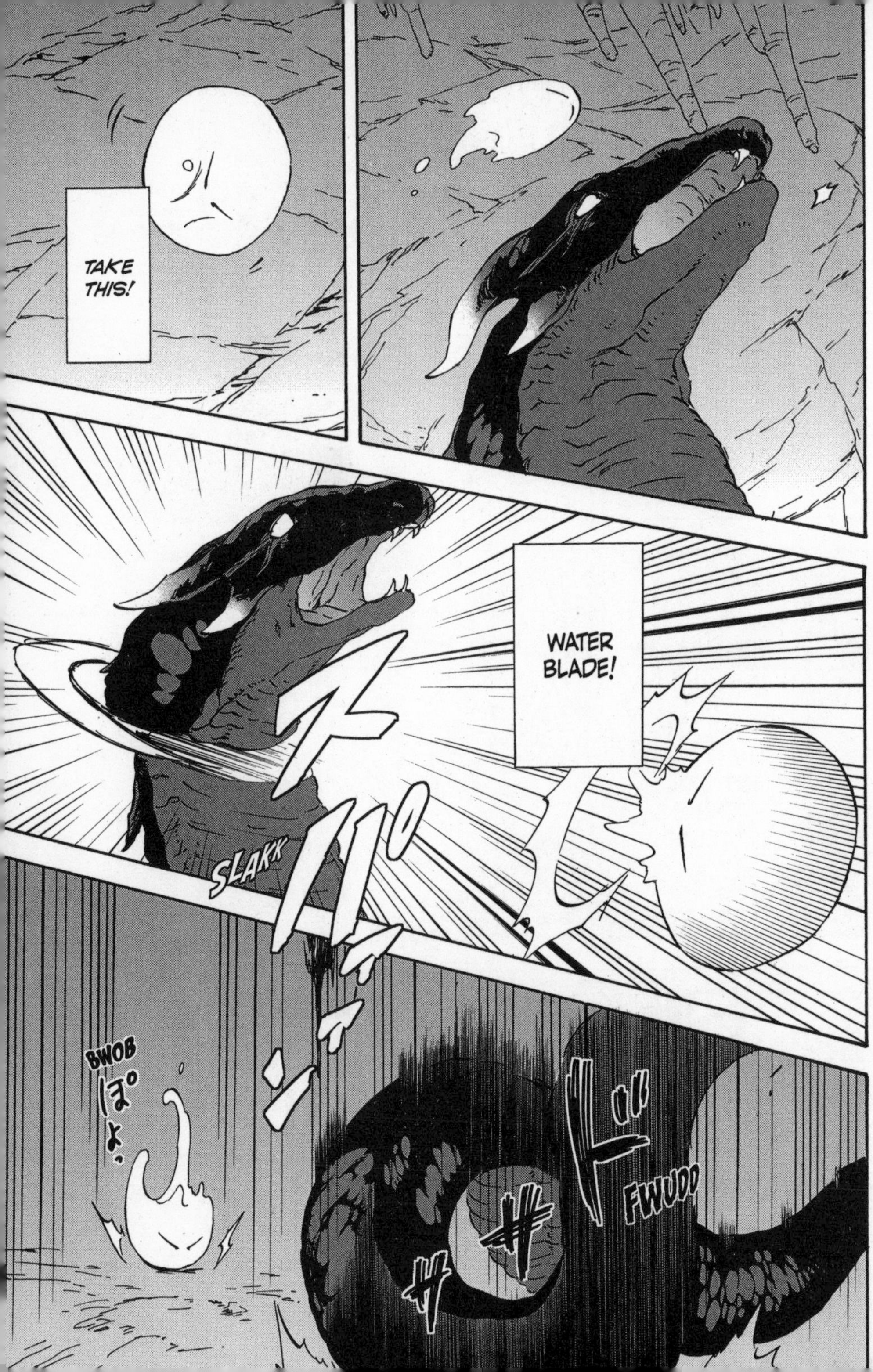
TAKE THIS!
WATER BLADE!
SLAKK
FWUDD
BWOB
ぽよ

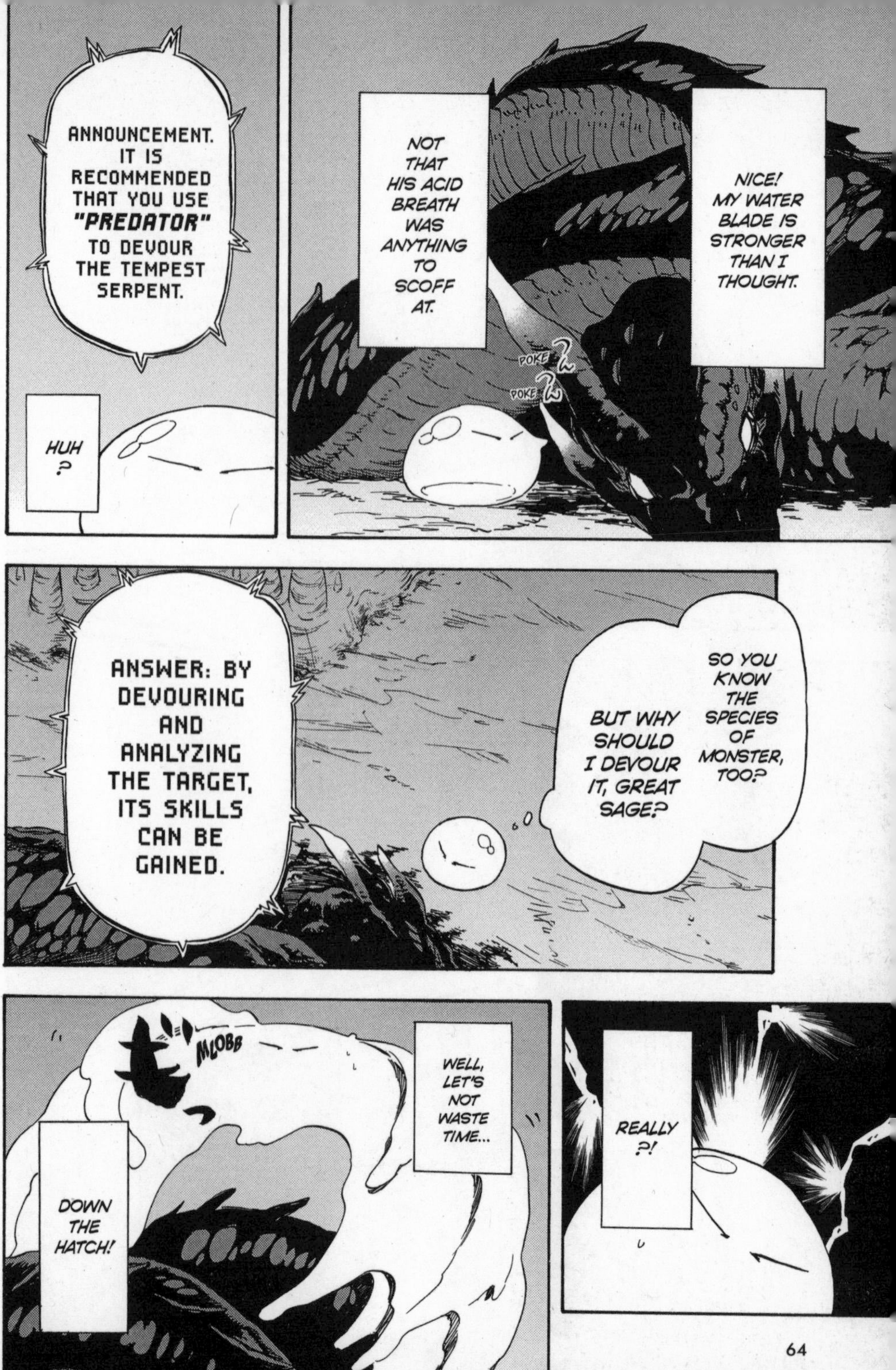
NICE! MY WATER BLADE IS STRONGER THAN I THOUGHT.
NOT THAT HIS ACID BREATH WAS ANYTHING TO SCOFF AT.
POKE
POKE
ANNOUNCEMENT. IT IS RECOMMENDED THAT YOU USE "PREDATOR" TO DEVOUR THE TEMPEST SERPENT.
HUH?
SO YOU KNOW THE SPECIES OF MONSTER, TOO?
BUT WHY SHOULD I DEVOUR IT, GREAT SAGE?
ANSWER: BY DEVOURING AND ANALYZING THE TARGET, ITS SKILLS CAN BE GAINED.
REALLY?!
WELL, LET'S NOT WASTE TIME...
MLOBB
DOWN THE HATCH!

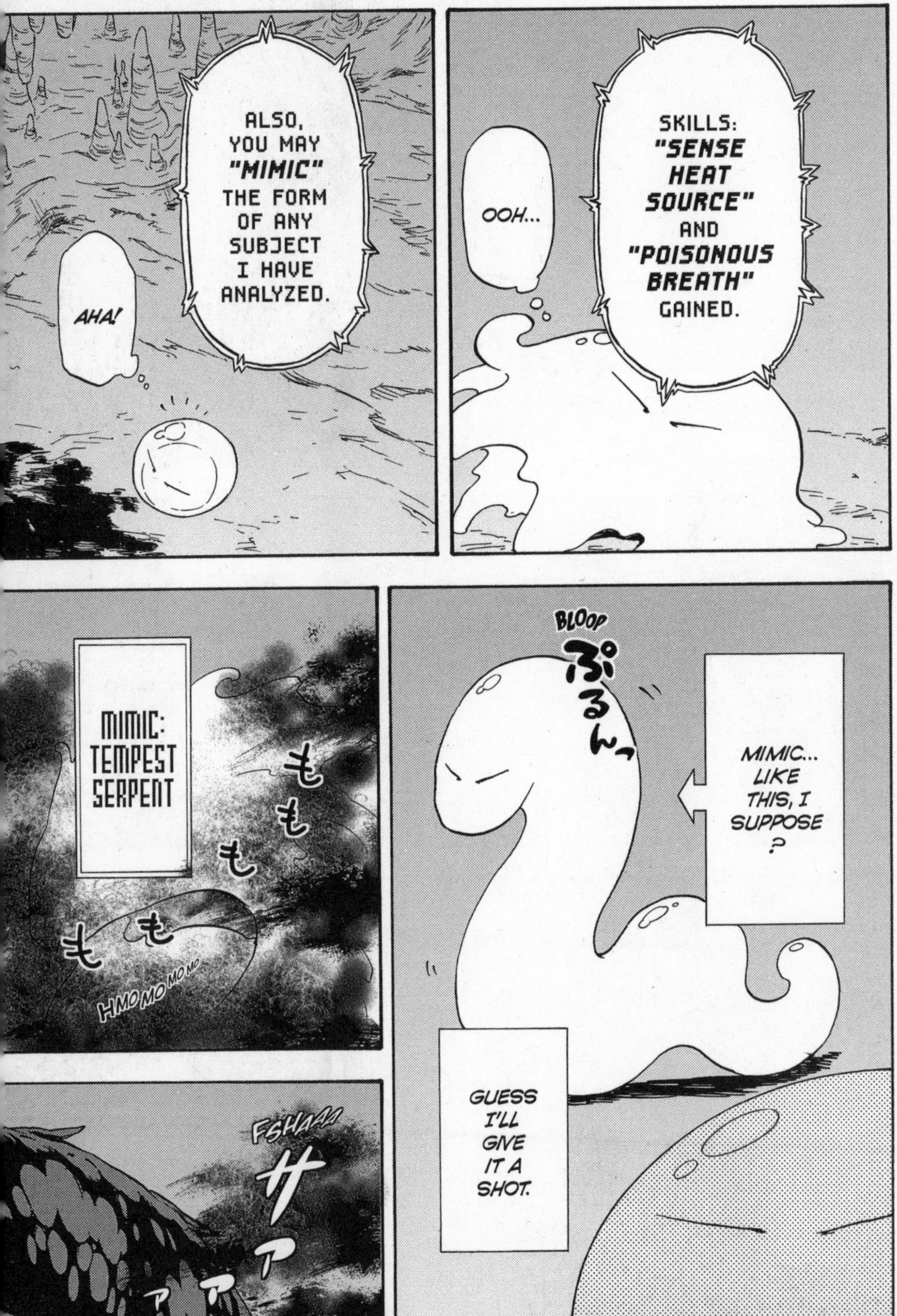
SKILLS: "SENSE HEAT SOURCE" AND "POISONOUS BREATH" GAINED.
OOH...
ALSO, YOU MAY "MIMIC" THE FORM OF ANY SUBJECT I HAVE ANALYZED.
AHA!
BLOOP
ぷるん
MIMIC... LIKE THIS, I SUPPOSE?
GUESS I'LL GIVE IT A SHOT.
MIMIC: TEMPEST SERPENT
もももももも
HMO MO MO MO
FSHAAA
サァァ

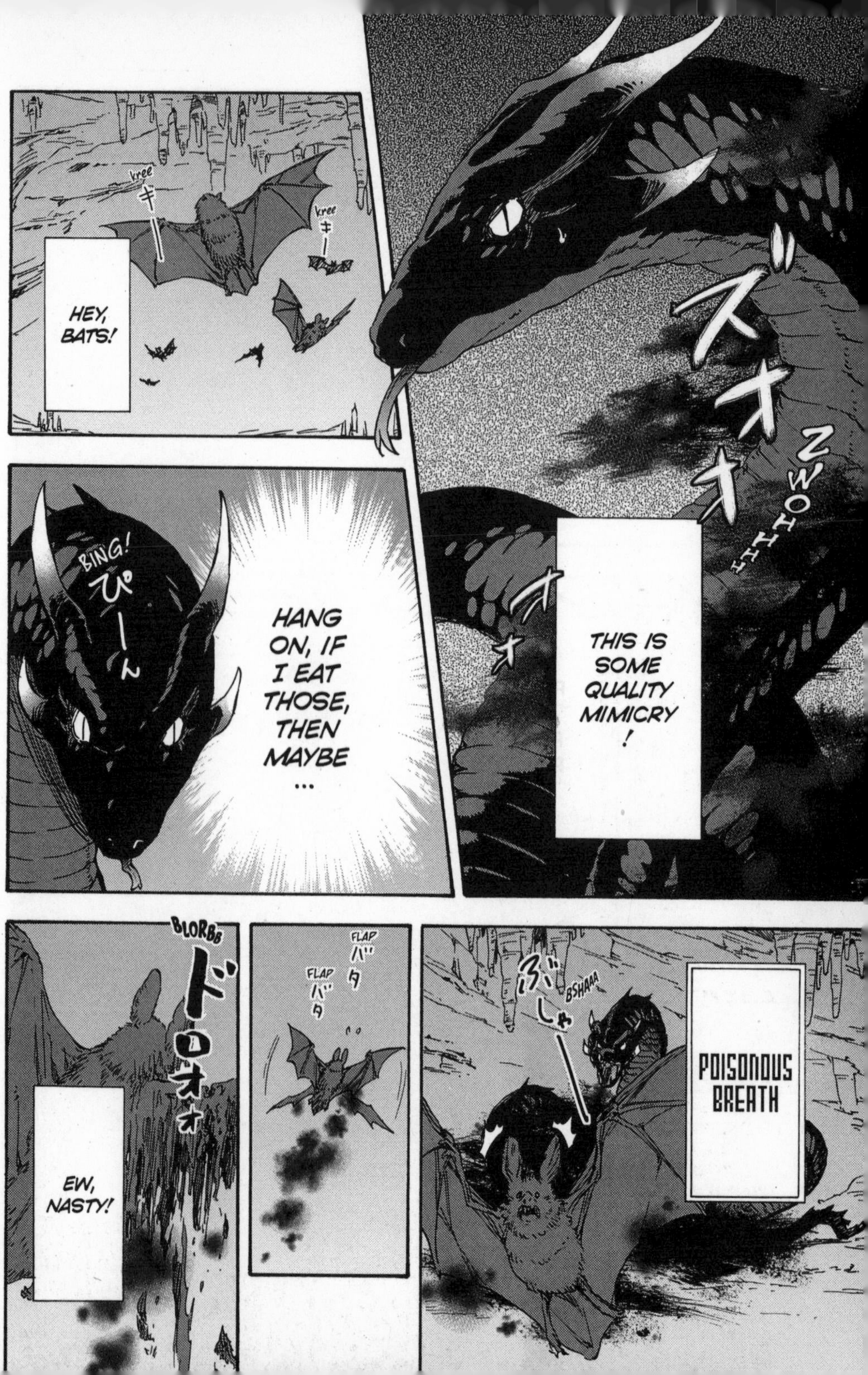
ズオオオオオ
ZWOHHHH
THIS IS SOME QUALITY MIMICRY!
kree
キー
kree
キー
HEY, BATS!
BING!
ぴーん
HANG ON, IF I EAT THOSE, THEN MAYBE...
POISONOUS BREATH
ぶしゃー
BSHAAA
FLAP
バタ
FLAP
バタ
BLORBB
ドロォォ
EW, NASTY!

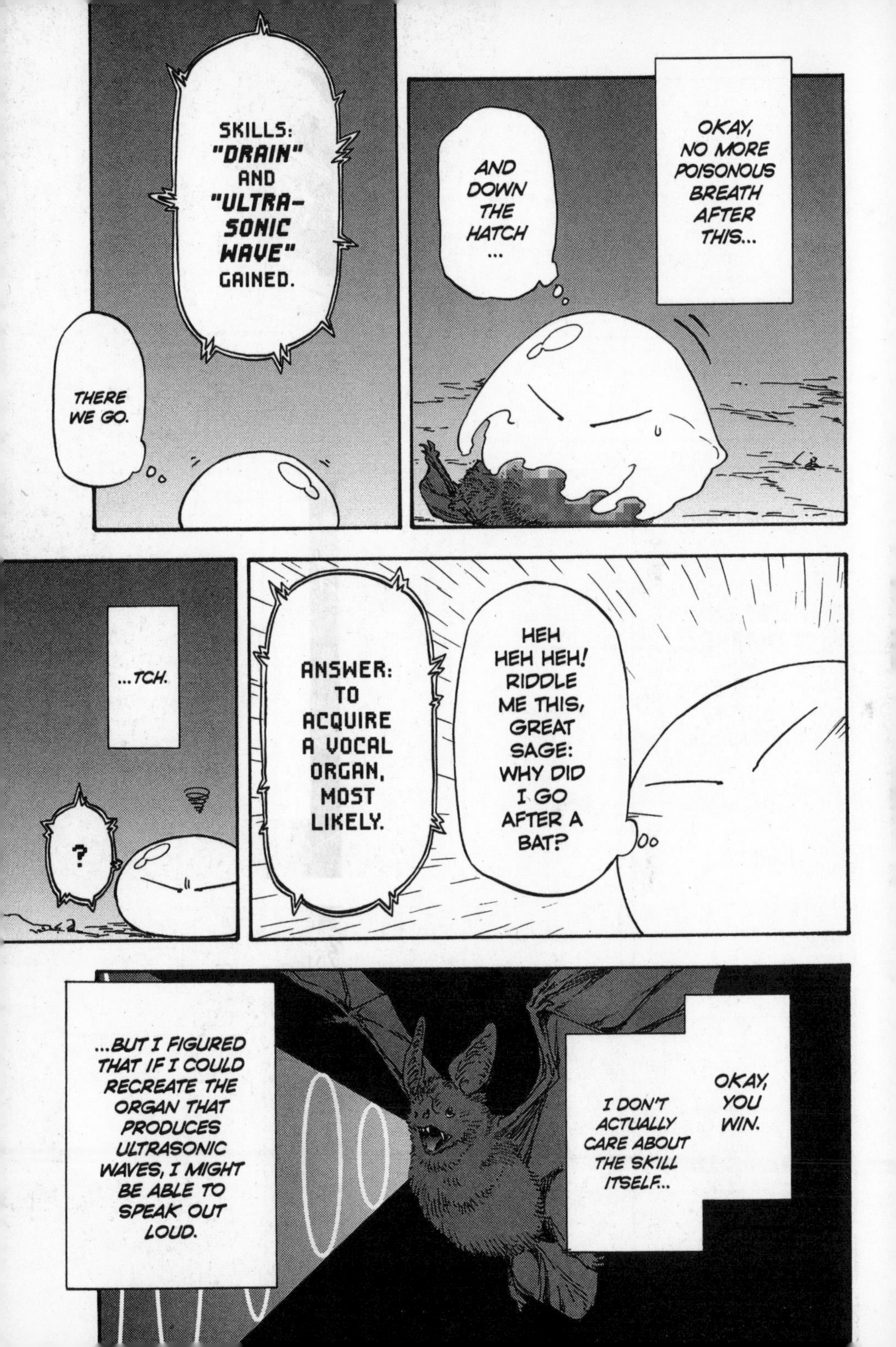
OKAY, NO MORE POISONOUS BREATH AFTER THIS...
AND DOWN THE HATCH ...
SKILLS: "DRAIN" AND "ULTRA-SONIC WAVE" GAINED.
THERE WE GO.
HEH HEH HEH! RIDDLE ME THIS, GREAT SAGE: WHY DID I GO AFTER A BAT?
ANSWER: TO ACQUIRE A VOCAL ORGAN, MOST LIKELY.
...TCH.
?
OKAY, YOU WIN.
I DON'T ACTUALLY CARE ABOUT THE SKILL ITSELF...
...BUT I FIGURED THAT IF I COULD RECREATE THE ORGAN THAT PRODUCES ULTRASONIC WAVES, I MIGHT BE ABLE TO SPEAK OUT LOUD.

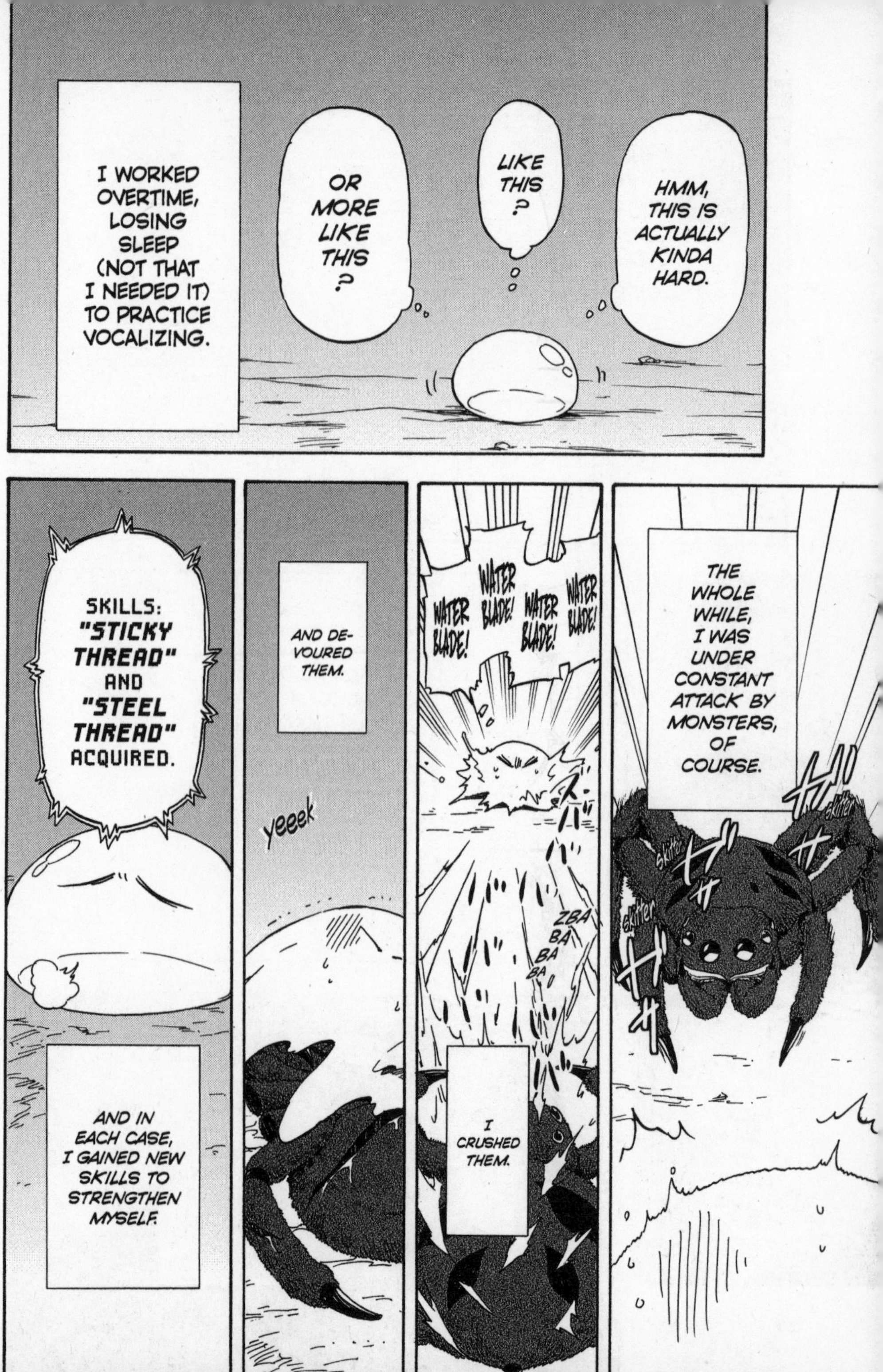
HMM, THIS IS ACTUALLY KINDA HARD.
LIKE THIS?
OR MORE LIKE THIS?
I WORKED OVERTIME, LOSING SLEEP (NOT THAT I NEEDED IT) TO PRACTICE VOCALIZING.
THE WHOLE WHILE, I WAS UNDER CONSTANT ATTACK BY MONSTERS, OF COURSE.
skitter
skitter
skitter
WATER BLADE!
WATER BLADE!
WATER BLADE!
WATER BLADE!
ZBA BA BA BA
I CRUSHED THEM.
AND DE-VOURED THEM.
yeeek
SKILLS: "STICKY THREAD" AND "STEEL THREAD" ACQUIRED.
AND IN EACH CASE, I GAINED NEW SKILLS TO STRENGTHEN MYSELF.

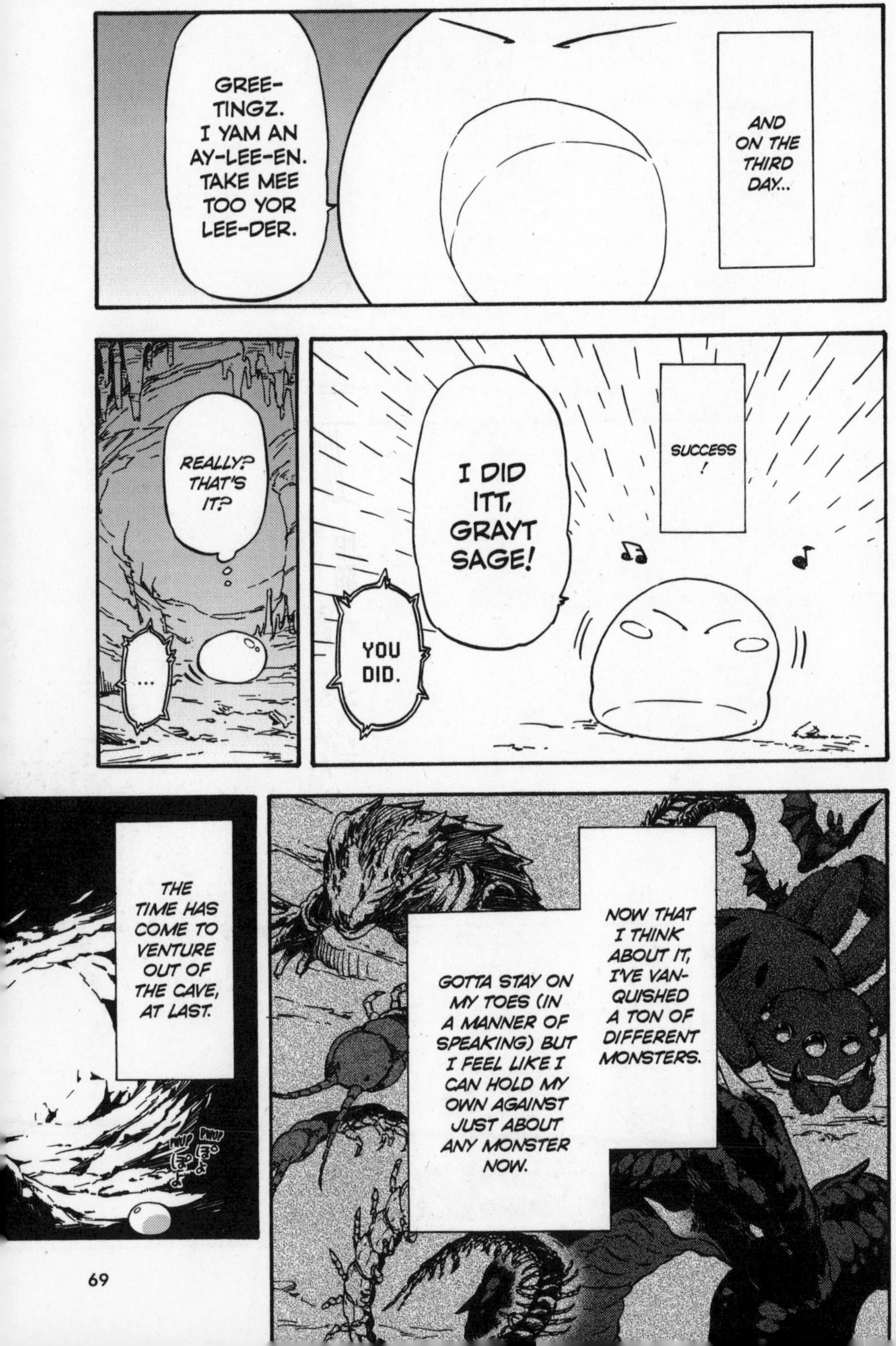
AND ON THE THIRD DAY...
GREE-TINGZ. I YAM AN AY-LEE-EN. TAKE MEE TOO YOR LEE-DER.
SUCCESS!
I DID ITT, GRAYT SAGE!
YOU DID.
REALLY? THAT'S IT?
...
NOW THAT I THINK ABOUT IT, I'VE VAN-QUISHED A TON OF DIFFERENT MONSTERS.
GOTTA STAY ON MY TOES (IN A MANNER OF SPEAKING) BUT I FEEL LIKE I CAN HOLD MY OWN AGAINST JUST ABOUT ANY MONSTER NOW.
THE TIME HAS COME TO VENTURE OUT OF THE CAVE, AT LAST.
PWUP PWUP

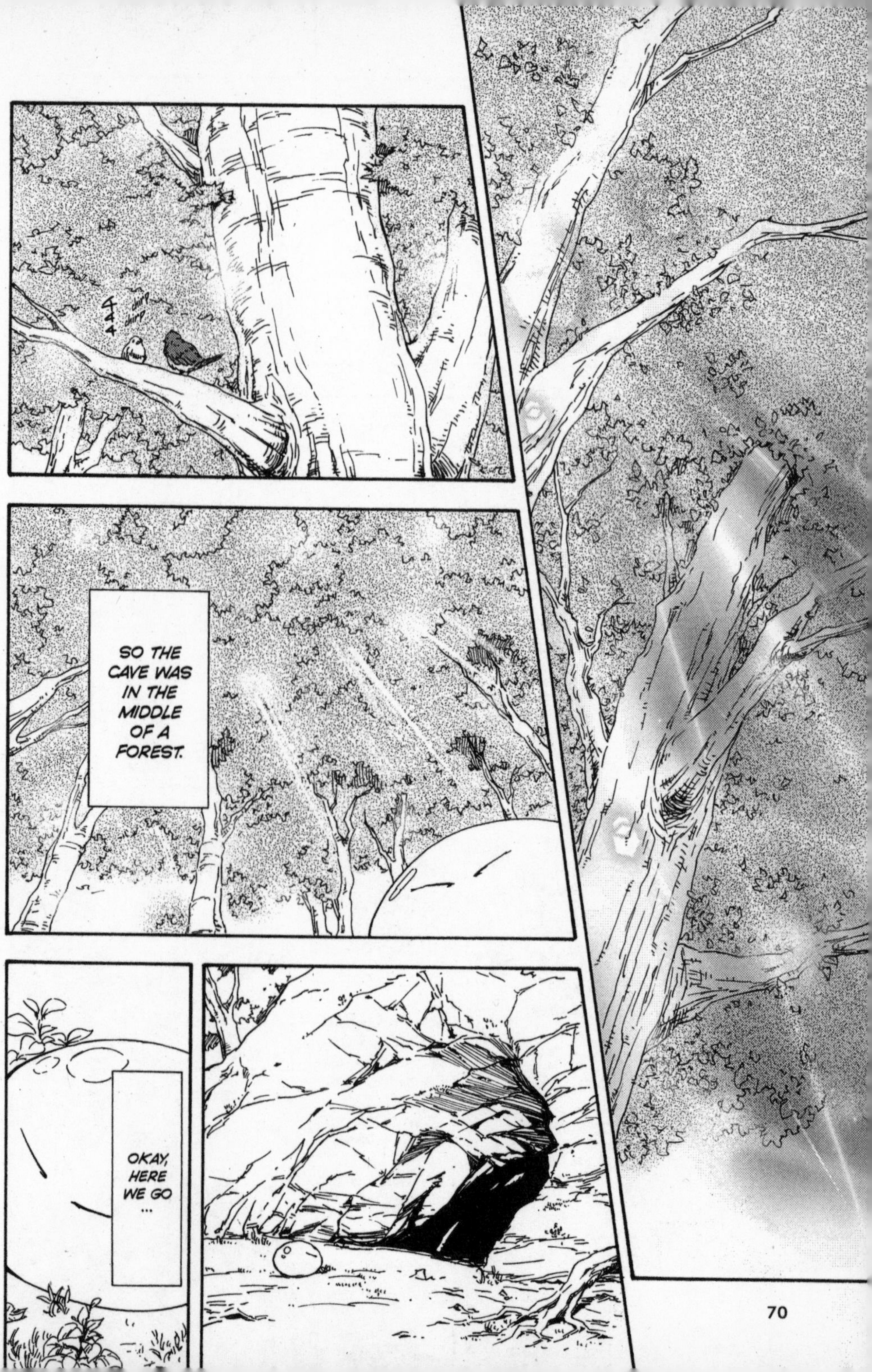
chirp chirp
SO THE CAVE WAS IN THE MIDDLE OF A FOREST.
OKAY, HERE WE GO ...

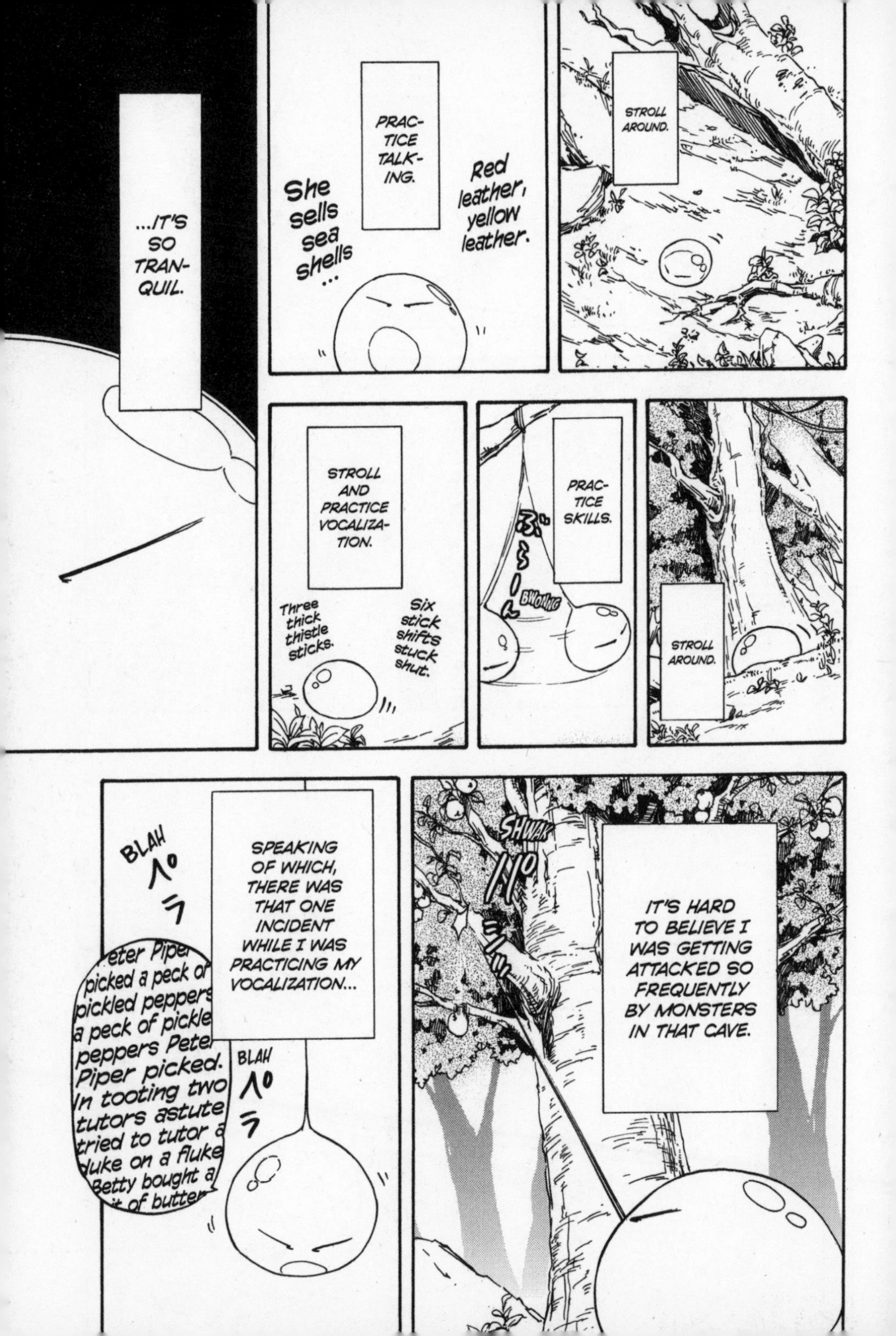
STROLL AROUND.
PRACTICE TALKING.
Red leather, yellow leather.
She sells sea shells...
STROLL AROUND.
PRACTICE SKILLS.
ぶーん
BWONNG
STROLL AND PRACTICE VOCALIZATION.
Six stick shifts stuck shut.
Three thick thistle sticks.
...IT'S SO TRANQUIL.
IT'S HARD TO BELIEVE I WAS GETTING ATTACKED SO FREQUENTLY BY MONSTERS IN THAT CAVE.
SHWAK
SPEAKING OF WHICH, THERE WAS THAT ONE INCIDENT WHILE I WAS PRACTICING MY VOCALIZATION...
BLAH
へら
Peter Piper picked a peck of pickled peppers a peck of pickled peppers Peter Piper picked. In tooting two tutors astute tried to tutor a duke on a fluke Betty bought a bit of butter
BLAH
へら

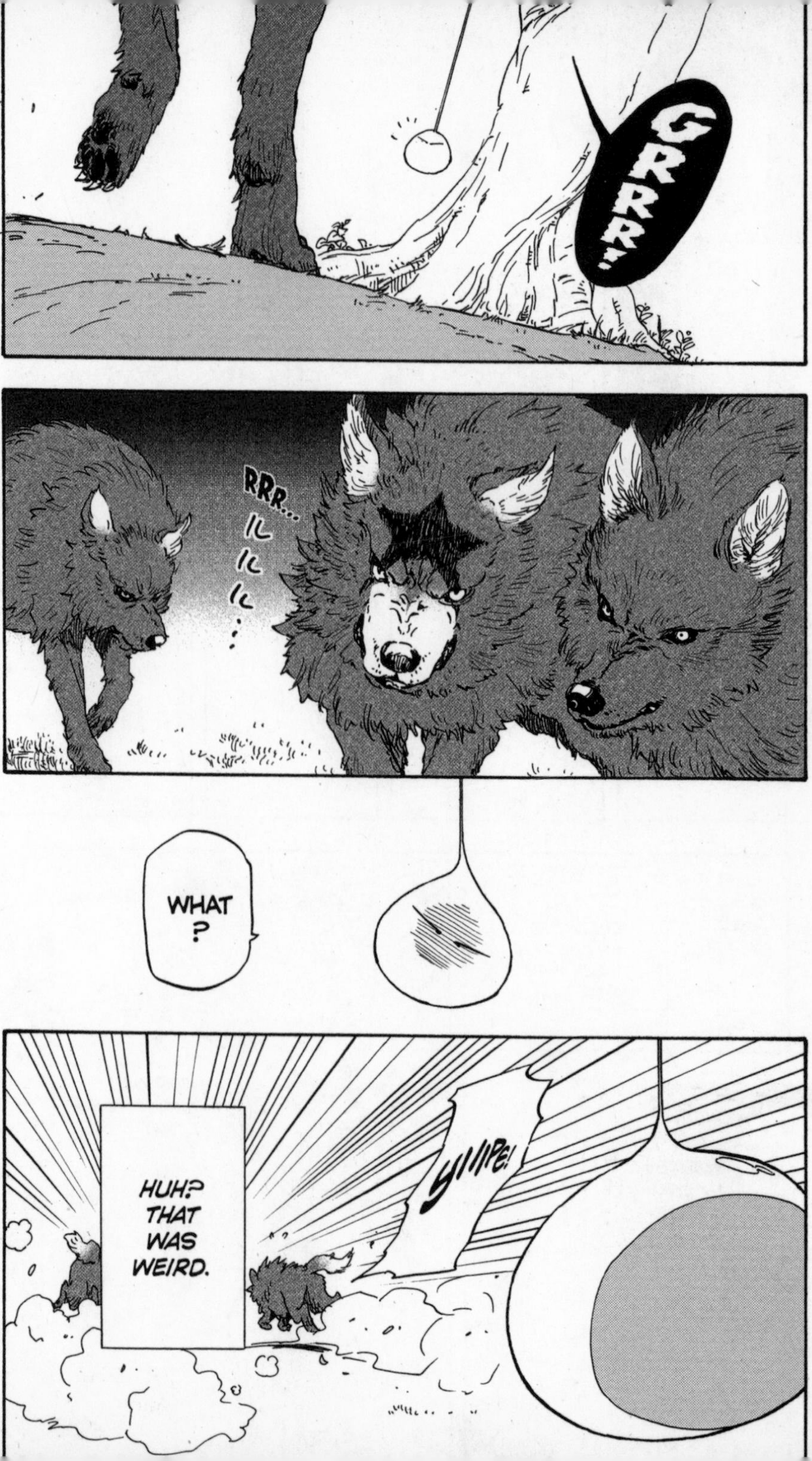
GRRR!
RRR...
ルルル...
WHAT?
SWIPE!
HUH? THAT WAS WEIRD.

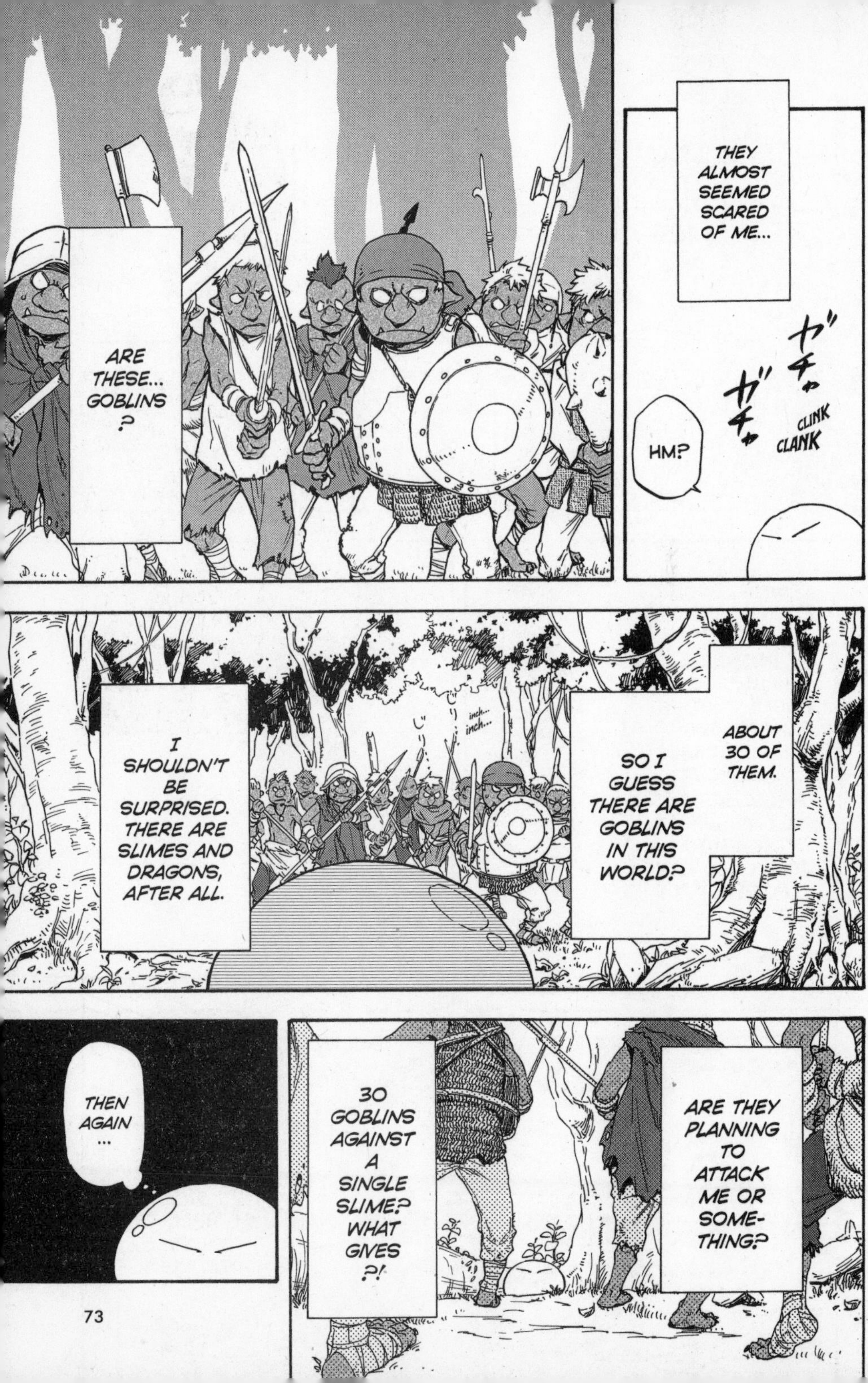
THEY ALMOST SEEMED SCARED OF ME...
ガチャ ガチャ
CLINK CLANK
HM?
ARE THESE... GOBLINS?
ABOUT 30 OF THEM.
SO I GUESS THERE ARE GOBLINS IN THIS WORLD?
inch... inch...
I SHOULDN'T BE SURPRISED. THERE ARE SLIMES AND DRAGONS, AFTER ALL.
ARE THEY PLANNING TO ATTACK ME OR SOME-THING?
30 GOBLINS AGAINST A SINGLE SLIME? WHAT GIVES?!
THEN AGAIN...

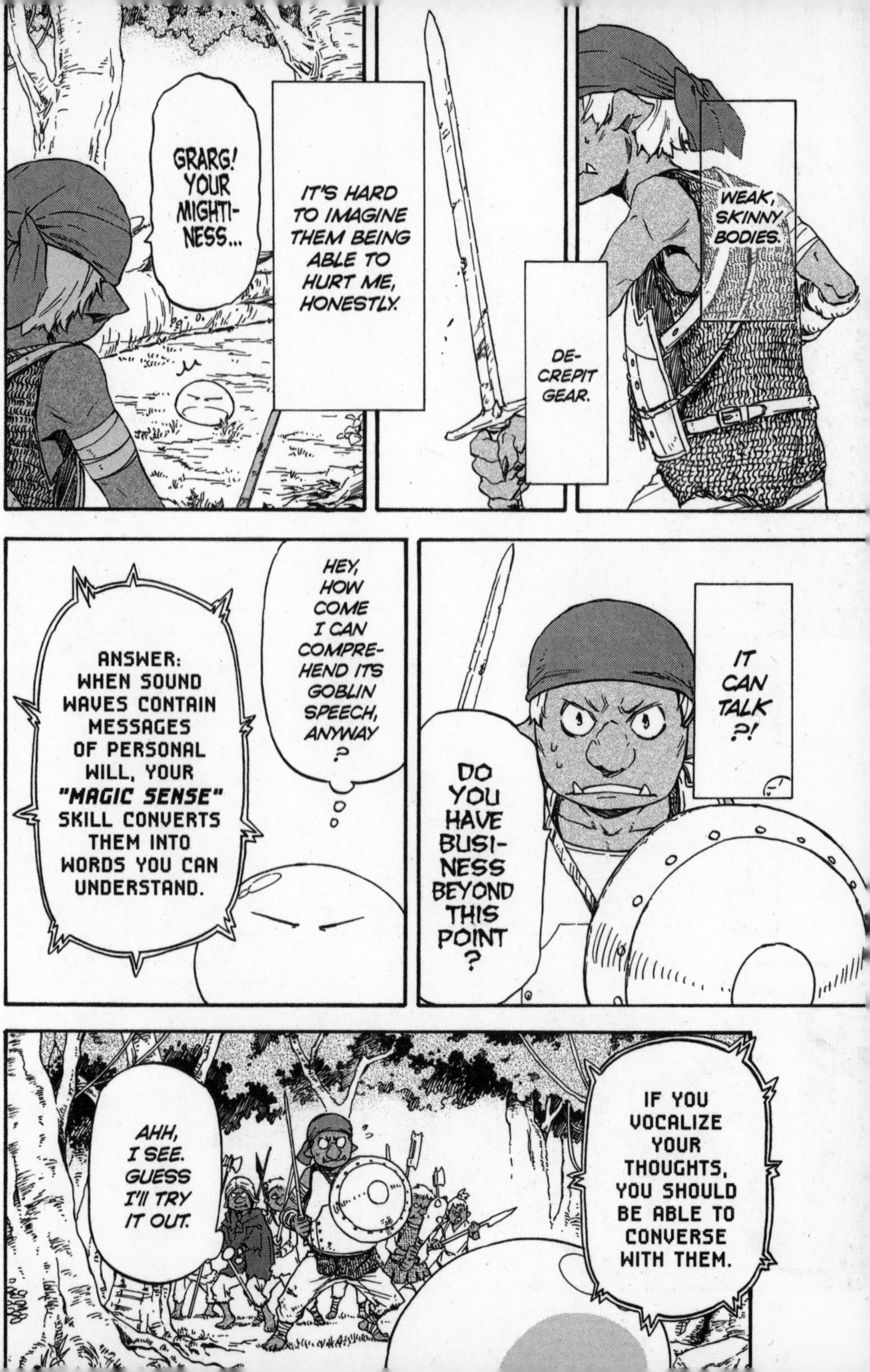
WEAK, SKINNY BODIES.
DE-CREPIT GEAR.
IT'S HARD TO IMAGINE THEM BEING ABLE TO HURT ME, HONESTLY.
GRARG! YOUR MIGHTI-NESS...
IT CAN TALK?!
DO YOU HAVE BUSI-NESS BEYOND THIS POINT?
HEY, HOW COME I CAN COMPRE-HEND ITS GOBLIN SPEECH, ANYWAY?
ANSWER: WHEN SOUND WAVES CONTAIN MESSAGES OF PERSONAL WILL, YOUR "MAGIC SENSE" SKILL CONVERTS THEM INTO WORDS YOU CAN UNDERSTAND.
IF YOU VOCALIZE YOUR THOUGHTS, YOU SHOULD BE ABLE TO CONVERSE WITH THEM.
AHH, I SEE. GUESS I'll TRY IT OUT.

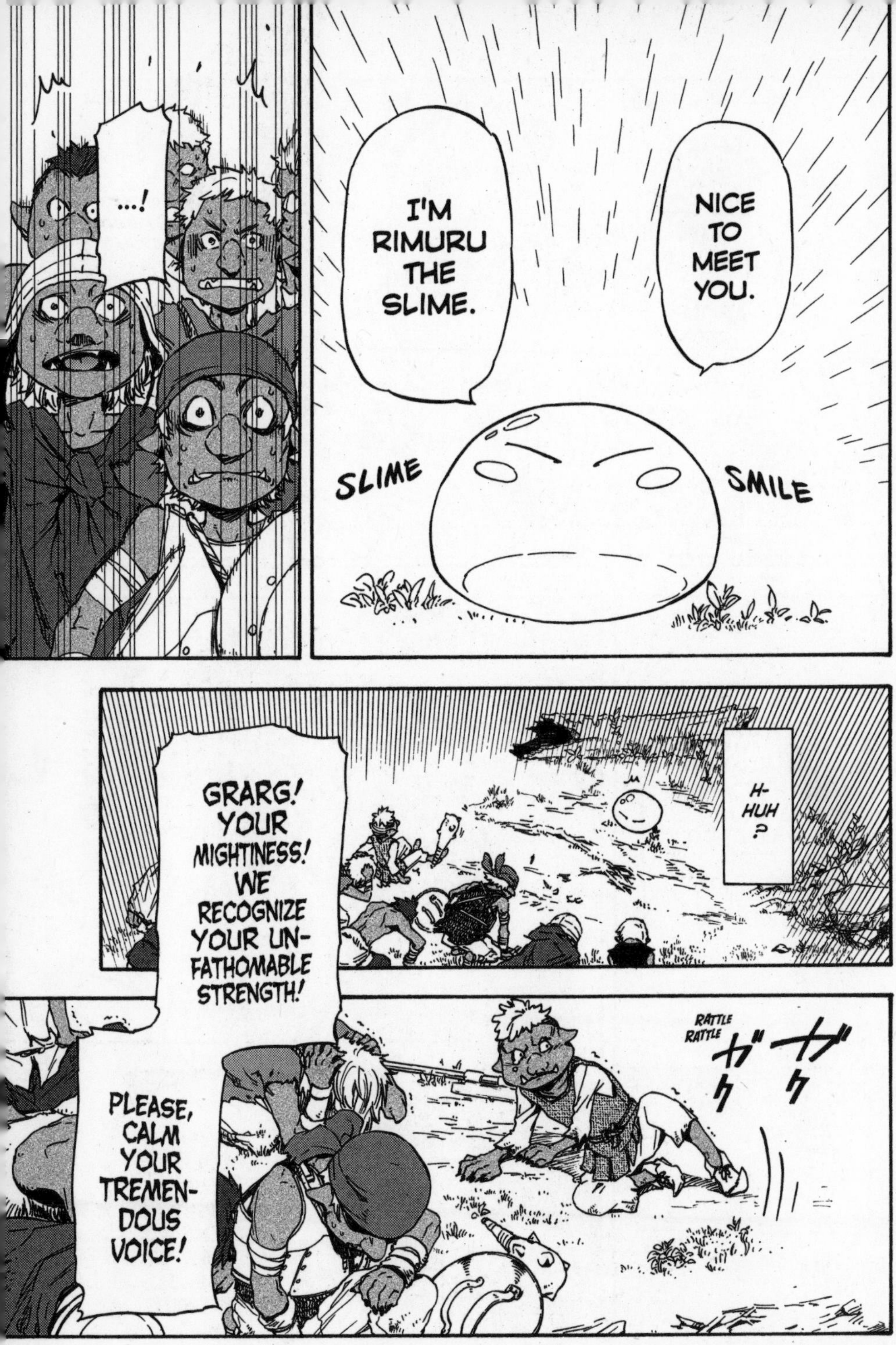
NICE TO MEET YOU.
I'M RIMURU THE SLIME.
SMILE
SLIME
...!
H-HUH?
GRARG! YOUR MIGHTINESS! WE RECOGNIZE YOUR UN-FATHOMABLE STRENGTH!
RATTLE RATTLE
ガク ガク
PLEASE, CALM YOUR TREMEN-DOUS VOICE!

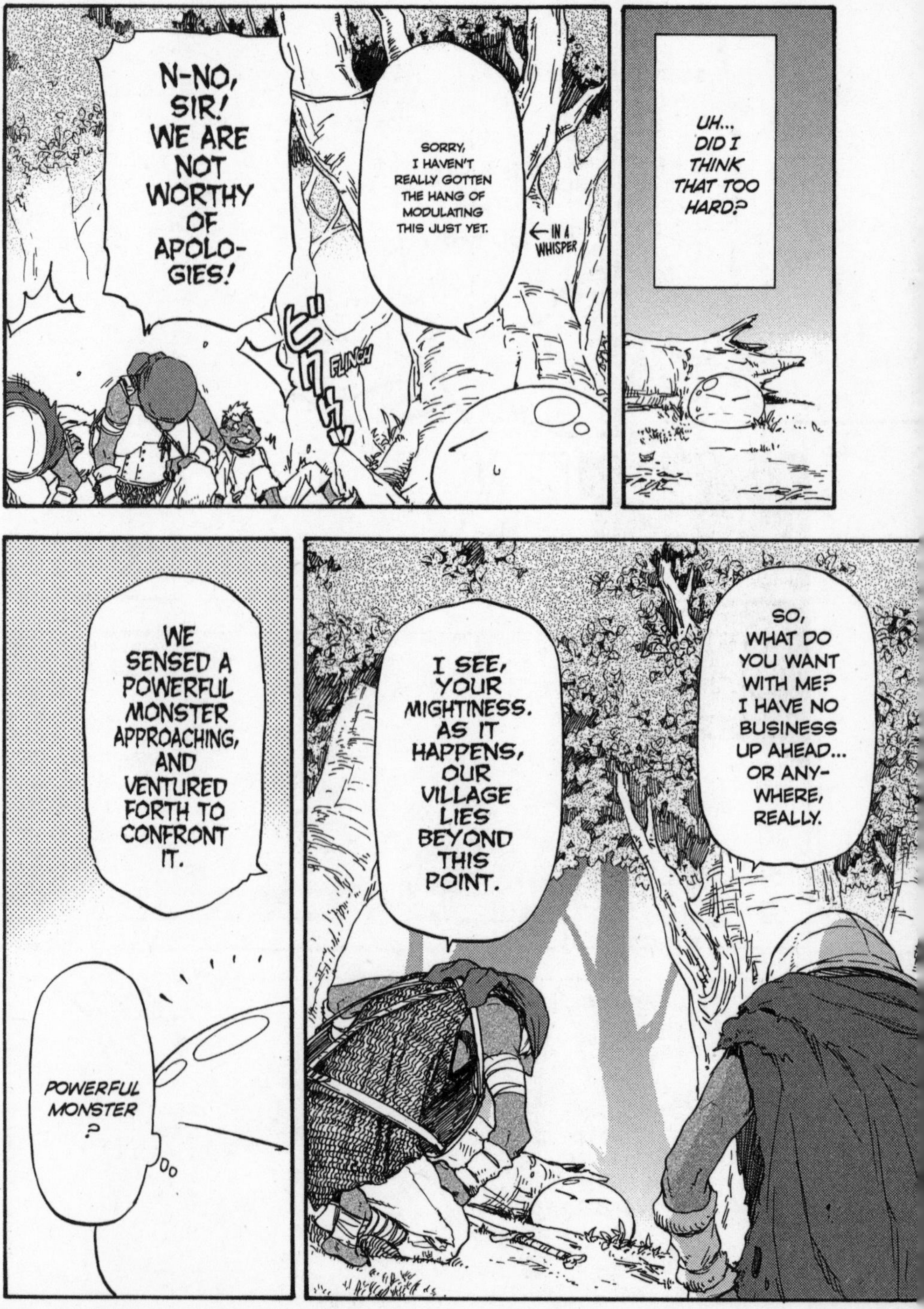
UH... DID I THINK THAT TOO HARD?
SORRY, I HAVEN'T REALLY GOTTEN THE HANG OF MODULATING THIS JUST YET.
← IN A WHISPER
FLINCH
N-NO, SIR! WE ARE NOT WORTHY OF APOLOGIES!
SO, WHAT DO YOU WANT WITH ME? I HAVE NO BUSINESS UP AHEAD... OR ANYWHERE, REALLY.
I SEE, YOUR MIGHTINESS. AS IT HAPPENS, OUR VILLAGE LIES BEYOND THIS POINT.
WE SENSED A POWERFUL MONSTER APPROACHING, AND VENTURED FORTH TO CONFRONT IT.
POWERFUL MONSTER?

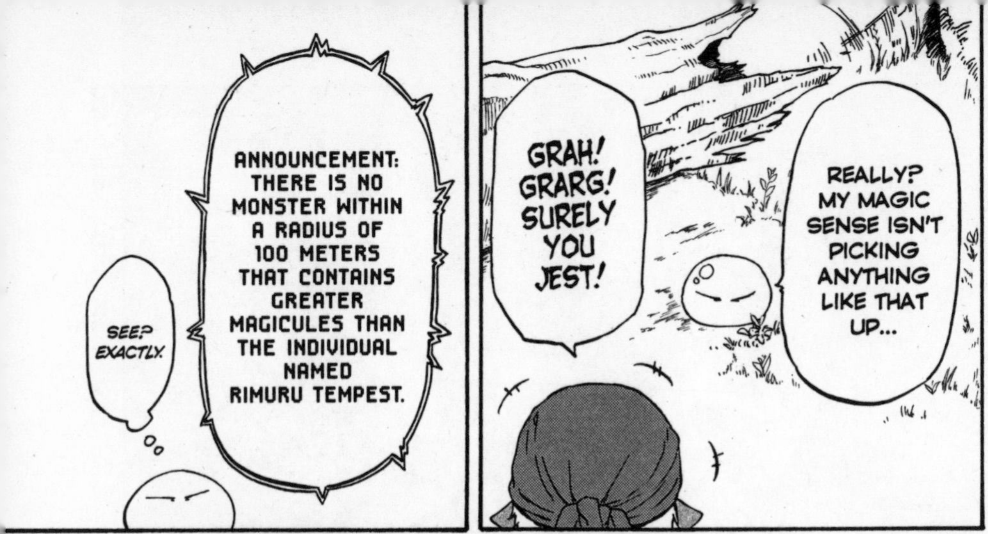
REALLY? MY MAGIC SENSE ISN'T PICKING ANYTHING LIKE THAT UP...
GRAH! GRARG! SURELY YOU JEST!
ANNOUNCEMENT: THERE IS NO MONSTER WITHIN A RADIUS OF 100 METERS THAT CONTAINS GREATER MAGICULES THAN THE INDIVIDUAL NAMED RIMURU TEMPEST.
SEE? EXACTLY.

100 meters = About 328 feet

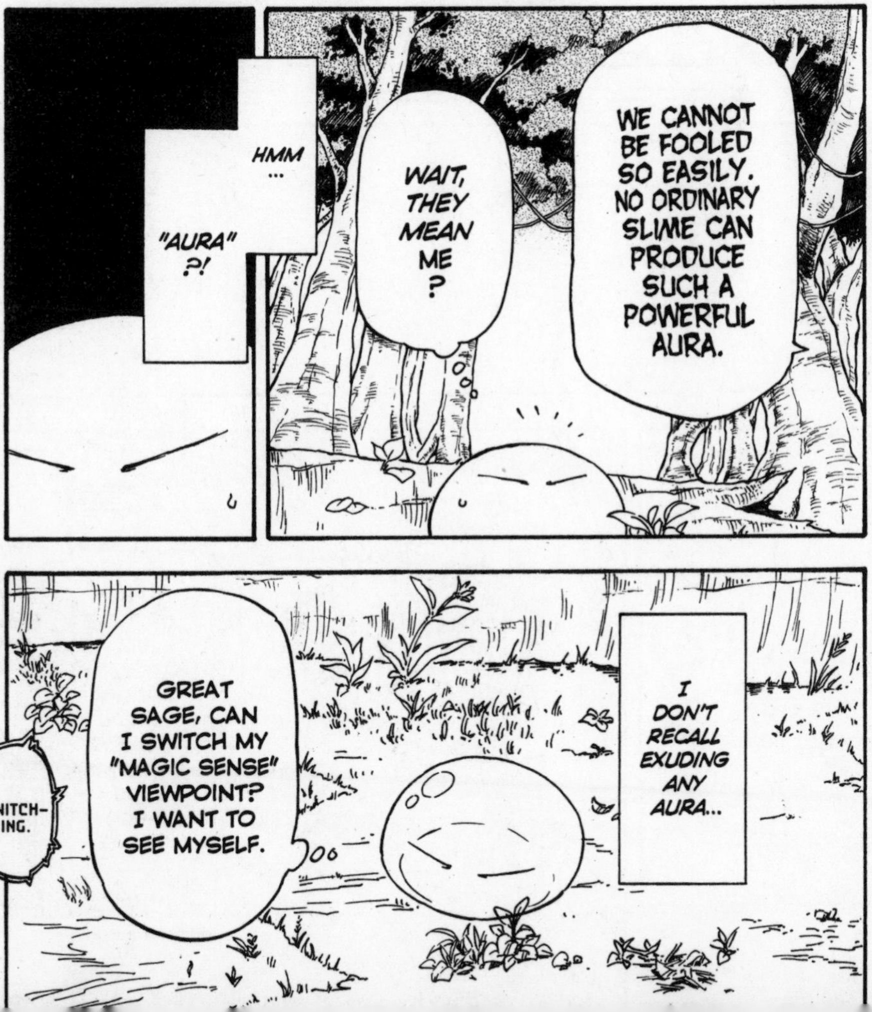
WE CANNOT BE FOOLED SO EASILY. NO ORDINARY SLIME CAN PRODUCE SUCH A POWERFUL AURA.
WAIT, THEY MEAN ME?
HMM...
"AURA"?!
I DON'T RECALL EXUDING ANY AURA...
GREAT SAGE, CAN I SWITCH MY "MAGIC SENSE" VIEWPOINT? I WANT TO SEE MYSELF.
SWITCH-ING.

Third-Person View
ZWAAAH
OH MY GOODNESS.
IT'S POURING OUT OF ME!
No wonder the wolves ran away.
THIS IS A LITTLE EMBARRASSING.
I FEEL LIKE I'VE BEEN STROLLING DOWN MAIN STREET WITH MY FLY DOWN OR SOMETHING.
HEH... HEH HEH. YOU CAN SEE THAT?
OF COURSE! IT IS IMPOSSIBLE FOR YOUR MIGHTINESS TO HIDE SUCH GRAND POWER!
Go back! Stop exuding!
OOH!

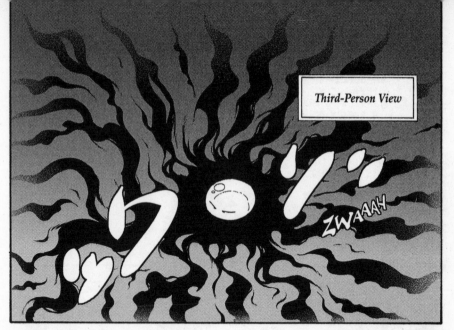

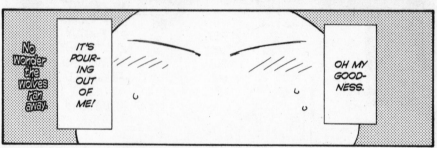

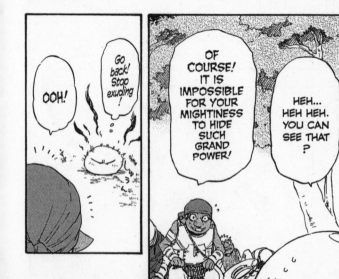

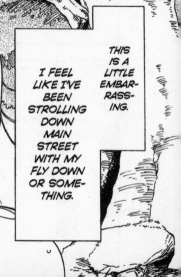

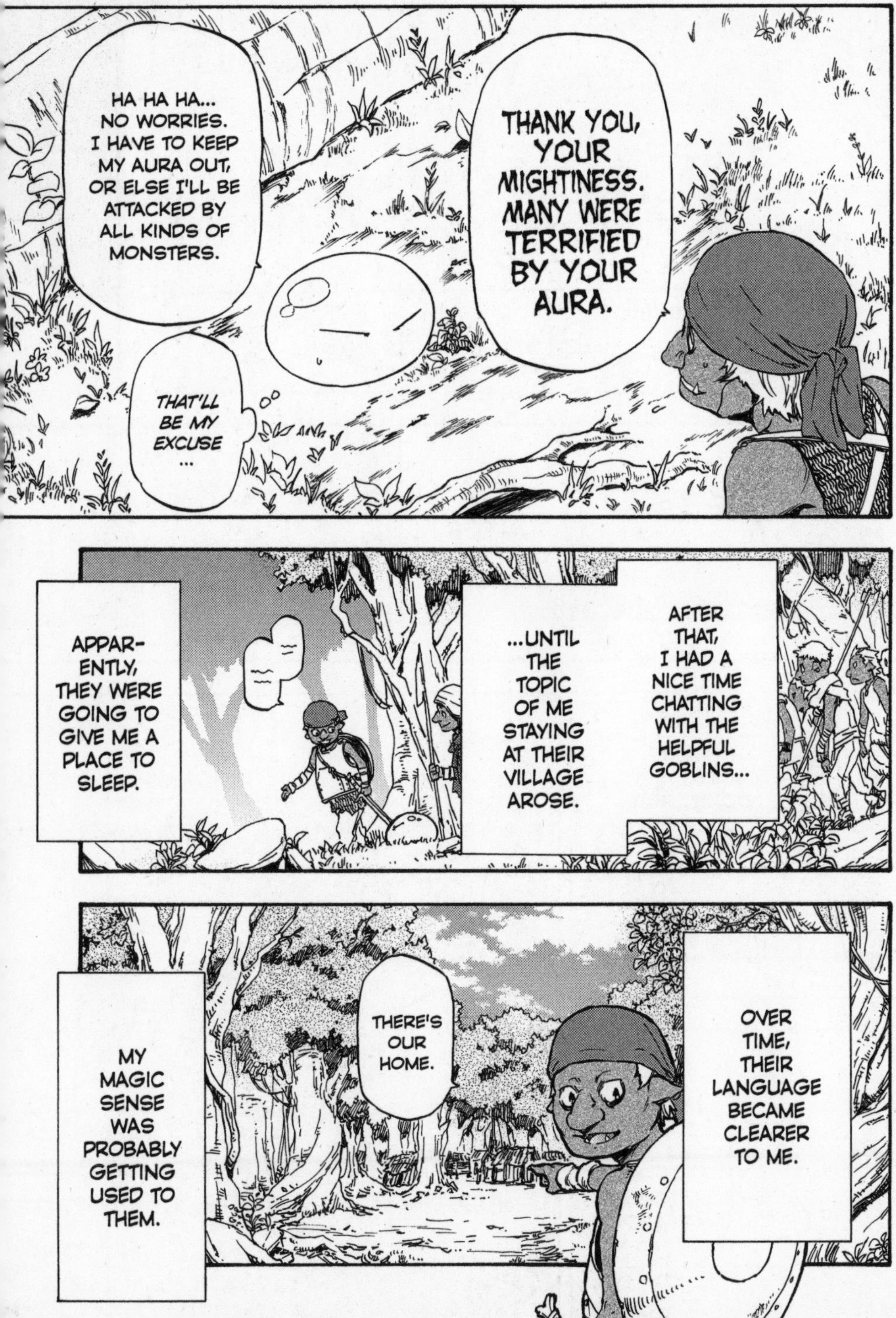

THANK YOU, YOUR MIGHTINESS. MANY WERE TERRIFIED BY YOUR AURA.
HA HA HA... NO WORRIES. I HAVE TO KEEP MY AURA OUT, OR ELSE I'LL BE ATTACKED BY ALL KINDS OF MONSTERS.
THAT'LL BE MY EXCUSE...
AFTER THAT, I HAD A NICE TIME CHATTING WITH THE HELPFUL GOBLINS...
...UNTIL THE TOPIC OF ME STAYING AT THEIR VILLAGE AROSE.
APPAR-ENTLY, THEY WERE GOING TO GIVE ME A PLACE TO SLEEP.
OVER TIME, THEIR LANGUAGE BECAME CLEARER TO ME.
THERE'S OUR HOME.
MY MAGIC SENSE WAS PROBABLY GETTING USED TO THEM.

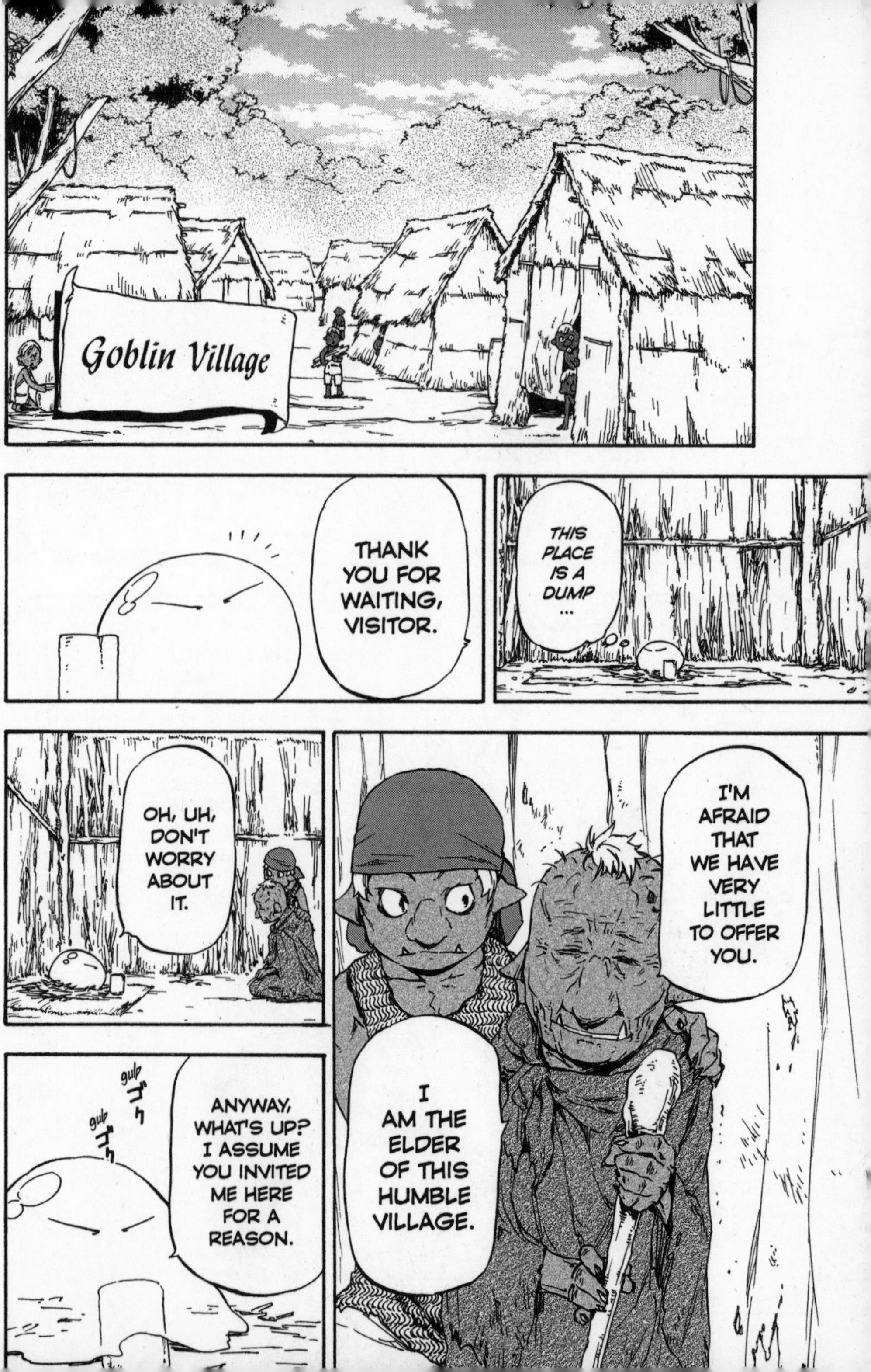
Goblin Village
THIS PLACE IS A DUMP ...
THANK YOU FOR WAITING, VISITOR.
I'M AFRAID THAT WE HAVE VERY LITTLE TO OFFER YOU.
I AM THE ELDER OF THIS HUMBLE VILLAGE.
OH, UH, DON'T WORRY ABOUT IT.
gulp ゴク
gulp ゴク
ANYWAY, WHAT'S UP? I ASSUME YOU INVITED ME HERE FOR A REASON.

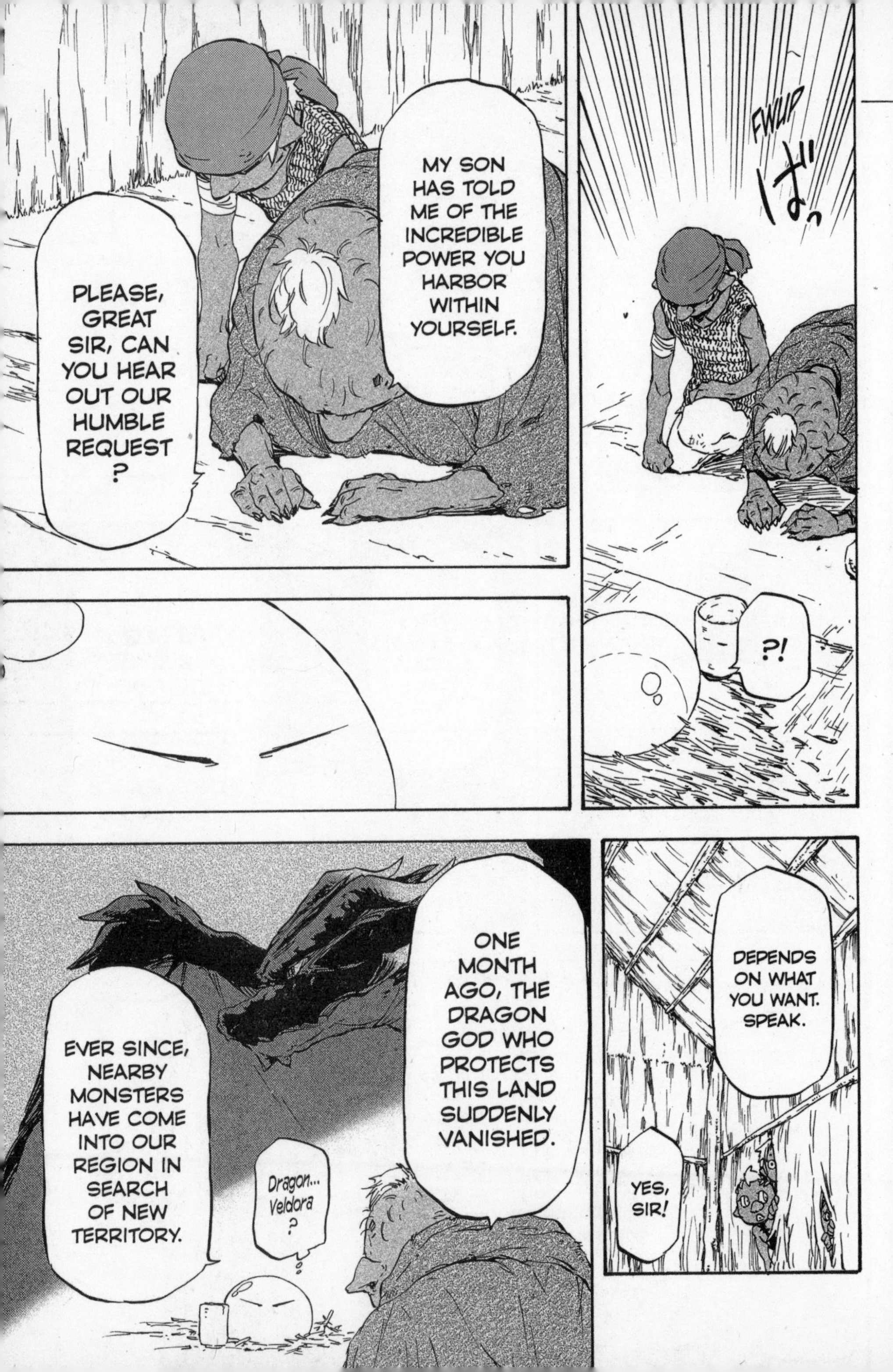
FWUP
ばっ
MY SON HAS TOLD ME OF THE INCREDIBLE POWER YOU HARBOR WITHIN YOURSELF.
PLEASE, GREAT SIR, CAN YOU HEAR OUT OUR HUMBLE REQUEST?
?!
DEPENDS ON WHAT YOU WANT. SPEAK.
YES, SIR!
ONE MONTH AGO, THE DRAGON GOD WHO PROTECTS THIS LAND SUDDENLY VANISHED.
EVER SINCE, NEARBY MONSTERS HAVE COME INTO OUR REGION IN SEARCH OF NEW TERRITORY.
Dragon... Veldora?

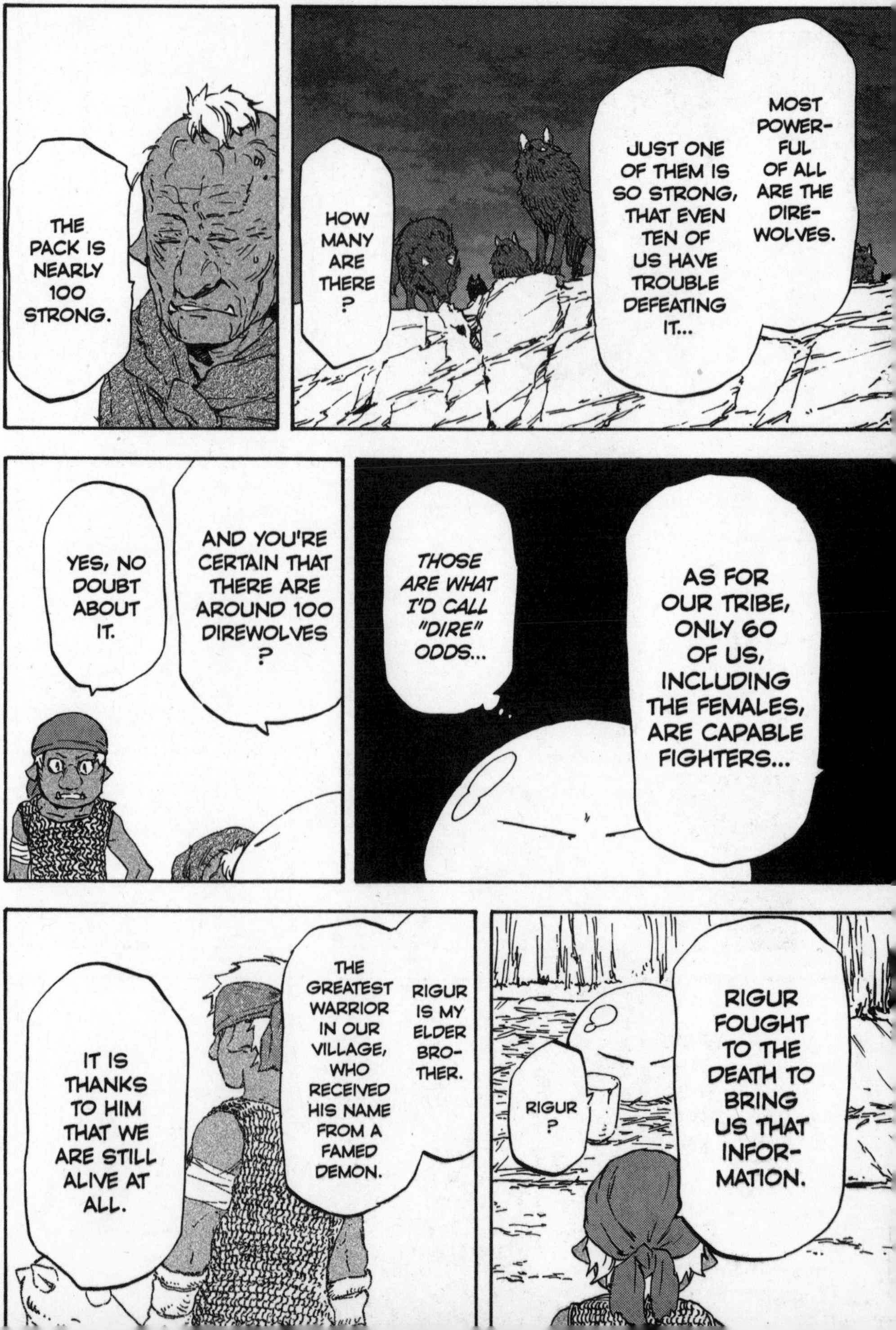
MOST POWERFUL OF ALL ARE THE DIREWOLVES.
JUST ONE OF THEM IS SO STRONG, THAT EVEN TEN OF US HAVE TROUBLE DEFEATING IT...
HOW MANY ARE THERE?
THE PACK IS NEARLY 100 STRONG.
AS FOR OUR TRIBE, ONLY 60 OF US, INCLUDING THE FEMALES, ARE CAPABLE FIGHTERS...
THOSE ARE WHAT I'D CALL "DIRE" ODDS...
AND YOU'RE CERTAIN THAT THERE ARE AROUND 100 DIREWOLVES?
YES, NO DOUBT ABOUT IT.
RIGUR FOUGHT TO THE DEATH TO BRING US THAT INFORMATION.
RIGUR?
RIGUR IS MY ELDER BROTHER.
THE GREATEST WARRIOR IN OUR VILLAGE, WHO RECEIVED HIS NAME FROM A FAMED DEMON.
IT IS THANKS TO HIM THAT WE ARE STILL ALIVE AT ALL.

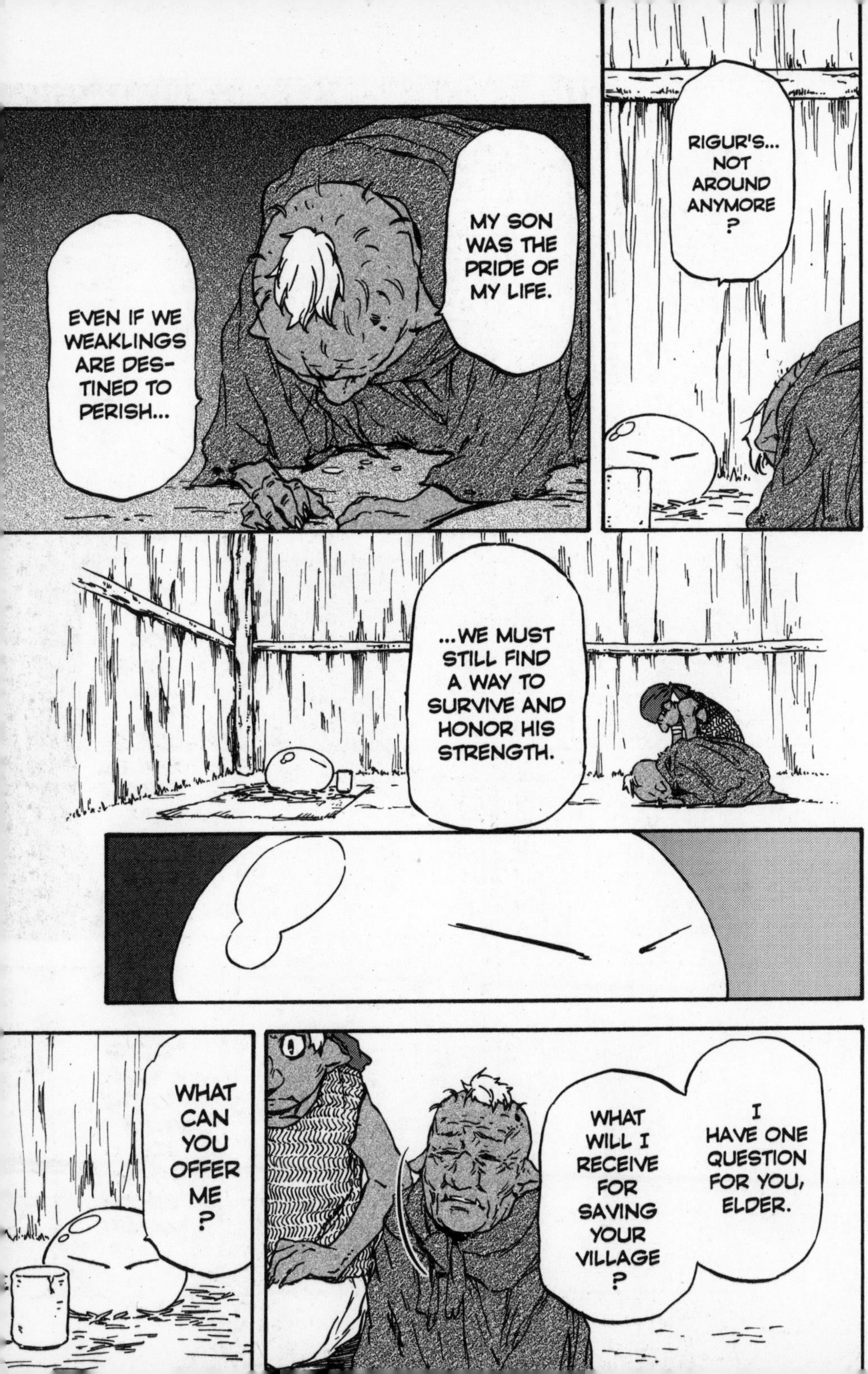

RIGUR'S... NOT AROUND ANYMORE?
MY SON WAS THE PRIDE OF MY LIFE.
EVEN IF WE WEAKLINGS ARE DES-TINED TO PERISH...
...WE MUST STILL FIND A WAY TO SURVIVE AND HONOR HIS STRENGTH.
I HAVE ONE QUESTION FOR YOU, ELDER.
WHAT WILL I RECEIVE FOR SAVING YOUR VILLAGE?
WHAT CAN YOU OFFER ME?

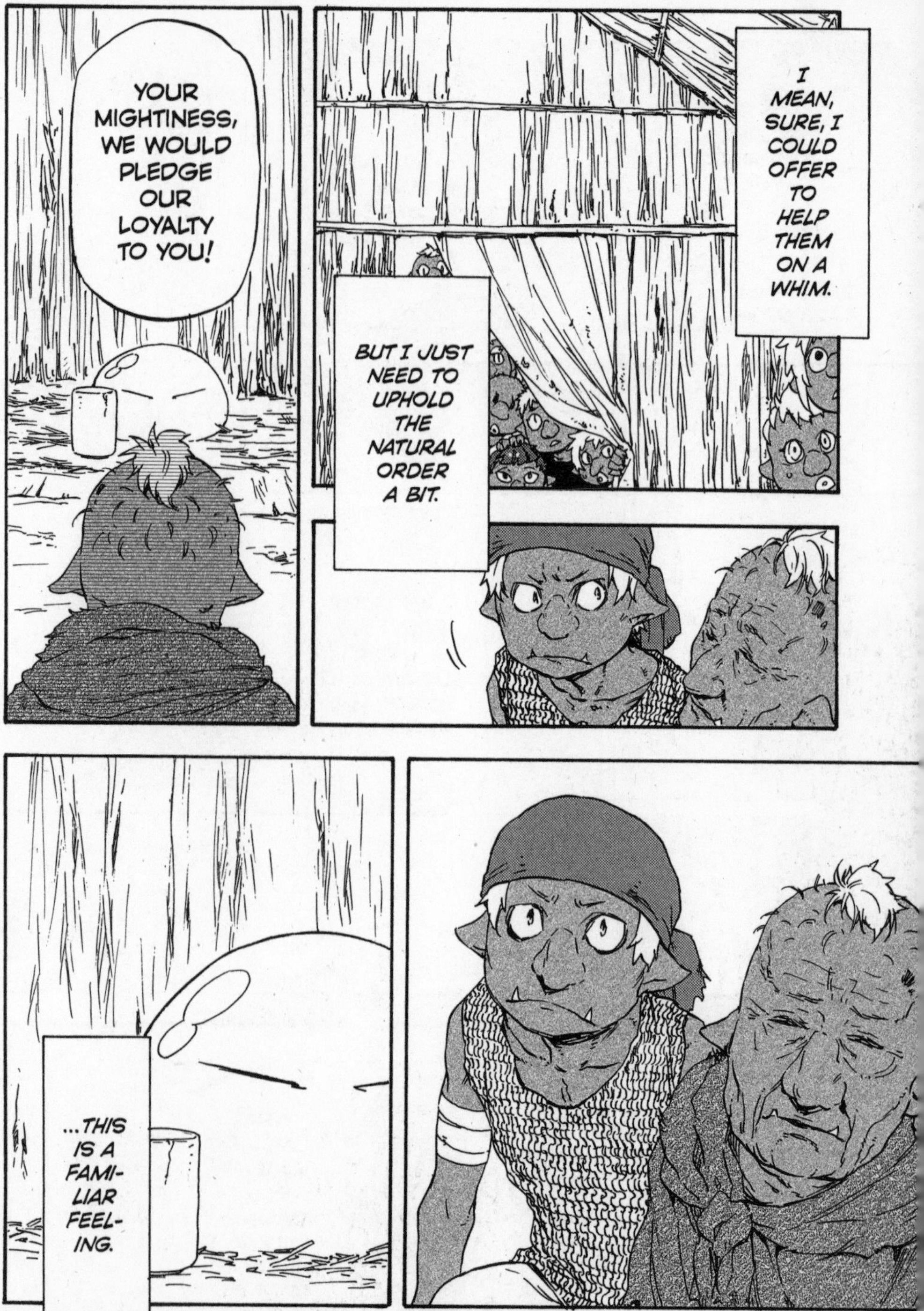
I MEAN, SURE, I COULD OFFER TO HELP THEM ON A WHIM.
BUT I JUST NEED TO UPHOLD THE NATURAL ORDER A BIT.
YOUR MIGHTINESS, WE WOULD PLEDGE OUR LOYALTY TO YOU!
...THIS IS A FAMILIAR FEELING.

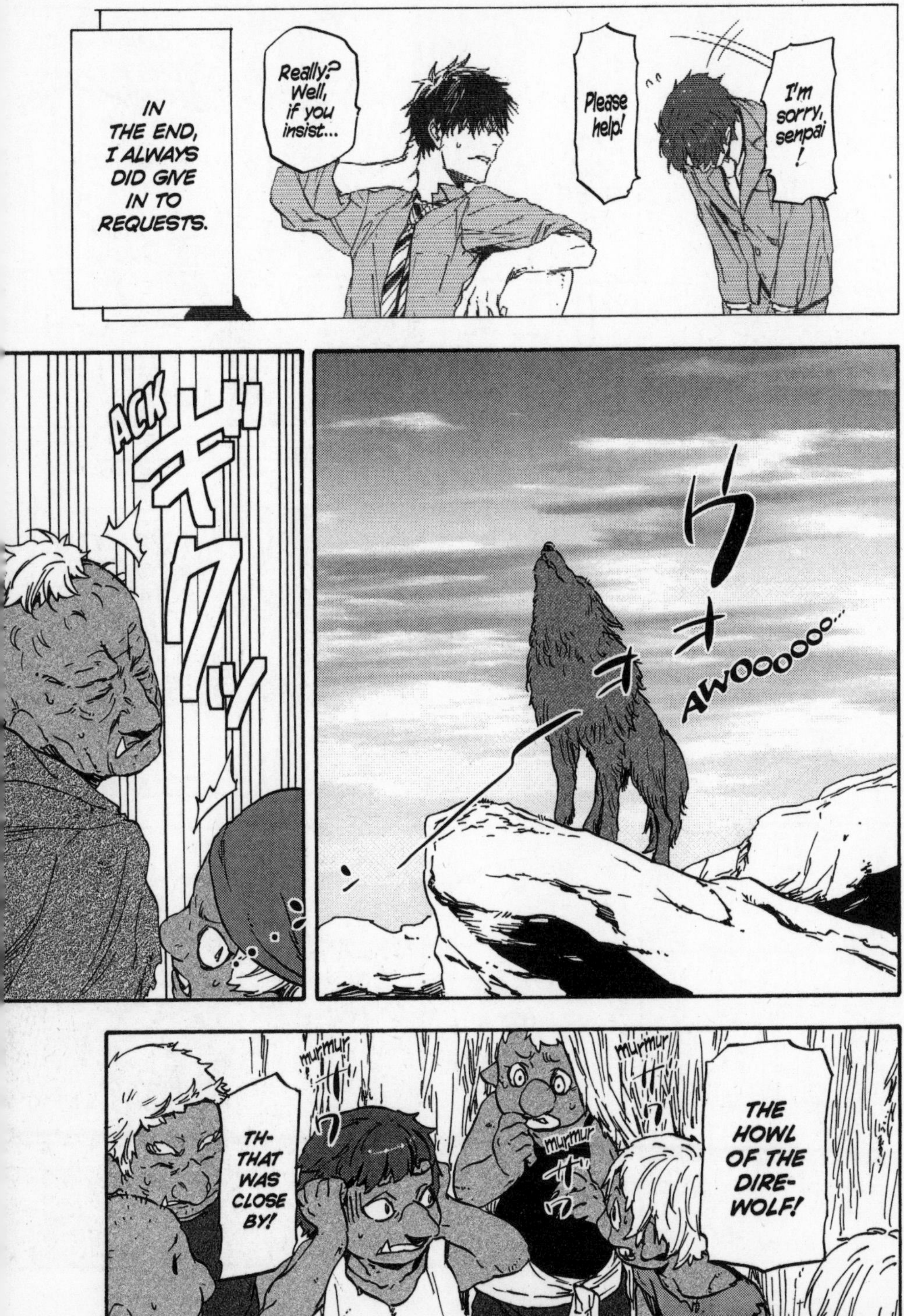
I'm sorry, senpai!
Please help!
Really? Well, if you insist...
IN THE END, I ALWAYS DID GIVE IN TO REQUESTS.
AWOOOOOO...
ACK
THE HOWL OF THE DIRE-WOLF!
murmur
murmur
TH-THAT WAS CLOSE BY!
murmur

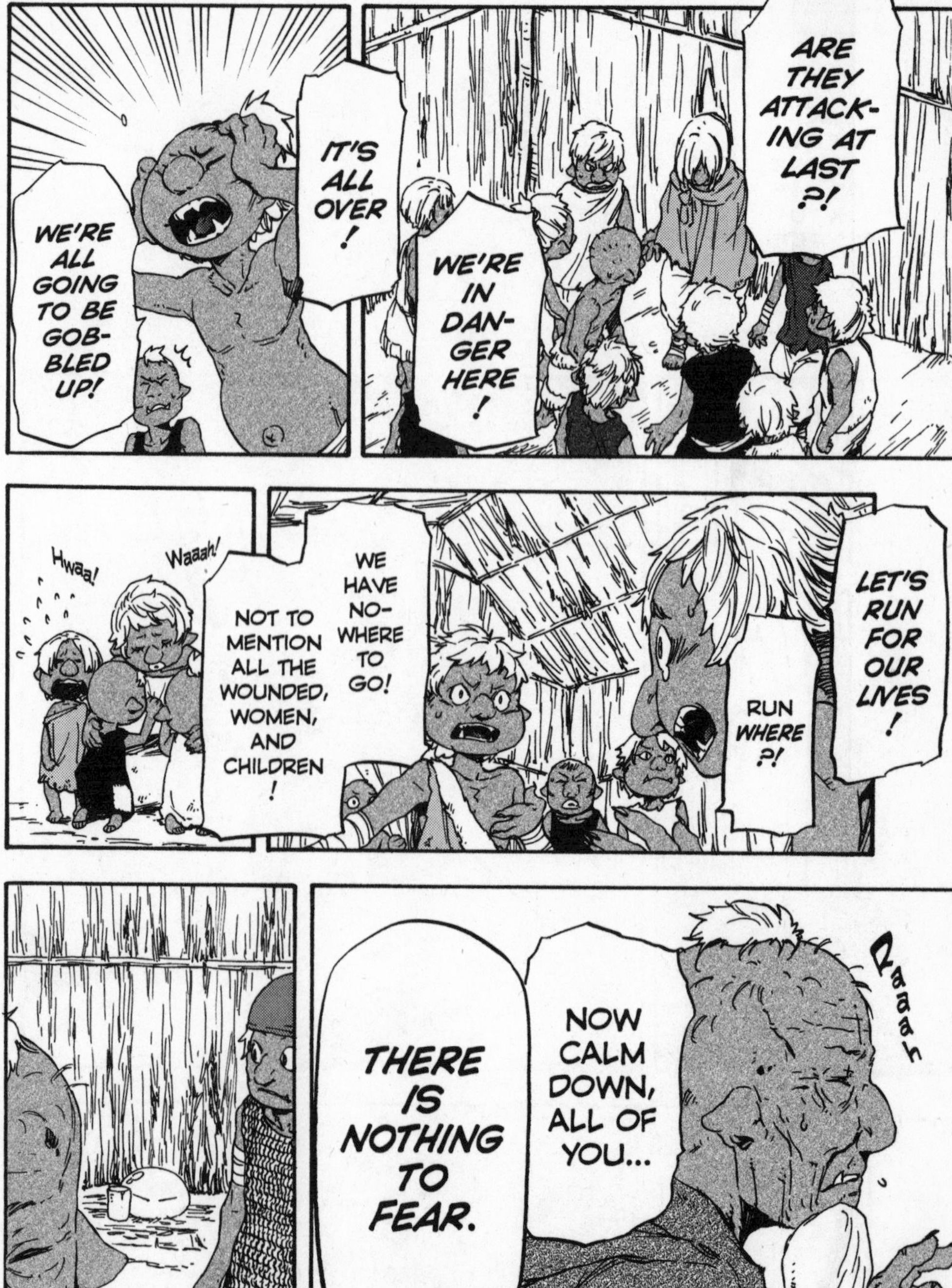
ARE THEY ATTACKING AT LAST?!
WE'RE IN DANGER HERE!
IT'S ALL OVER!
WE'RE ALL GOING TO BE GOBBLED UP!
LET'S RUN FOR OUR LIVES!
RUN WHERE?!
WE HAVE NOWHERE TO GO!
NOT TO MENTION ALL THE WOUNDED, WOMEN, AND CHILDREN!
Waaah!
Hwaa!
NOW CALM DOWN, ALL OF YOU...
THERE IS NOTHING TO FEAR.

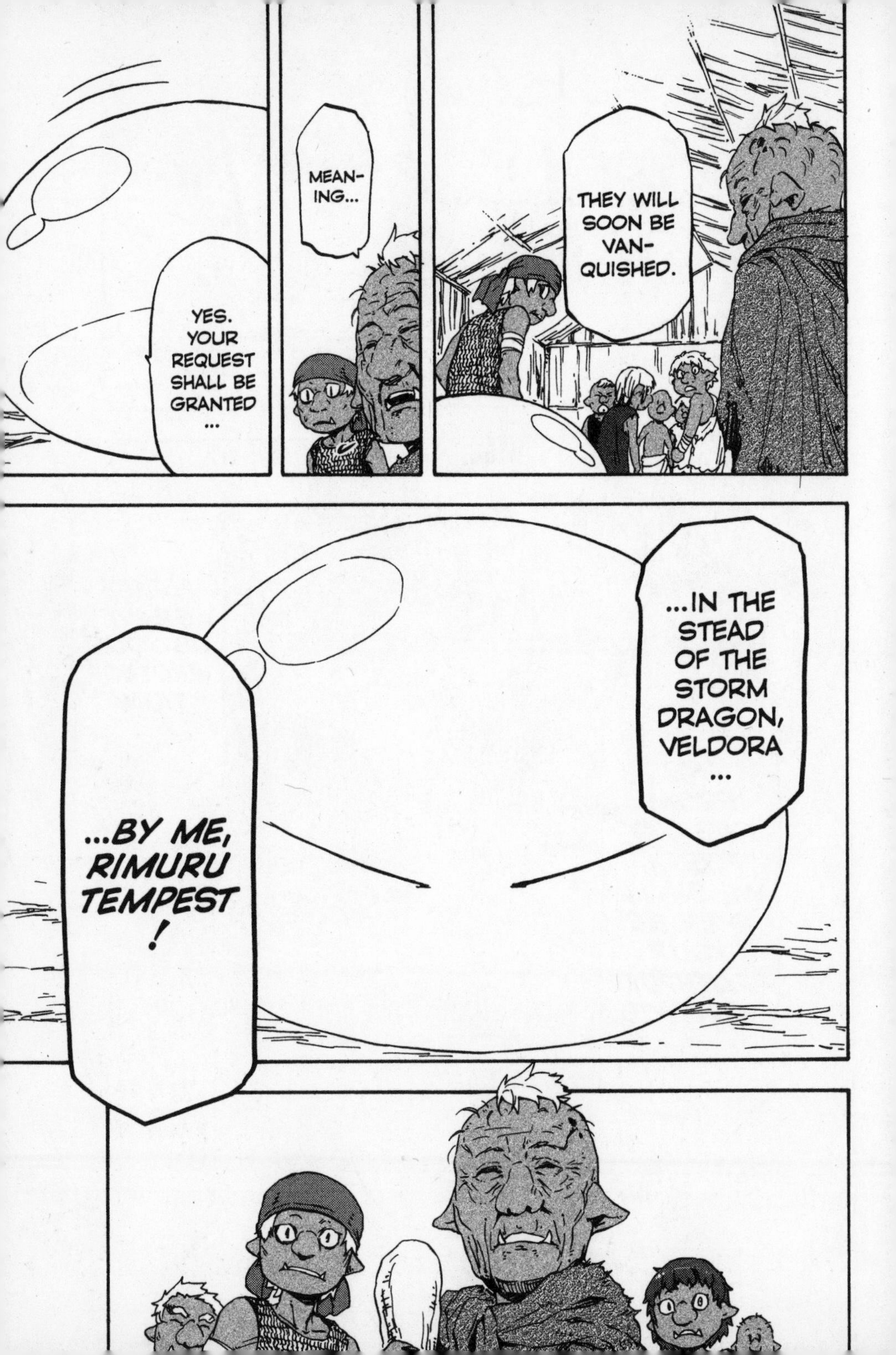
THEY WILL SOON BE VAN-QUISHED.
MEAN-ING...
YES. YOUR REQUEST SHALL BE GRANTED ...
...IN THE STEAD OF THE STORM DRAGON, VELDORA ...
...BY ME, RIMURU TEMPEST!

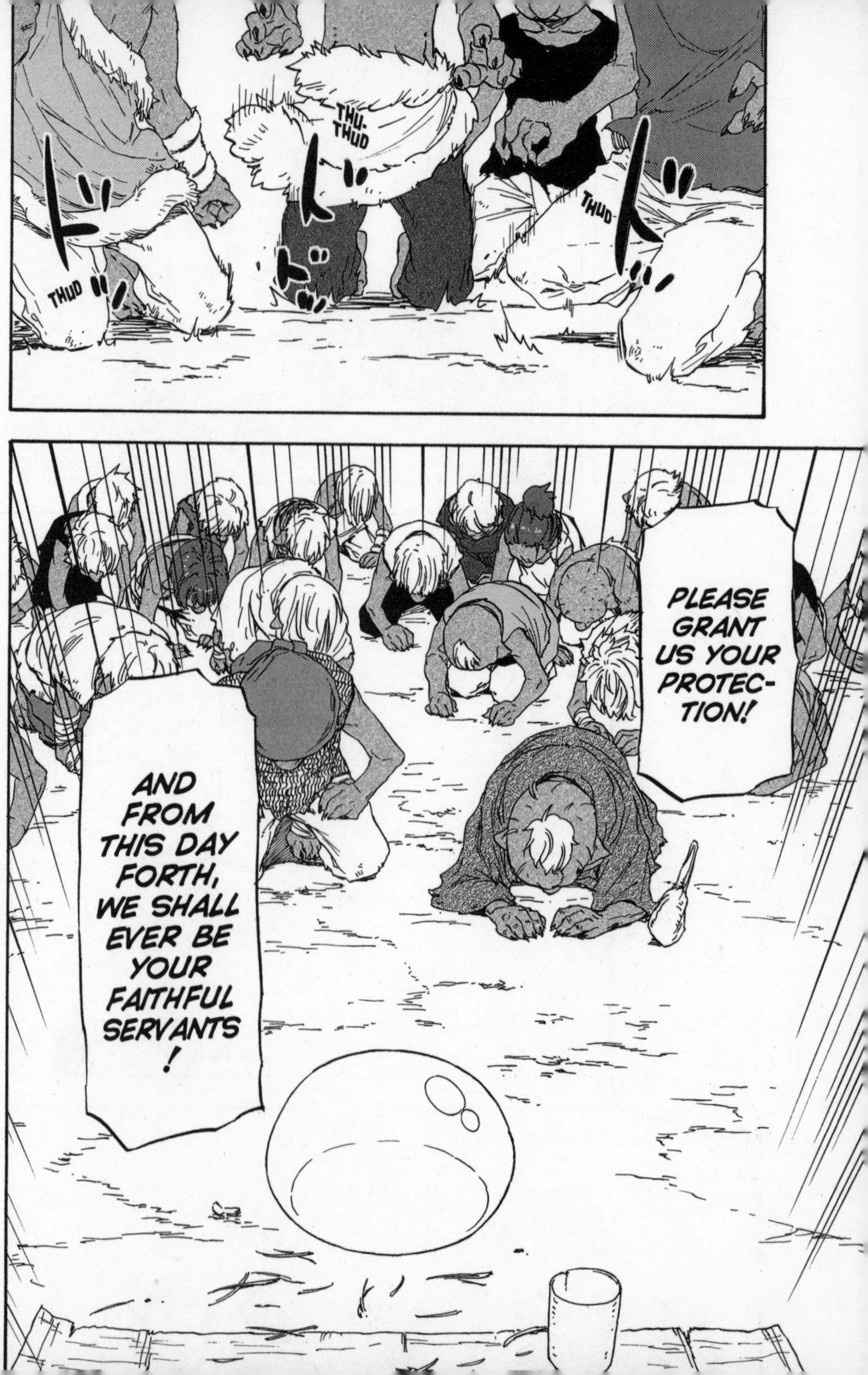
THUD
THU-THUD
THUD
PLEASE GRANT US YOUR PROTECTION!
AND FROM THIS DAY FORTH, WE SHALL EVER BE YOUR FAITHFUL SERVANTS!

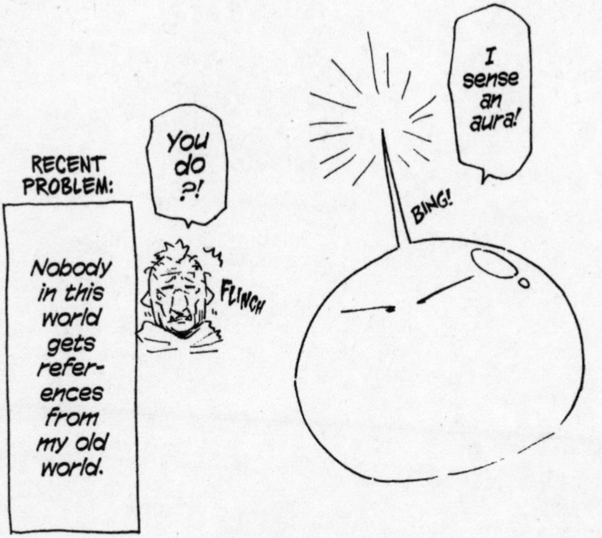
I sense an aura!
BING!
You do ?!
FLINCH
RECENT PROBLEM:
Nobody in this world gets refer- ences from my old world.

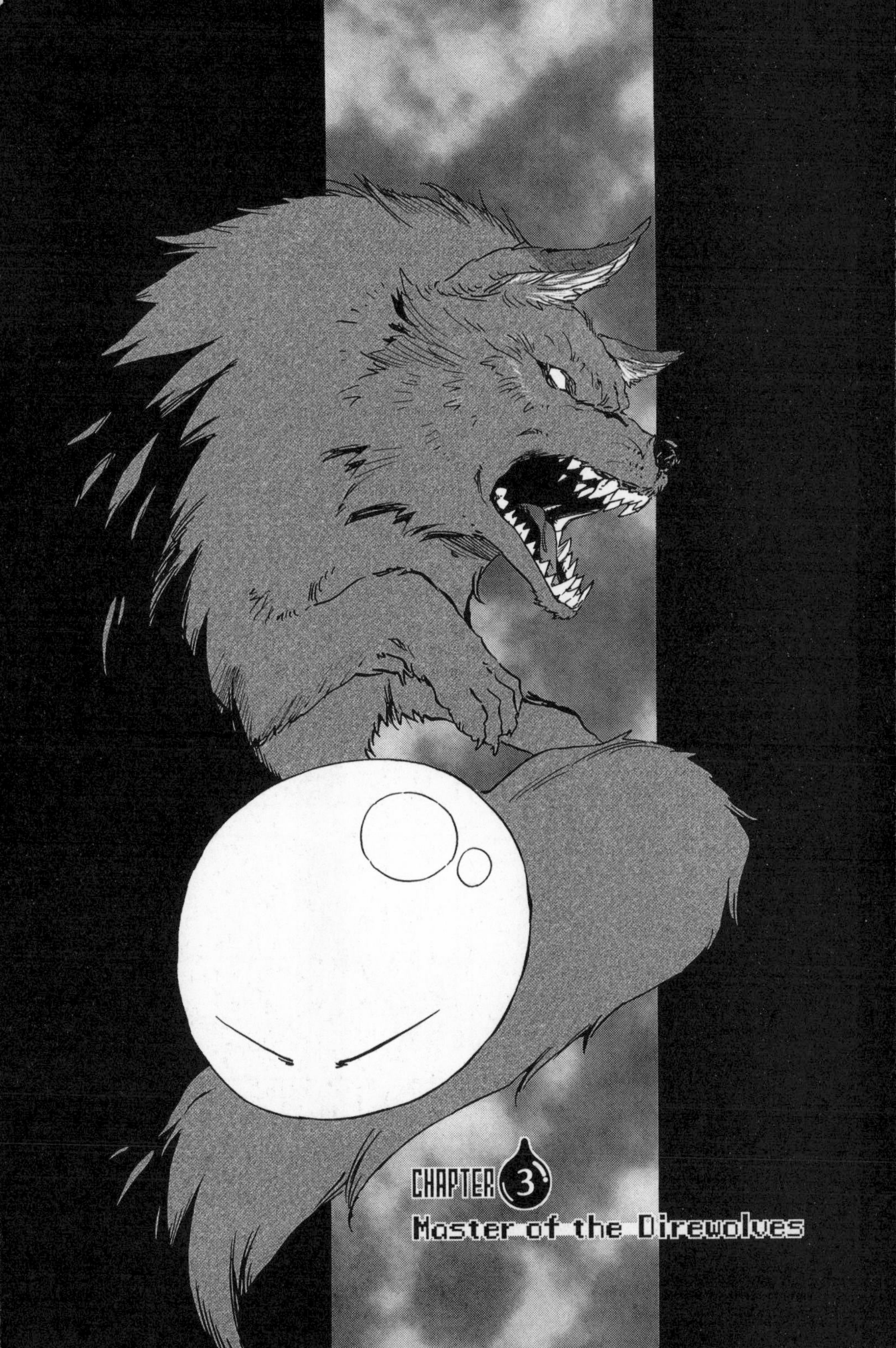
CHAPTER 3
Master of the Direwolves

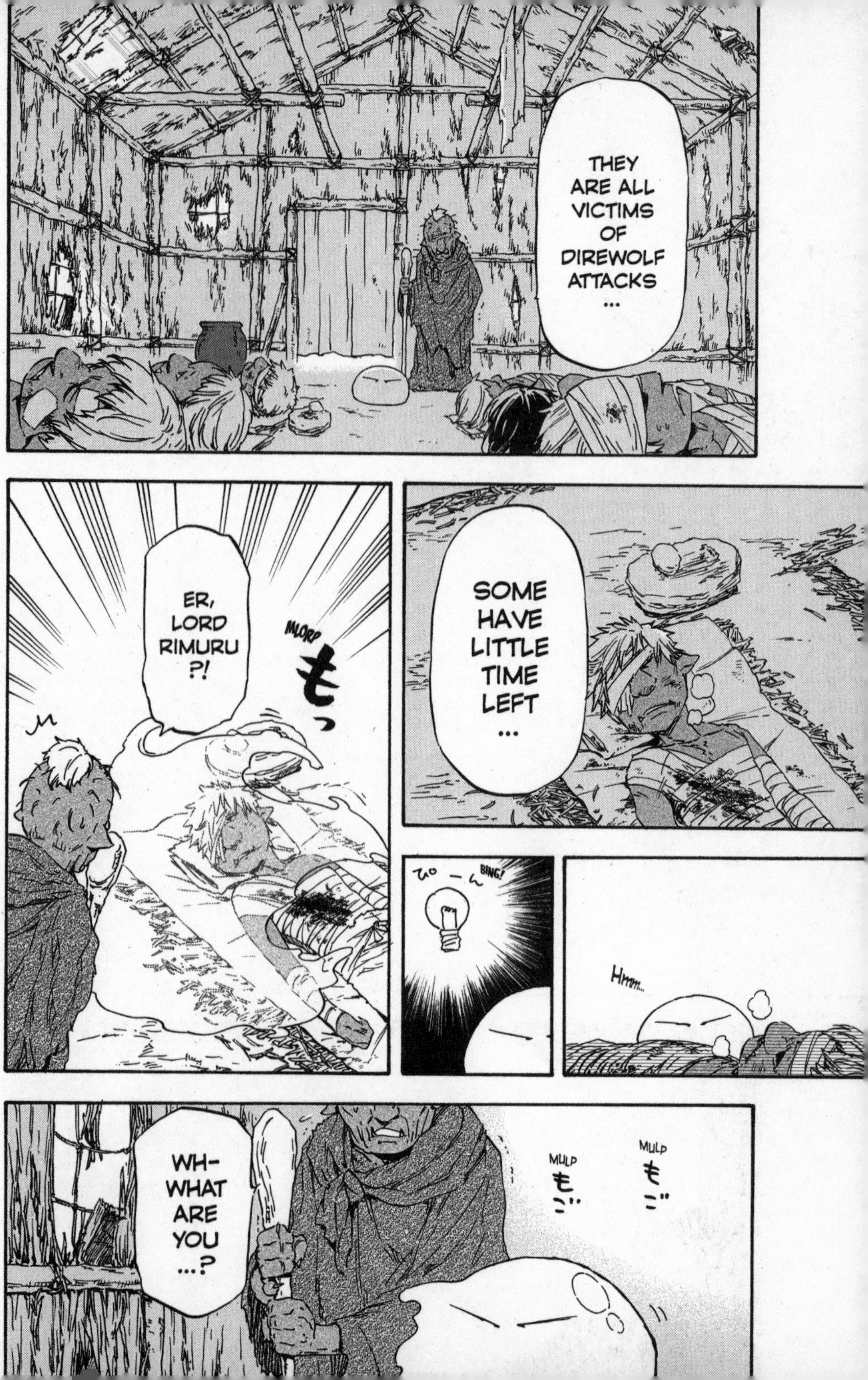
THEY ARE ALL VICTIMS OF DIREWOLF ATTACKS ...
SOME HAVE LITTLE TIME LEFT ...
Hmm...
ぴこーん
BING!
ER, LORD RIMURU ?!
MLORP
もっ
MULP
もご
MULP
もご
WH- WHAT ARE YOU ...?

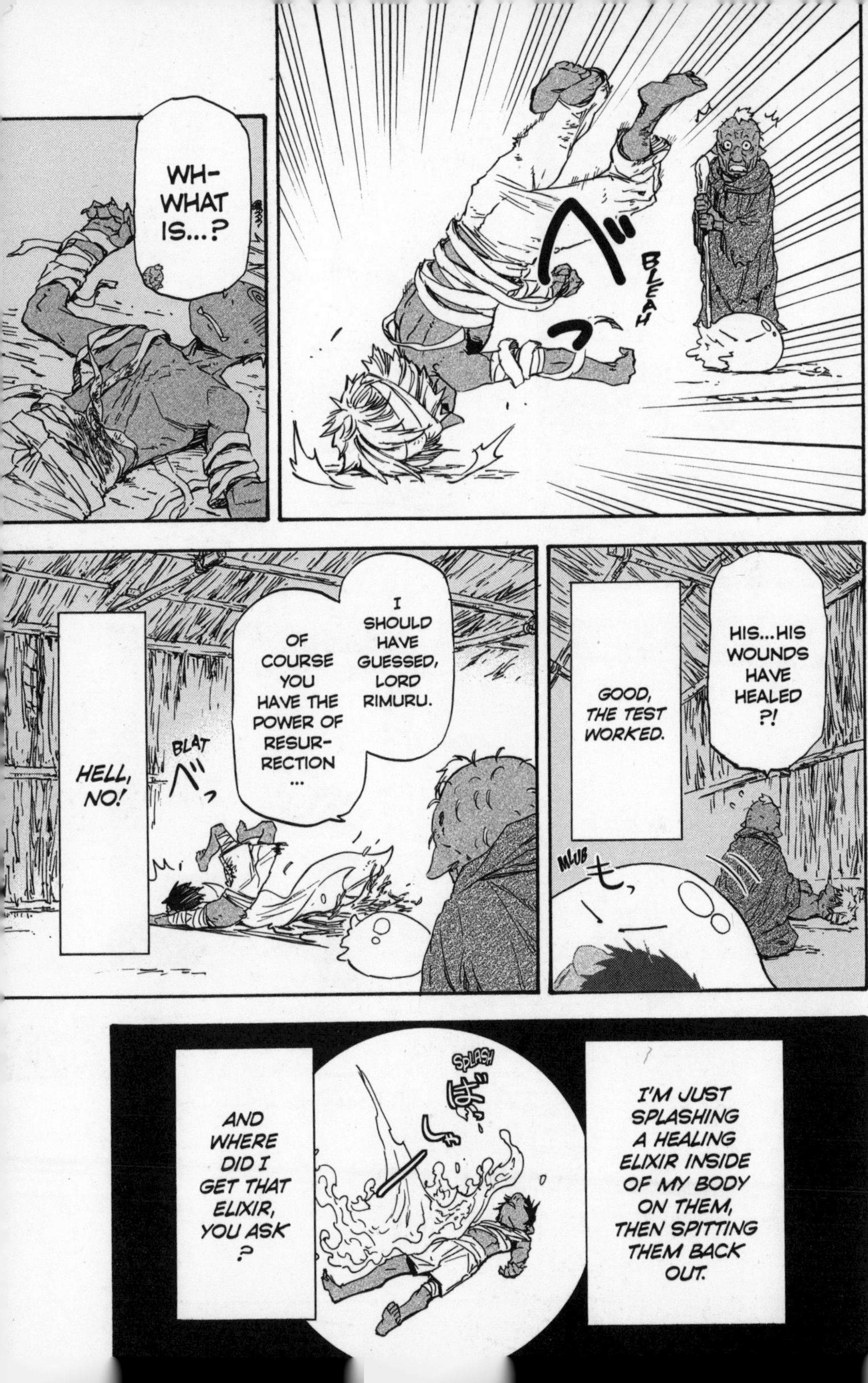
BLEAH
WH-WHAT IS...?
HIS...HIS WOUNDS HAVE HEALED?!
GOOD, THE TEST WORKED.
MLUB
I SHOULD HAVE GUESSED, LORD RIMURU.
OF COURSE YOU HAVE THE POWER OF RESURRECTION...
BLAT
HELL, NO!
I'M JUST SPLASHING A HEALING ELIXIR INSIDE OF MY BODY ON THEM, THEN SPITTING THEM BACK OUT.
SPLASH
AND WHERE DID I GET THAT ELIXIR, YOU ASK?

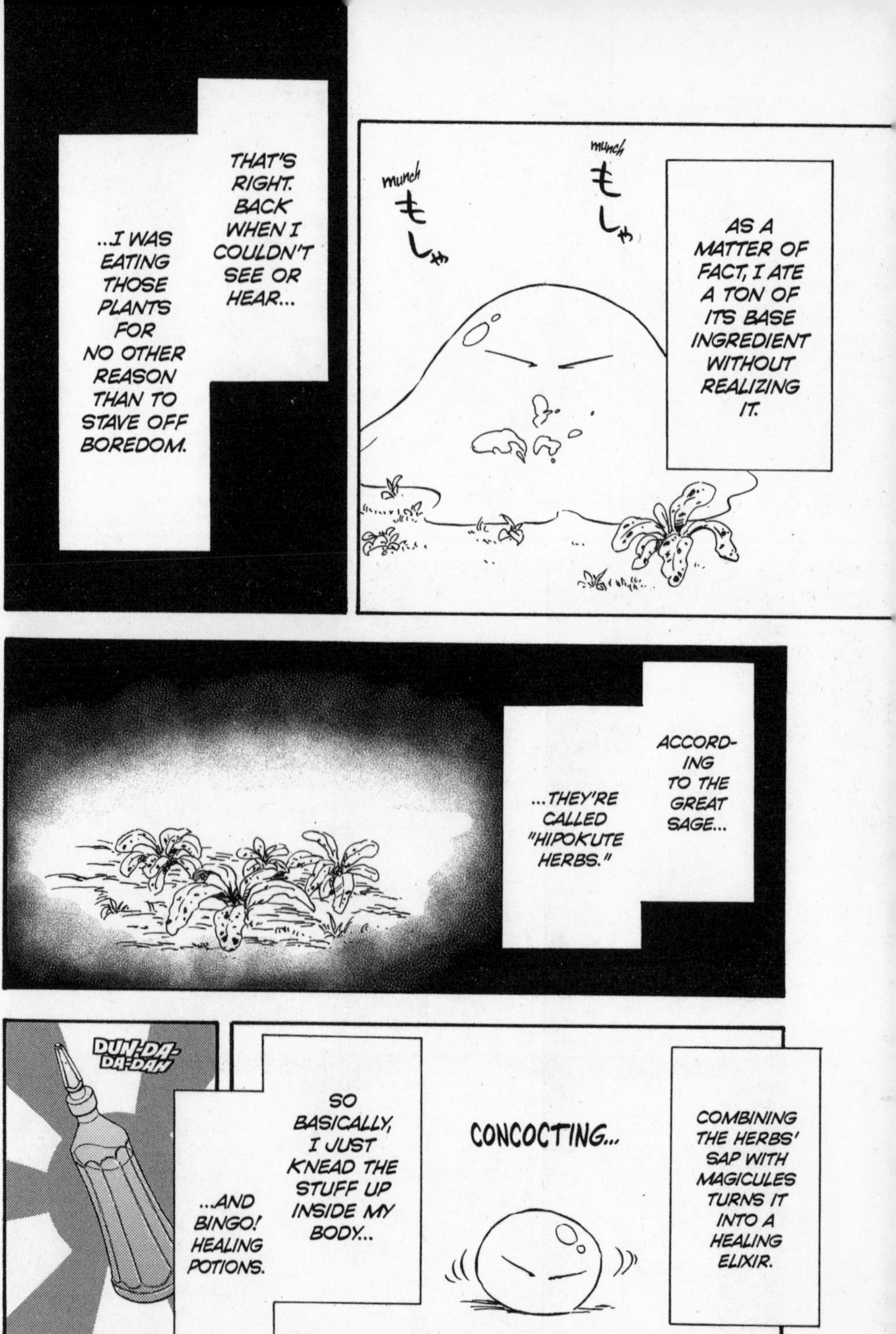
munch もしゃ
munch もしゃ
AS A MATTER OF FACT, I ATE A TON OF ITS BASE INGREDIENT WITHOUT REALIZING IT.
THAT'S RIGHT. BACK WHEN I COULDN'T SEE OR HEAR...
...I WAS EATING THOSE PLANTS FOR NO OTHER REASON THAN TO STAVE OFF BOREDOM.
ACCORD-ING TO THE GREAT SAGE...
...THEY'RE CALLED "HIPOKUTE HERBS."
COMBINING THE HERBS' SAP WITH MAGICULES TURNS IT INTO A HEALING ELIXIR.
CONCOCTING...
SO BASICALLY, I JUST KNEAD THE STUFF UP INSIDE MY BODY...
...AND BINGO! HEALING POTIONS.
DUN-DA-DA-DAH

*Bottle not included

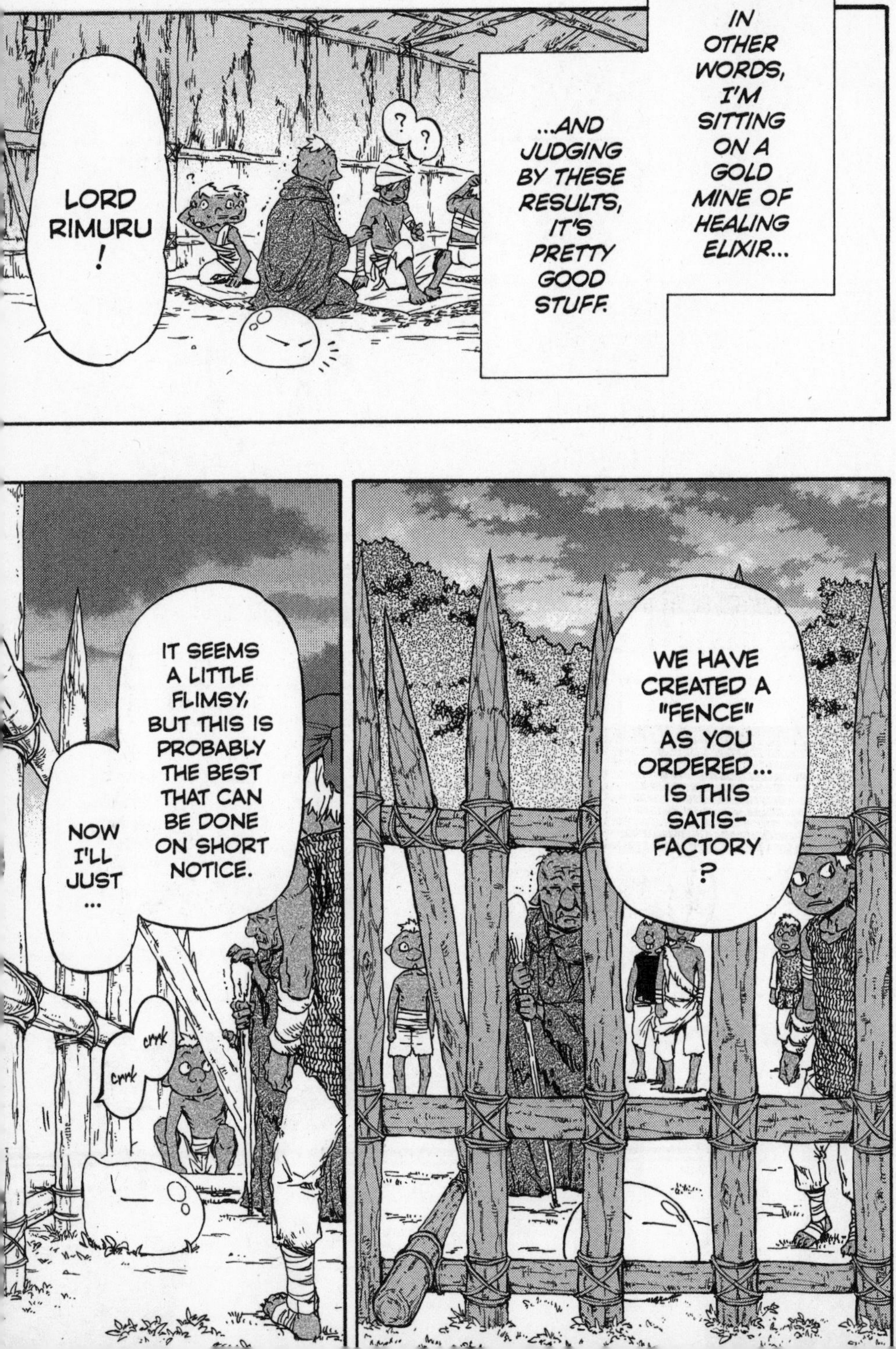
IN OTHER WORDS, I'M SITTING ON A GOLD MINE OF HEALING ELIXIR...
...AND JUDGING BY THESE RESULTS, IT'S PRETTY GOOD STUFF.
? ?
LORD RIMURU!
WE HAVE CREATED A "FENCE" AS YOU ORDERED... IS THIS SATIS-FACTORY?
IT SEEMS A LITTLE FLIMSY, BUT THIS IS PROBABLY THE BEST THAT CAN BE DONE ON SHORT NOTICE.
NOW I'LL JUST ...
crrk crrk

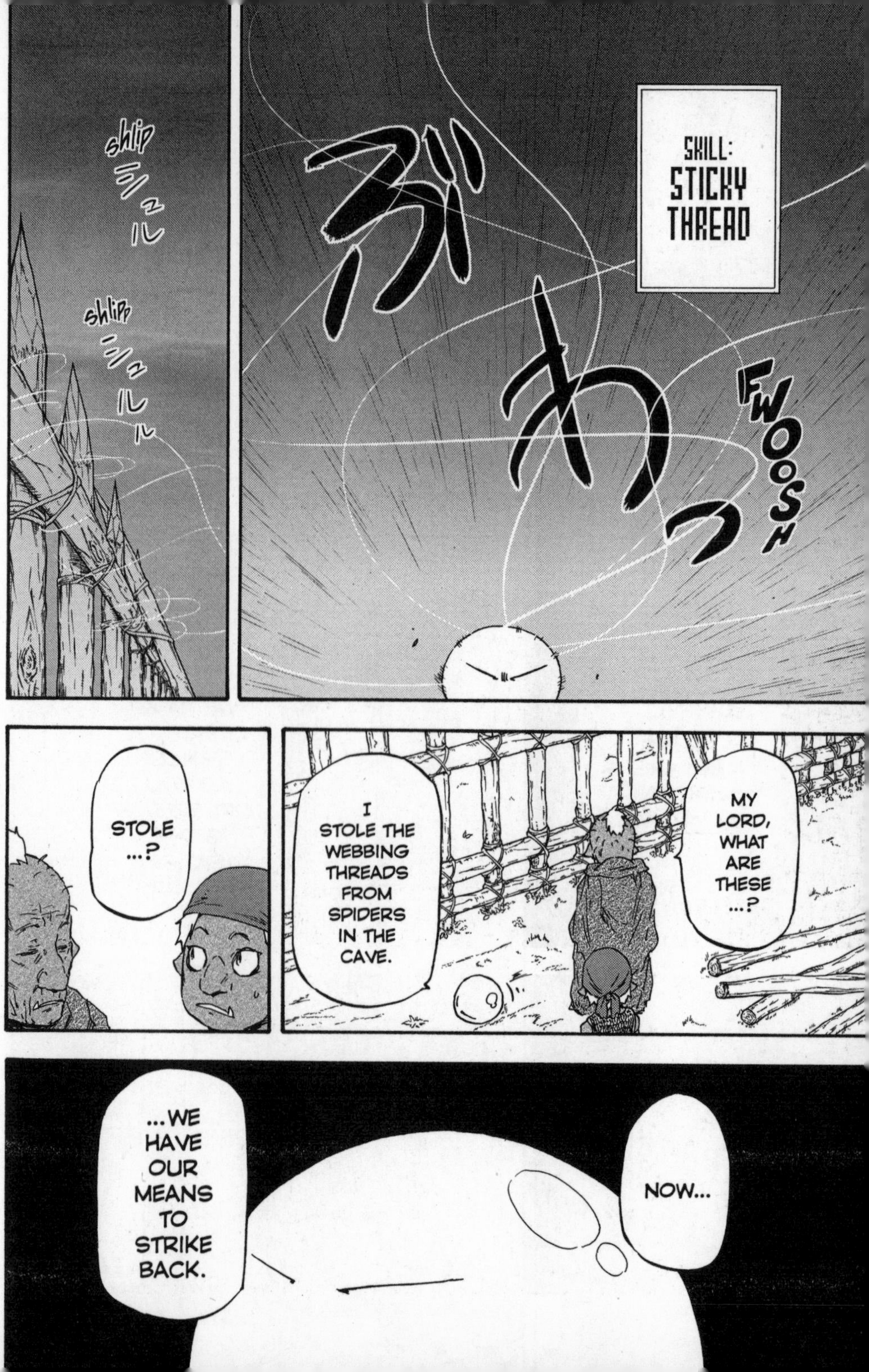
SKILL: STICKY THREAD
ぶわっ
FWOOSH
shlip
シュル
shlipp
シュルルル
MY LORD, WHAT ARE THESE ...?
I STOLE THE WEBBING THREADS FROM SPIDERS IN THE CAVE.
STOLE ...?
NOW...
...WE HAVE OUR MEANS TO STRIKE BACK.

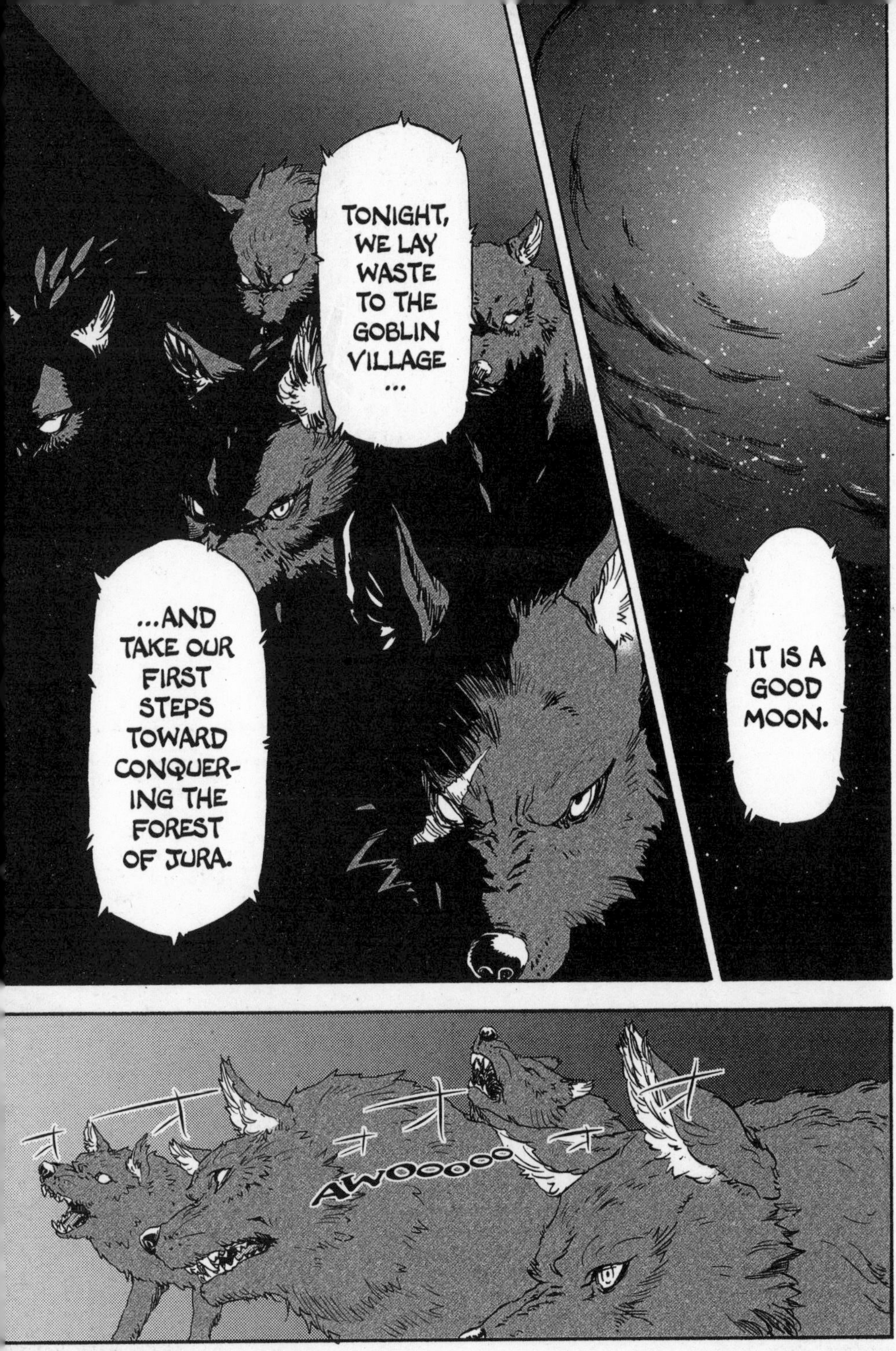
IT IS A GOOD MOON.
TONIGHT, WE LAY WASTE TO THE GOBLIN VILLAGE ...
...AND TAKE OUR FIRST STEPS TOWARD CONQUER-ING THE FOREST OF JURA.
AWOOOOOO

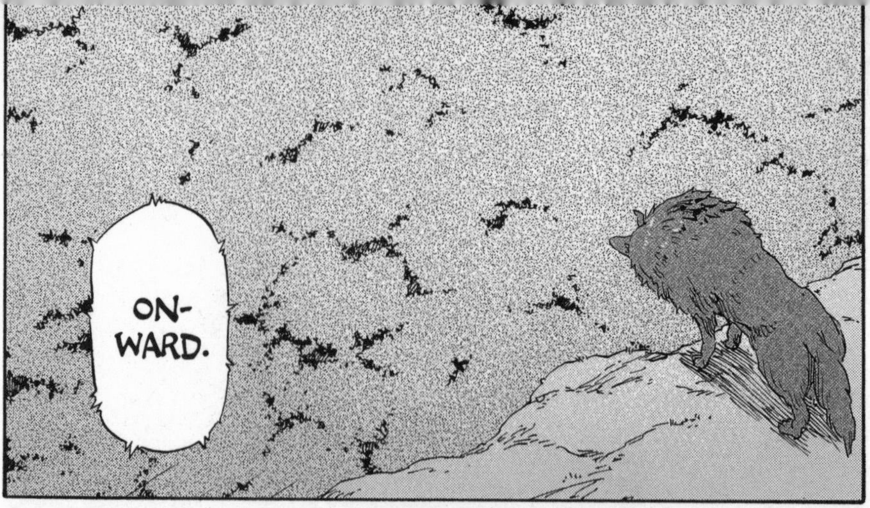
ON-
WARD.
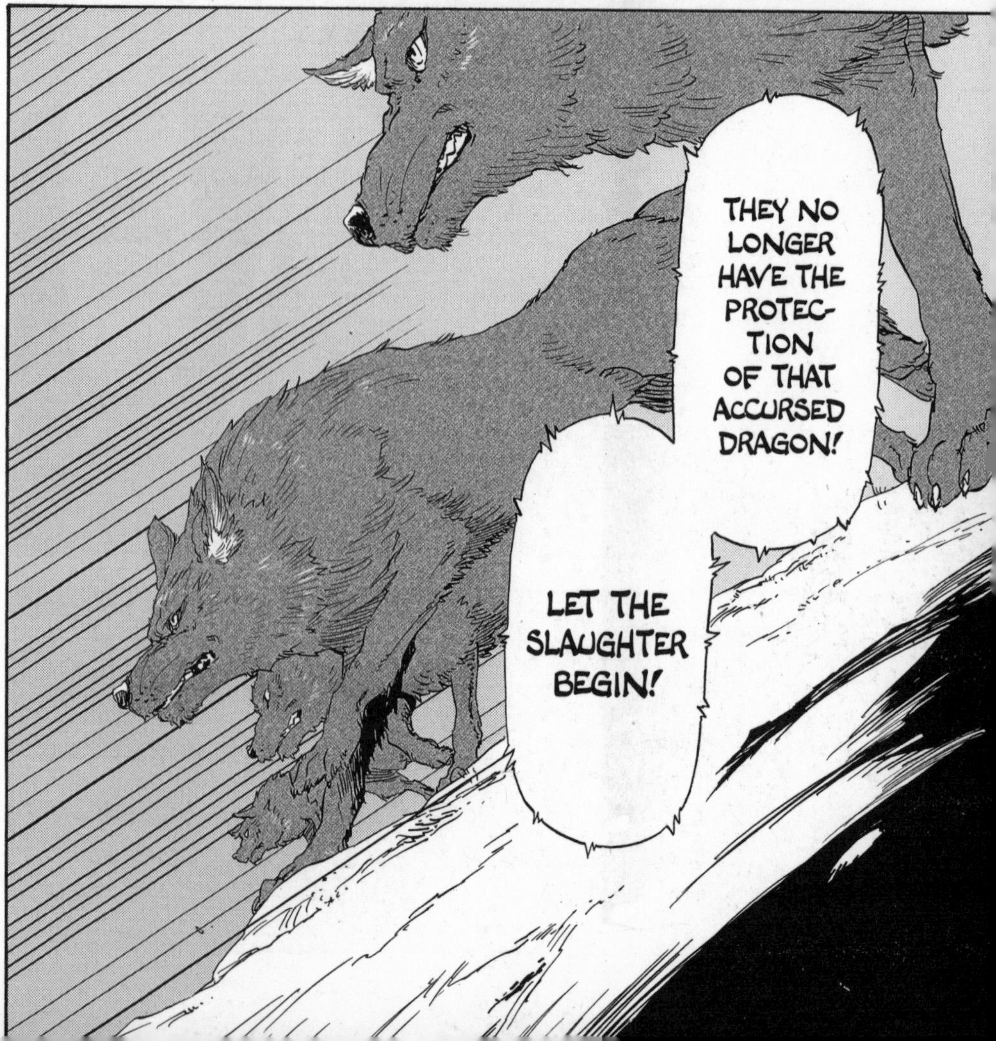
THEY NO LONGER HAVE THE PROTECTION OF THAT ACCURSED DRAGON!
LET THE SLAUGHTER BEGIN!

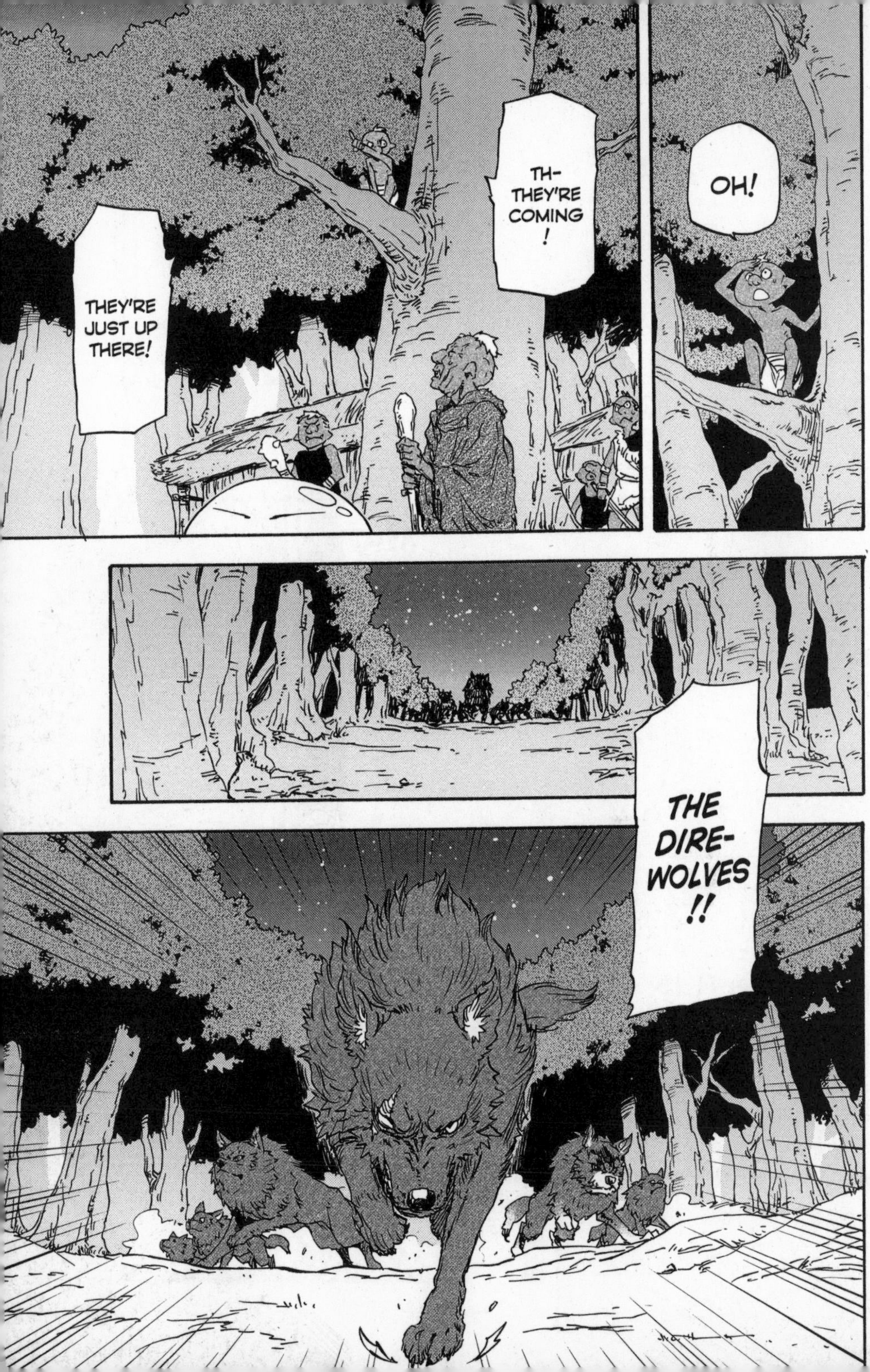
OH!
TH- THEY'RE COMING!
THEY'RE JUST UP THERE!
THE DIRE-WOLVES!!

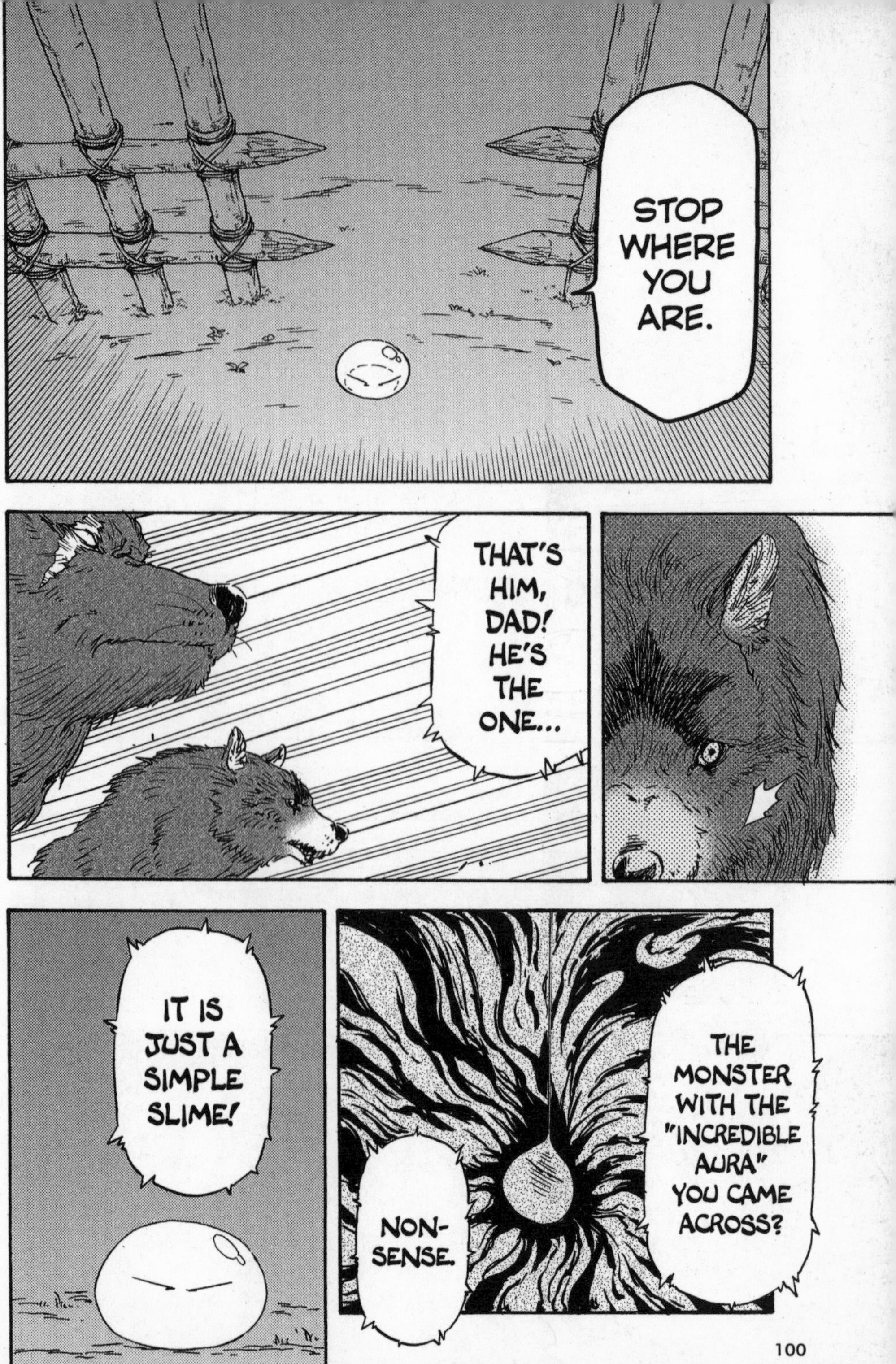
STOP WHERE YOU ARE.
THAT'S HIM, DAD! HE'S THE ONE...
THE MONSTER WITH THE "INCREDIBLE AURA" YOU CAME ACROSS?
NON-SENSE.
IT IS JUST A SIMPLE SLIME!

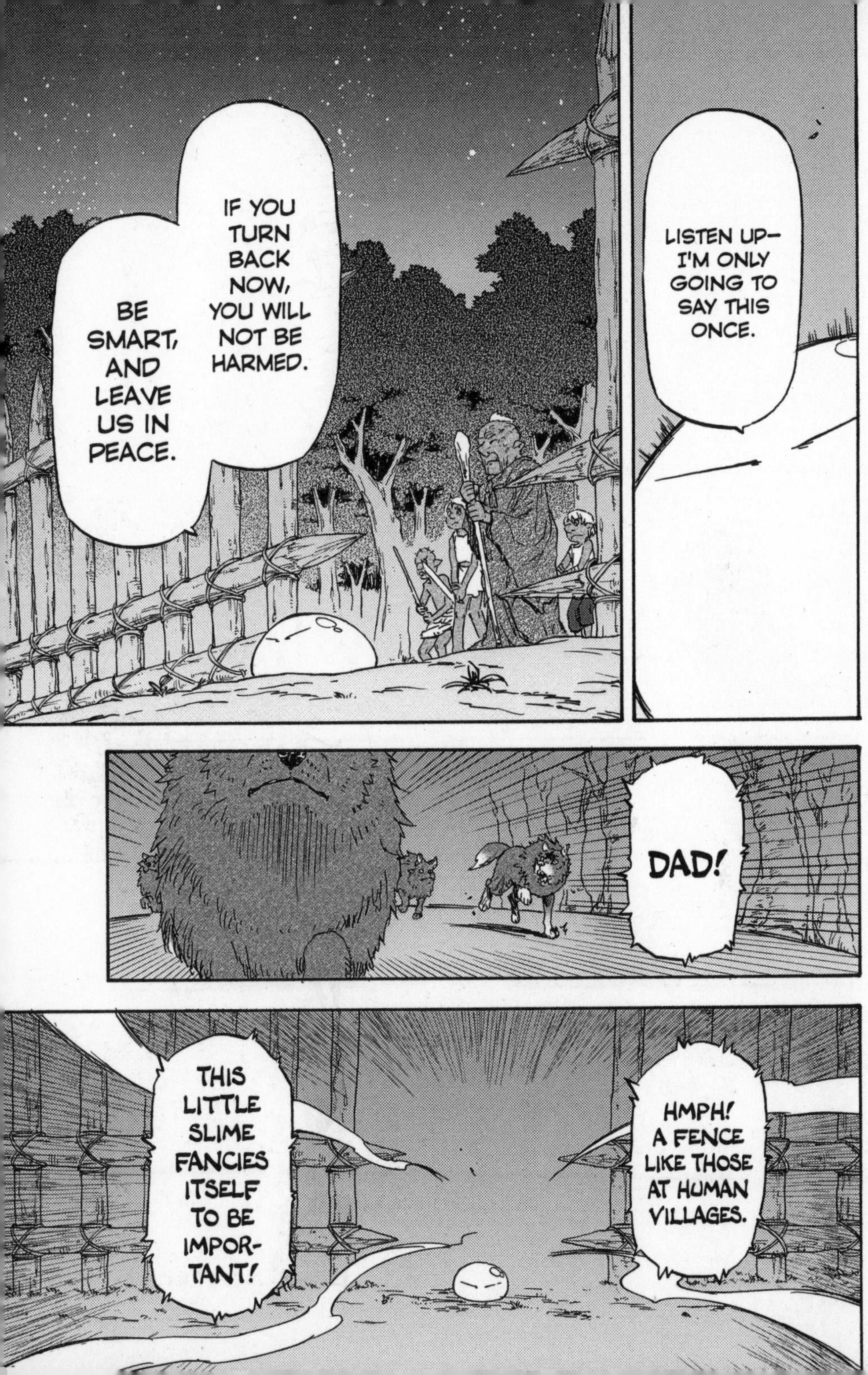
LISTEN UP— I'M ONLY GOING TO SAY THIS ONCE.
IF YOU TURN BACK NOW, YOU WILL NOT BE HARMED.
BE SMART, AND LEAVE US IN PEACE.
DAD!
HMPH! A FENCE LIKE THOSE AT HUMAN VILLAGES.
THIS LITTLE SLIME FANCIES ITSELF TO BE IMPOR-TANT!

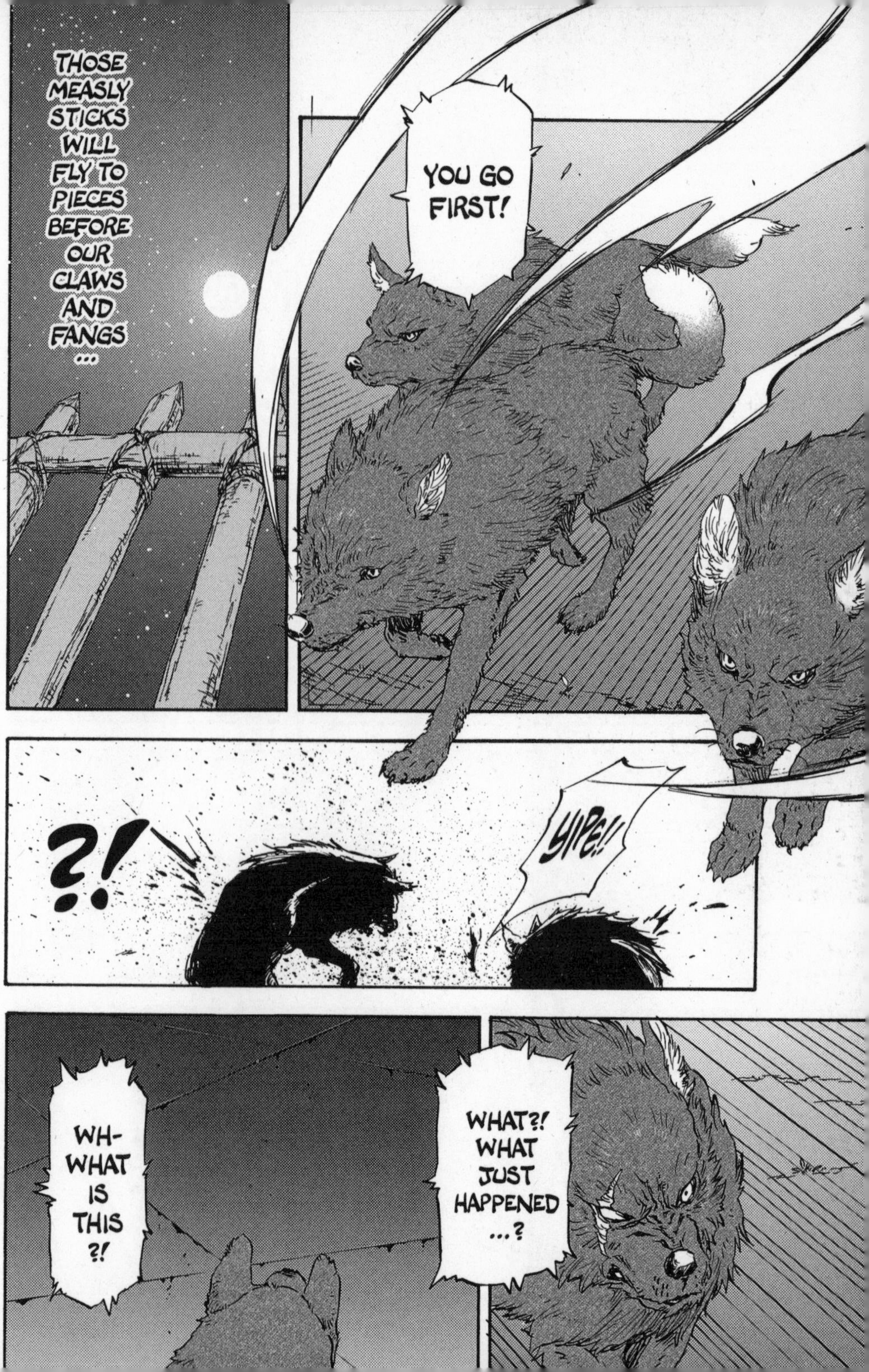
YOU GO FIRST!
THOSE MEASLY STICKS WILL FLY TO PIECES BEFORE OUR CLAWS AND FANGS...
YIPE!!
?!
WHAT?! WHAT JUST HAPPENED...?
WH-WHAT IS THIS?!

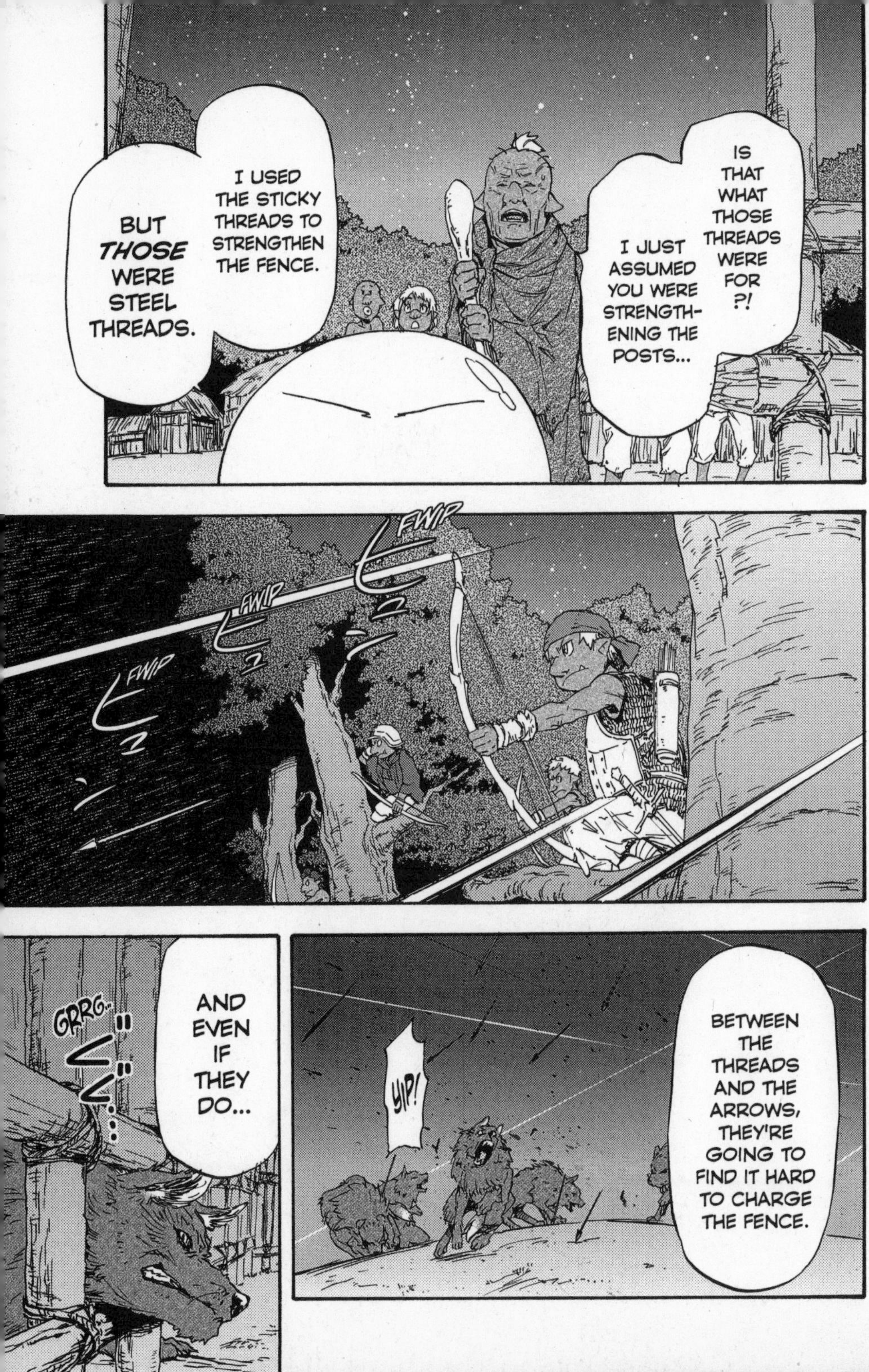

IS THAT WHAT THOSE THREADS WERE FOR?!
I JUST ASSUMED YOU WERE STRENGTH-ENING THE POSTS...
I USED THE STICKY THREADS TO STRENGTHEN THE FENCE.
BUT *THOSE* WERE STEEL THREADS.
FWIP
FWIP
FWIP
BETWEEN THE THREADS AND THE ARROWS, THEY'RE GOING TO FIND IT HARD TO CHARGE THE FENCE.
YIP!
AND EVEN IF THEY DO...
GRRG...

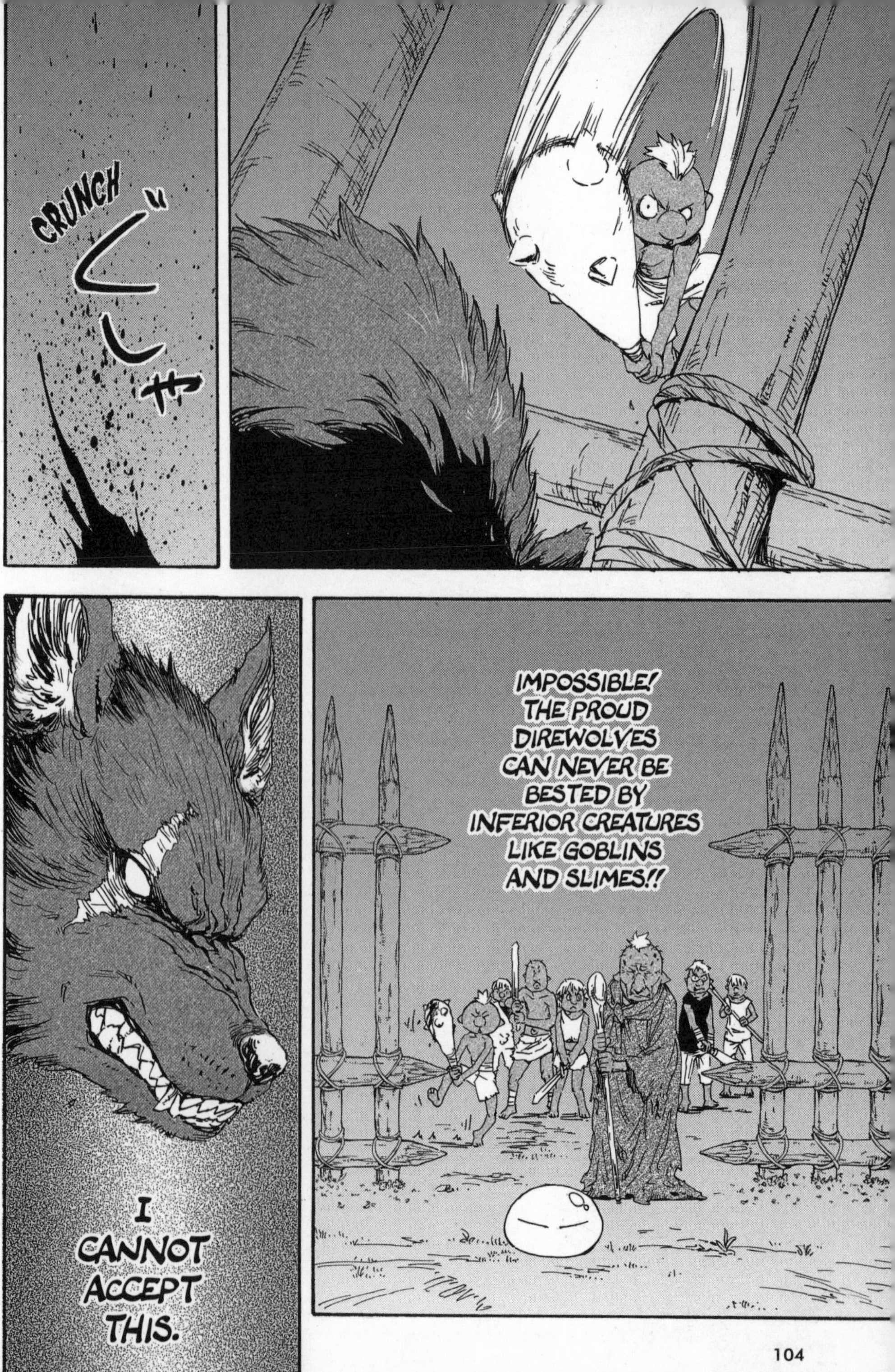
CRUNCH
ぐしゃ
IMPOSSIBLE! THE PROUD DIREWOLVES CAN NEVER BE BESTED BY INFERIOR CREATURES LIKE GOBLINS AND SLIMES!!
I CANNOT ACCEPT THIS.

DAD
?!

THE BLOOD
OF MY
FELLOW
WOLVES
ALLOWS ME
TO SEE THE
STRINGS...

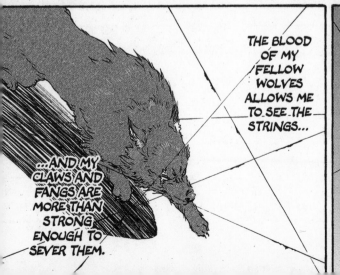

...AND MY
CLAWS AND
FANGS ARE
MORE THAN
STRONG
ENOUGH TO
SEVER THEM.

MERE
TRICKS.

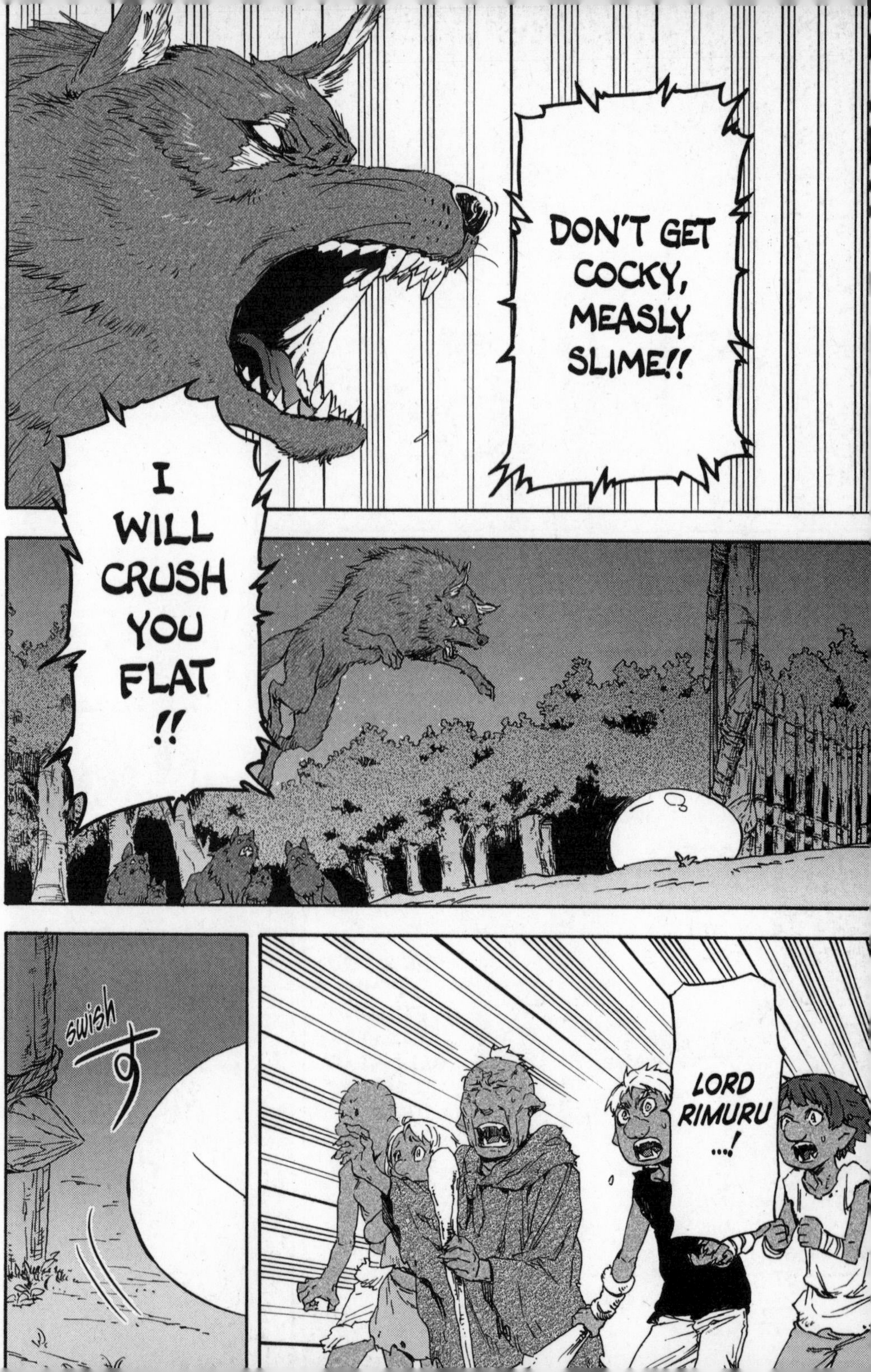
DON'T GET COCKY, MEASLY SLIME!!
I WILL CRUSH YOU FLAT!!
LORD RIMURU...!
swish
す

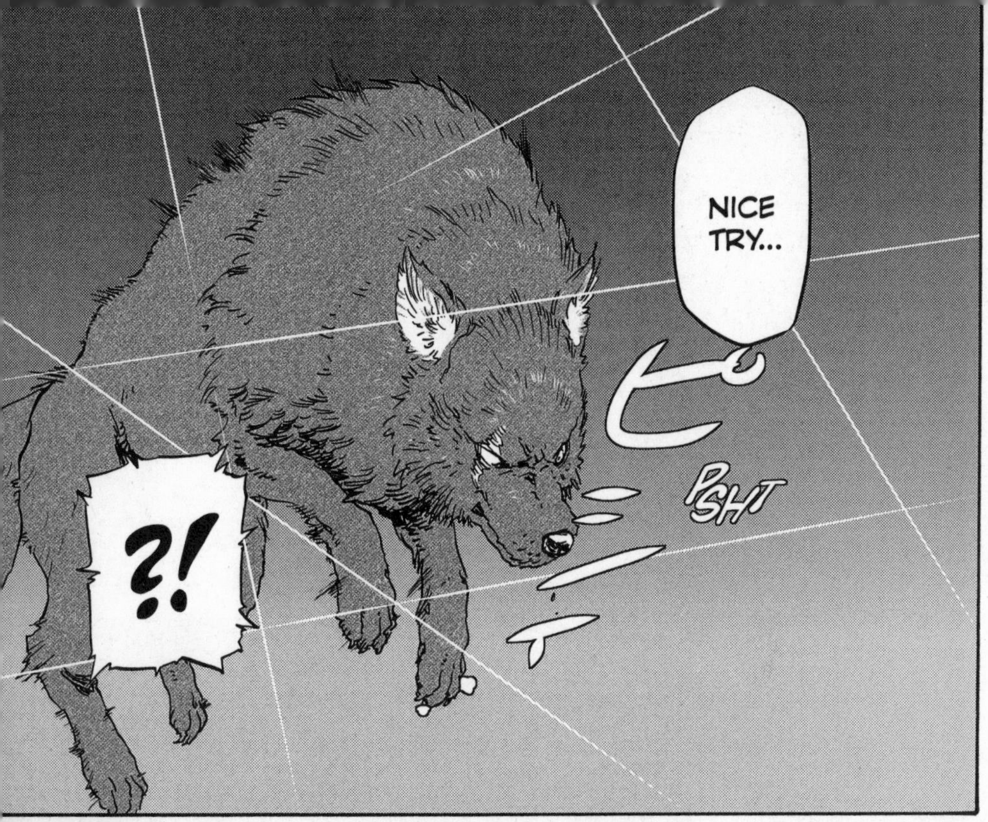
NICE TRY...
PSHT
?!

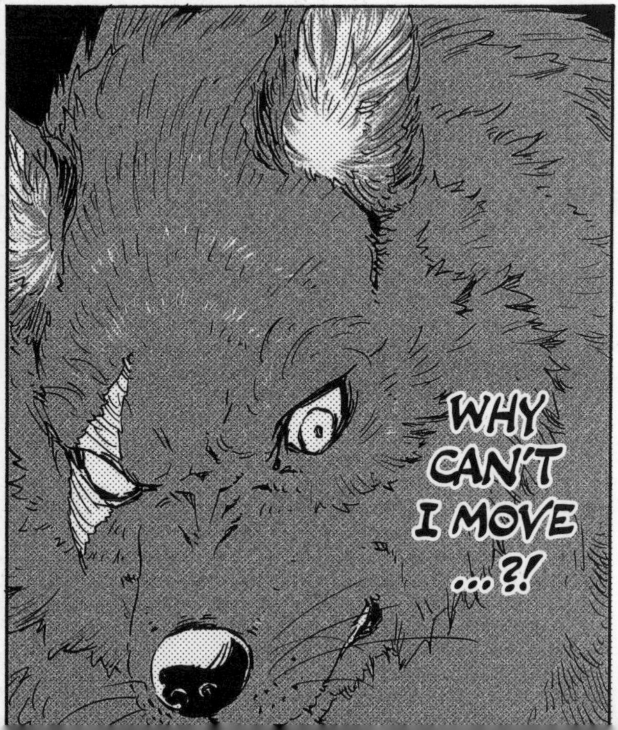
WHY CAN'T I MOVE ...?!

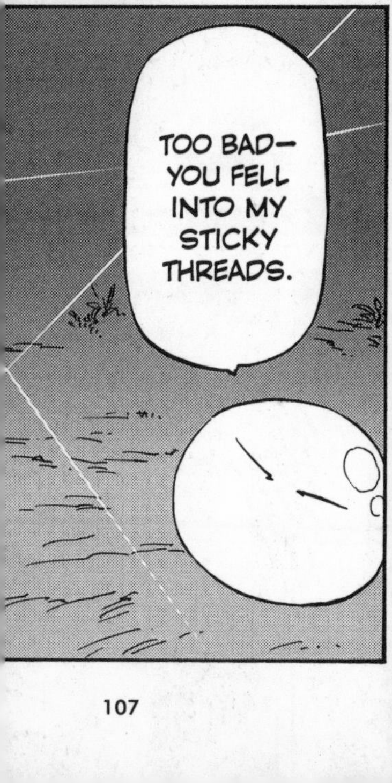
TOO BAD—YOU FELL INTO MY STICKY THREADS.

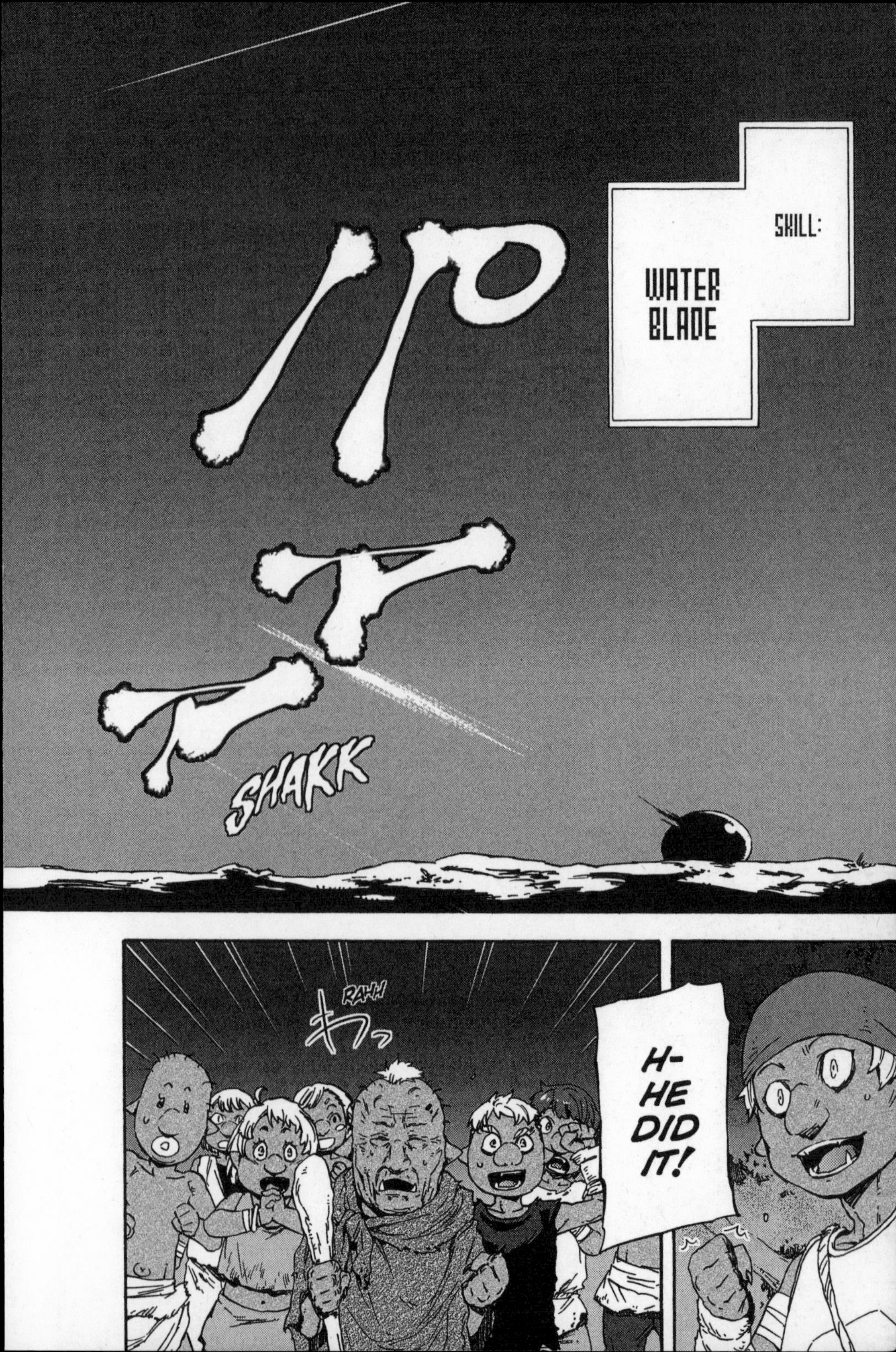
SKILL:
WATER BLADE
SHAKK
H- HE DID IT!
RAWH
わっ

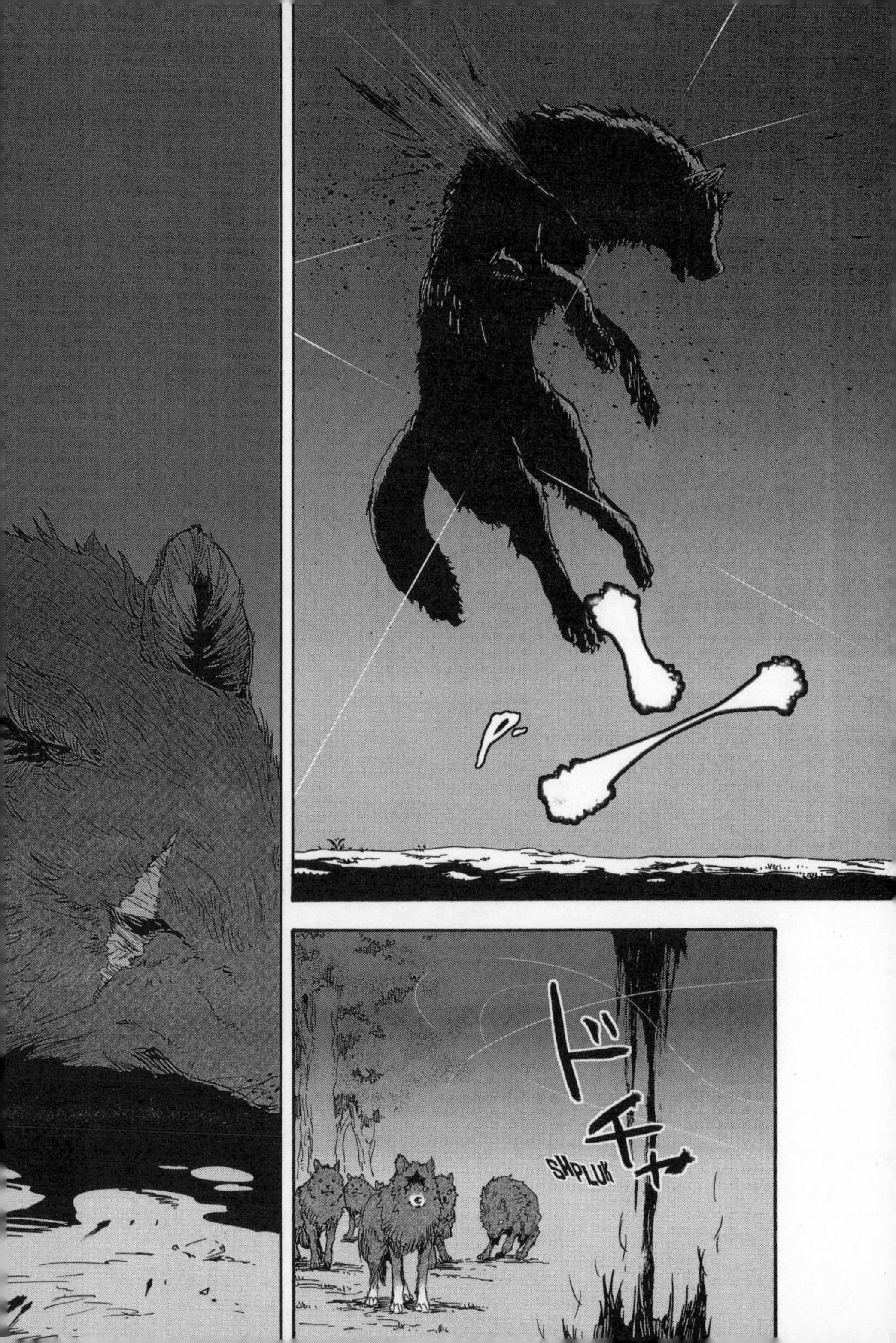
ドチャ
SHPLUK

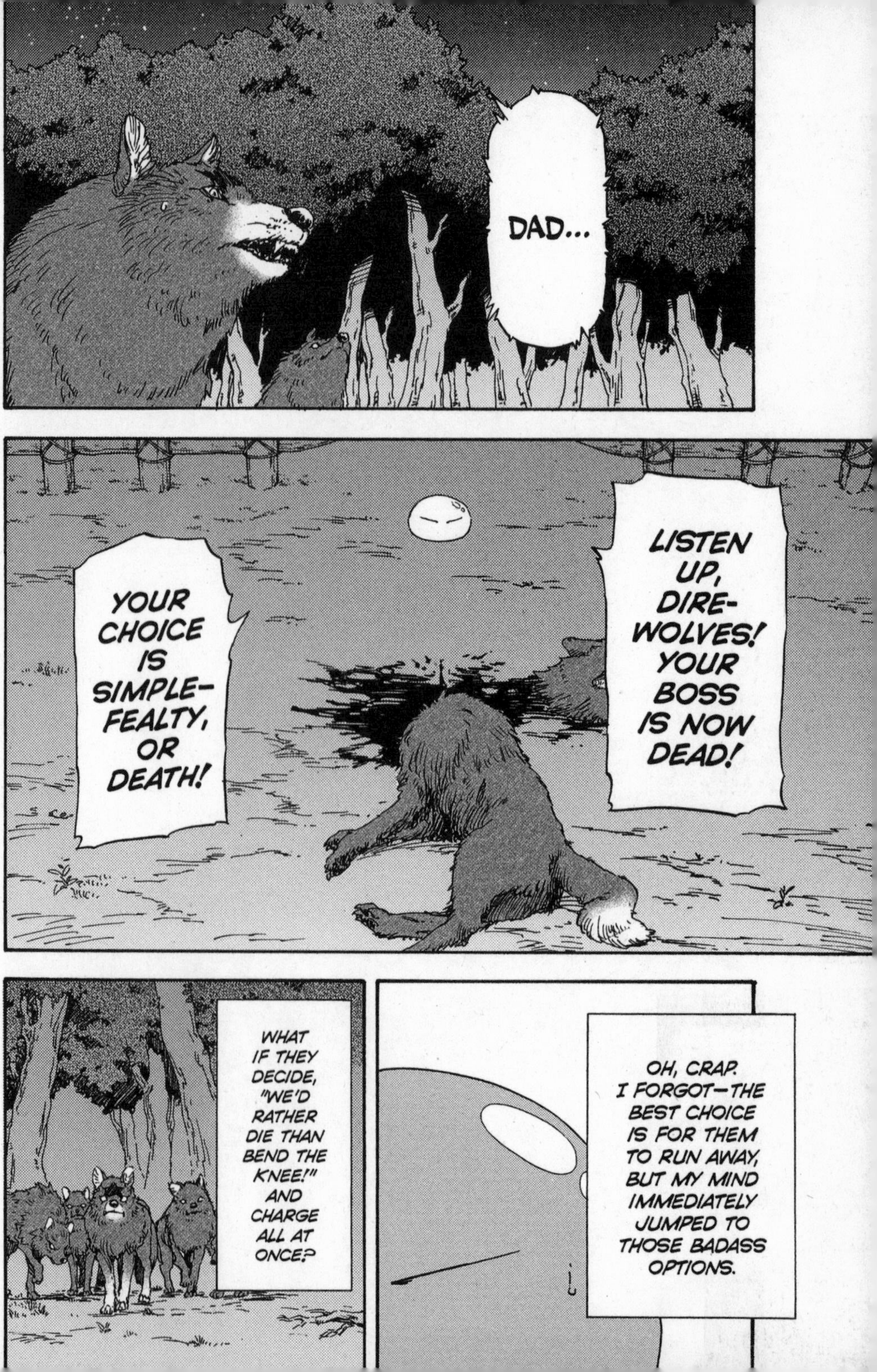
DAD...
LISTEN UP, DIRE-WOLVES! YOUR BOSS IS NOW DEAD!
YOUR CHOICE IS SIMPLE—FEALTY, OR DEATH!
OH, CRAP. I FORGOT—THE BEST CHOICE IS FOR THEM TO RUN AWAY, BUT MY MIND IMMEDIATELY JUMPED TO THOSE BADASS OPTIONS.
WHAT IF THEY DECIDE, "WE'D RATHER DIE THAN BEND THE KNEE!" AND CHARGE ALL AT ONCE?

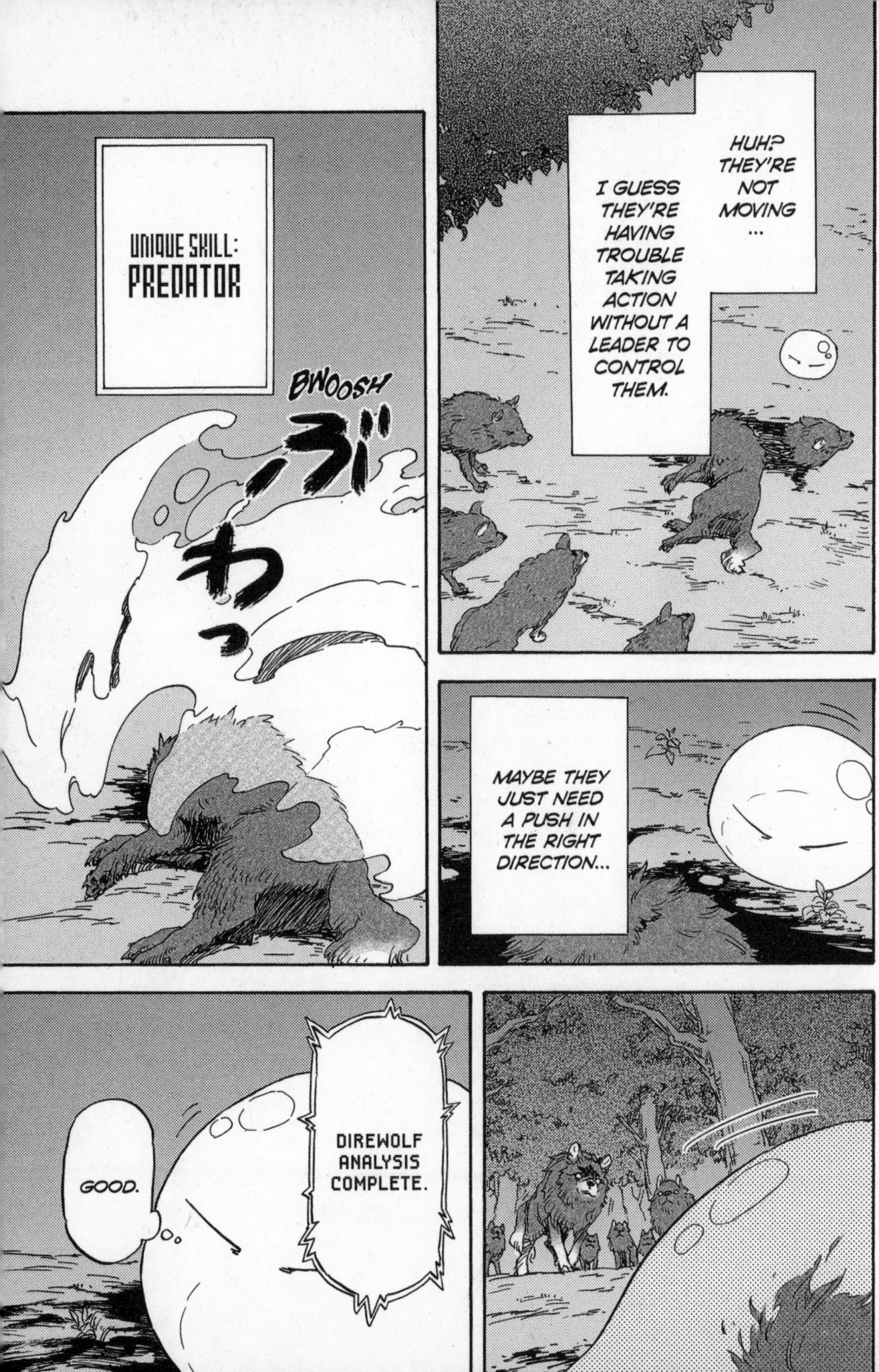
HUH? THEY'RE NOT MOVING ...
I GUESS THEY'RE HAVING TROUBLE TAKING ACTION WITHOUT A LEADER TO CONTROL THEM.
MAYBE THEY JUST NEED A PUSH IN THE RIGHT DIRECTION...
UNIQUE SKILL: PREDATOR
BWOOSH
DIREWOLF ANALYSIS COMPLETE.
GOOD.

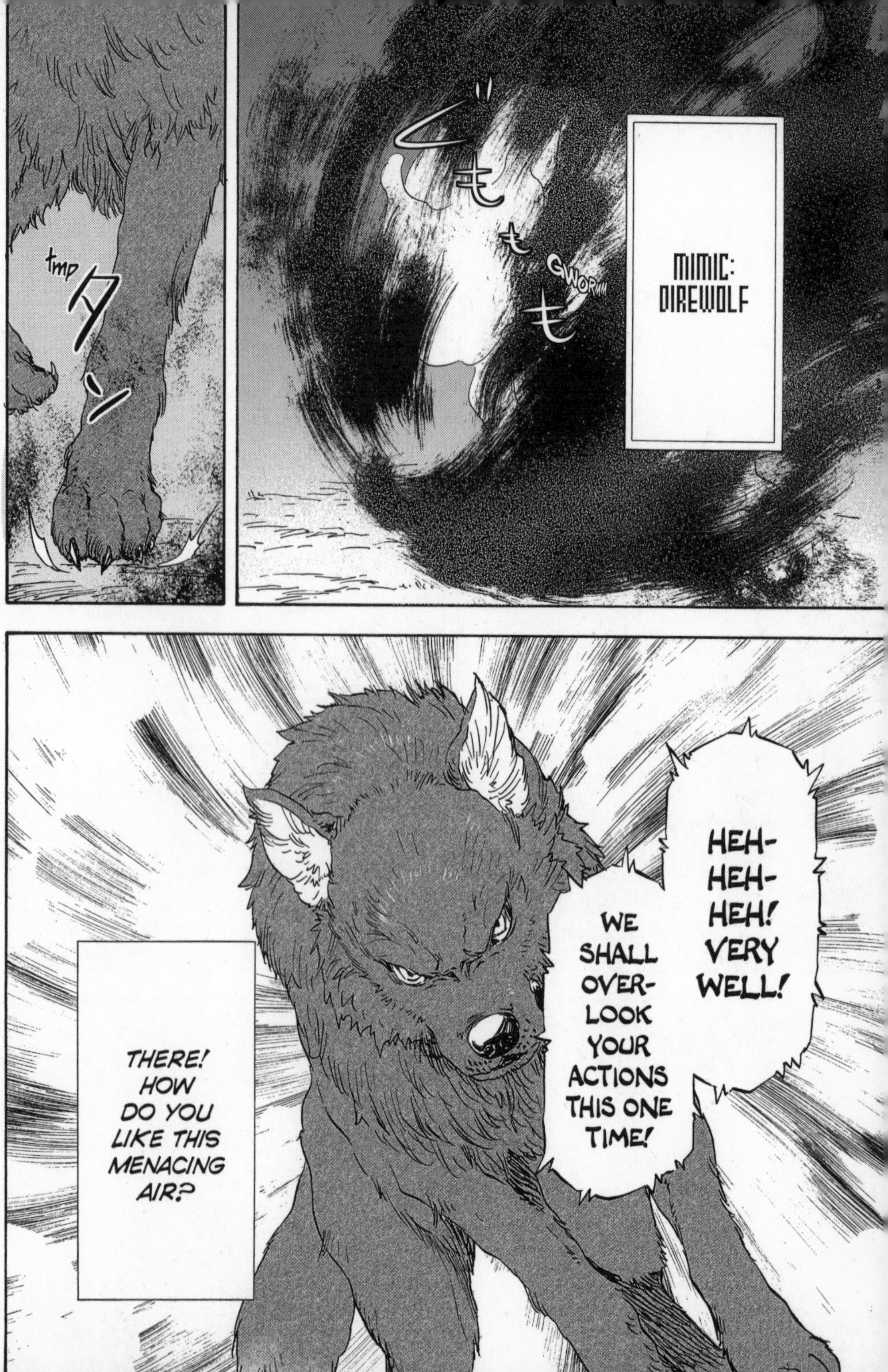
ごもももも
GWORMM
MIMIC: DIREWOLF
tmp
タン
HEH-HEH-HEH! VERY WELL!
WE SHALL OVER-LOOK YOUR ACTIONS THIS ONE TIME!
THERE! HOW DO YOU LIKE THIS MENACING AIR?

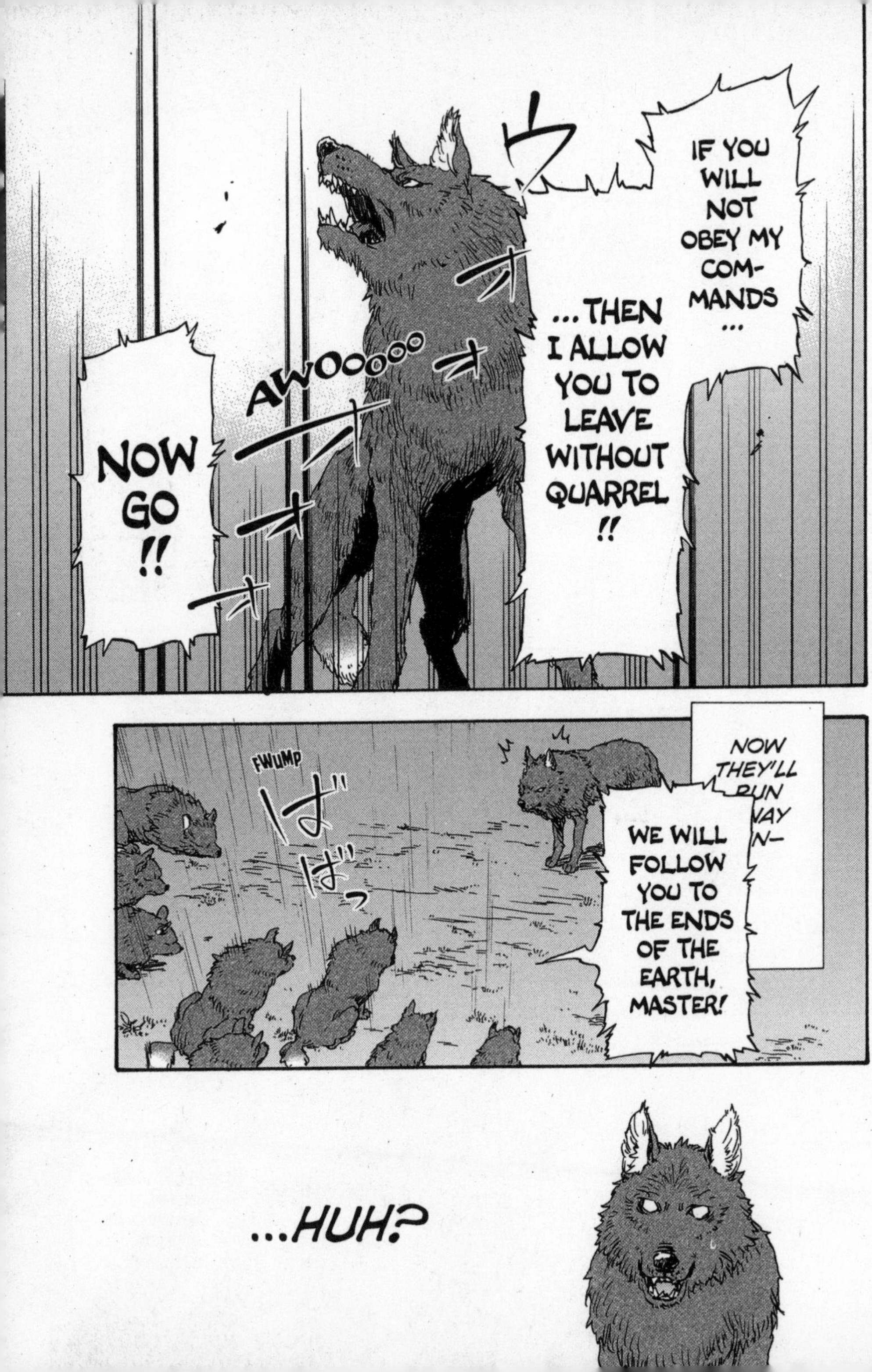
IF YOU WILL NOT OBEY MY COM-MANDS ...
...THEN I ALLOW YOU TO LEAVE WITHOUT QUARREL !!
AWOOOOOO
NOW GO !!
NOW THEY'LL RUN
WE WILL FOLLOW YOU TO THE ENDS OF THE EARTH, MASTER!
FWUMP
ばばっ
...HUH?

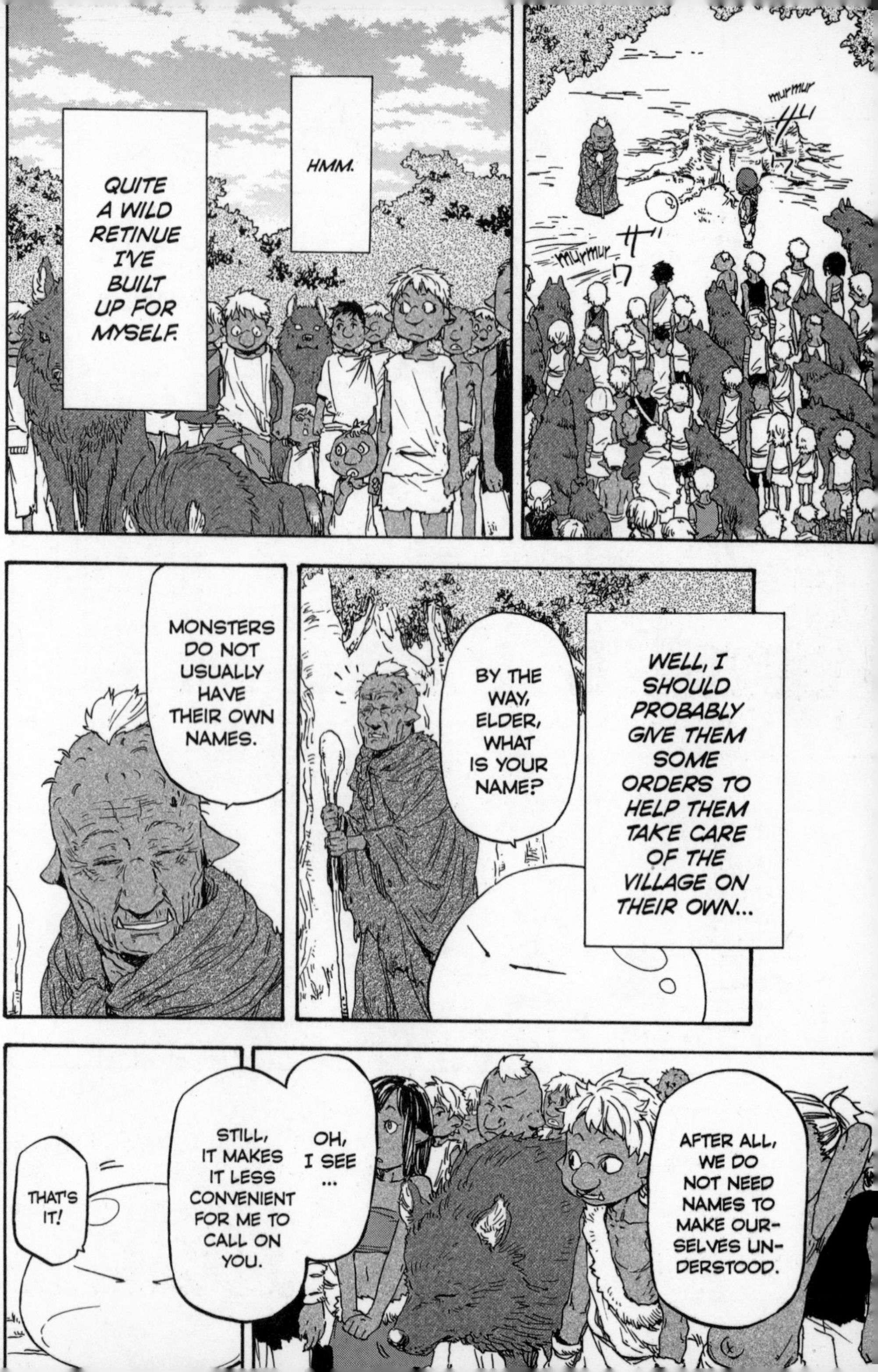
murmur
murmur
HMM.
QUITE A WILD RETINUE I'VE BUILT UP FOR MYSELF.
WELL, I SHOULD PROBABLY GIVE THEM SOME ORDERS TO HELP THEM TAKE CARE OF THE VILLAGE ON THEIR OWN...
BY THE WAY, ELDER, WHAT IS YOUR NAME?
MONSTERS DO NOT USUALLY HAVE THEIR OWN NAMES.
AFTER ALL, WE DO NOT NEED NAMES TO MAKE OUR-SELVES UN-DERSTOOD.
OH, I SEE ...
STILL, IT MAKES IT LESS CONVENIENT FOR ME TO CALL ON YOU.
THAT'S IT!

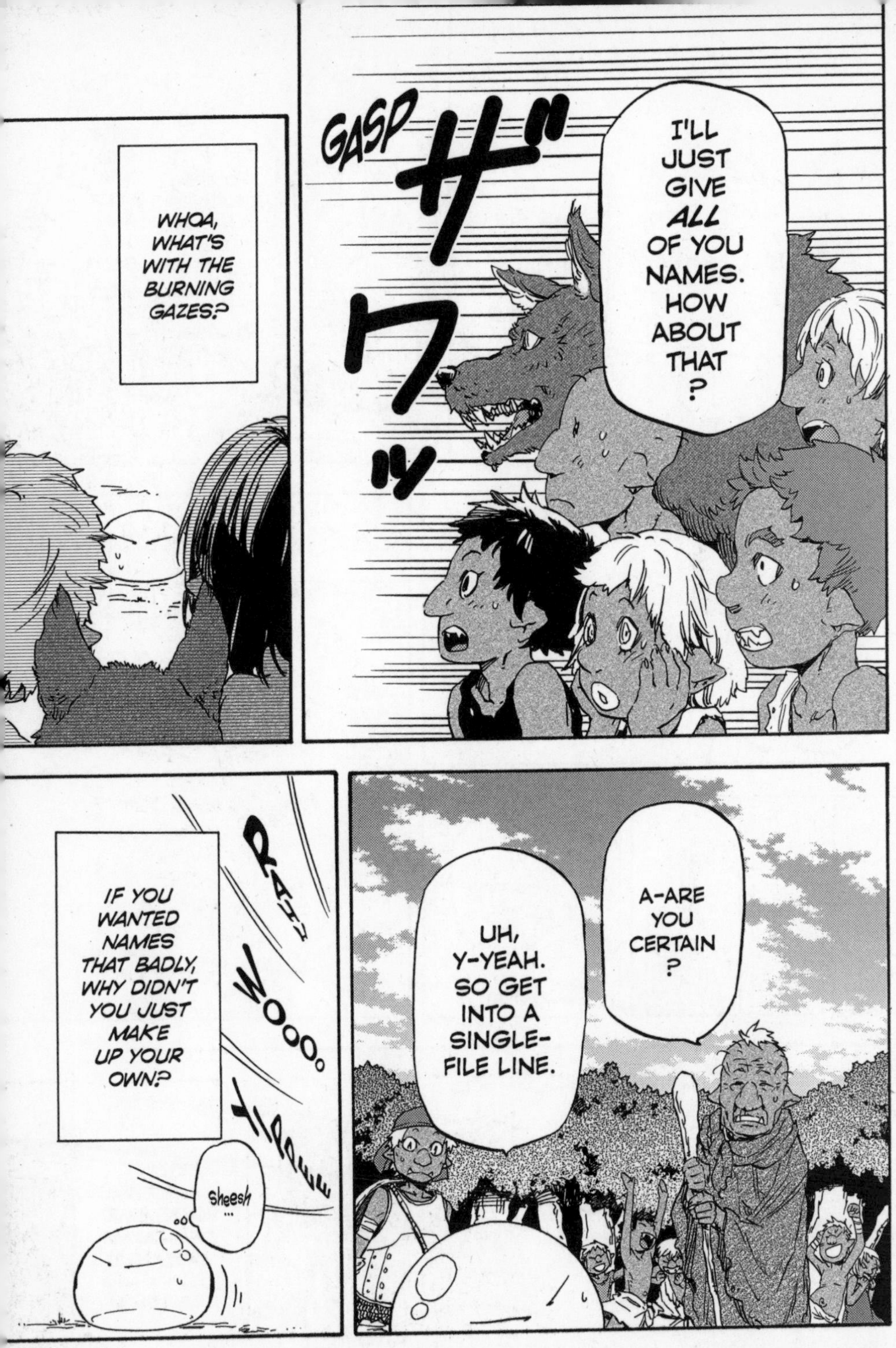
I'LL JUST GIVE ALL OF YOU NAMES. HOW ABOUT THAT?
GASP
ザワッ
WHOA, WHAT'S WITH THE BURNING GAZES?
A-ARE YOU CERTAIN?
UH, Y-YEAH. SO GET INTO A SINGLE-FILE LINE.
IF YOU WANTED NAMES THAT BADLY, WHY DIDN'T YOU JUST MAKE UP YOUR OWN?
RAHH
WOOOO
sheesh...

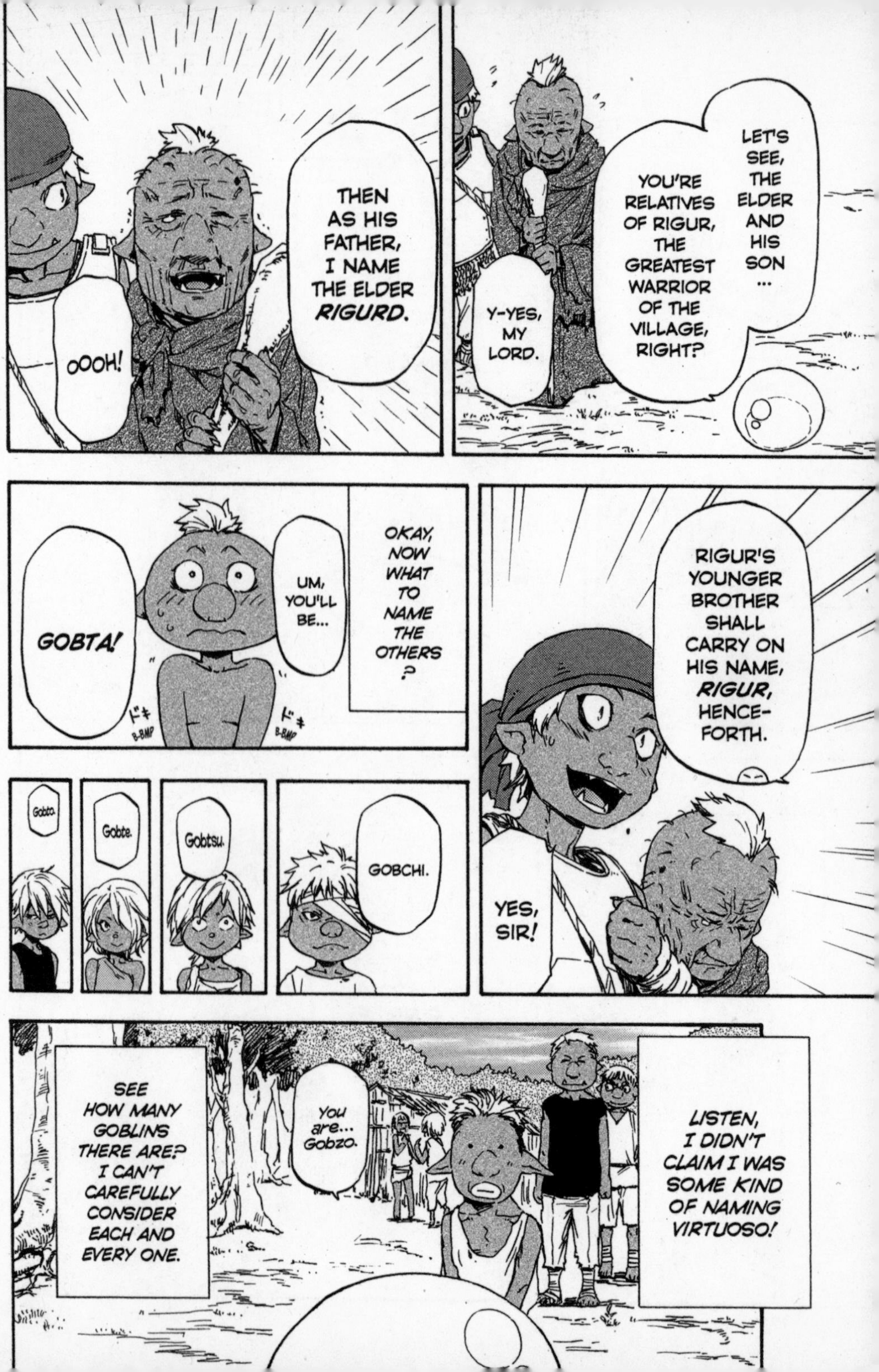
LET'S SEE, THE ELDER AND HIS SON...
YOU'RE RELATIVES OF RIGUR, THE GREATEST WARRIOR OF THE VILLAGE, RIGHT?
Y-YES, MY LORD.
THEN AS HIS FATHER, I NAME THE ELDER *RIGURD*.
OOOH!
RIGUR'S YOUNGER BROTHER SHALL CARRY ON HIS NAME, *RIGUR*, HENCE-FORTH.
YES, SIR!
OKAY, NOW WHAT TO NAME THE OTHERS?
UM, YOU'LL BE...
GOBTA!
ドキ B-BMP
ドキ B-BMP
GOBCHI.
Gobtsu.
Gobte.
Gobto.
LISTEN, I DIDN'T CLAIM I WAS SOME KIND OF NAMING VIRTUOSO!
You are... Gobzo.
SEE HOW MANY GOBLINS THERE ARE? I CAN'T CAREFULLY CONSIDER EACH AND EVERY ONE.

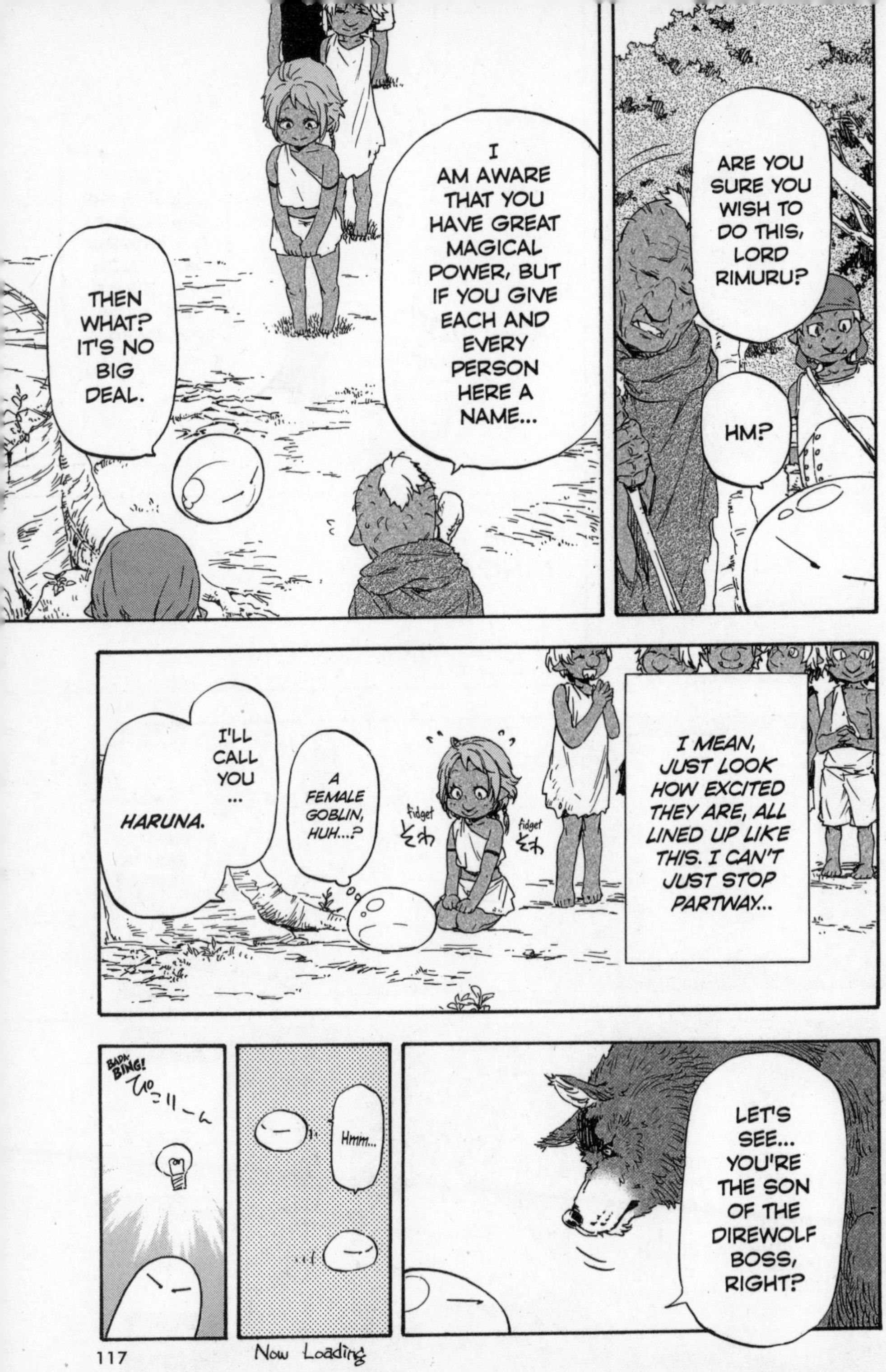

ARE YOU SURE YOU WISH TO DO THIS, LORD RIMURU?
HM?
I AM AWARE THAT YOU HAVE GREAT MAGICAL POWER, BUT IF YOU GIVE EACH AND EVERY PERSON HERE A NAME...
THEN WHAT? IT'S NO BIG DEAL.
I MEAN, JUST LOOK HOW EXCITED THEY ARE, ALL LINED UP LIKE THIS. I CAN'T JUST STOP PARTWAY...
fidget
fidget
A FEMALE GOBLIN, HUH...?
I'LL CALL YOU ... HARUNA.
LET'S SEE... YOU'RE THE SON OF THE DIREWOLF BOSS, RIGHT?
Hmm...
Now Loading
BADA-BING!

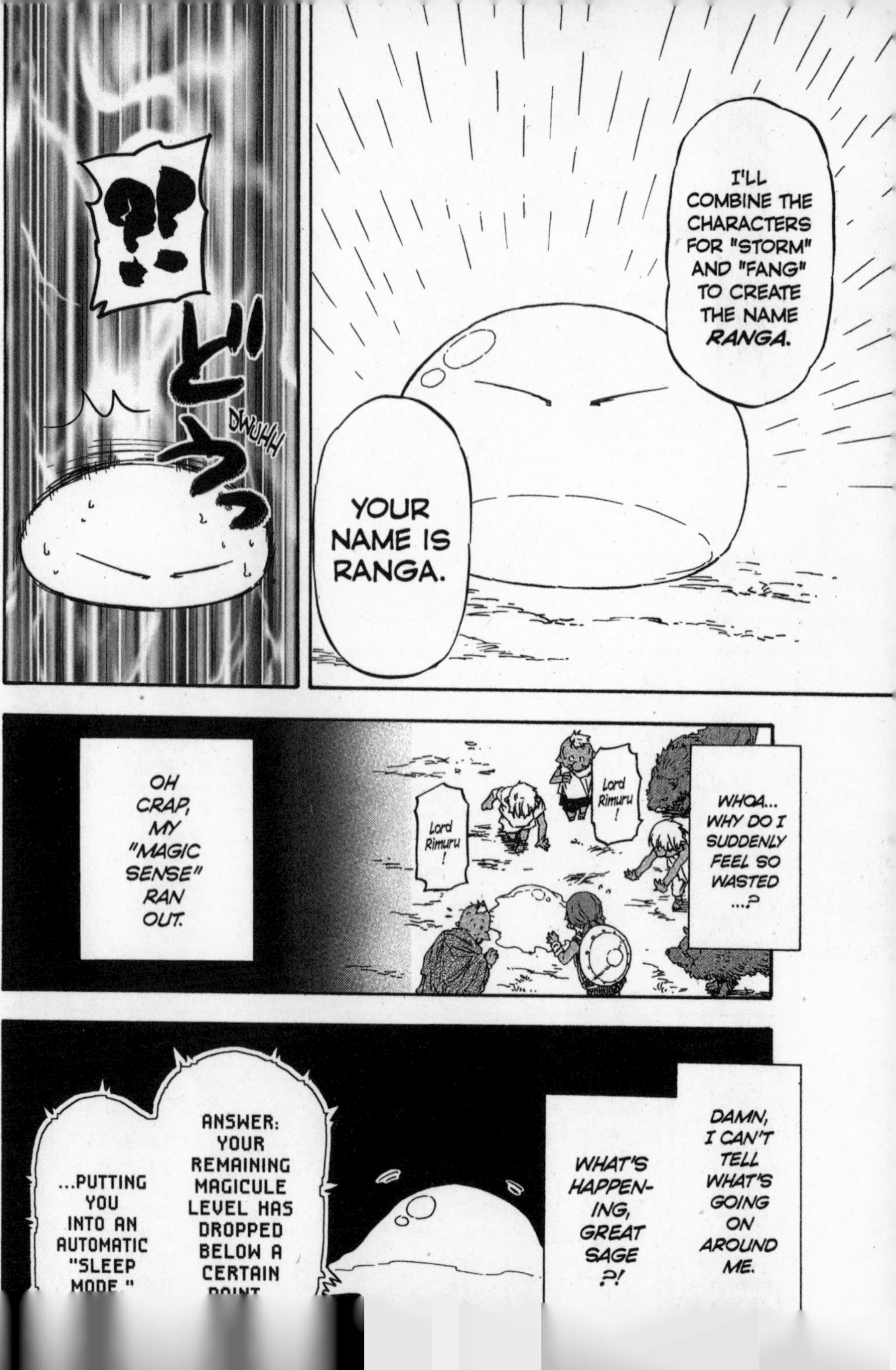
I'LL COMBINE THE CHARACTERS FOR "STORM" AND "FANG" TO CREATE THE NAME RANGA.
YOUR NAME IS RANGA.
?!
DWUHH
WHOA... WHY DO I SUDDENLY FEEL SO WASTED ...?
Lord Rimuru!
Lord Rimuru!
OH CRAP, MY "MAGIC SENSE" RAN OUT.
DAMN, I CAN'T TELL WHAT'S GOING ON AROUND ME.
WHAT'S HAPPEN-ING, GREAT SAGE?!
ANSWER: YOUR REMAINING MAGICULE LEVEL HAS DROPPED BELOW A CERTAIN
...PUTTING YOU INTO AN AUTOMATIC "SLEEP

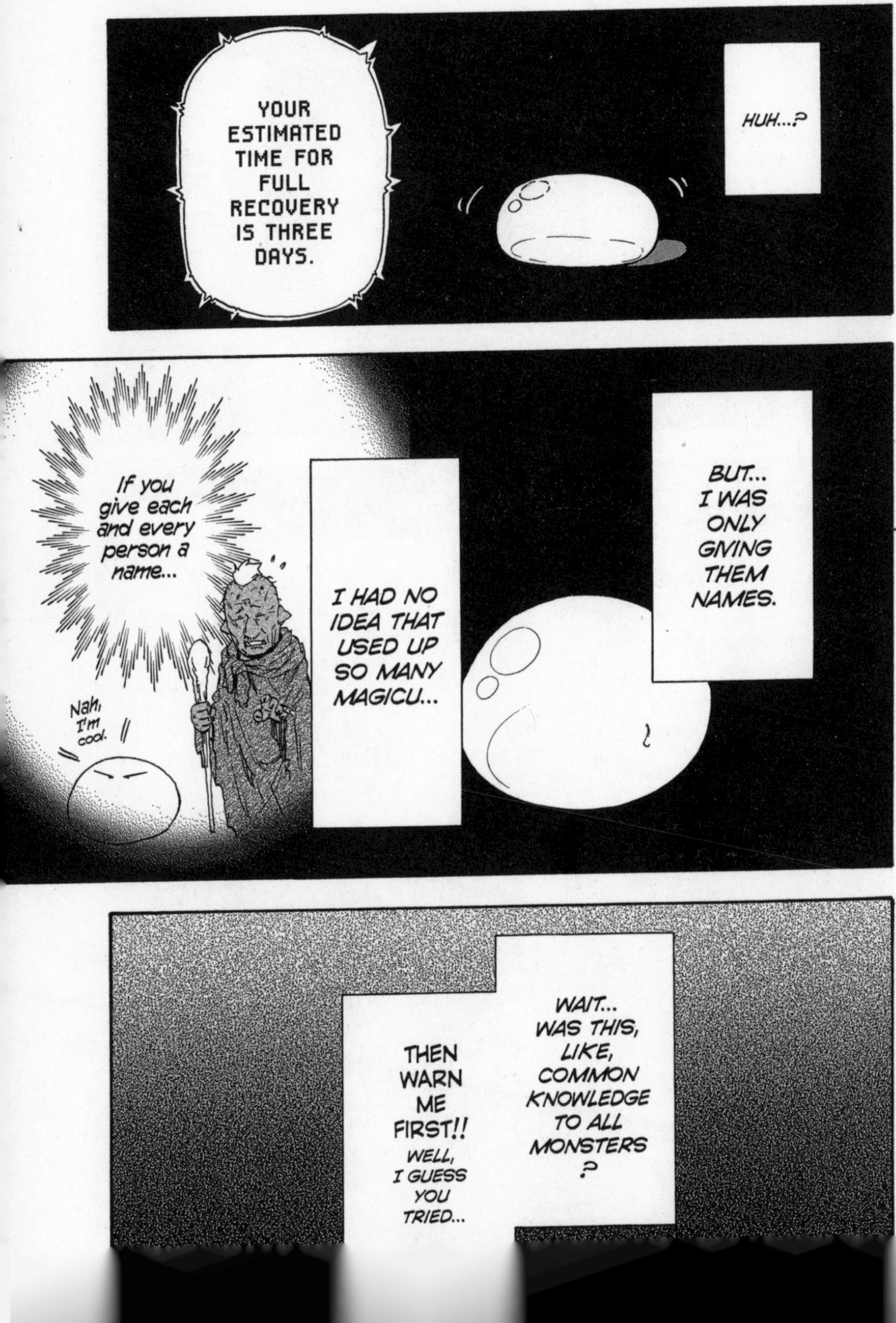
HUH...?
YOUR ESTIMATED TIME FOR FULL RECOVERY IS THREE DAYS.
BUT... I WAS ONLY GIVING THEM NAMES.
I HAD NO IDEA THAT USED UP SO MANY MAGICU...
If you give each and every person a name...
Nah, I'm cool.
WAIT... WAS THIS, LIKE, COMMON KNOWLEDGE TO ALL MONSTERS ?
THEN WARN ME FIRST!!
WELL, I GUESS YOU TRIED...

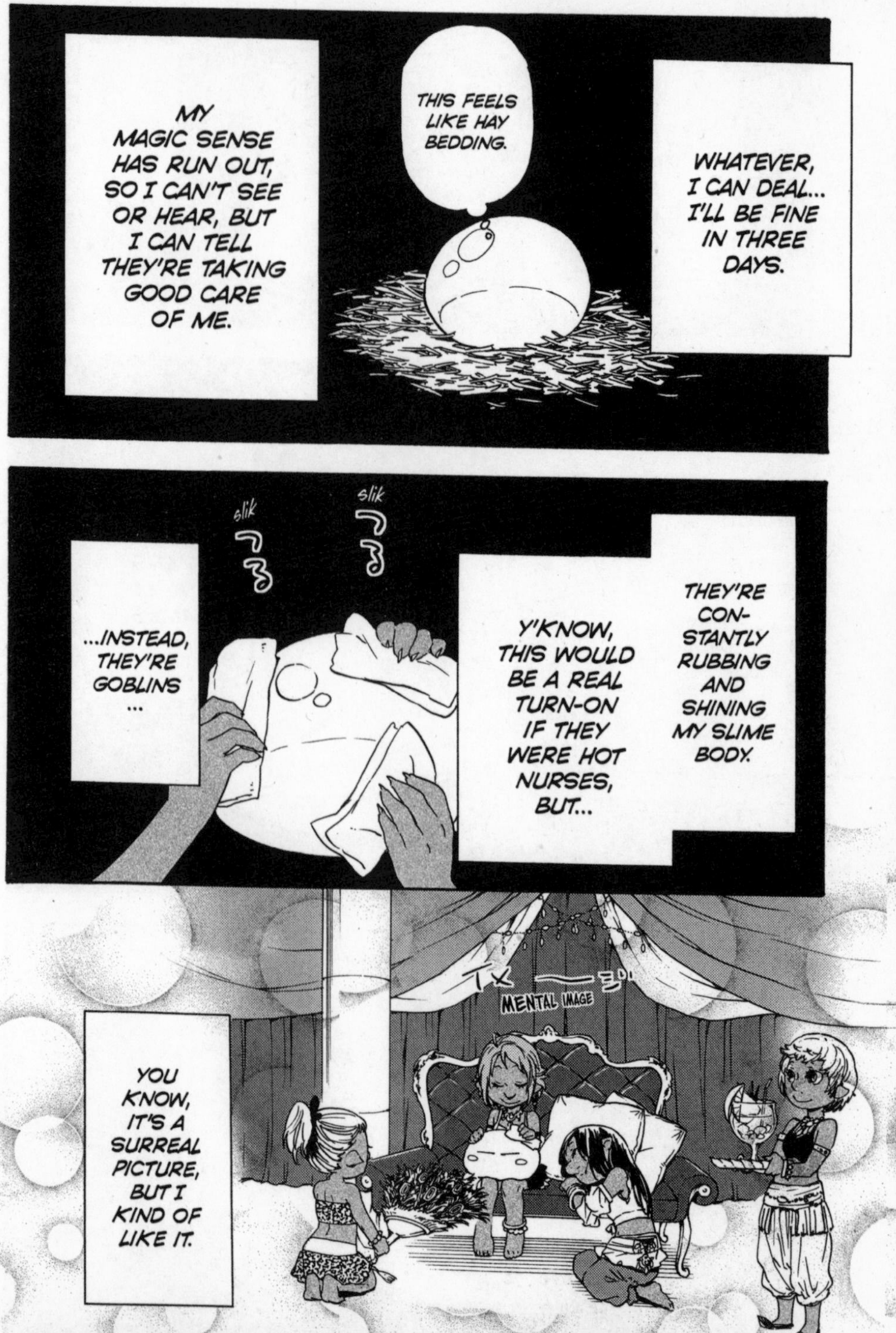

WHATEVER, I CAN DEAL... I'LL BE FINE IN THREE DAYS.
THIS FEELS LIKE HAY BEDDING.
MY MAGIC SENSE HAS RUN OUT, SO I CAN'T SEE OR HEAR, BUT I CAN TELL THEY'RE TAKING GOOD CARE OF ME.
THEY'RE CON-STANTLY RUBBING AND SHINING MY SLIME BODY.
Y'KNOW, THIS WOULD BE A REAL TURN-ON IF THEY WERE HOT NURSES, BUT...
slik
slik
...INSTEAD, THEY'RE GOBLINS ...
MENTAL IMAGE
YOU KNOW, IT'S A SURREAL PICTURE, BUT I KIND OF LIKE IT.

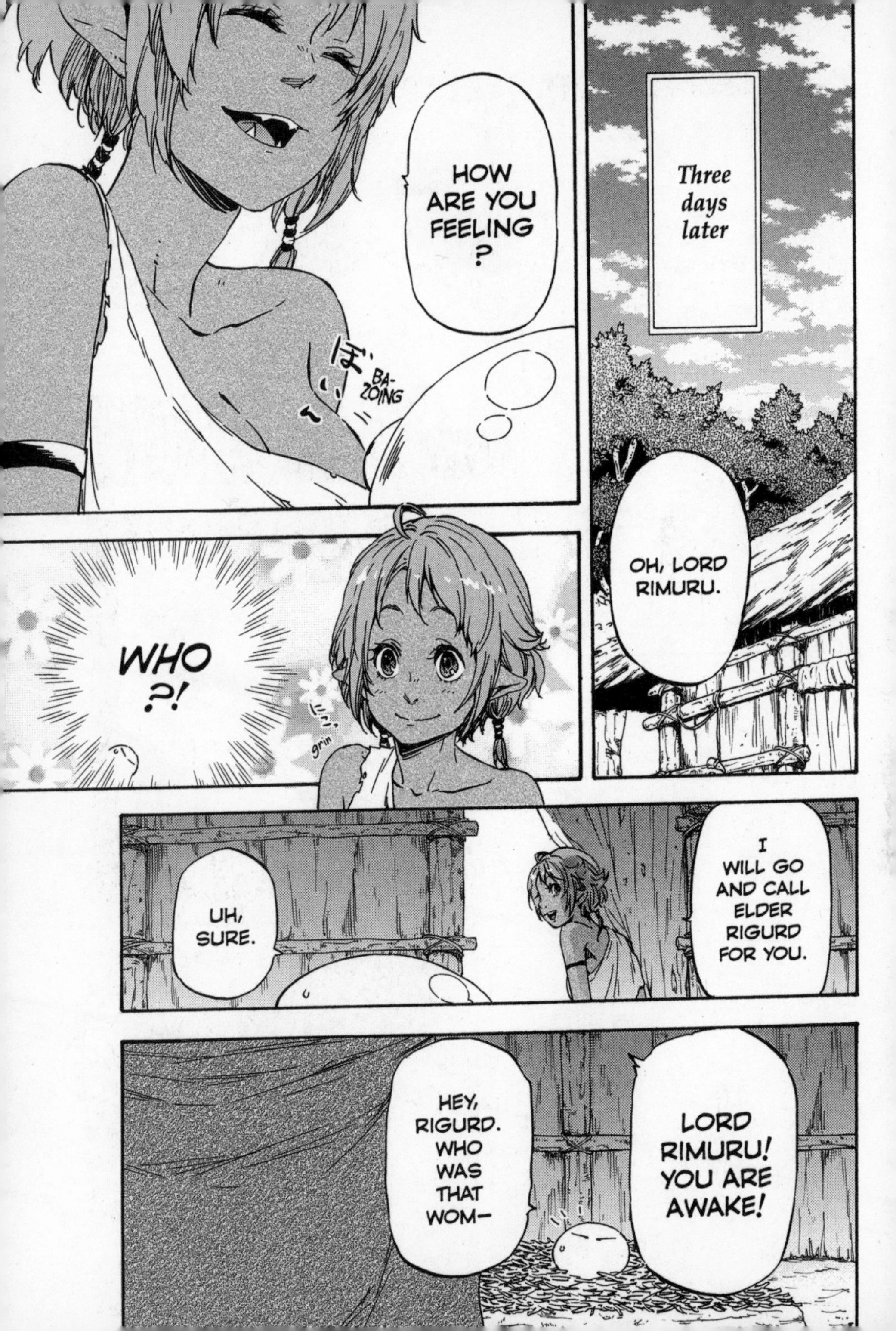
Three days later
OH, LORD RIMURU.
HOW ARE YOU FEELING?
BA-ZOING
WHO?!
grin
I WILL GO AND CALL ELDER RIGURD FOR YOU.
UH, SURE.
LORD RIMURU! YOU ARE AWAKE!
HEY, RIGURD. WHO WAS THAT WOM—

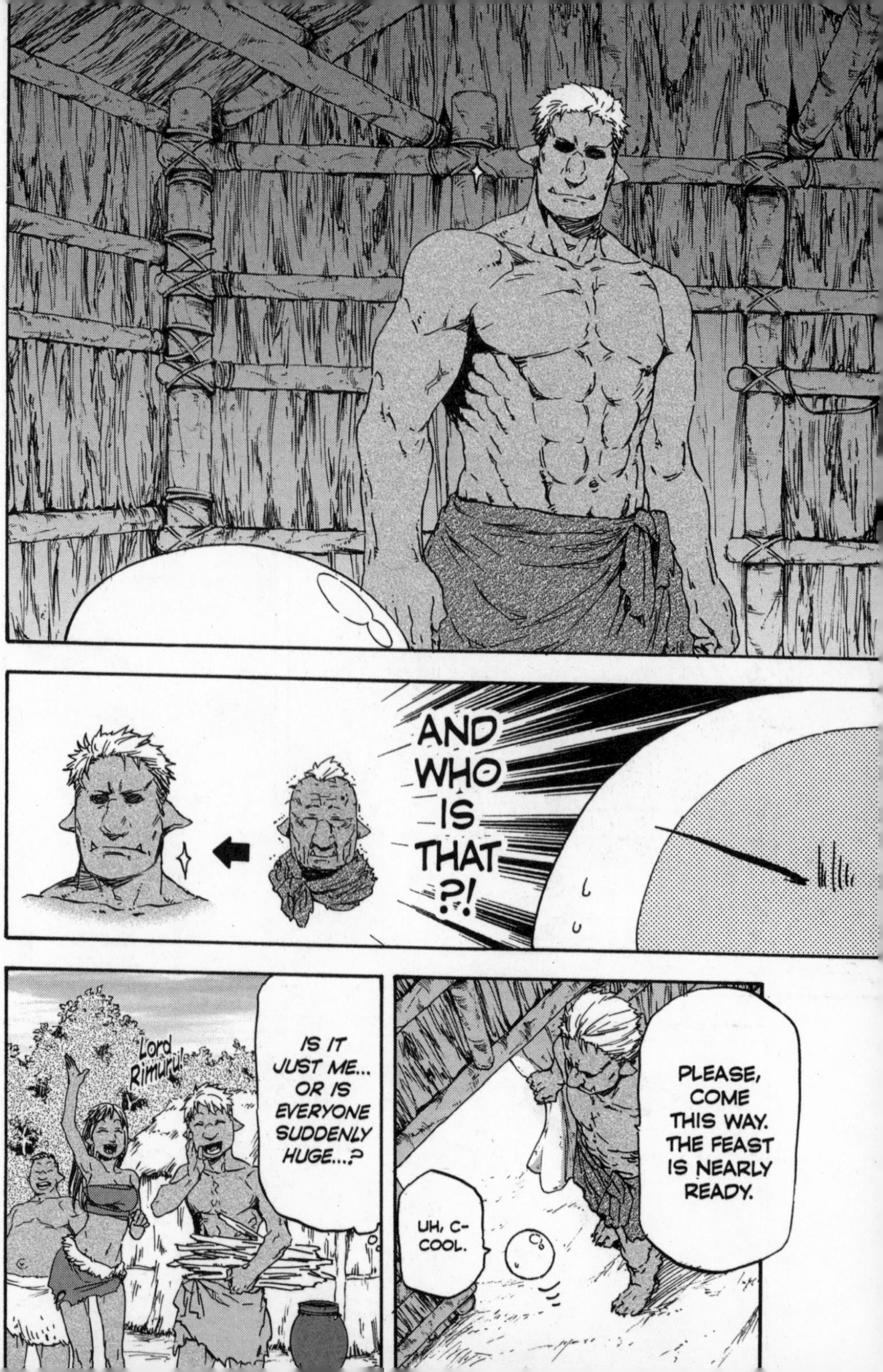
AND WHO IS THAT?!
PLEASE, COME THIS WAY. THE FEAST IS NEARLY READY.
UH, C-COOL.
IS IT JUST ME... OR IS EVERYONE SUDDENLY HUGE...?
Lord Rimuru!!

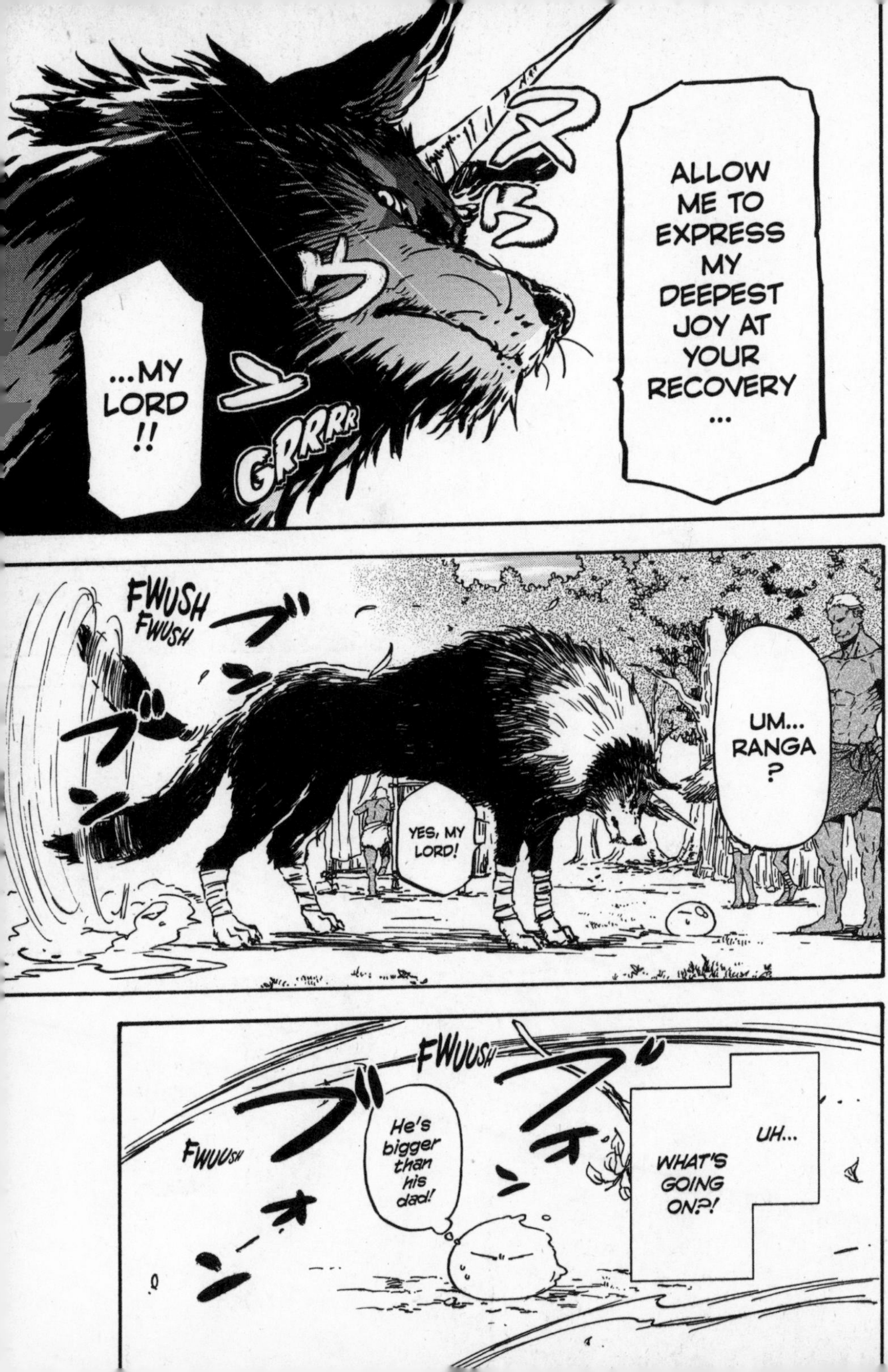
ALLOW ME TO EXPRESS MY DEEPEST JOY AT YOUR RECOVERY ...
...MY LORD !!
GRRRR
UM... RANGA ?
FWUSH FWUSH
YES, MY LORD!
UH... WHAT'S GOING ON?!
FWUUSH
He's bigger than his dad!
FWUUSH

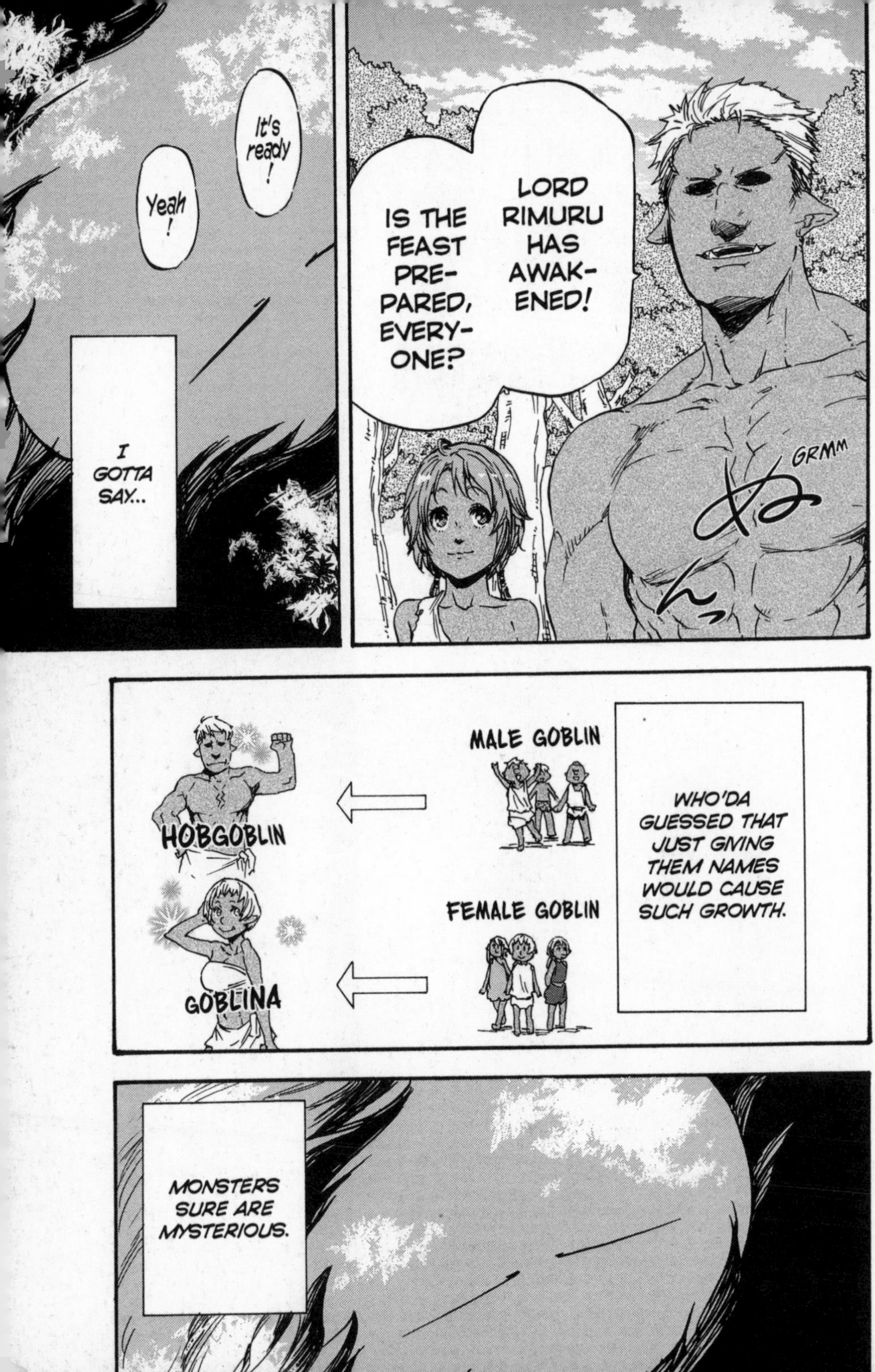
LORD RIMURU HAS AWAKENED!
IS THE FEAST PREPARED, EVERYONE?
GRMM
It's ready!
Yeah!
I GOTTA SAY...
WHO'DA GUESSED THAT JUST GIVING THEM NAMES WOULD CAUSE SUCH GROWTH.
MALE GOBLIN
HOBGOBLIN
FEMALE GOBLIN
GOBLINA
MONSTERS SURE ARE MYSTERIOUS.

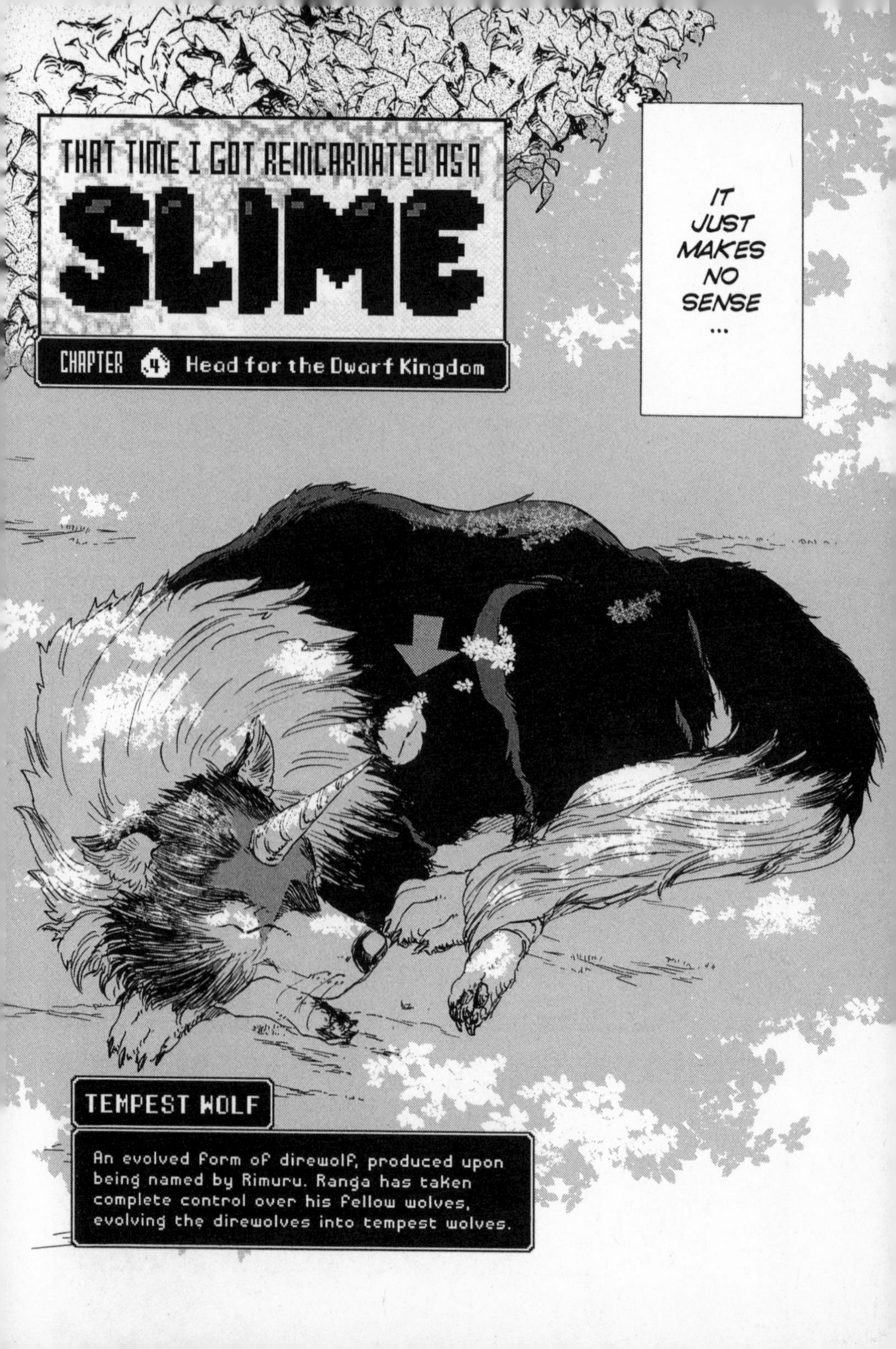

THAT TIME I GOT REINCARNATED AS A
SLIME
CHAPTER 4 Head for the Dwarf Kingdom
IT JUST MAKES NO SENSE ...
TEMPEST WOLF
An evolved form of direwolf, produced upon being named by Rimuru. Ranga has taken complete control over his fellow wolves, evolving the direwolves into tempest wolves.

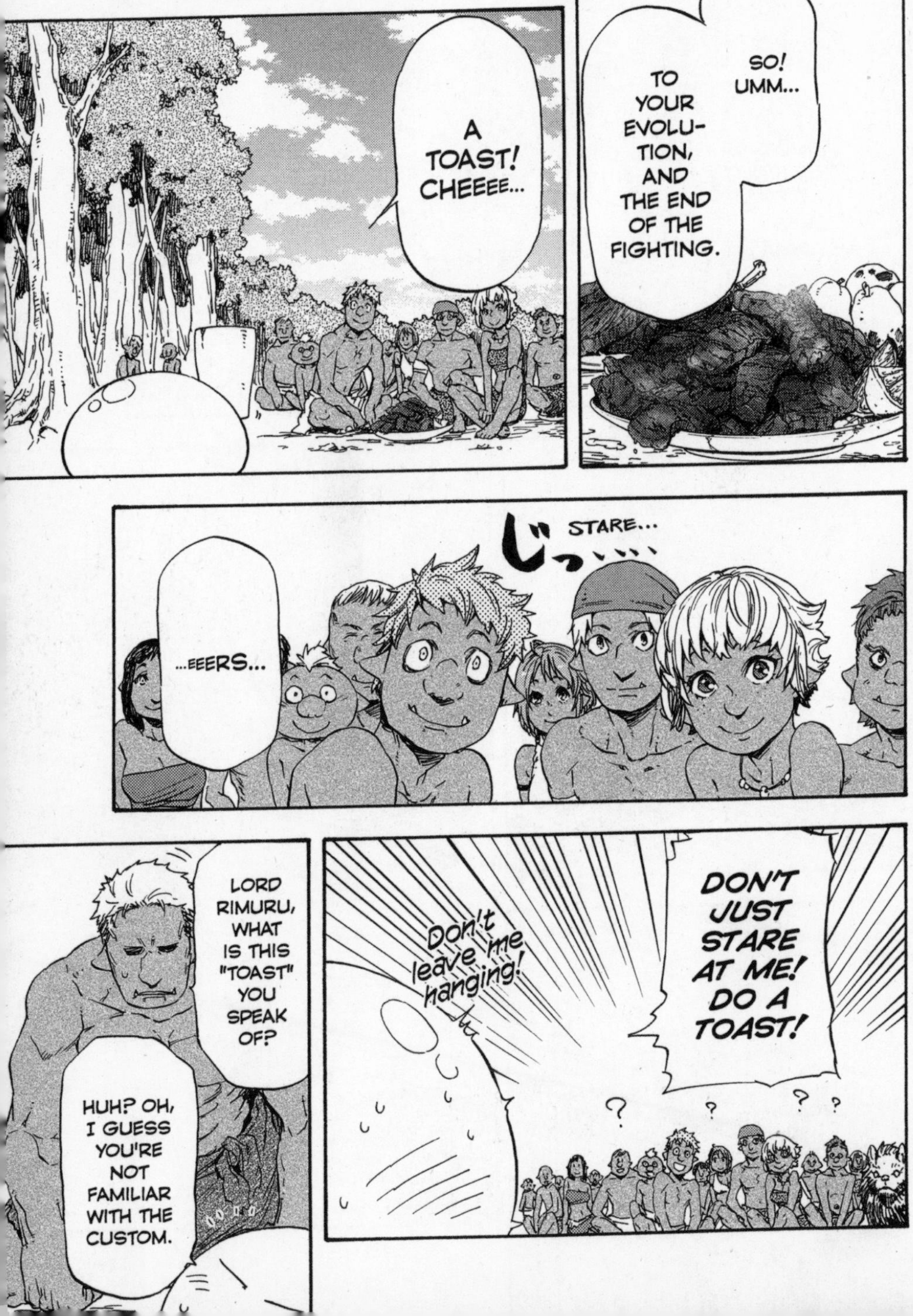
SO! UMM... TO YOUR EVOLUTION, AND THE END OF THE FIGHTING.
A TOAST! CHEEEEE...
じっ…
STARE...
...EEERS...
DON'T JUST STARE AT ME! DO A TOAST!
Don't leave me hanging!
LORD RIMURU, WHAT IS THIS "TOAST" YOU SPEAK OF?
HUH? OH, I GUESS YOU'RE NOT FAMILIAR WITH THE CUSTOM.

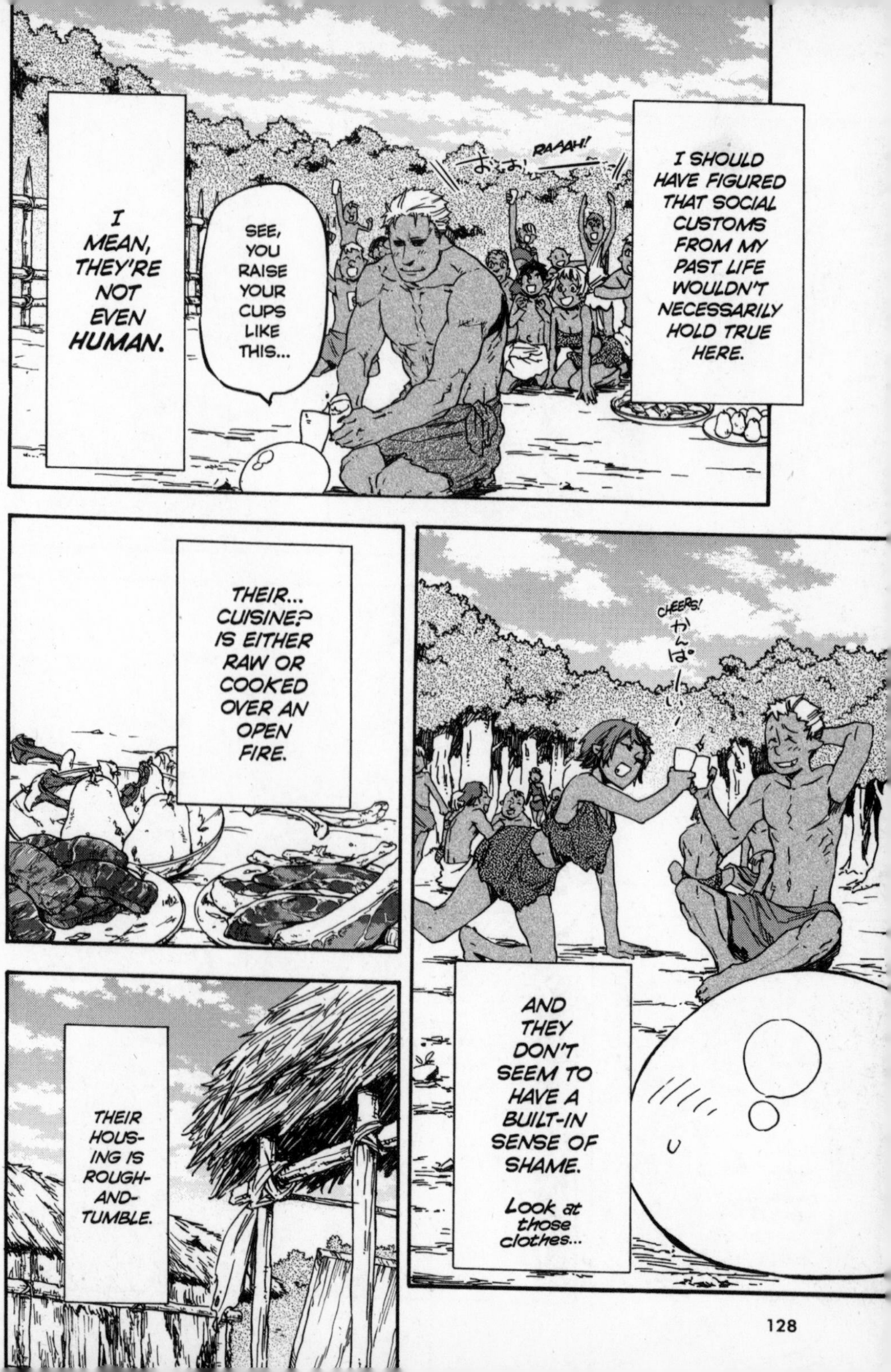
I SHOULD HAVE FIGURED THAT SOCIAL CUSTOMS FROM MY PAST LIFE WOULDN'T NECESSARILY HOLD TRUE HERE.
RAAAH!
おぉぉ!
SEE, YOU RAISE YOUR CUPS LIKE THIS...
I MEAN, THEY'RE NOT EVEN HUMAN.
CHEERS!
かんぱーい!
AND THEY DON'T SEEM TO HAVE A BUILT-IN SENSE OF SHAME.
Look at those clothes...
THEIR... CUISINE? IS EITHER RAW OR COOKED OVER AN OPEN FIRE.
THEIR HOUSING IS ROUGH-AND-TUMBLE.

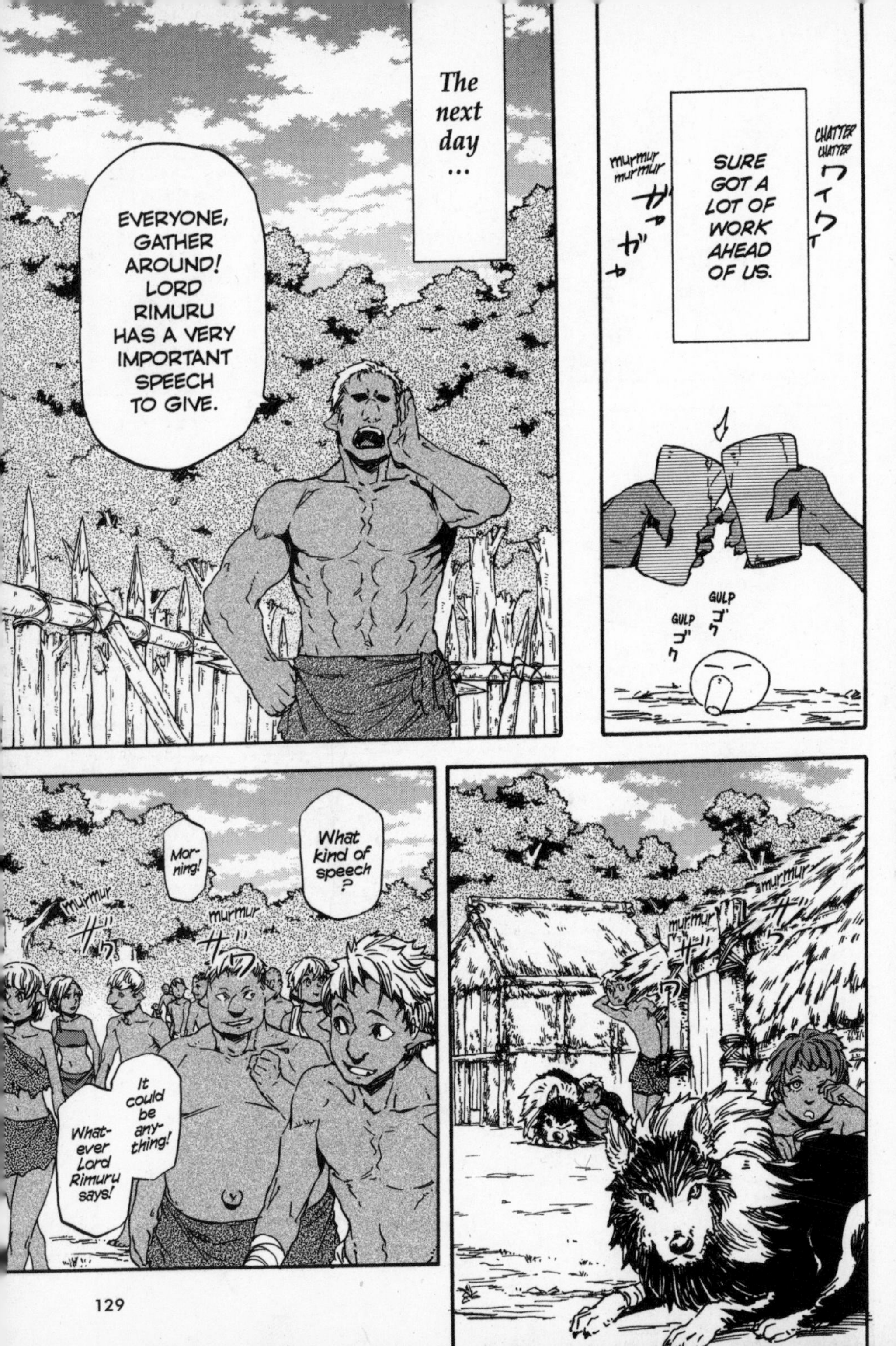
CHATTER CHATTER
murmur murmur
SURE GOT A LOT OF WORK AHEAD OF US.
GULP GULP
The next day ...
EVERYONE, GATHER AROUND! LORD RIMURU HAS A VERY IMPORTANT SPEECH TO GIVE.
murmur
murmur
What kind of speech?
Mor-ning!
murmur
murmur
It could be any-thing!
What-ever Lord Rimuru says!

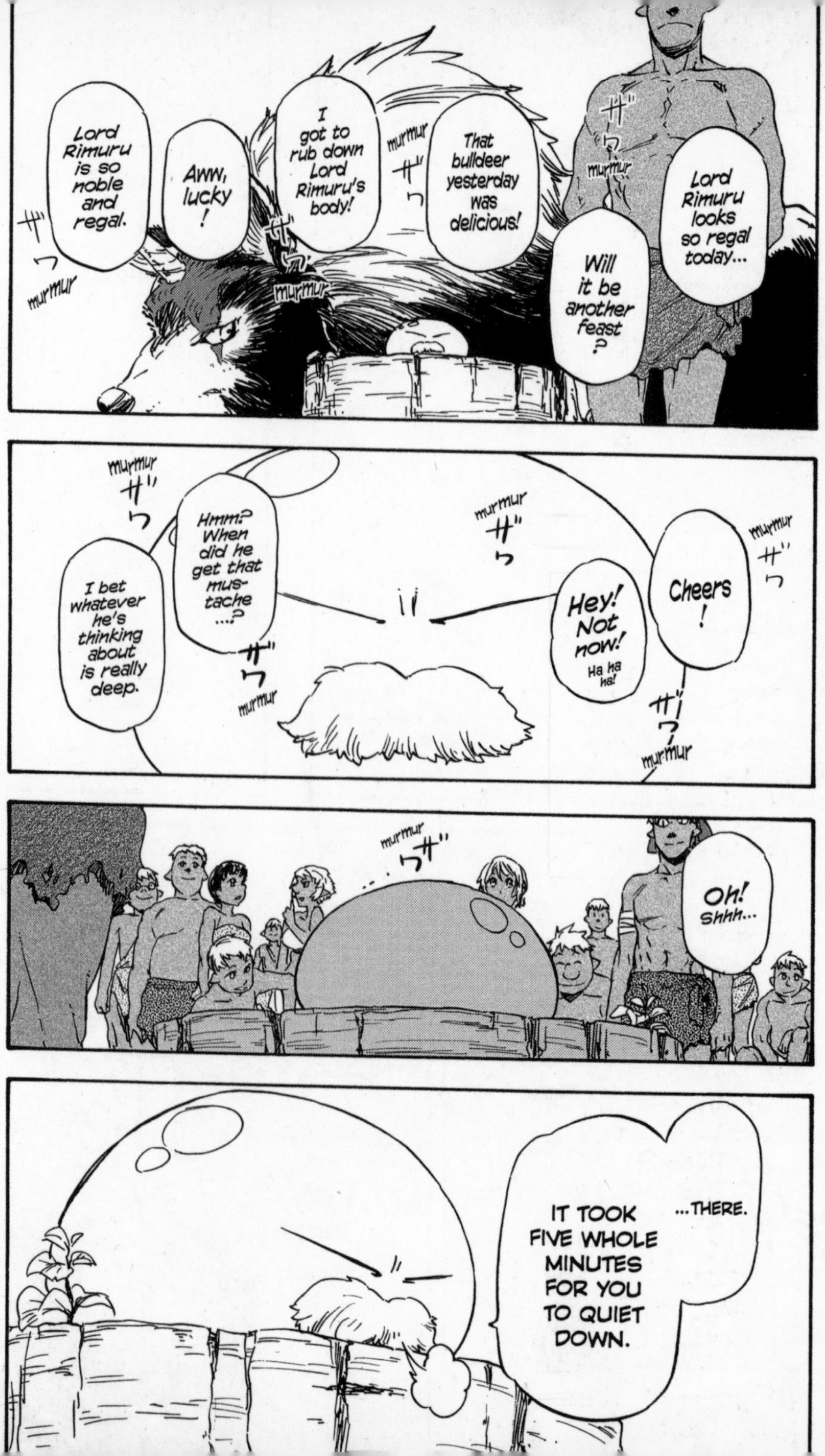
Lord Rimuru looks so regal today...
Will it be another feast?
murmur
That bulldeer yesterday was delicious!
murmur
I got to rub down Lord Rimuru's body!
murmur
Aww, lucky!
Lord Rimuru is so noble and regal.
murmur
murmur
Cheers!
Hey! Not now!
Ha ha ha!
murmur
murmur
Hmm? When did he get that mus-tache ...?
murmur
I bet whatever he's thinking about is really deep.
murmur
Oh! shhh...
murmur
...THERE.
IT TOOK FIVE WHOLE MINUTES FOR YOU TO QUIET DOWN.

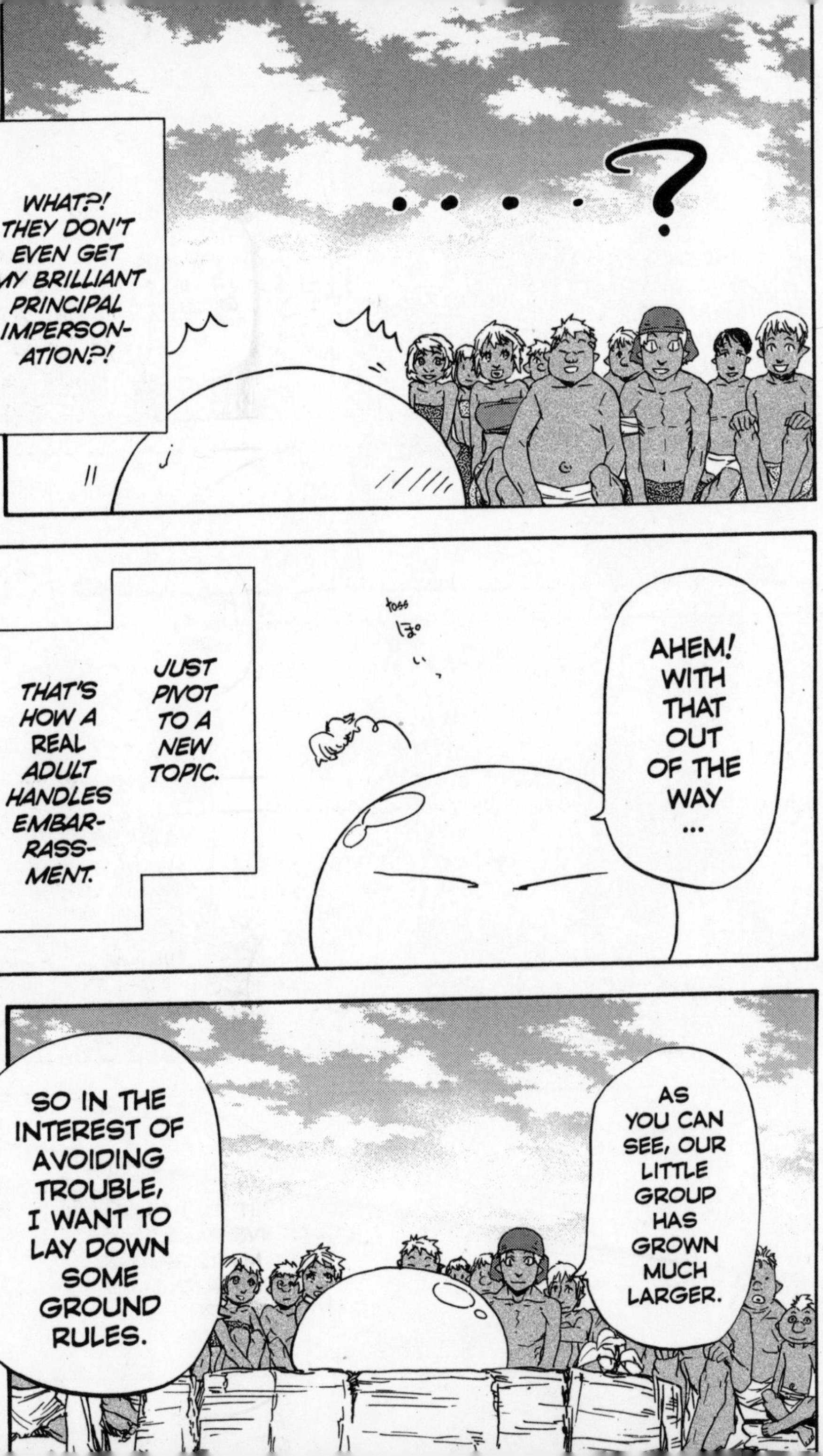
...?
WHAT?! THEY DON'T EVEN GET MY BRILLIANT PRINCIPAL IMPERSON-ATION?!
AHEM! WITH THAT OUT OF THE WAY...
toss
JUST PIVOT TO A NEW TOPIC.
THAT'S HOW A REAL ADULT HANDLES EMBAR-RASS-MENT.
AS YOU CAN SEE, OUR LITTLE GROUP HAS GROWN MUCH LARGER.
SO IN THE INTEREST OF AVOIDING TROUBLE, I WANT TO LAY DOWN SOME GROUND RULES.

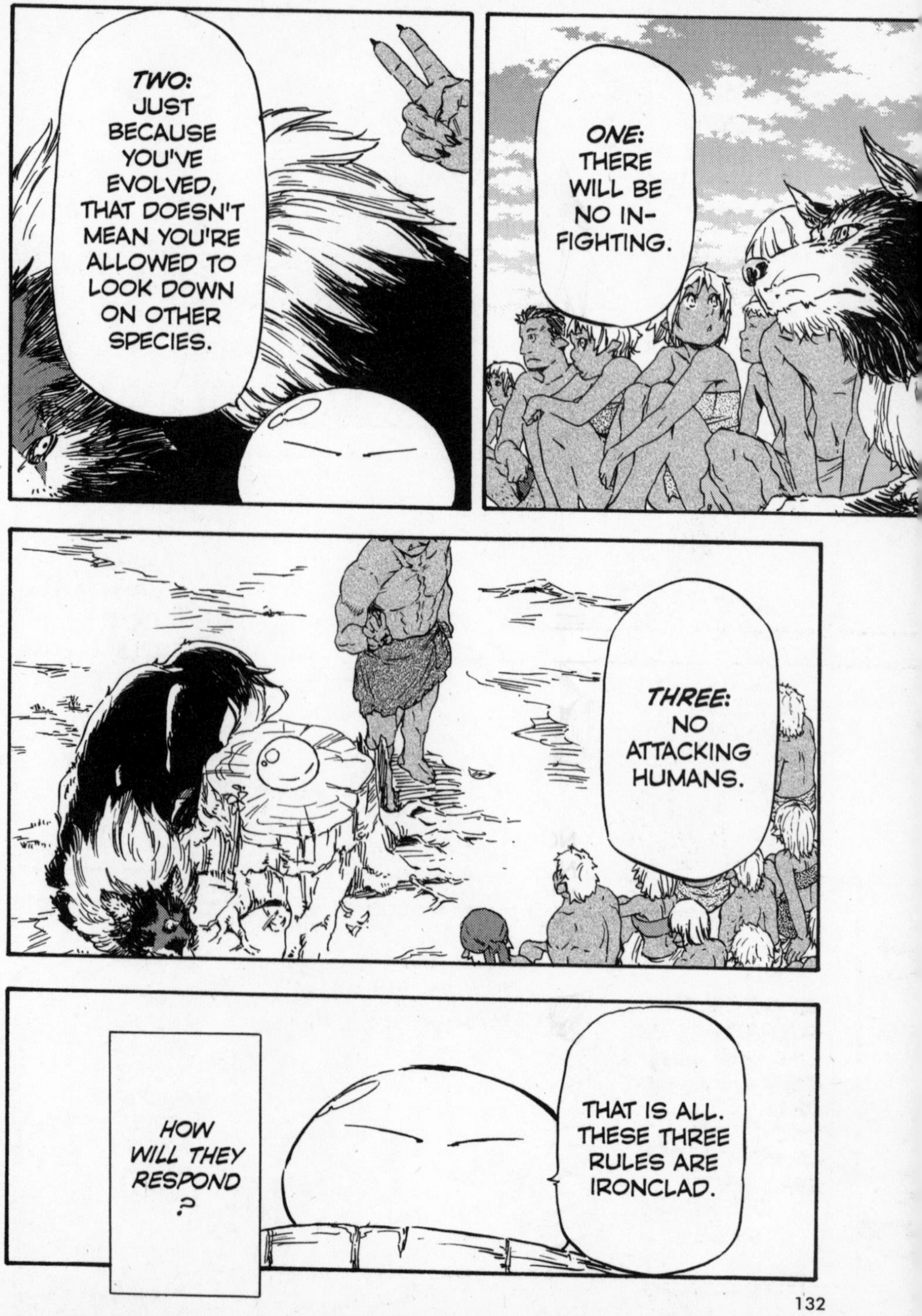
ONE: THERE WILL BE NO IN-FIGHTING.
TWO: JUST BECAUSE YOU'VE EVOLVED, THAT DOESN'T MEAN YOU'RE ALLOWED TO LOOK DOWN ON OTHER SPECIES.
THREE: NO ATTACKING HUMANS.
THAT IS ALL. THESE THREE RULES ARE IRONCLAD.
HOW WILL THEY RESPOND?

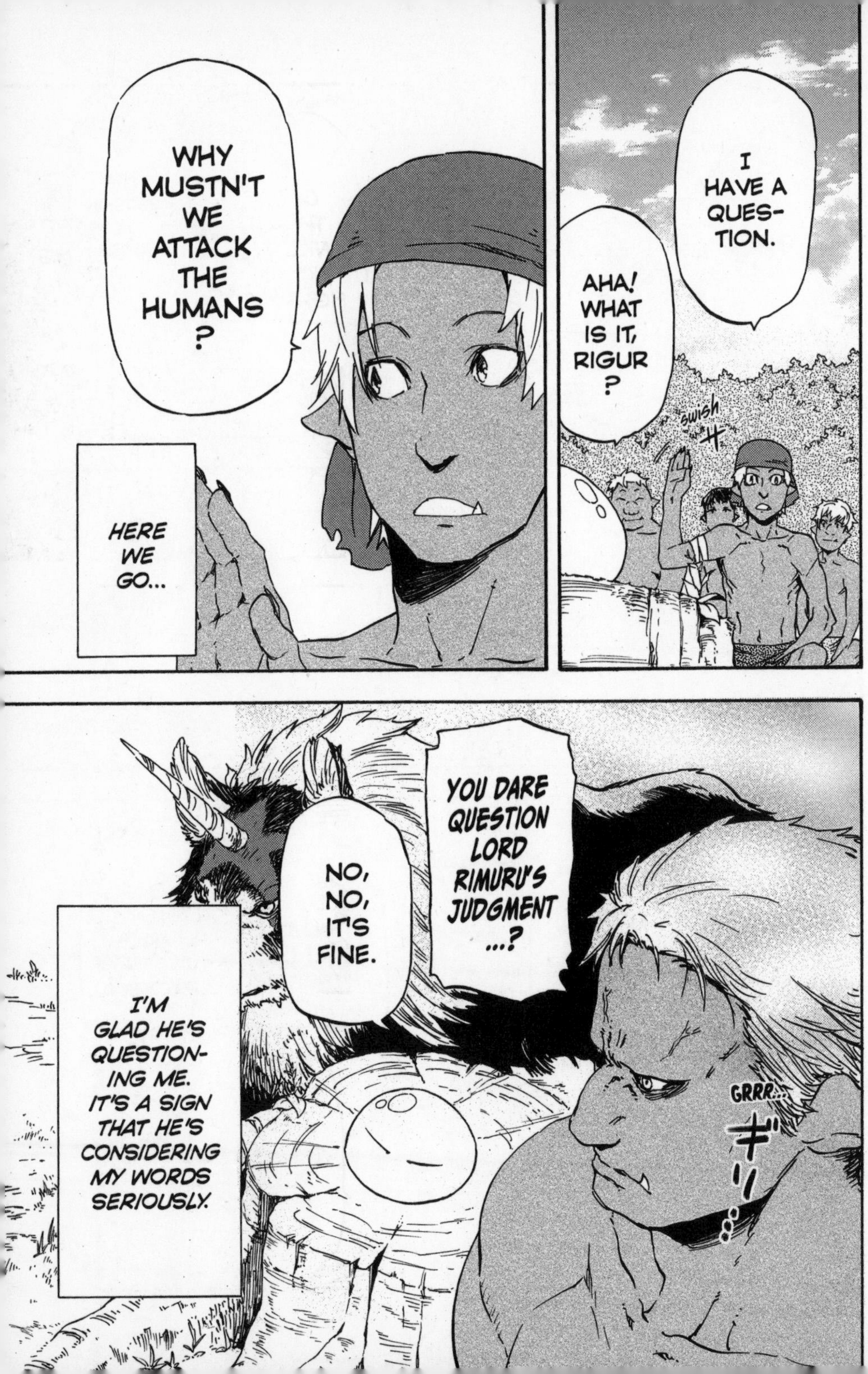
I HAVE A QUES-TION.
AHA! WHAT IS IT, RIGUR?
SWISH
WHY MUSTN'T WE ATTACK THE HUMANS?
HERE WE GO...
YOU DARE QUESTION LORD RIMURU'S JUDGMENT...?
GRRR...
NO, NO, IT'S FINE.
I'M GLAD HE'S QUESTION-ING ME. IT'S A SIGN THAT HE'S CONSIDERING MY WORDS SERIOUSLY.

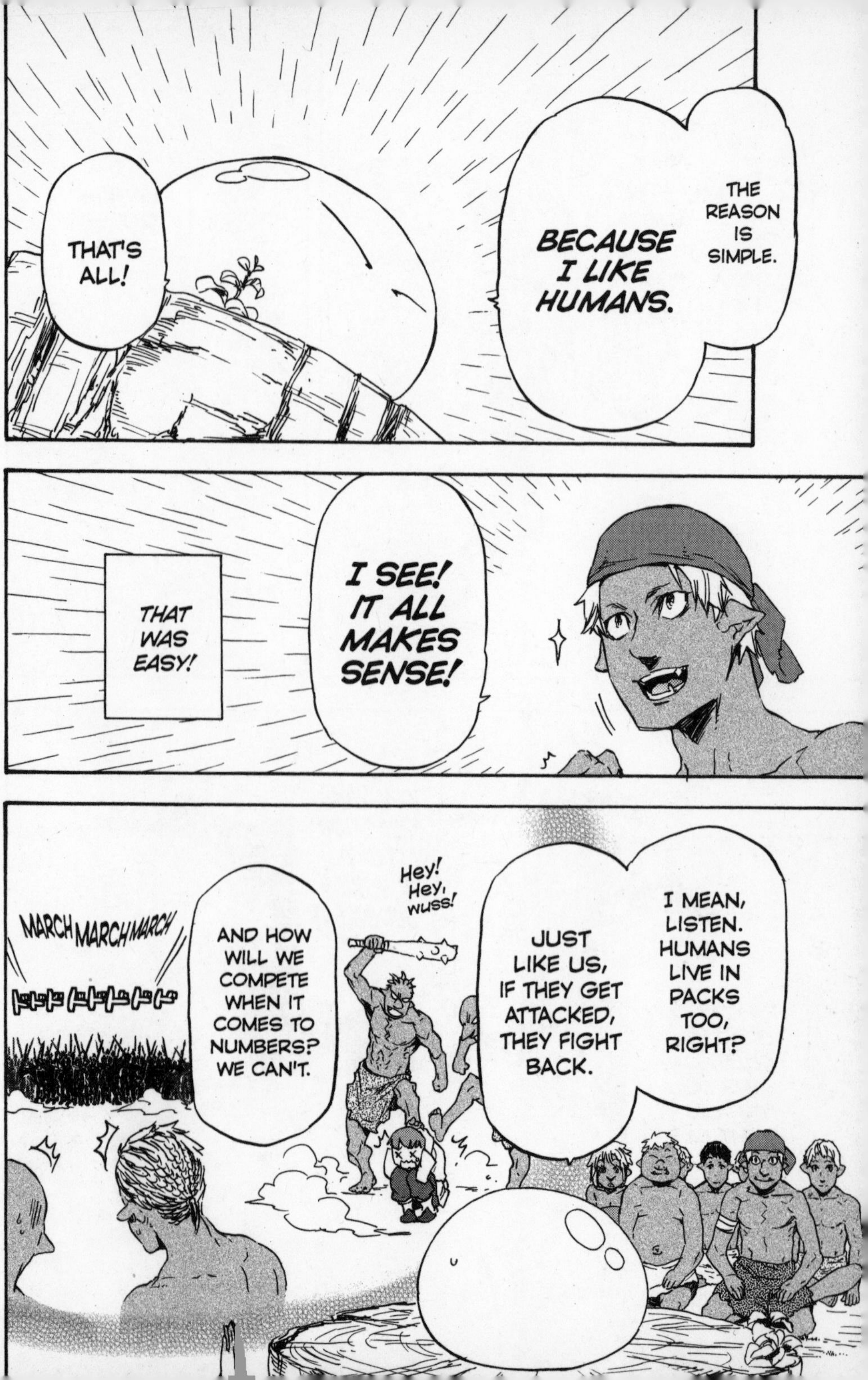
THE REASON IS SIMPLE.
BECAUSE I LIKE HUMANS.
THAT'S ALL!
I SEE! IT ALL MAKES SENSE!
THAT WAS EASY!
I MEAN, LISTEN. HUMANS LIVE IN PACKS TOO, RIGHT?
JUST LIKE US, IF THEY GET ATTACKED, THEY FIGHT BACK.
Hey! Hey, wuss!
AND HOW WILL WE COMPETE WHEN IT COMES TO NUMBERS? WE CAN'T.
MARCH MARCH MARCH
ドドド ドドドドド

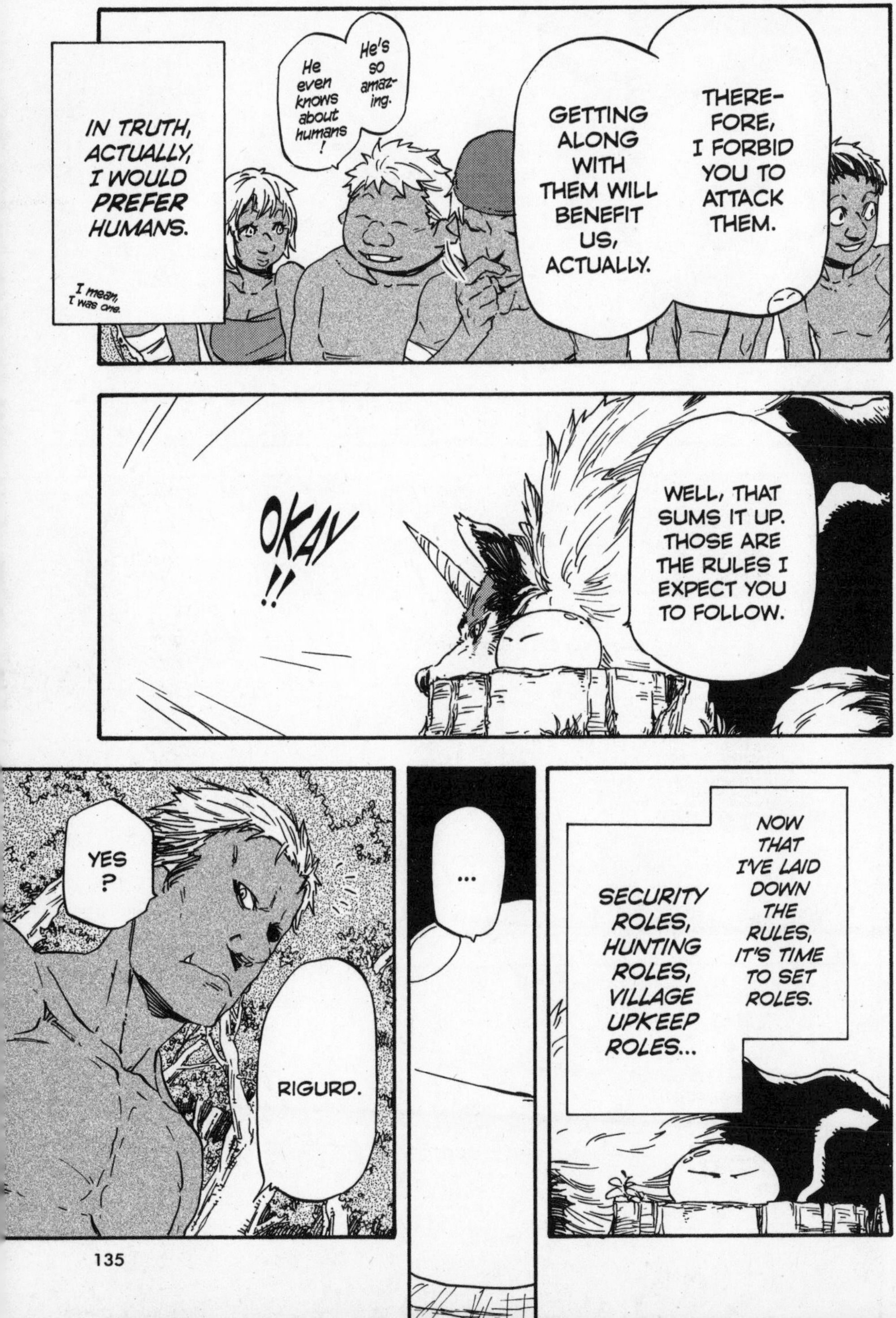
THEREFORE, I FORBID YOU TO ATTACK THEM.
GETTING ALONG WITH THEM WILL BENEFIT US, ACTUALLY.
He's so amazing.
He even knows about humans!
IN TRUTH, ACTUALLY, I WOULD PREFER HUMANS.
I mean, I was one.
WELL, THAT SUMS IT UP. THOSE ARE THE RULES I EXPECT YOU TO FOLLOW.
OKAY!!
NOW THAT I'VE LAID DOWN THE RULES, IT'S TIME TO SET ROLES.
SECURITY ROLES, HUNTING ROLES, VILLAGE UPKEEP ROLES...
...
RIGURD.
YES?

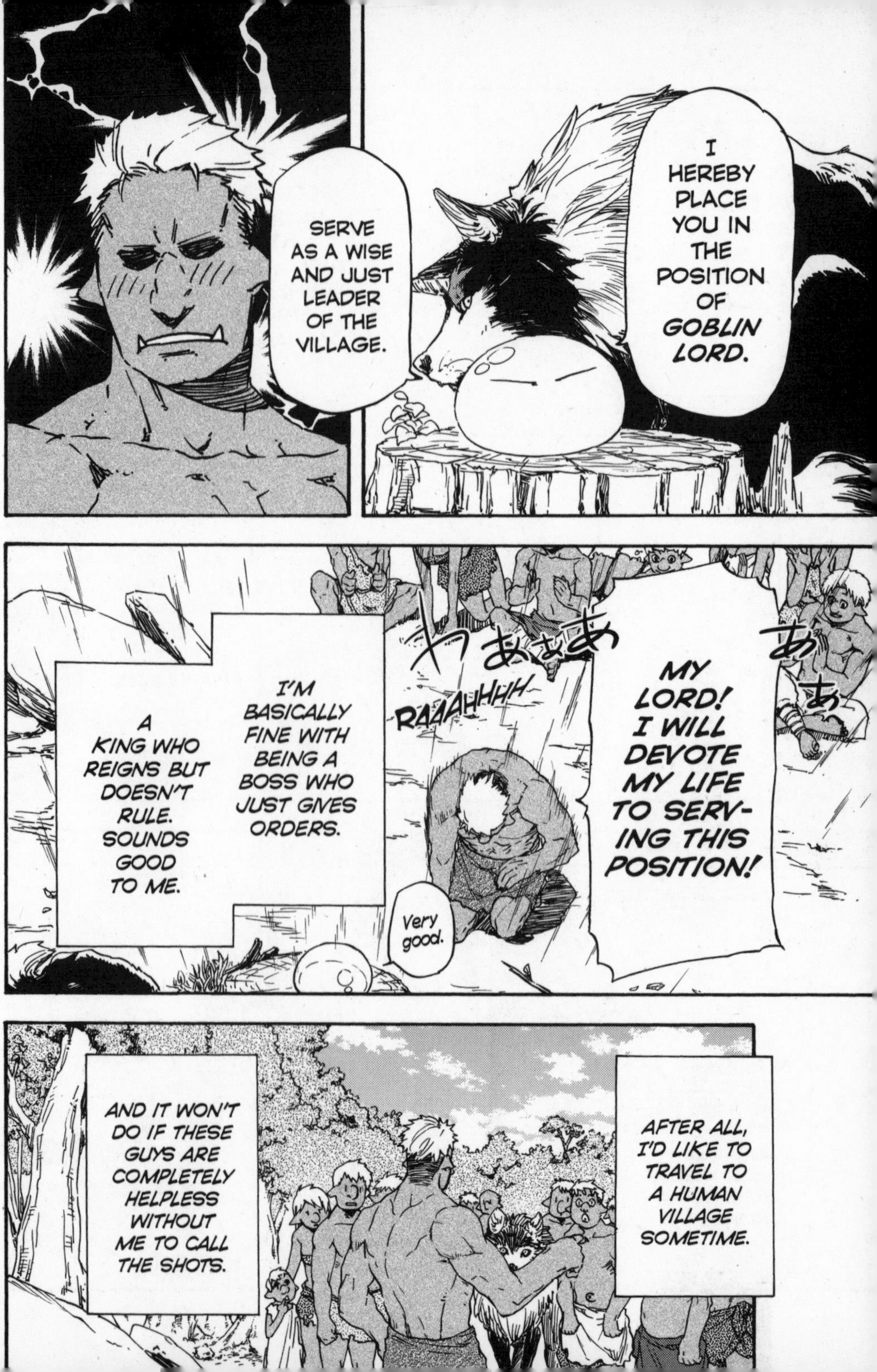
I HEREBY PLACE YOU IN THE POSITION OF GOBLIN LORD.
SERVE AS A WISE AND JUST LEADER OF THE VILLAGE.
MY LORD! I WILL DEVOTE MY LIFE TO SERV-ING THIS POSITION!
RAAAHHHH
Very good.
I'M BASICALLY FINE WITH BEING A BOSS WHO JUST GIVES ORDERS.
A KING WHO REIGNS BUT DOESN'T RULE. SOUNDS GOOD TO ME.
AFTER ALL, I'D LIKE TO TRAVEL TO A HUMAN VILLAGE SOMETIME.
AND IT WON'T DO IF THESE GUYS ARE COMPLETELY HELPLESS WITHOUT ME TO CALL THE SHOTS.

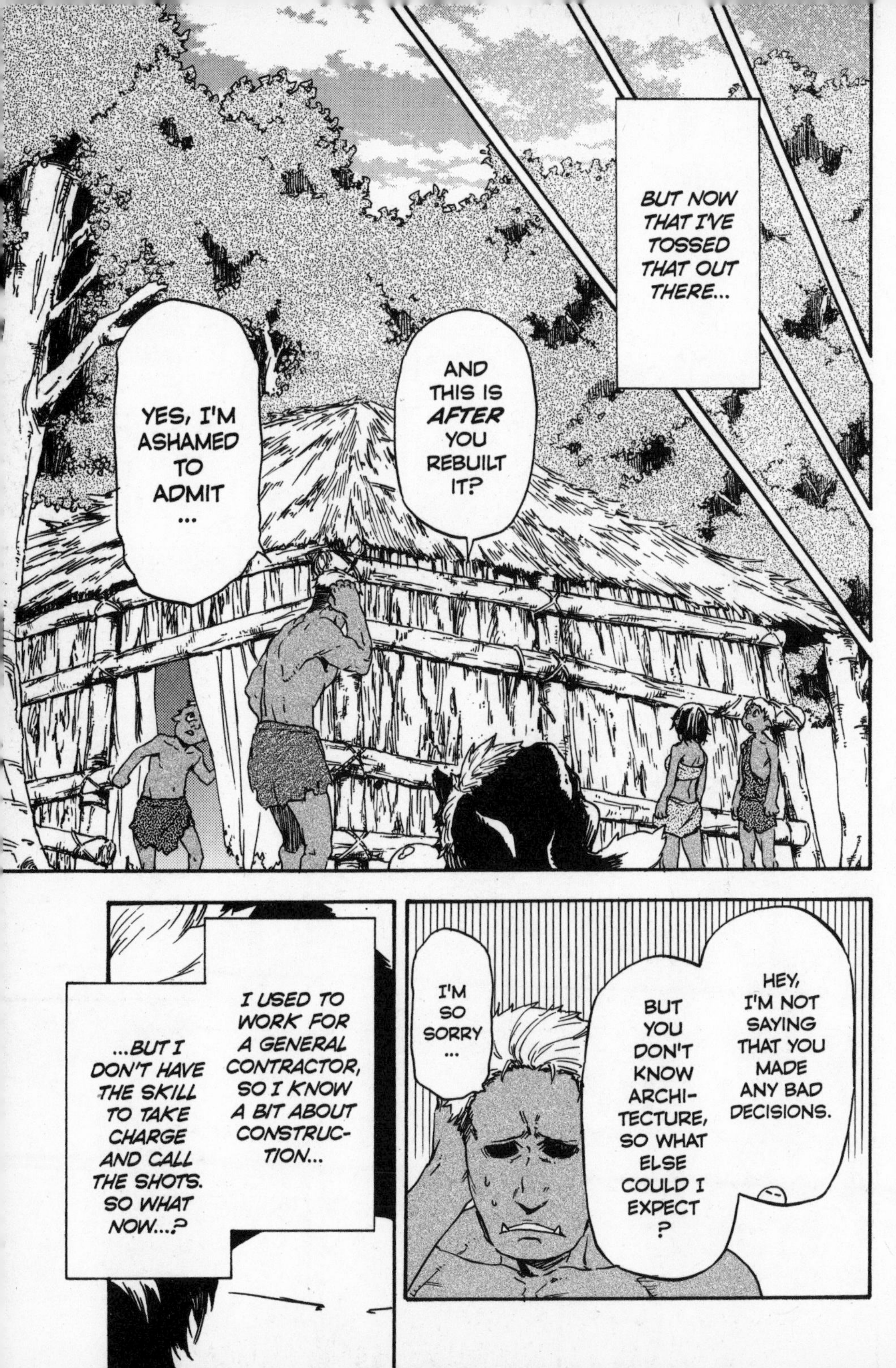
BUT NOW THAT I'VE TOSSED THAT OUT THERE...
AND THIS IS *AFTER* YOU REBUILT IT?
YES, I'M ASHAMED TO ADMIT ...
HEY, I'M NOT SAYING THAT YOU MADE ANY BAD DECISIONS.
BUT YOU DON'T KNOW ARCHITECTURE, SO WHAT ELSE COULD I EXPECT?
I'M SO SORRY ...
I USED TO WORK FOR A GENERAL CONTRACTOR, SO I KNOW A BIT ABOUT CONSTRUCTION...
...BUT I DON'T HAVE THE SKILL TO TAKE CHARGE AND CALL THE SHOTS. SO WHAT NOW...?

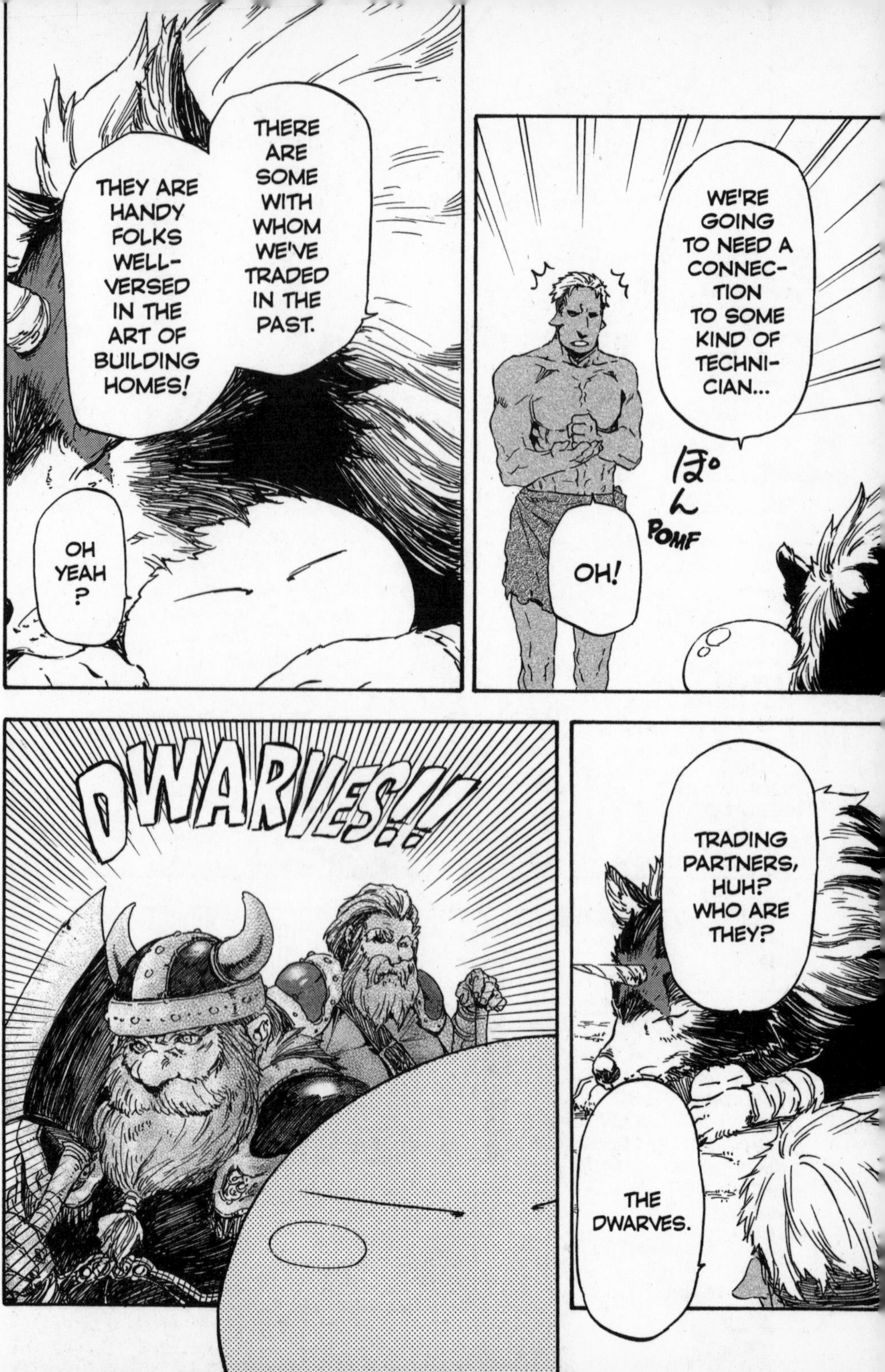
WE'RE GOING TO NEED A CONNECTION TO SOME KIND OF TECHNICIAN...
ぽん
POMF
OH!
THERE ARE SOME WITH WHOM WE'VE TRADED IN THE PAST.
THEY ARE HANDY FOLKS WELL-VERSED IN THE ART OF BUILDING HOMES!
OH YEAH?
TRADING PARTNERS, HUH? WHO ARE THEY?
THE DWARVES.
DWARVES!!

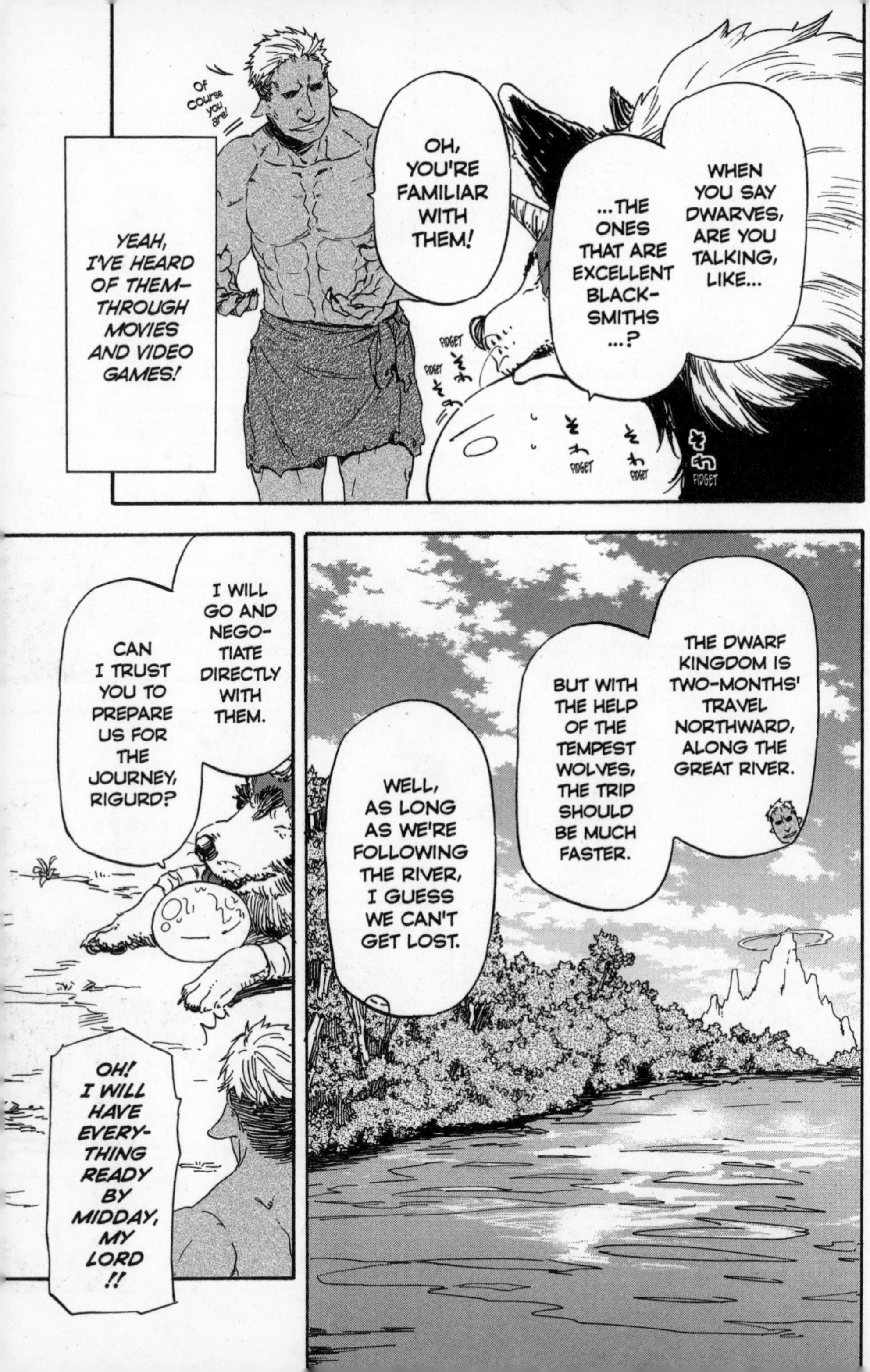
WHEN YOU SAY DWARVES, ARE YOU TALKING, LIKE...
...THE ONES THAT ARE EXCELLENT BLACK-SMITHS ...?
FIDGET FIDGET FIDGET FIDGET FIDGET
OH, YOU'RE FAMILIAR WITH THEM!
Of course you are!
YEAH, I'VE HEARD OF THEM—THROUGH MOVIES AND VIDEO GAMES!
THE DWARF KINGDOM IS TWO-MONTHS' TRAVEL NORTHWARD, ALONG THE GREAT RIVER.
BUT WITH THE HELP OF THE TEMPEST WOLVES, THE TRIP SHOULD BE MUCH FASTER.
WELL, AS LONG AS WE'RE FOLLOWING THE RIVER, I GUESS WE CAN'T GET LOST.
I WILL GO AND NEGO-TIATE DIRECTLY WITH THEM.
CAN I TRUST YOU TO PREPARE US FOR THE JOURNEY, RIGURD?
OH! I WILL HAVE EVERY-THING READY BY MIDDAY, MY LORD!!

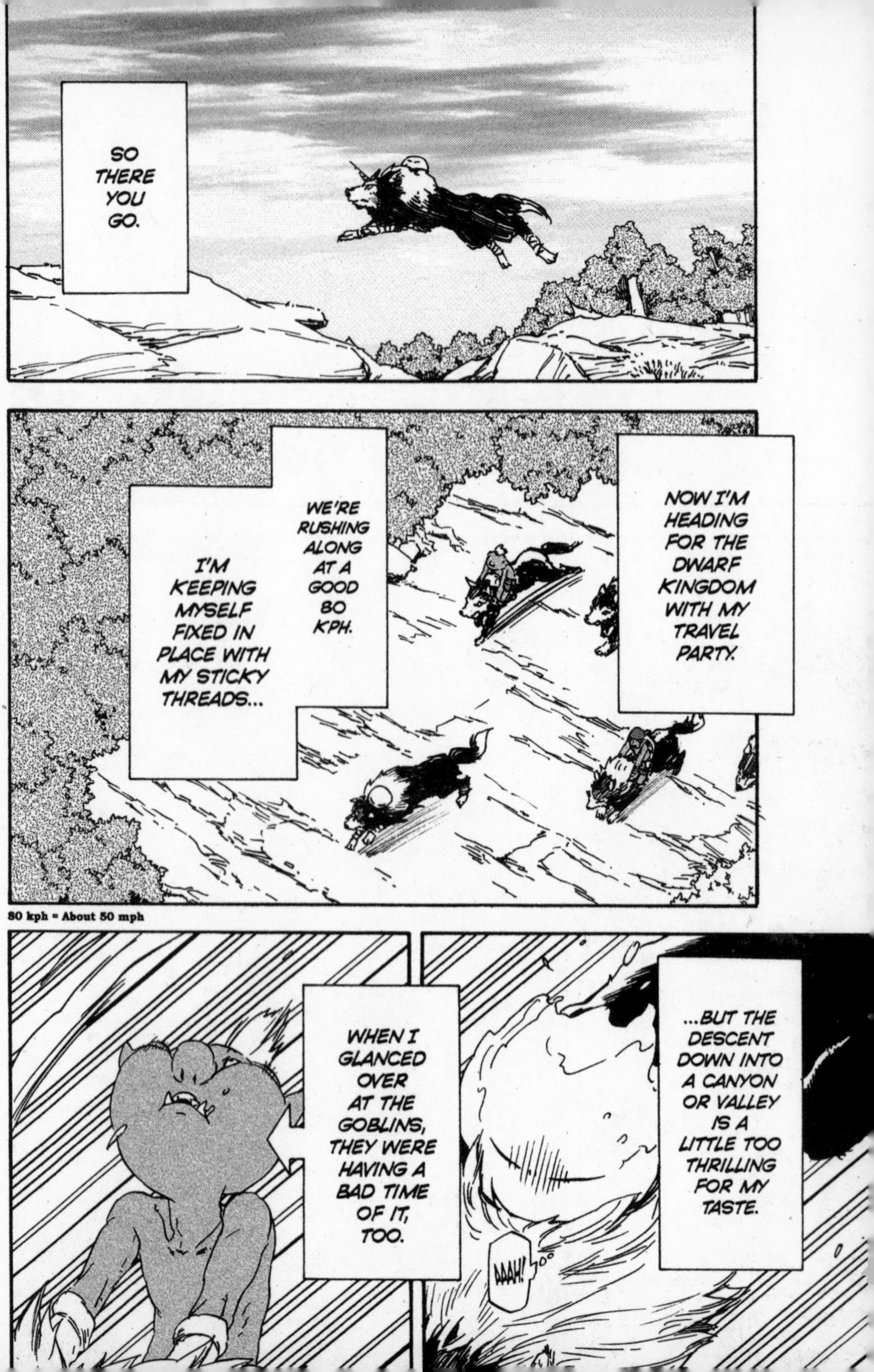
SO THERE YOU GO.
NOW I'M HEADING FOR THE DWARF KINGDOM WITH MY TRAVEL PARTY.
WE'RE RUSHING ALONG AT A GOOD 80 KPH.
I'M KEEPING MYSELF FIXED IN PLACE WITH MY STICKY THREADS...
...BUT THE DESCENT DOWN INTO A CANYON OR VALLEY IS A LITTLE TOO THRILLING FOR MY TASTE.
AAAH!
WHEN I GLANCED OVER AT THE GOBLINS, THEY WERE HAVING A BAD TIME OF IT, TOO.

80 kph = About 50 mph

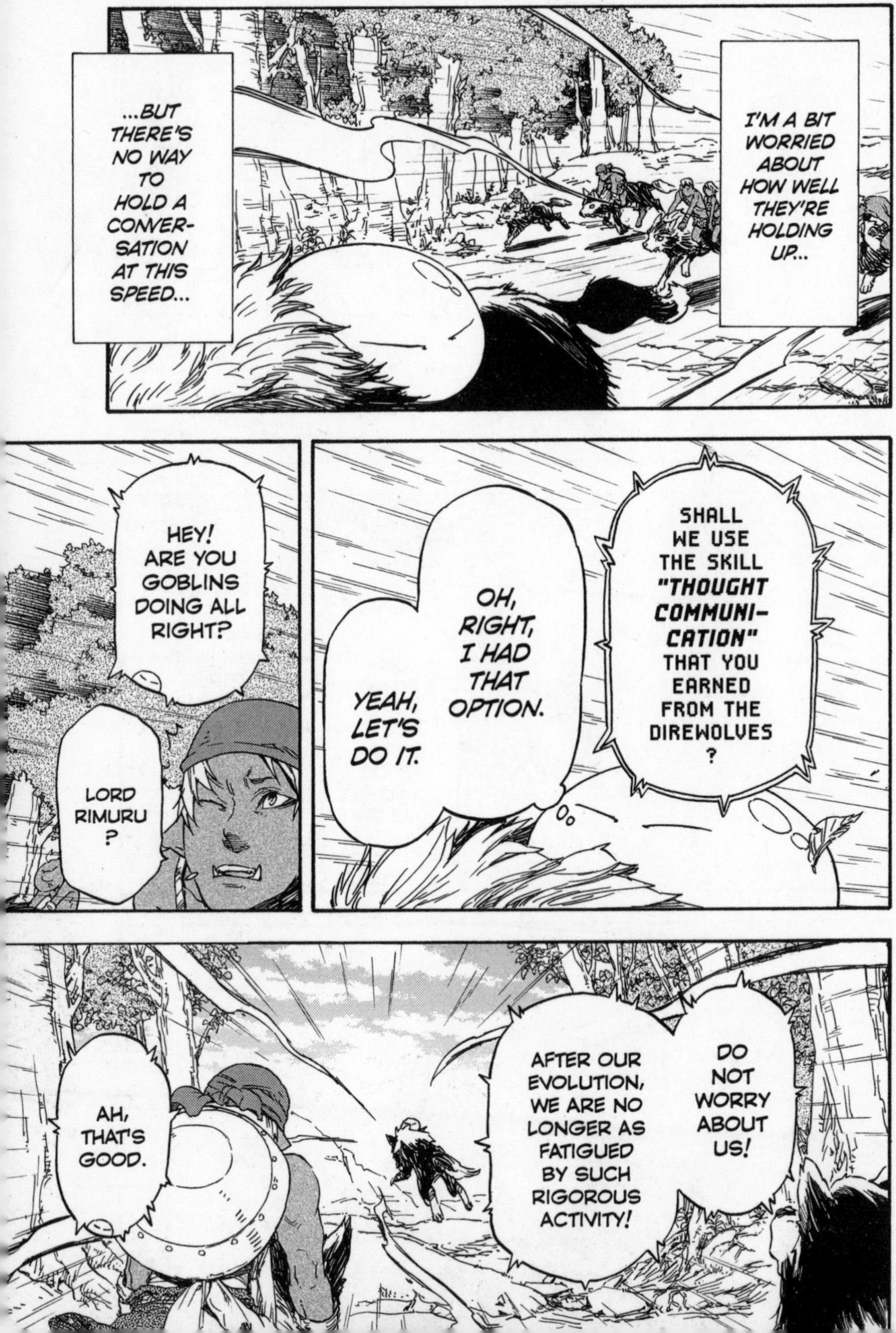
I'M A BIT WORRIED ABOUT HOW WELL THEY'RE HOLDING UP...
...BUT THERE'S NO WAY TO HOLD A CONVER-SATION AT THIS SPEED...
SHALL WE USE THE SKILL "THOUGHT COMMUNI-CATION" THAT YOU EARNED FROM THE DIREWOLVES ?
OH, RIGHT, I HAD THAT OPTION.
YEAH, LET'S DO IT.
HEY! ARE YOU GOBLINS DOING ALL RIGHT?
LORD RIMURU ?
DO NOT WORRY ABOUT US!
AFTER OUR EVOLUTION, WE ARE NO LONGER AS FATIGUED BY SUCH RIGOROUS ACTIVITY!
AH, THAT'S GOOD.

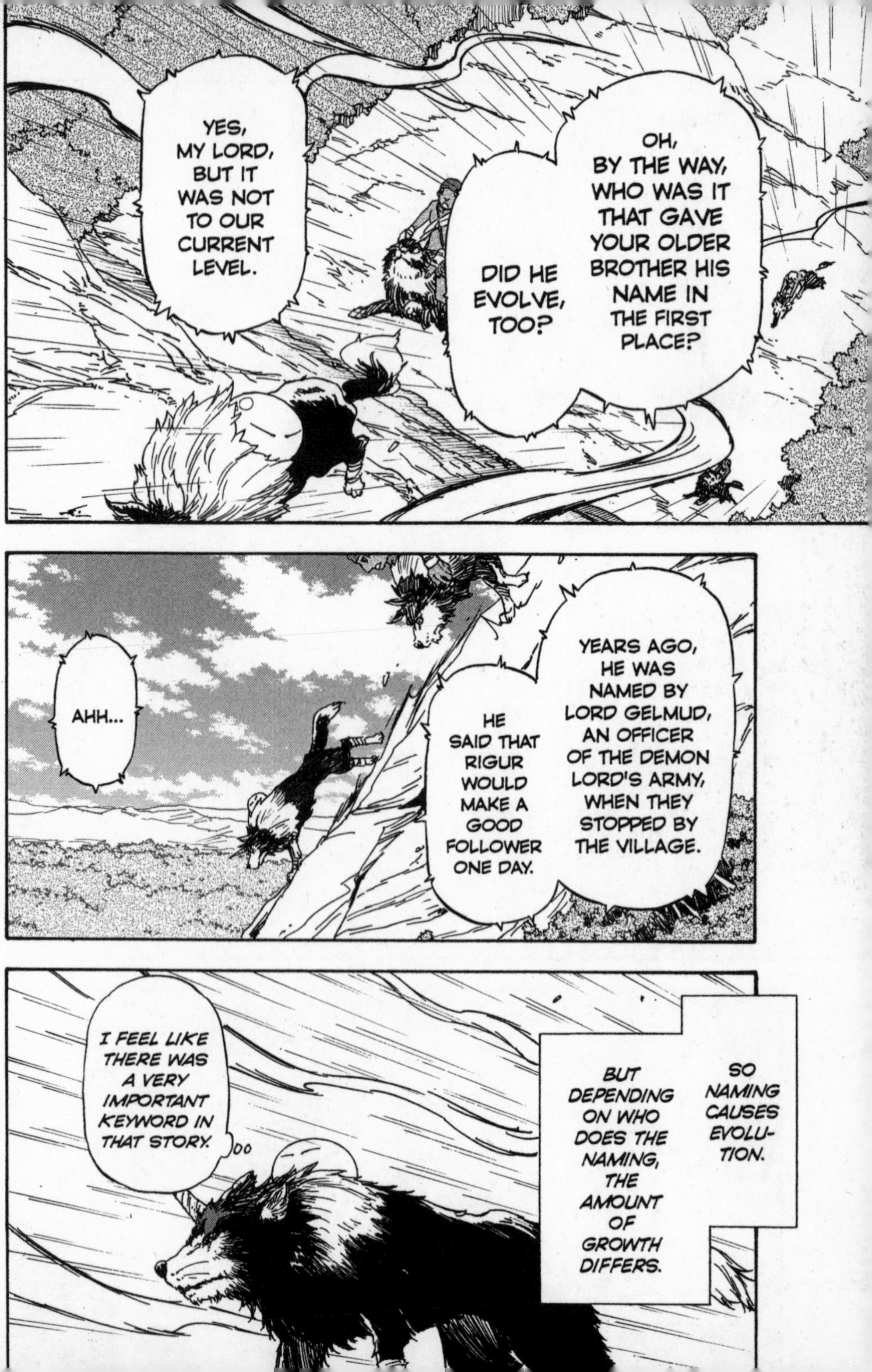
DID HE EVOLVE, TOO?
YES, MY LORD, BUT IT WAS NOT TO OUR CURRENT LEVEL.
OH, BY THE WAY, WHO WAS IT THAT GAVE YOUR OLDER BROTHER HIS NAME IN THE FIRST PLACE?
YEARS AGO, HE WAS NAMED BY LORD GELMUD, AN OFFICER OF THE DEMON LORD'S ARMY, WHEN THEY STOPPED BY THE VILLAGE.
HE SAID THAT RIGUR WOULD MAKE A GOOD FOLLOWER ONE DAY.
AHH...
SO NAMING CAUSES EVOLUTION.
BUT DEPENDING ON WHO DOES THE NAMING, THE AMOUNT OF GROWTH DIFFERS.
I FEEL LIKE THERE WAS A VERY IMPORTANT KEYWORD IN THAT STORY.

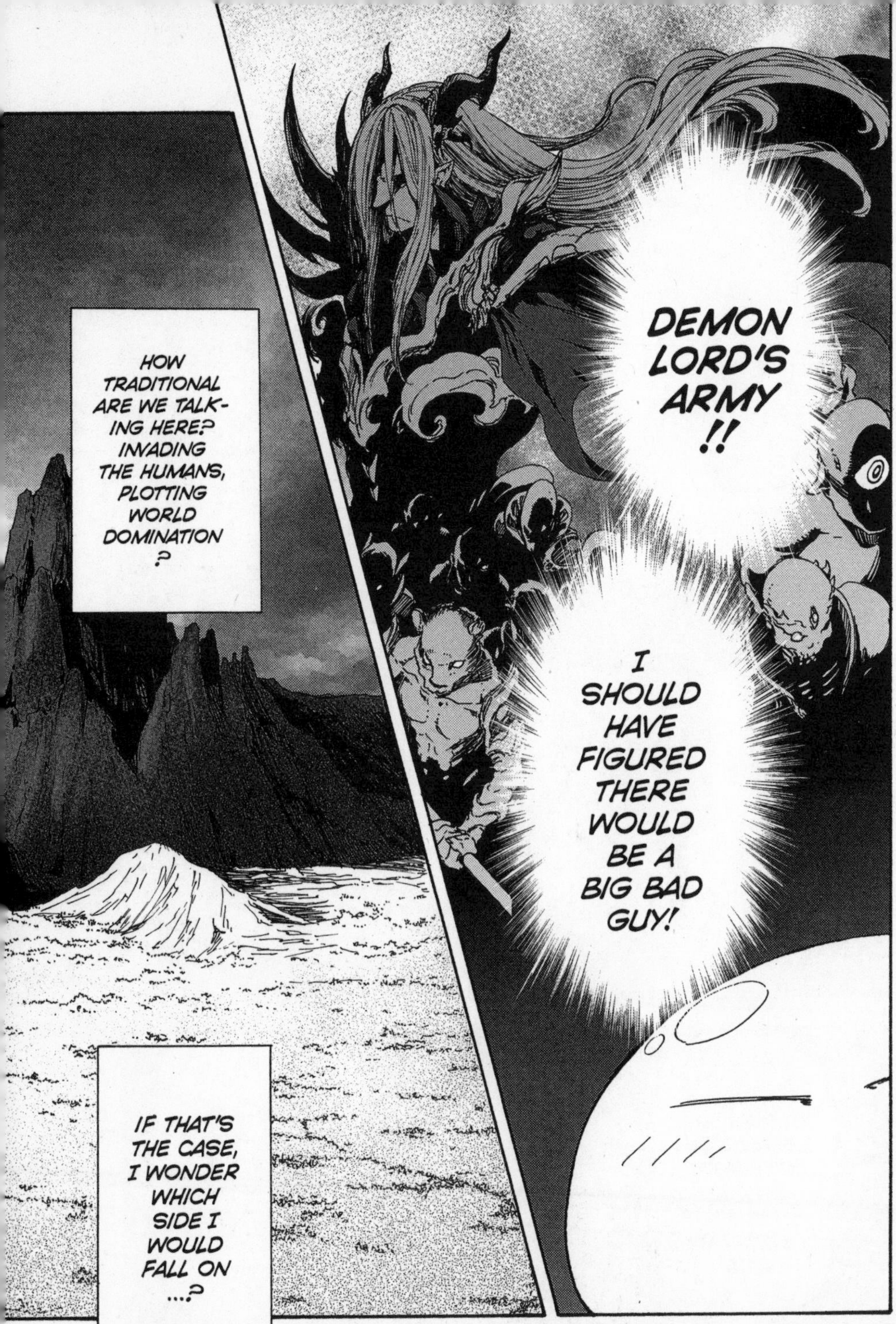
DEMON LORD'S ARMY!!
I SHOULD HAVE FIGURED THERE WOULD BE A BIG BAD GUY!
HOW TRADITIONAL ARE WE TALKING HERE? INVADING THE HUMANS, PLOTTING WORLD DOMINATION?
IF THAT'S THE CASE, I WONDER WHICH SIDE I WOULD FALL ON ...?

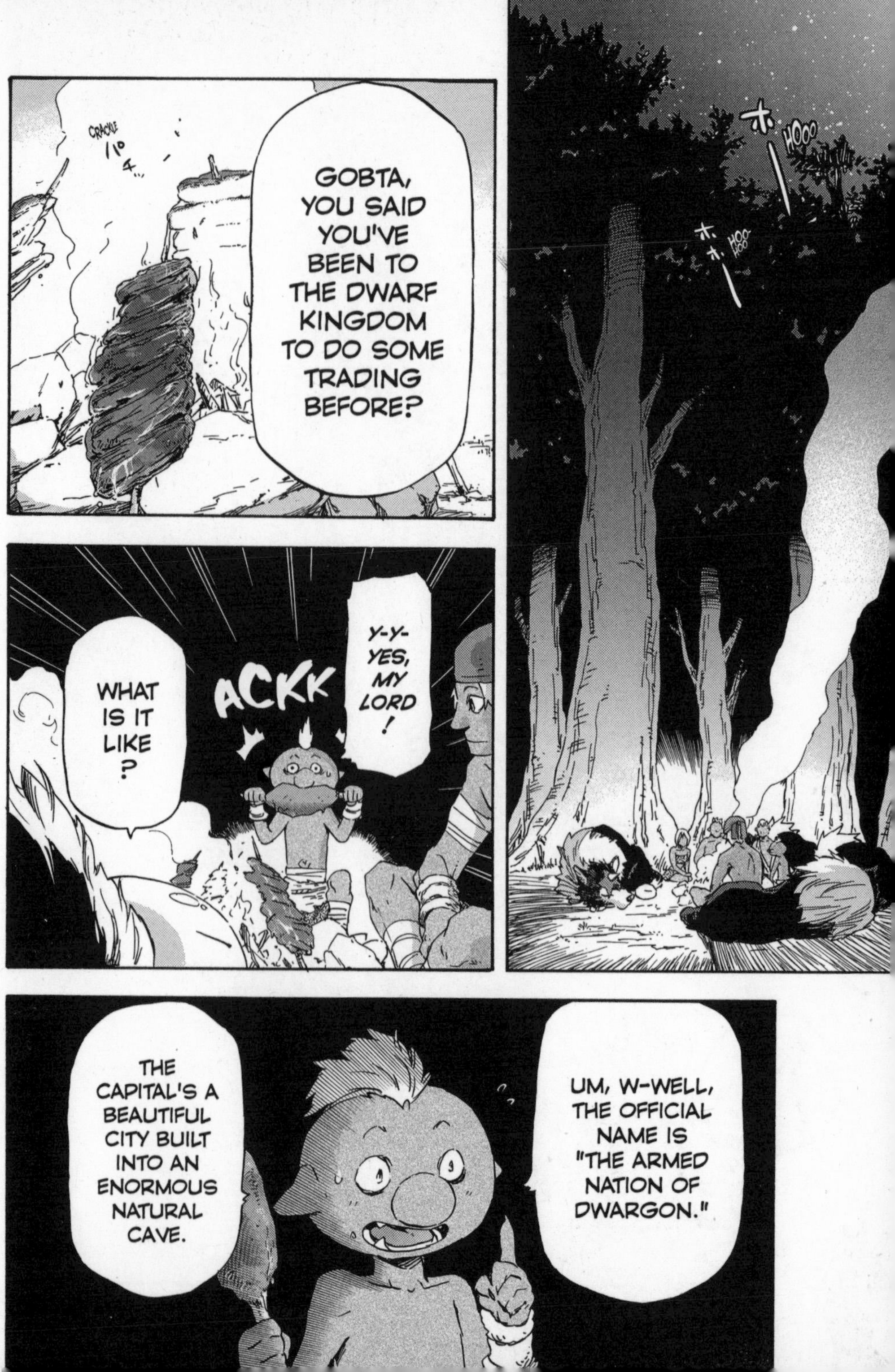
HOOO
HOO HOO
CRACKLE
GOBTA, YOU SAID YOU'VE BEEN TO THE DWARF KINGDOM TO DO SOME TRADING BEFORE?
Y-Y-YES, MY LORD!
ACKK
WHAT IS IT LIKE?
UM, W-WELL, THE OFFICIAL NAME IS "THE ARMED NATION OF DWARGON."
THE CAPITAL'S A BEAUTIFUL CITY BUILT INTO AN ENORMOUS NATURAL CAVE.

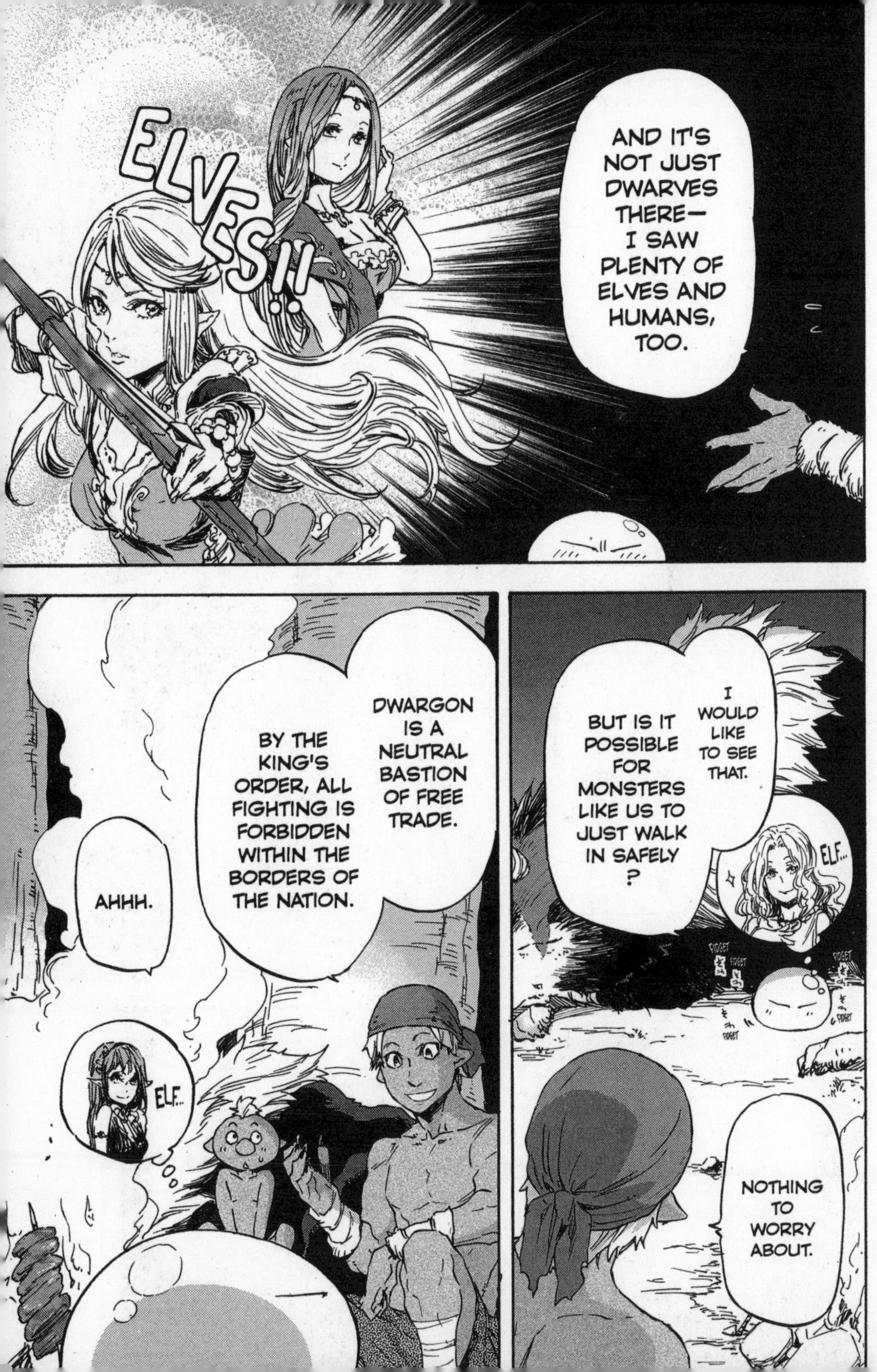
AND IT'S NOT JUST DWARVES THERE—I SAW PLENTY OF ELVES AND HUMANS, TOO.
ELVES!!
I WOULD LIKE TO SEE THAT.
BUT IS IT POSSIBLE FOR MONSTERS LIKE US TO JUST WALK IN SAFELY?
ELF...
FIDGET FIDGET FIDGET FIDGET FIDGET
NOTHING TO WORRY ABOUT.
DWARGON IS A NEUTRAL BASTION OF FREE TRADE.
BY THE KING'S ORDER, ALL FIGHTING IS FORBIDDEN WITHIN THE BORDERS OF THE NATION.
AHHH.
ELF...

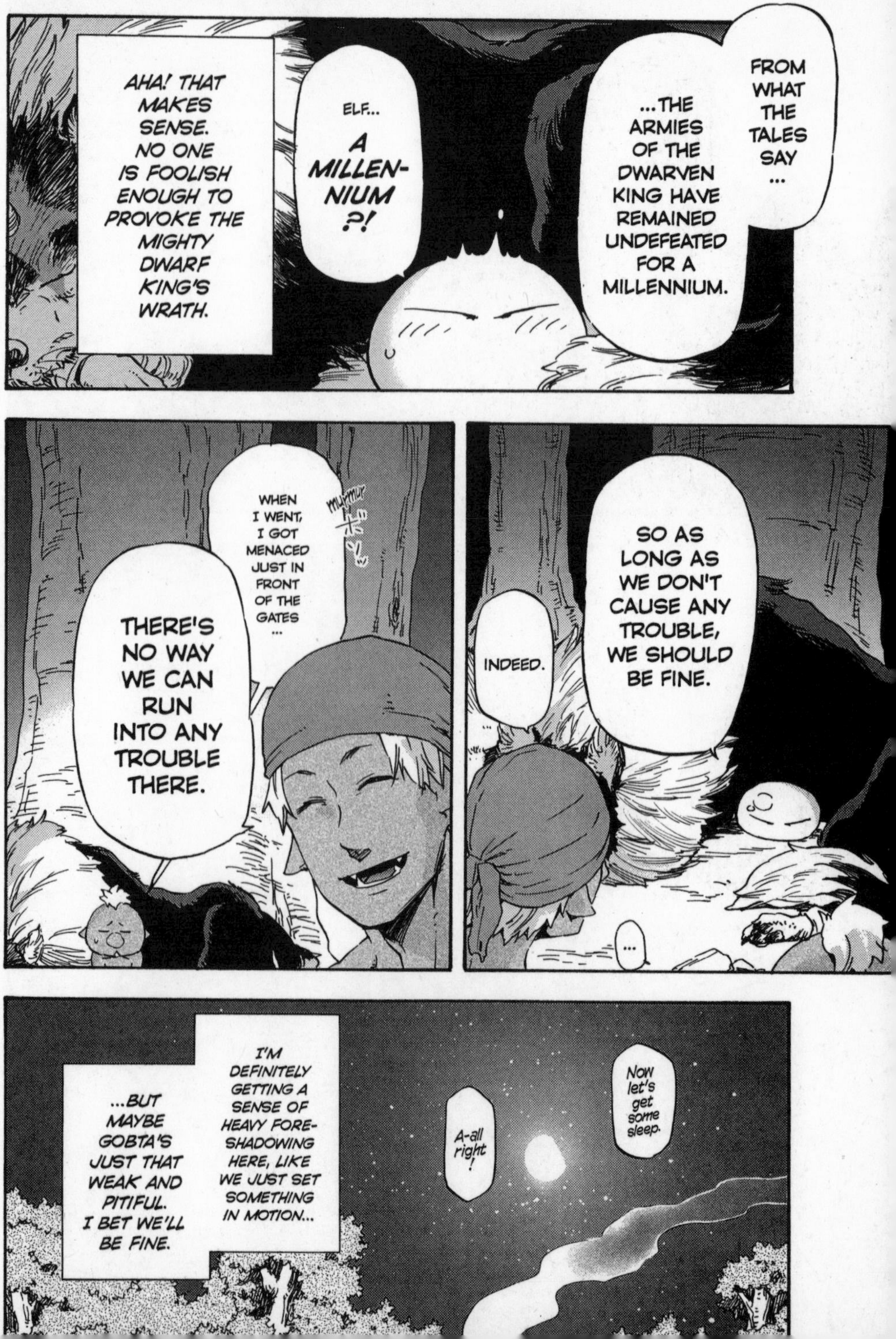
FROM WHAT THE TALES SAY...
...THE ARMIES OF THE DWARVEN KING HAVE REMAINED UNDEFEATED FOR A MILLENNIUM.
ELF... A MILLENNIUM?!
AHA! THAT MAKES SENSE. NO ONE IS FOOLISH ENOUGH TO PROVOKE THE MIGHTY DWARF KING'S WRATH.
SO AS LONG AS WE DON'T CAUSE ANY TROUBLE, WE SHOULD BE FINE.
INDEED.
...
...
WHEN I WENT, I GOT MENACED JUST IN FRONT OF THE GATES...
murmur
THERE'S NO WAY WE CAN RUN INTO ANY TROUBLE THERE.
Now let's get some sleep.
A-all right!
I'M DEFINITELY GETTING A SENSE OF HEAVY FORE-SHADOWING HERE, LIKE WE JUST SET SOMETHING IN MOTION...
...BUT MAYBE GOBTA'S JUST THAT WEAK AND PITIFUL. I BET WE'LL BE FINE.

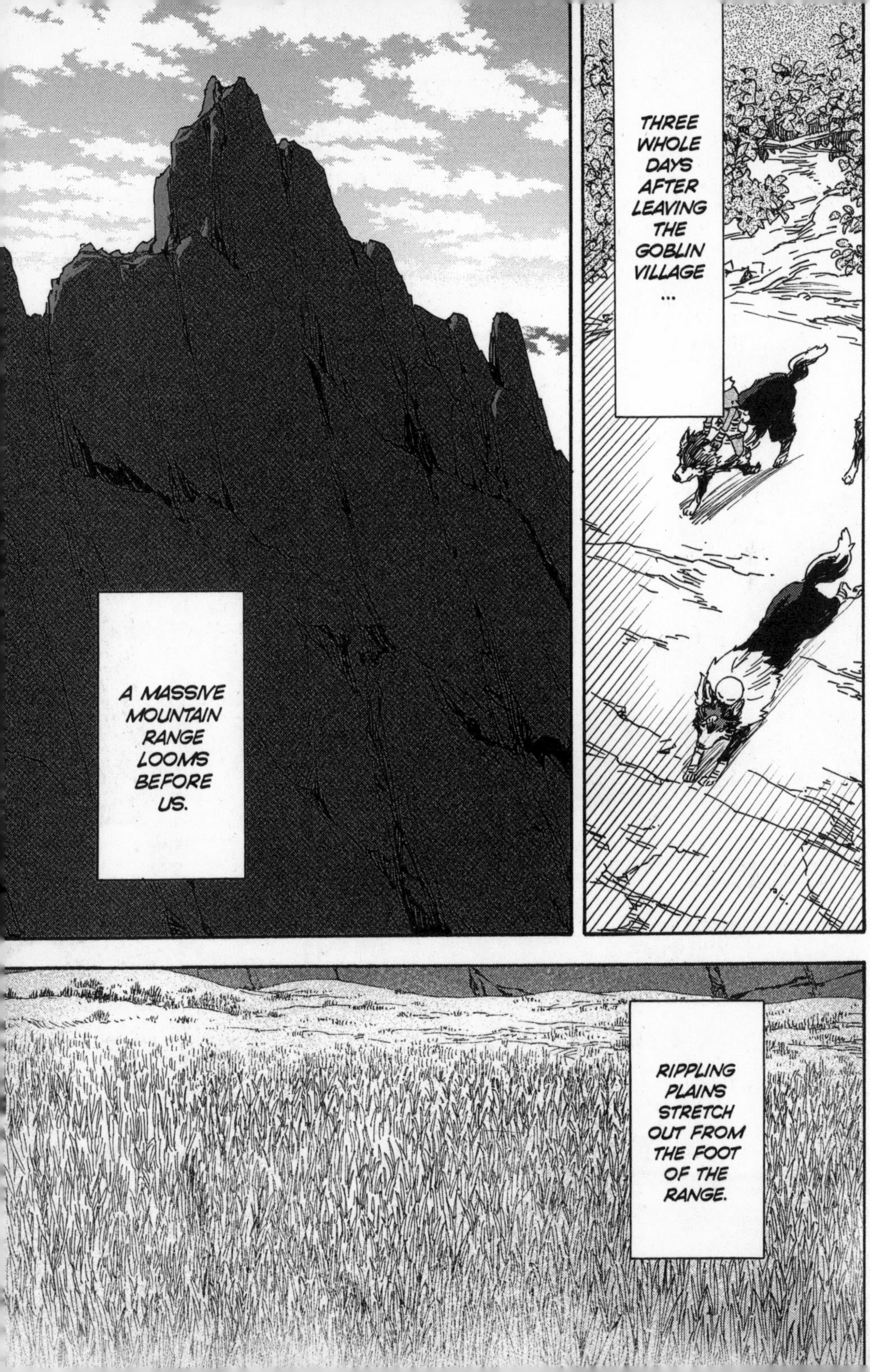
THREE WHOLE DAYS AFTER LEAVING THE GOBLIN VILLAGE ...
A MASSIVE MOUNTAIN RANGE LOOMS BEFORE US.
RIPPLING PLAINS STRETCH OUT FROM THE FOOT OF THE RANGE.

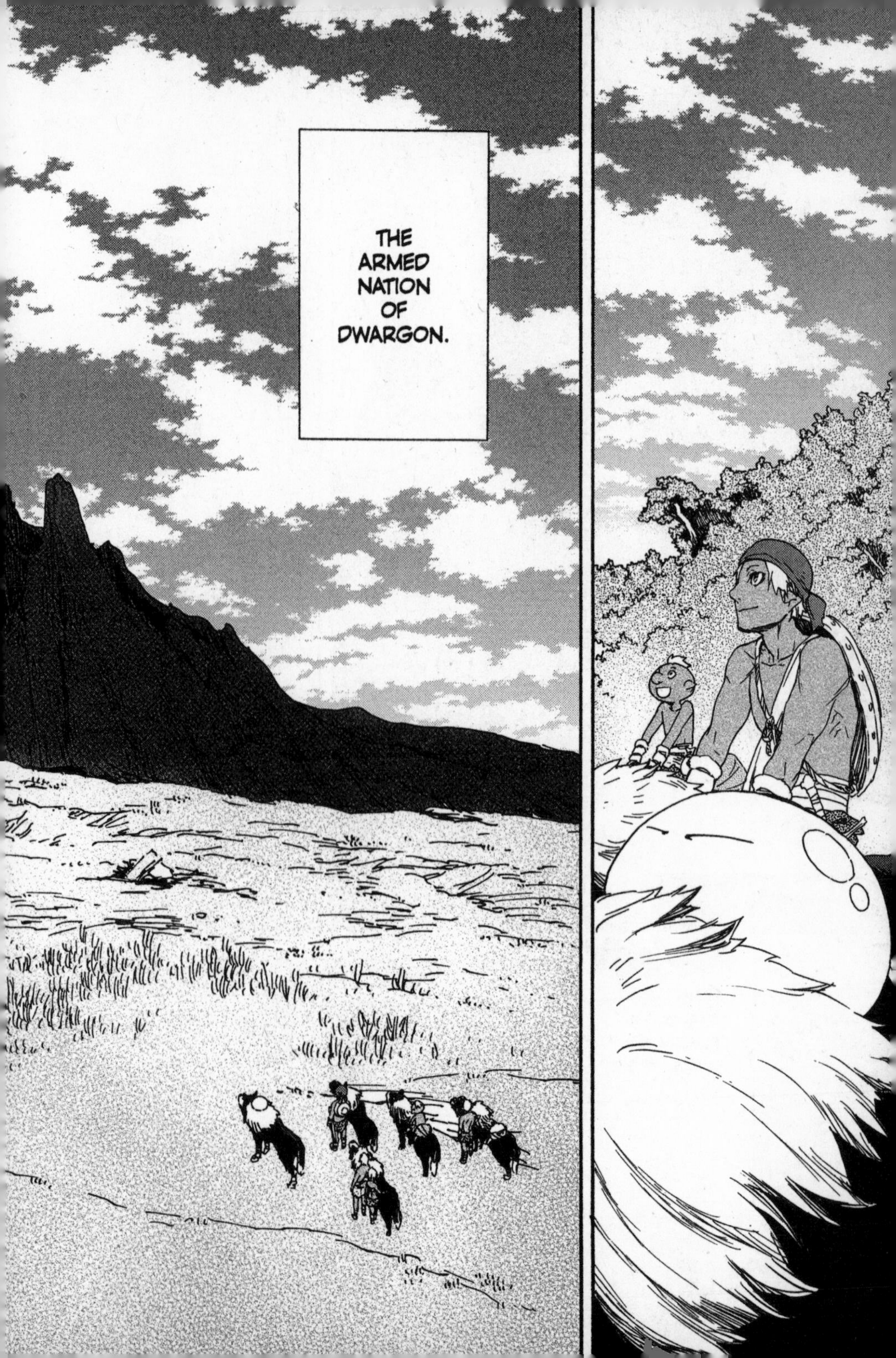
THE ARMED NATION OF DWARGON.

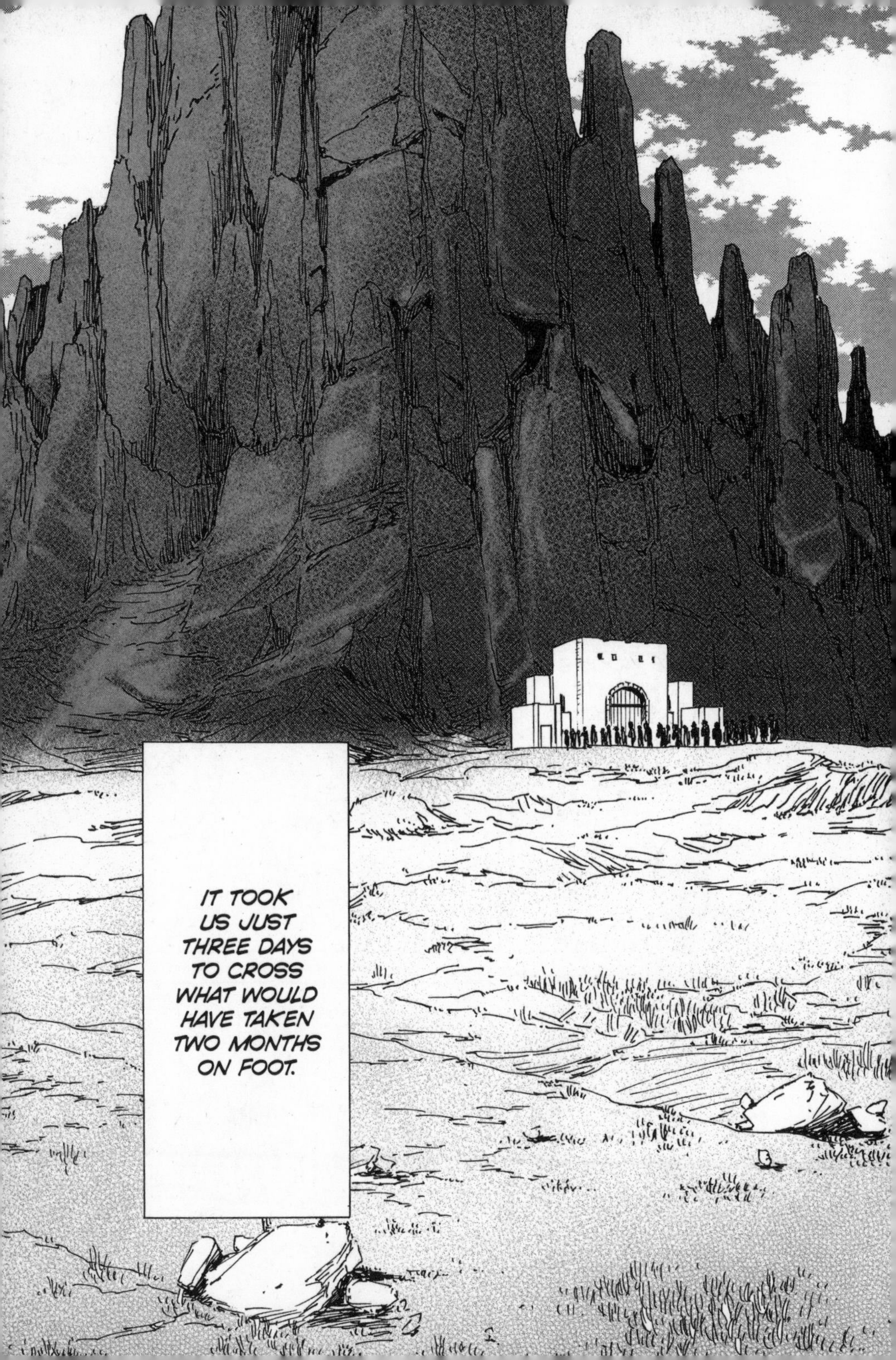
IT TOOK US JUST THREE DAYS TO CROSS WHAT WOULD HAVE TAKEN TWO MONTHS ON FOOT.

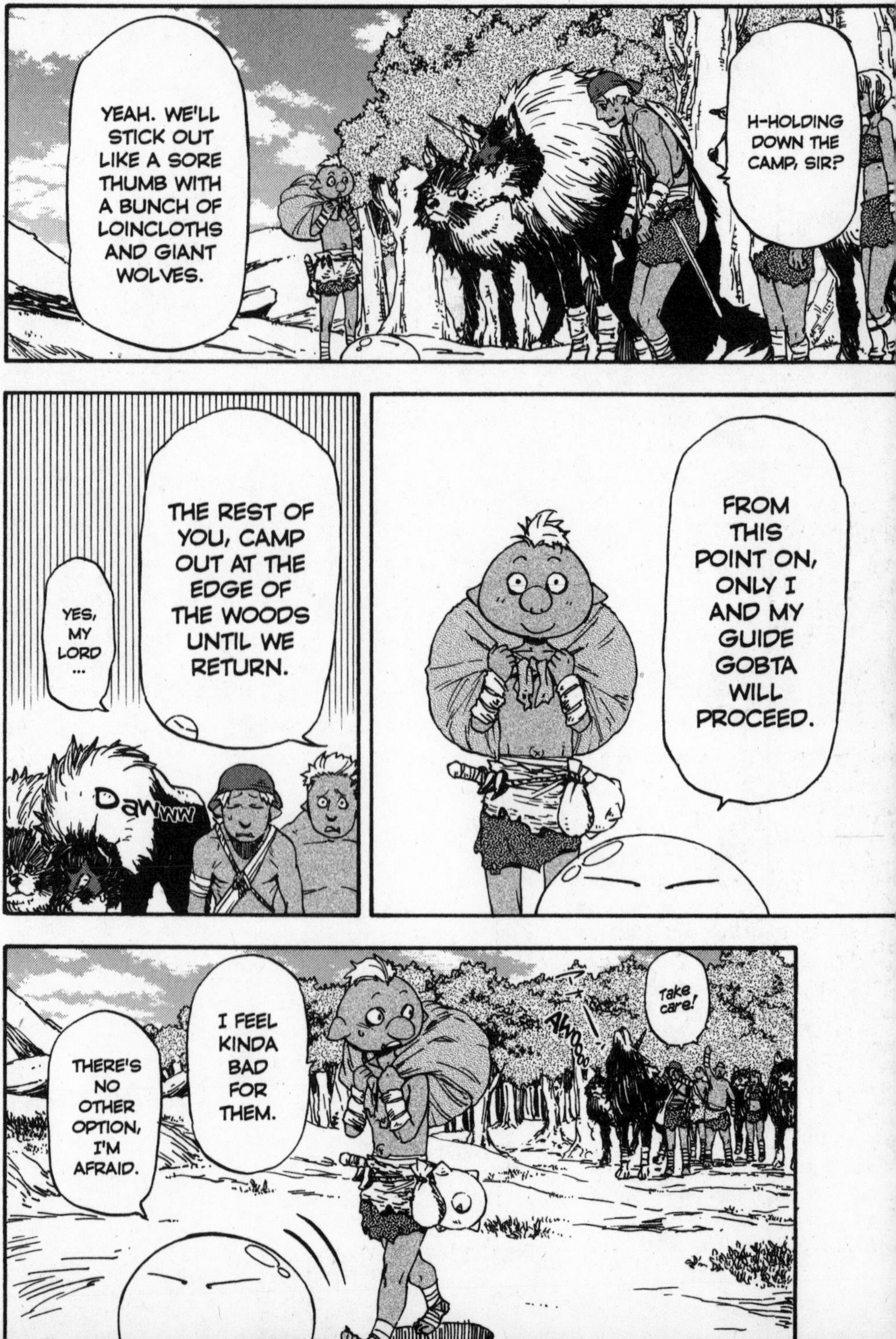
H-HOLDING DOWN THE CAMP, SIR?
YEAH. WE'LL STICK OUT LIKE A SORE THUMB WITH A BUNCH OF LOINCLOTHS AND GIANT WOLVES.
FROM THIS POINT ON, ONLY I AND MY GUIDE GOBTA WILL PROCEED.
THE REST OF YOU, CAMP OUT AT THE EDGE OF THE WOODS UNTIL WE RETURN.
YES, MY LORD ...
Dawww
Take care!
AWOOooo
I FEEL KINDA BAD FOR THEM.
THERE'S NO OTHER OPTION, I'M AFRAID.

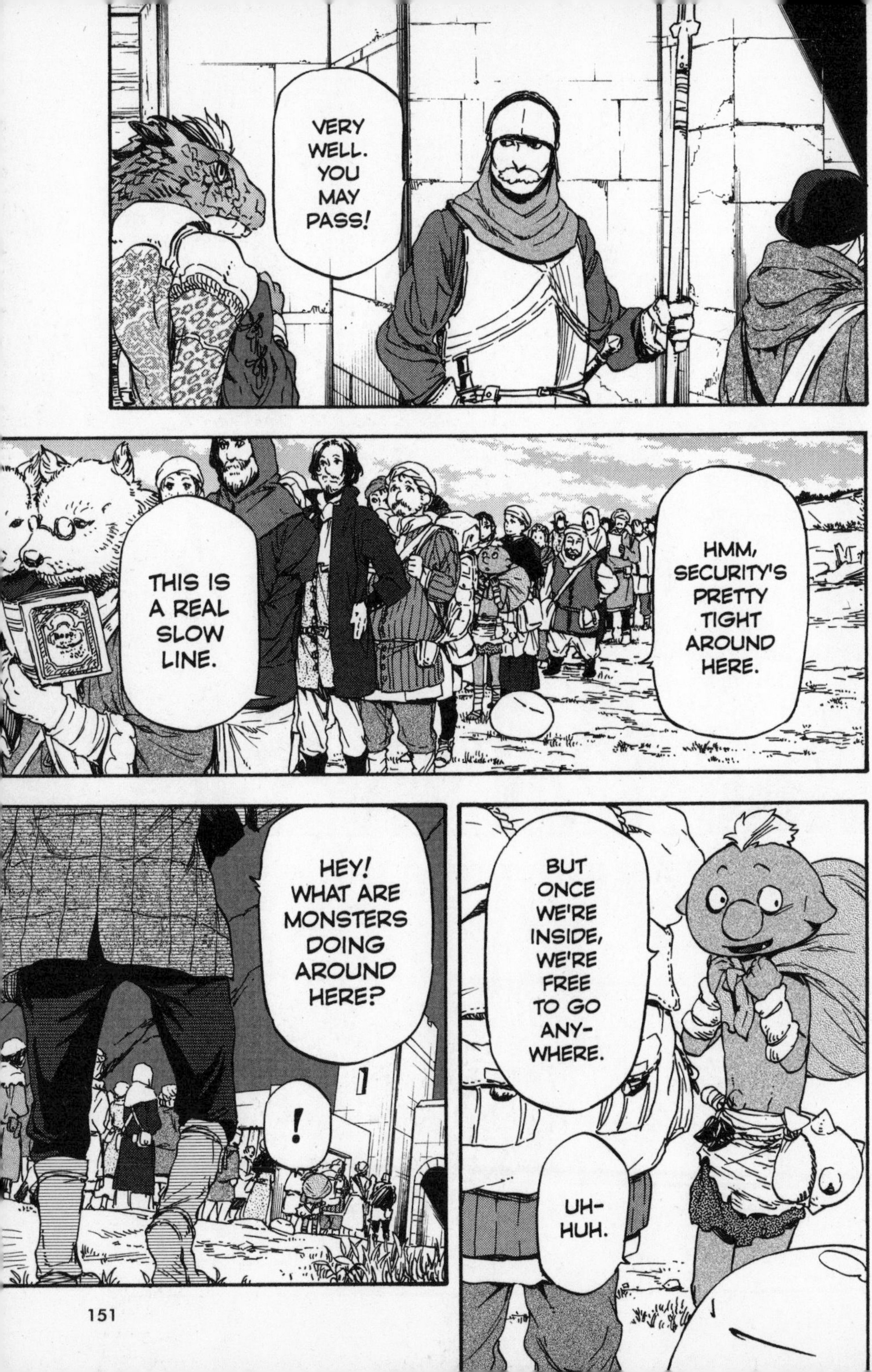
VERY WELL. YOU MAY PASS!
HMM, SECURITY'S PRETTY TIGHT AROUND HERE.
THIS IS A REAL SLOW LINE.
BUT ONCE WE'RE INSIDE, WE'RE FREE TO GO ANY-WHERE.
UH-HUH.
HEY! WHAT ARE MONSTERS DOING AROUND HERE?
!

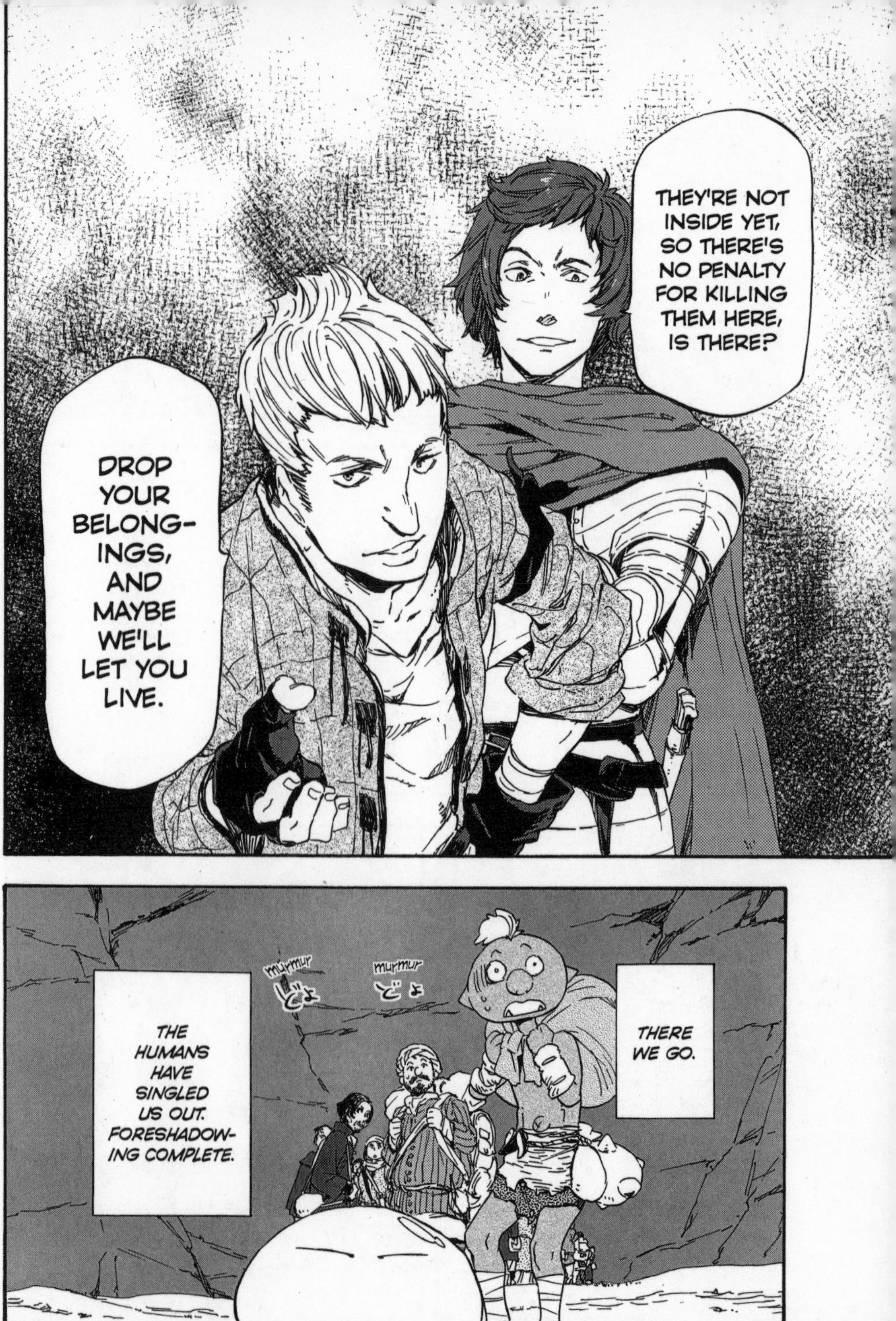
THEY'RE NOT INSIDE YET, SO THERE'S NO PENALTY FOR KILLING THEM HERE, IS THERE?
DROP YOUR BELONG-INGS, AND MAYBE WE'LL LET YOU LIVE.
THERE WE GO.
murmur どよ
murmur どよ
THE HUMANS HAVE SINGLED US OUT. FORESHADOW-ING COMPLETE.

Why does he
look basically
the same as
before his
evolution
....?

GOBTA.

*My growth was more
of the symbolic type!!*

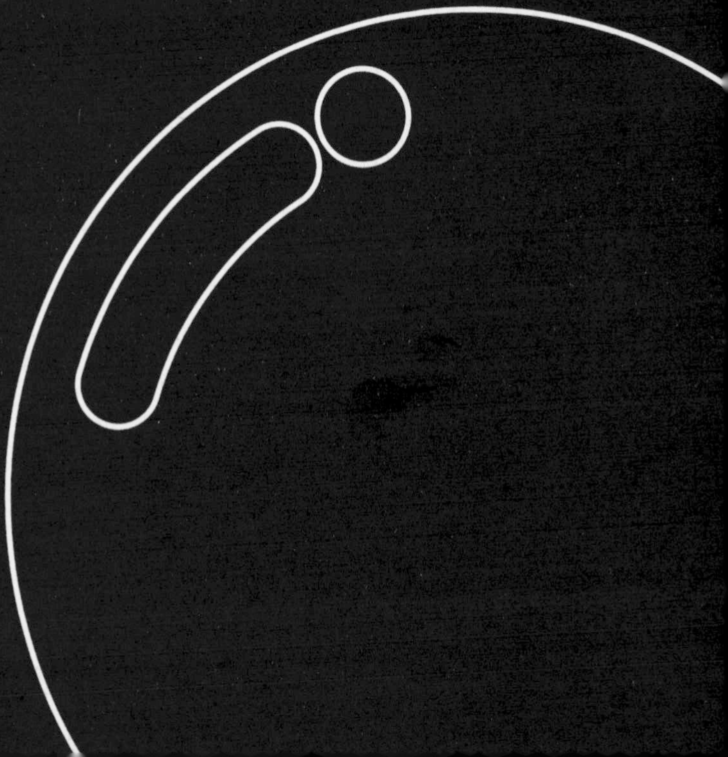

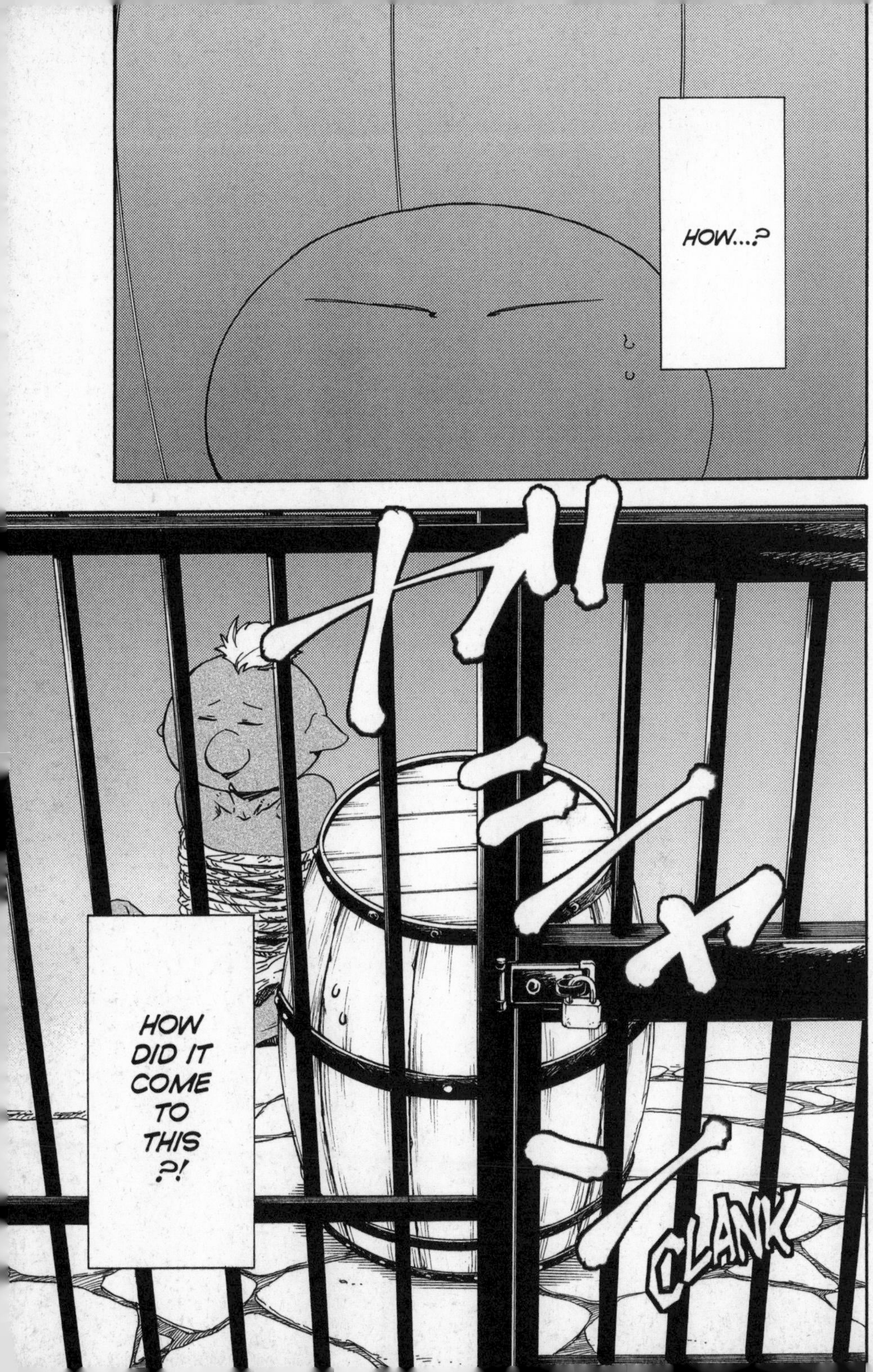
HOW...?
HOW DID IT COME TO THIS?!
CLANK

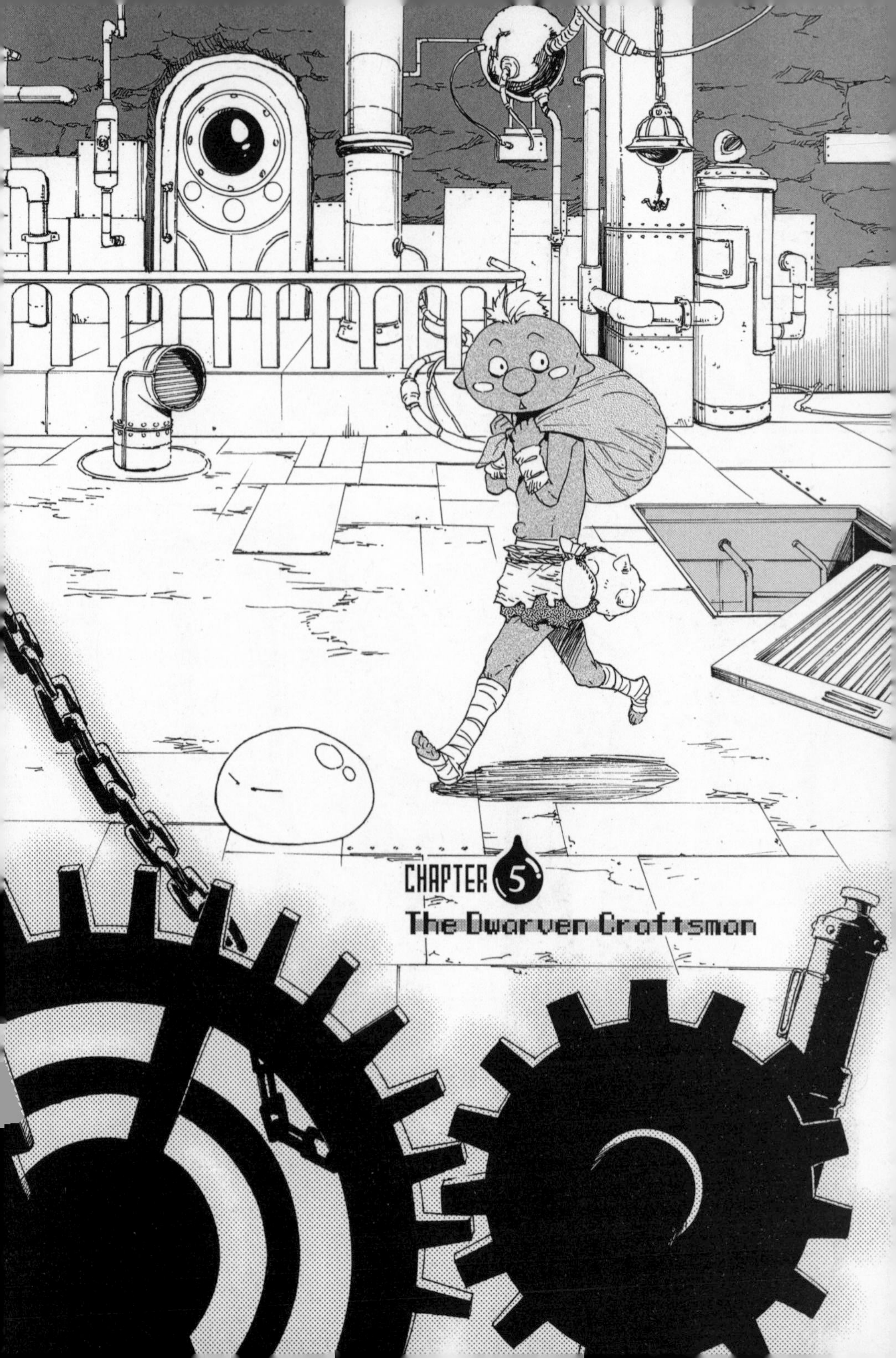

CHAPTER 5
The Dwarven Craftsman

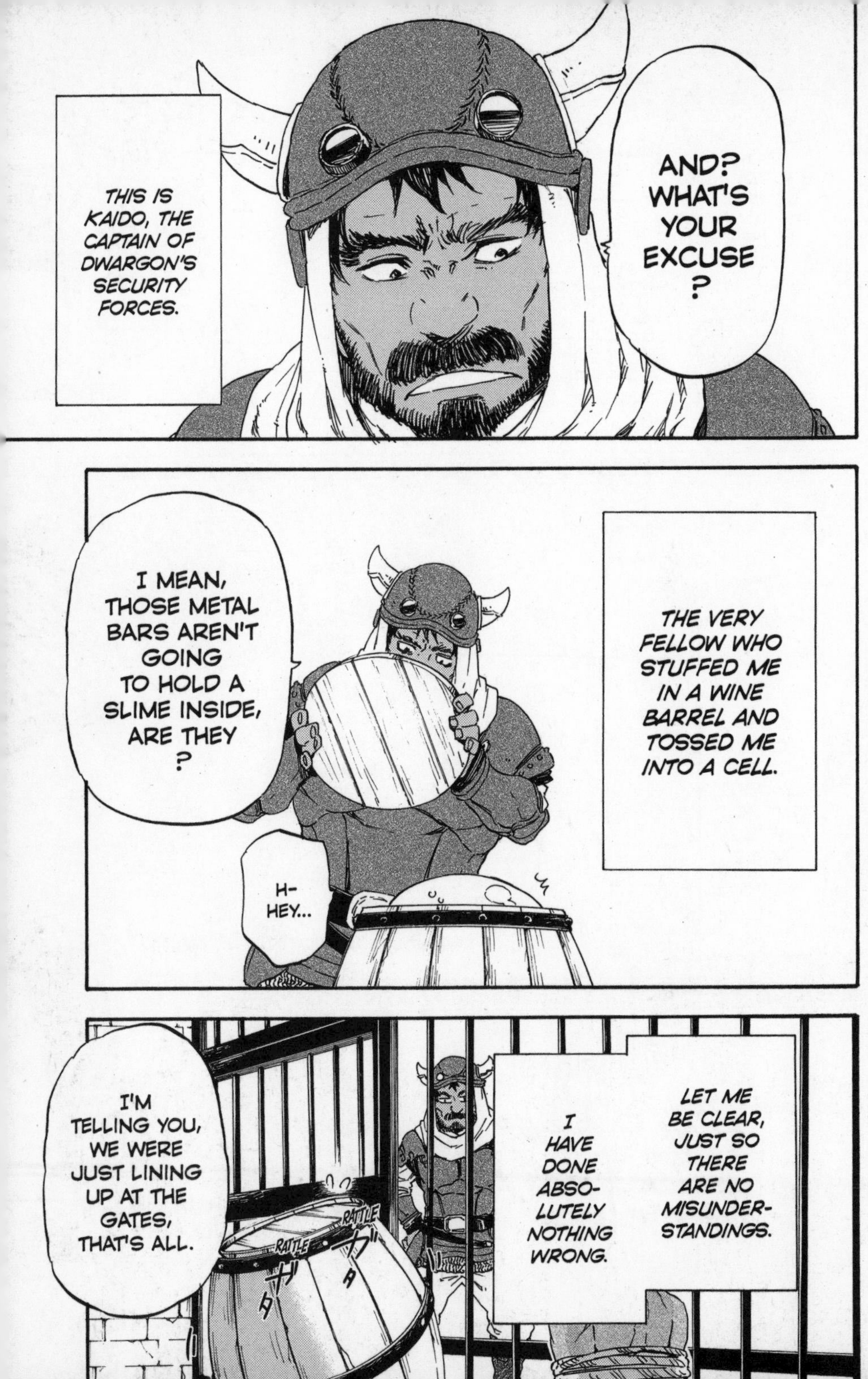
AND? WHAT'S YOUR EXCUSE?
THIS IS KAIDO, THE CAPTAIN OF DWARGON'S SECURITY FORCES.
THE VERY FELLOW WHO STUFFED ME IN A WINE BARREL AND TOSSED ME INTO A CELL.
I MEAN, THOSE METAL BARS AREN'T GOING TO HOLD A SLIME INSIDE, ARE THEY?
H-HEY...
LET ME BE CLEAR, JUST SO THERE ARE NO MISUNDERSTANDINGS.
I HAVE DONE ABSOLUTELY NOTHING WRONG.
RATTLE
RATTLE
I'M TELLING YOU, WE WERE JUST LINING UP AT THE GATES, THAT'S ALL.

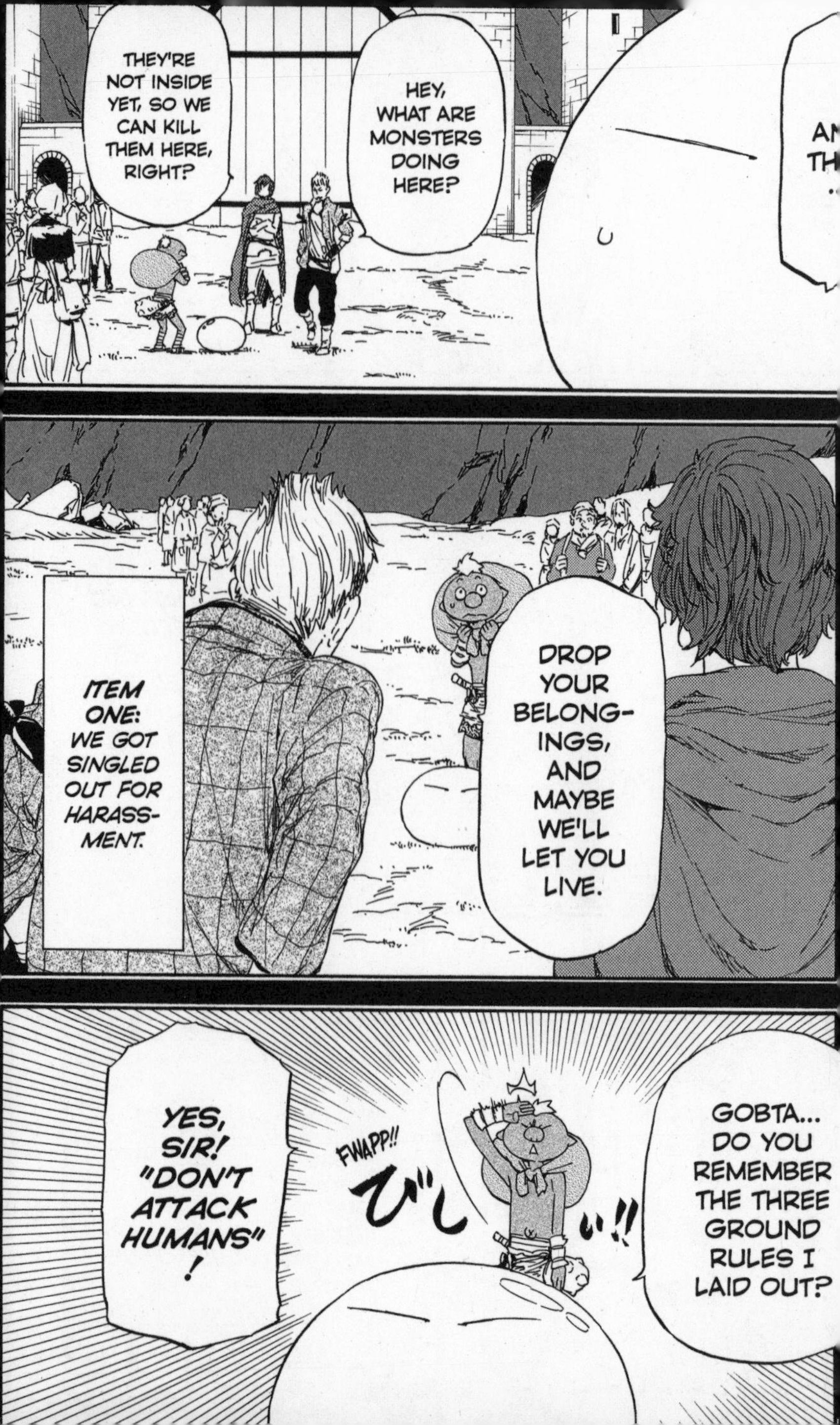
HEY, WHAT ARE MONSTERS DOING HERE?
THEY'RE NOT INSIDE YET, SO WE CAN KILL THEM HERE, RIGHT?
DROP YOUR BELONGINGS, AND MAYBE WE'LL LET YOU LIVE.
ITEM ONE: WE GOT SINGLED OUT FOR HARASSMENT.
GOBTA... DO YOU REMEMBER THE THREE GROUND RULES I LAID OUT?
びしぃ!!
FWAPP!!
YES, SIR! "DON'T ATTACK HUMANS"!

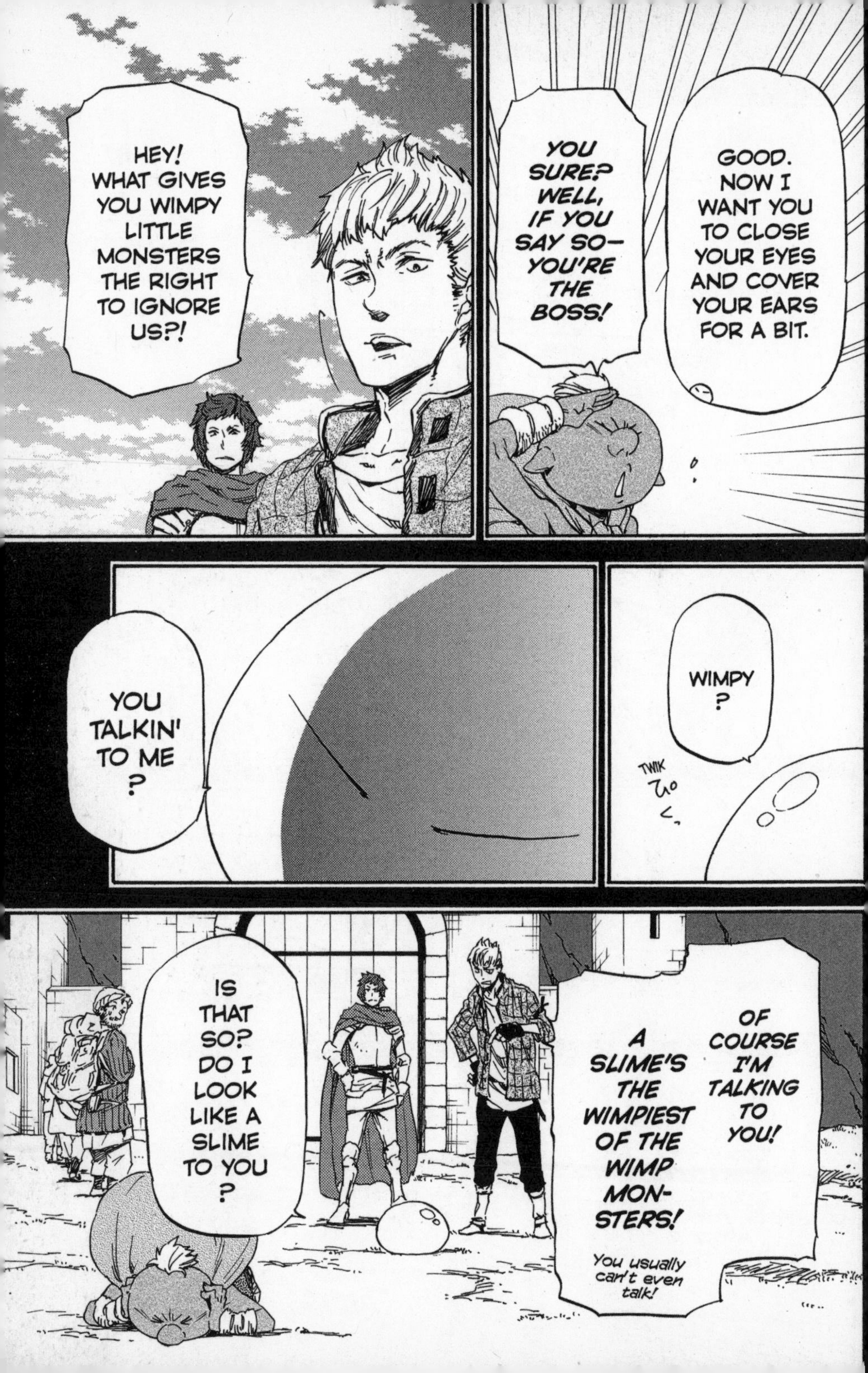
GOOD. NOW I WANT YOU TO CLOSE YOUR EYES AND COVER YOUR EARS FOR A BIT.
YOU SURE? WELL, IF YOU SAY SO— YOU'RE THE BOSS!
HEY! WHAT GIVES YOU WIMPY LITTLE MONSTERS THE RIGHT TO IGNORE US?!
WIMPY ?
TWIK
YOU TALKIN' TO ME ?
OF COURSE I'M TALKING TO YOU!
A SLIME'S THE WIMPIEST OF THE WIMP MON-STERS!
You usually can't even talk!
IS THAT SO? DO I LOOK LIKE A SLIME TO YOU ?

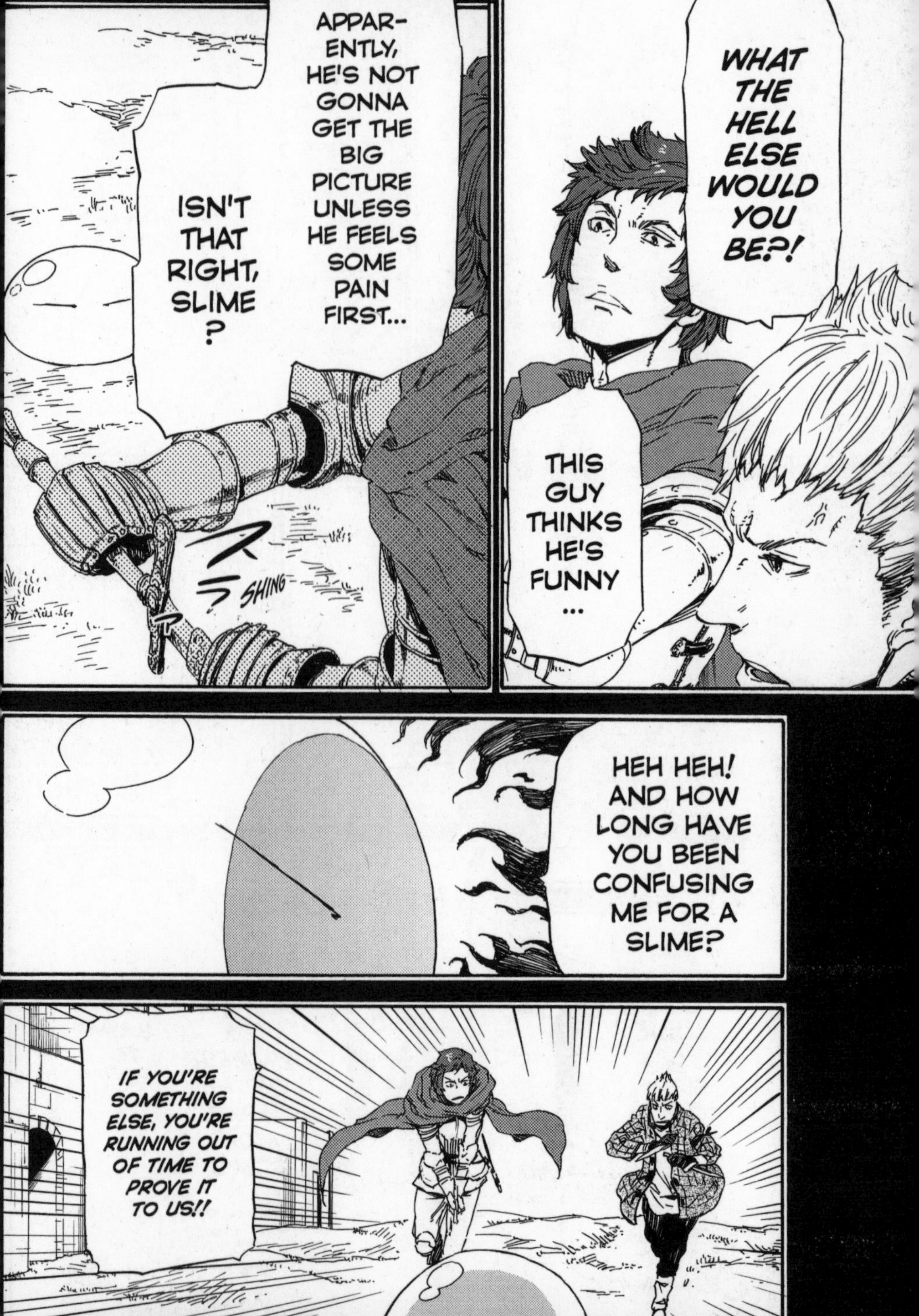
WHAT THE HELL ELSE WOULD YOU BE?!
THIS GUY THINKS HE'S FUNNY...
APPARENTLY, HE'S NOT GONNA GET THE BIG PICTURE UNLESS HE FEELS SOME PAIN FIRST...
ISN'T THAT RIGHT, SLIME?
SHING
HEH HEH! AND HOW LONG HAVE YOU BEEN CONFUSING ME FOR A SLIME?
IF YOU'RE SOMETHING ELSE, YOU'RE RUNNING OUT OF TIME TO PROVE IT TO US!!

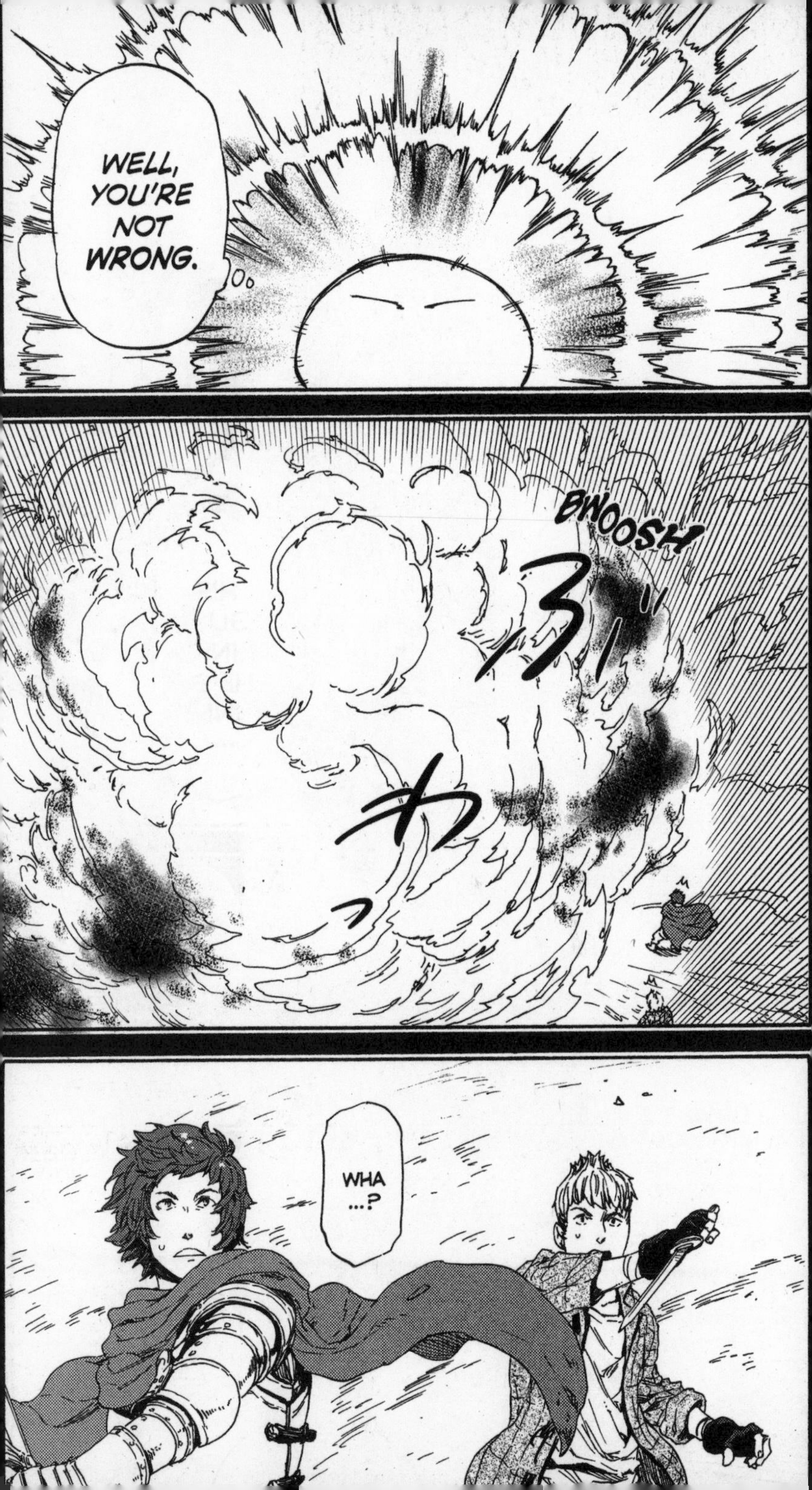
WELL, YOU'RE NOT WRONG.
BWOOSH
WHA ...?

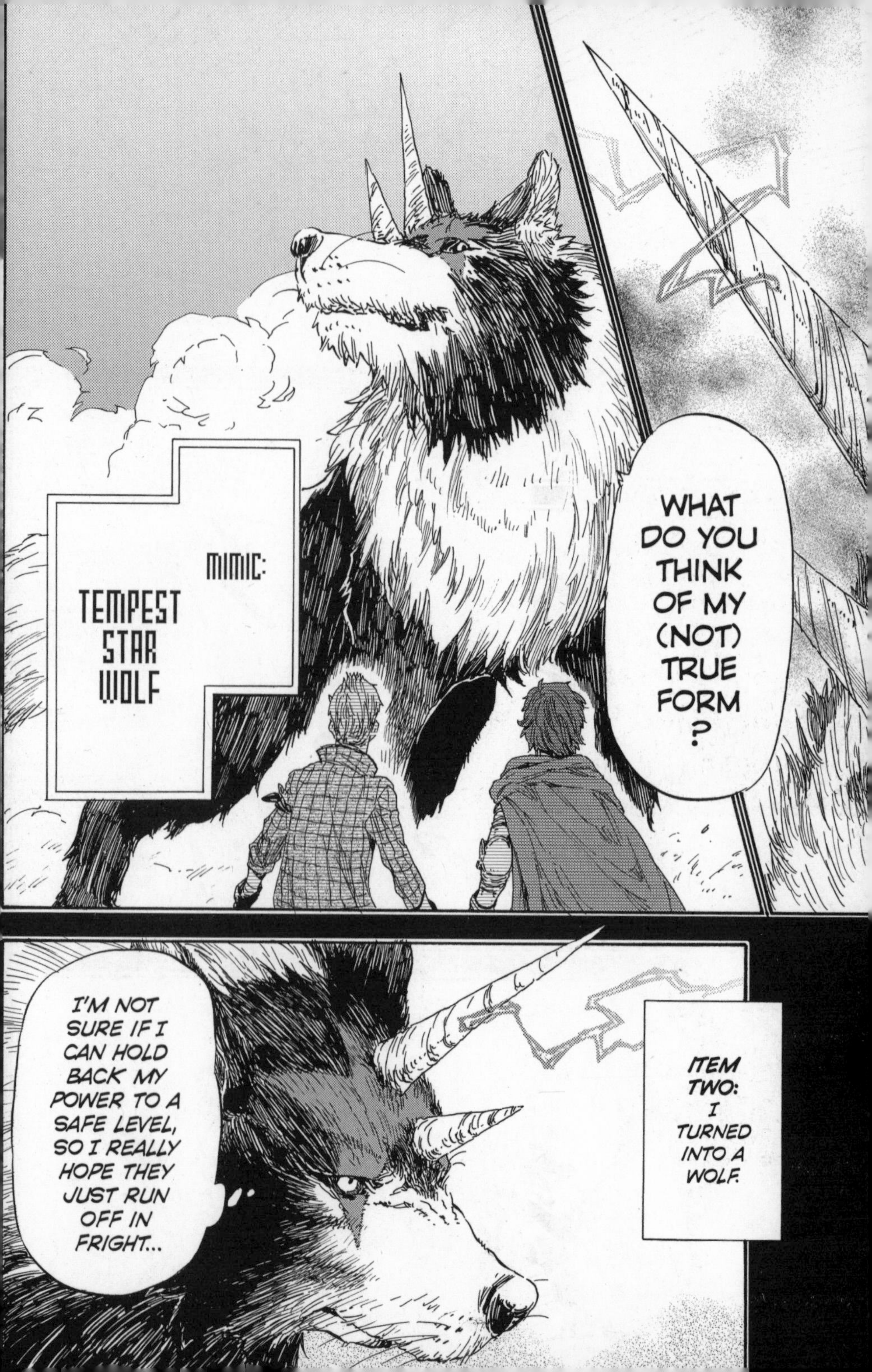
WHAT DO YOU THINK OF MY (NOT) TRUE FORM?
MIMIC: TEMPEST STAR WOLF
ITEM TWO: I TURNED INTO A WOLF.
I'M NOT SURE IF I CAN HOLD BACK MY POWER TO A SAFE LEVEL, SO I REALLY HOPE THEY JUST RUN OFF IN FRIGHT...

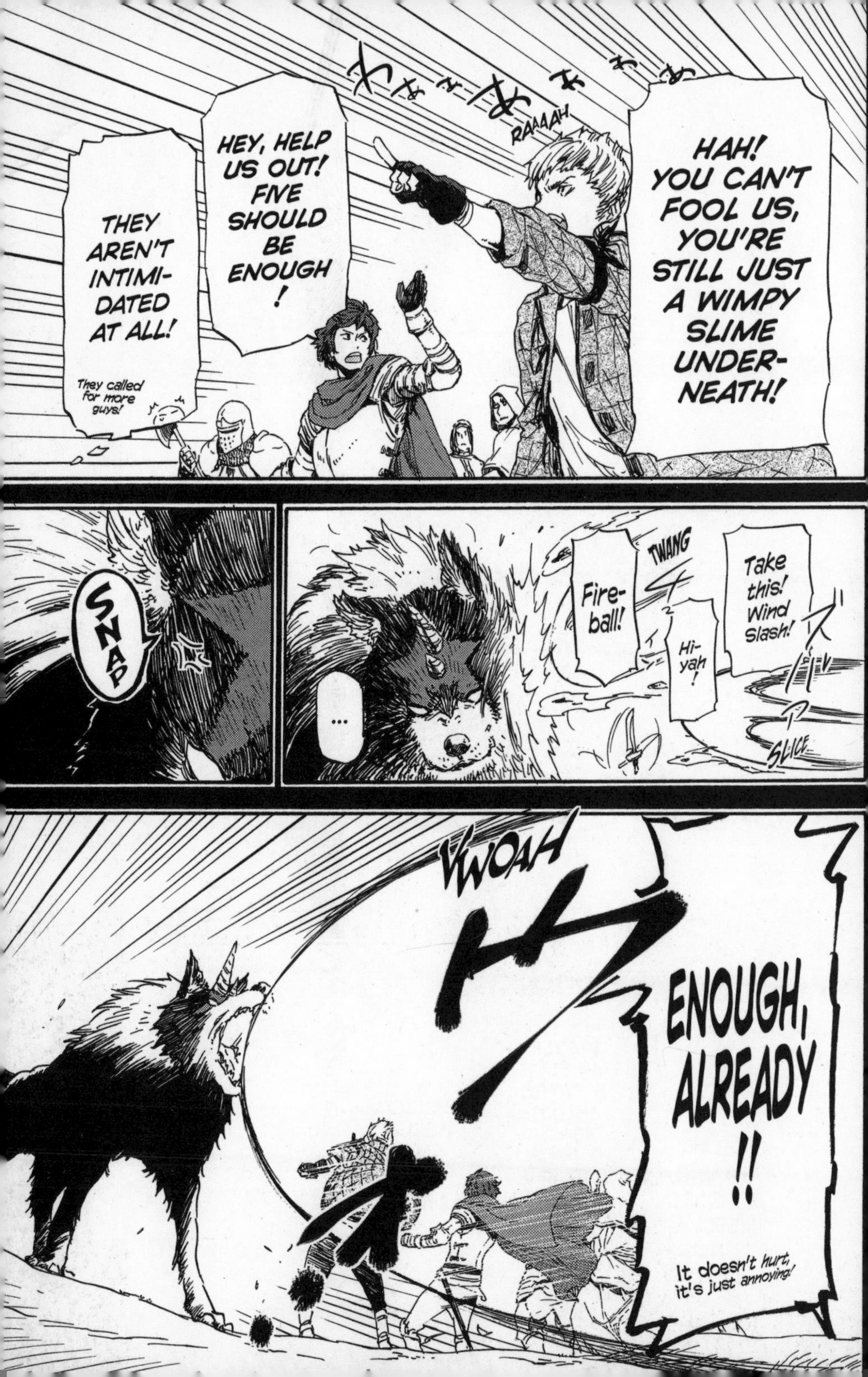
HAH! YOU CAN'T FOOL US, YOU'RE STILL JUST A WIMPY SLIME UNDERNEATH!
RAAAAH
HEY, HELP US OUT! FIVE SHOULD BE ENOUGH!
THEY AREN'T INTIMIDATED AT ALL!
They called for more guys!
Take this! Wind Slash!
SLICE
Hi-yah!
TWANG
Fireball!
...
SNAP
ENOUGH, ALREADY!!
It doesn't hurt, it's just annoying!
VWOAH

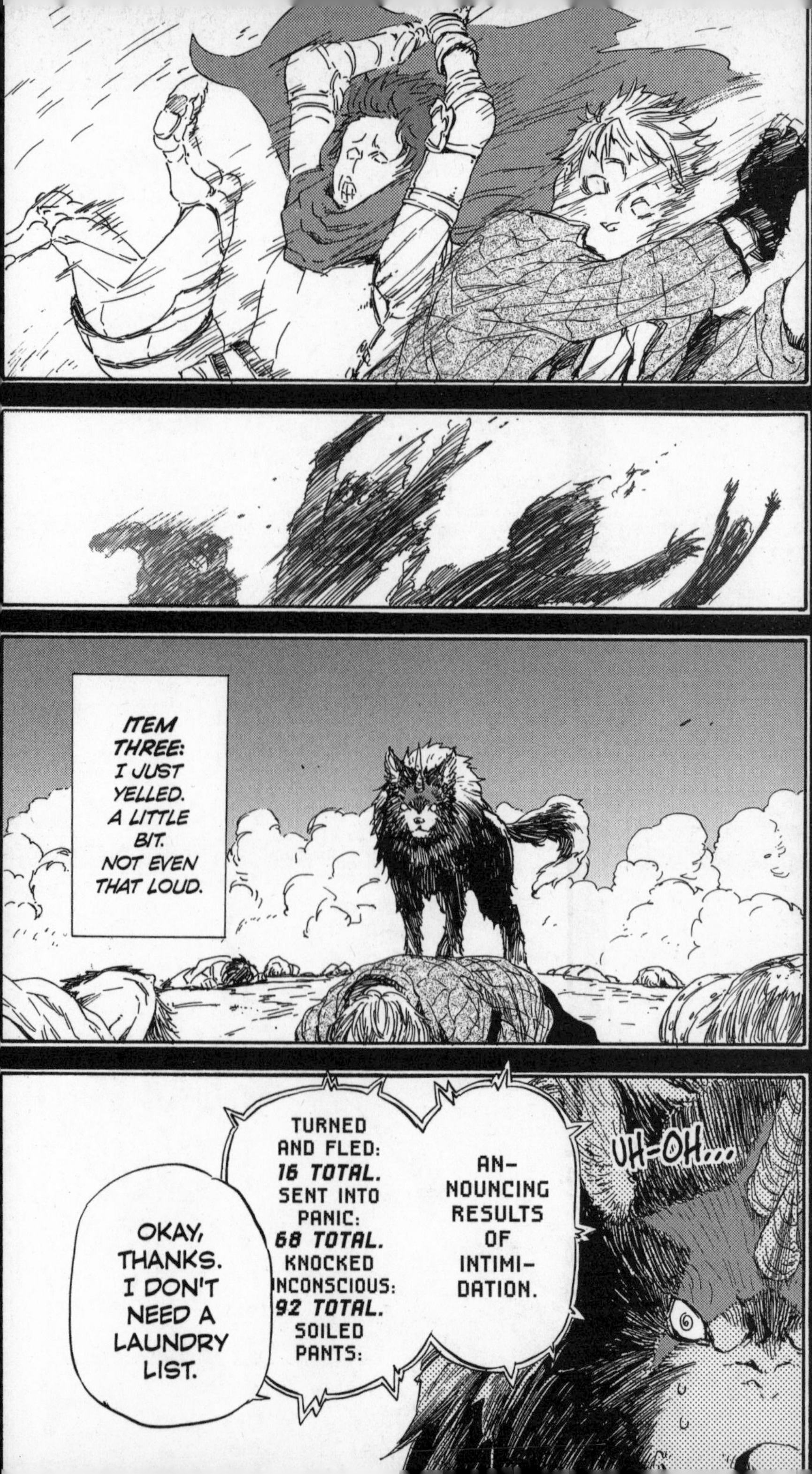
ITEM THREE: I JUST YELLED. A LITTLE BIT. NOT EVEN THAT LOUD.
UH-OH...
AN-NOUNCING RESULTS OF INTIMI-DATION.
TURNED AND FLED: 16 TOTAL. SENT INTO PANIC: 68 TOTAL. KNOCKED UNCONSCIOUS: 92 TOTAL. SOILED PANTS:
OKAY, THANKS. I DON'T NEED A LAUNDRY LIST.

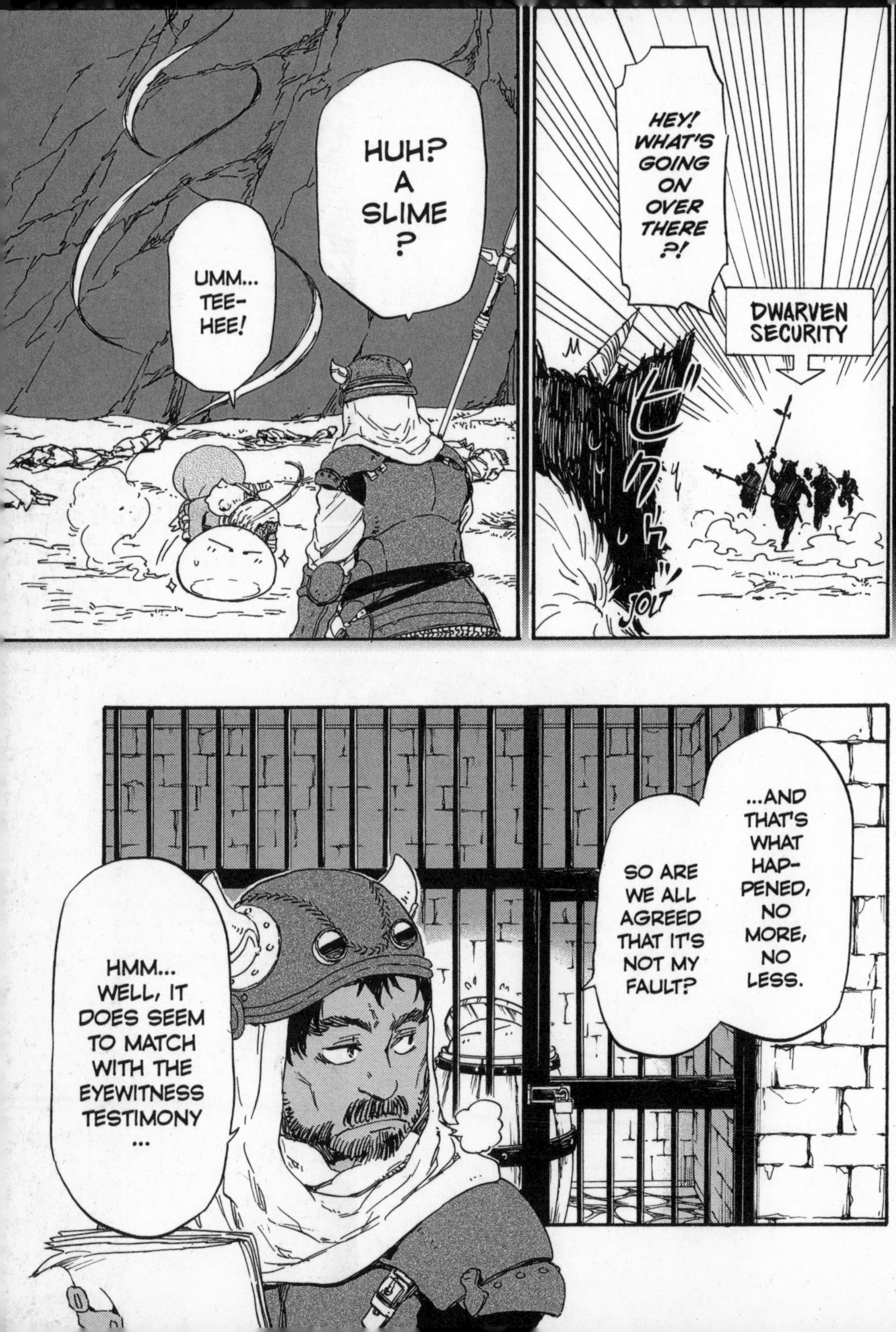
HEY! WHAT'S GOING ON OVER THERE?!
DWARVEN SECURITY
JOLT
HUH? A SLIME?
UMM... TEE-HEE!
...AND THAT'S WHAT HAPPENED, NO MORE, NO LESS.
SO ARE WE ALL AGREED THAT IT'S NOT MY FAULT?
HMM... WELL, IT DOES SEEM TO MATCH WITH THE EYEWITNESS TESTIMONY...

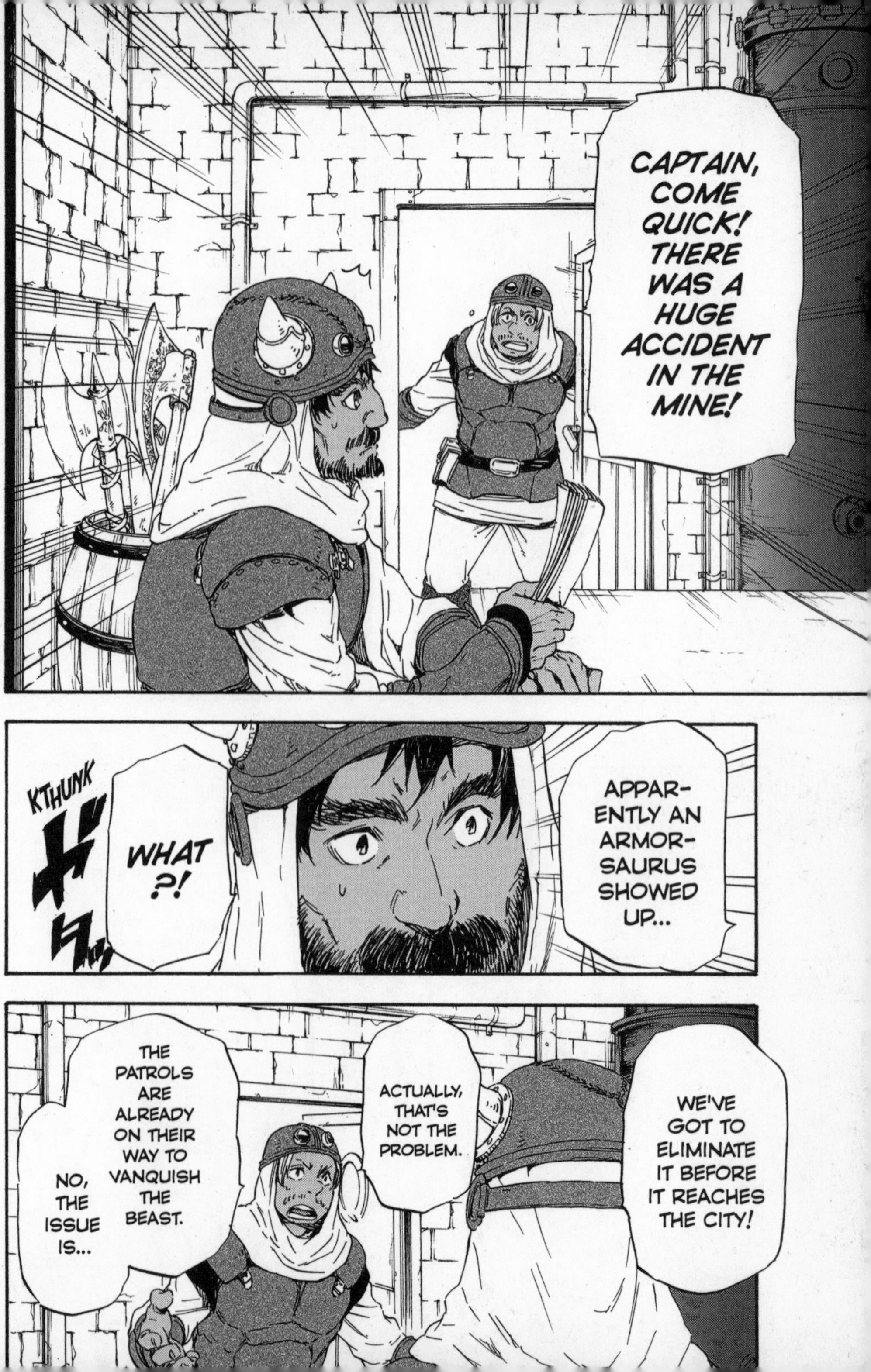

CAPTAIN, COME QUICK! THERE WAS A HUGE ACCIDENT IN THE MINE!
APPAR-ENTLY AN ARMOR-SAURUS SHOWED UP...
WHAT?!
KTHUNK
WE'VE GOT TO ELIMINATE IT BEFORE IT REACHES THE CITY!
ACTUALLY, THAT'S NOT THE PROBLEM.
THE PATROLS ARE ALREADY ON THEIR WAY TO VANQUISH THE BEAST.
NO, THE ISSUE IS...

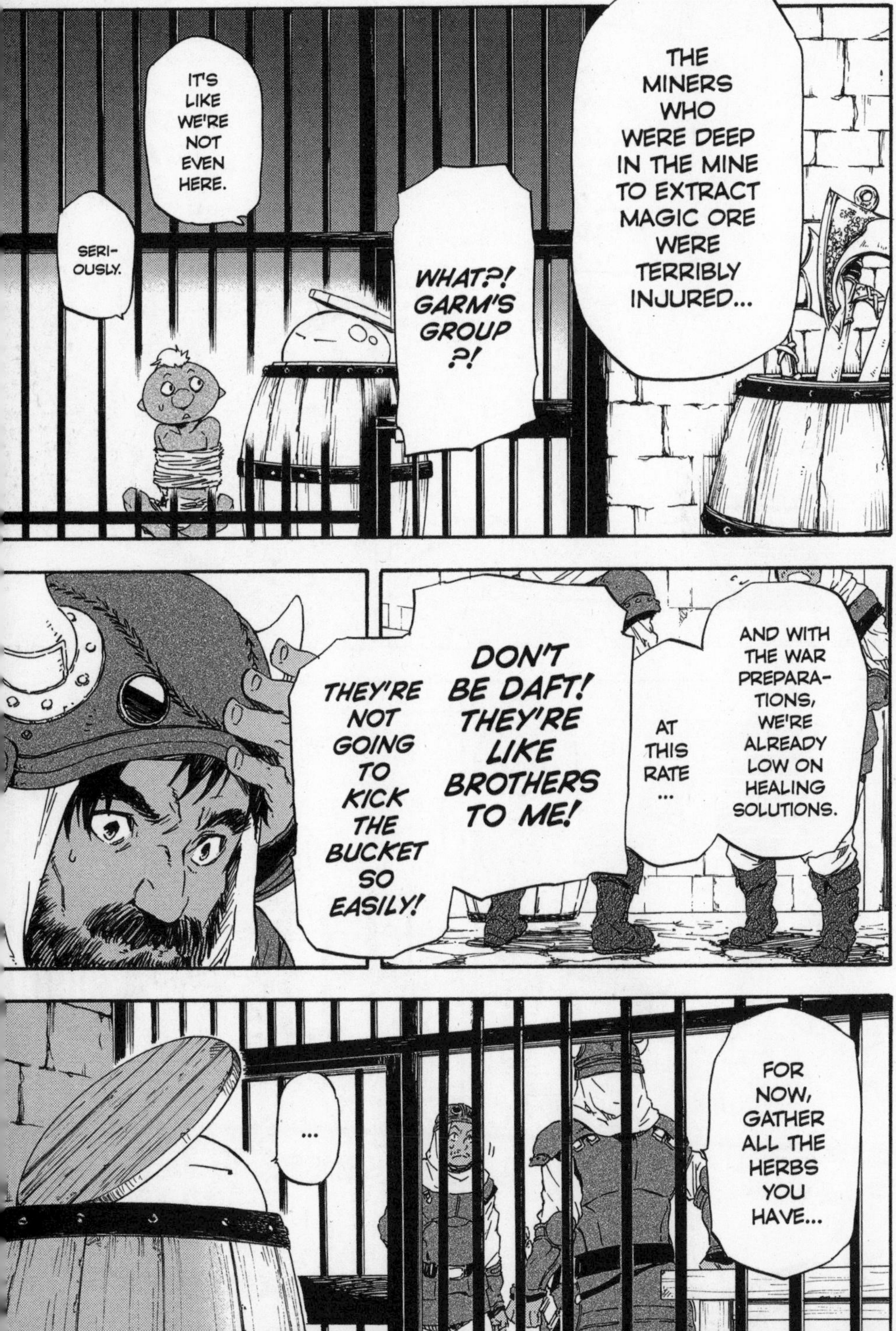
THE MINERS WHO WERE DEEP IN THE MINE TO EXTRACT MAGIC ORE WERE TERRIBLY INJURED...
WHAT?! GARM'S GROUP?!
IT'S LIKE WE'RE NOT EVEN HERE.
SERIOUSLY.
AND WITH THE WAR PREPARATIONS, WE'RE ALREADY LOW ON HEALING SOLUTIONS.
AT THIS RATE...
DON'T BE DAFT! THEY'RE LIKE BROTHERS TO ME!
THEY'RE NOT GOING TO KICK THE BUCKET SO EASILY!
FOR NOW, GATHER ALL THE HERBS YOU HAVE...
...

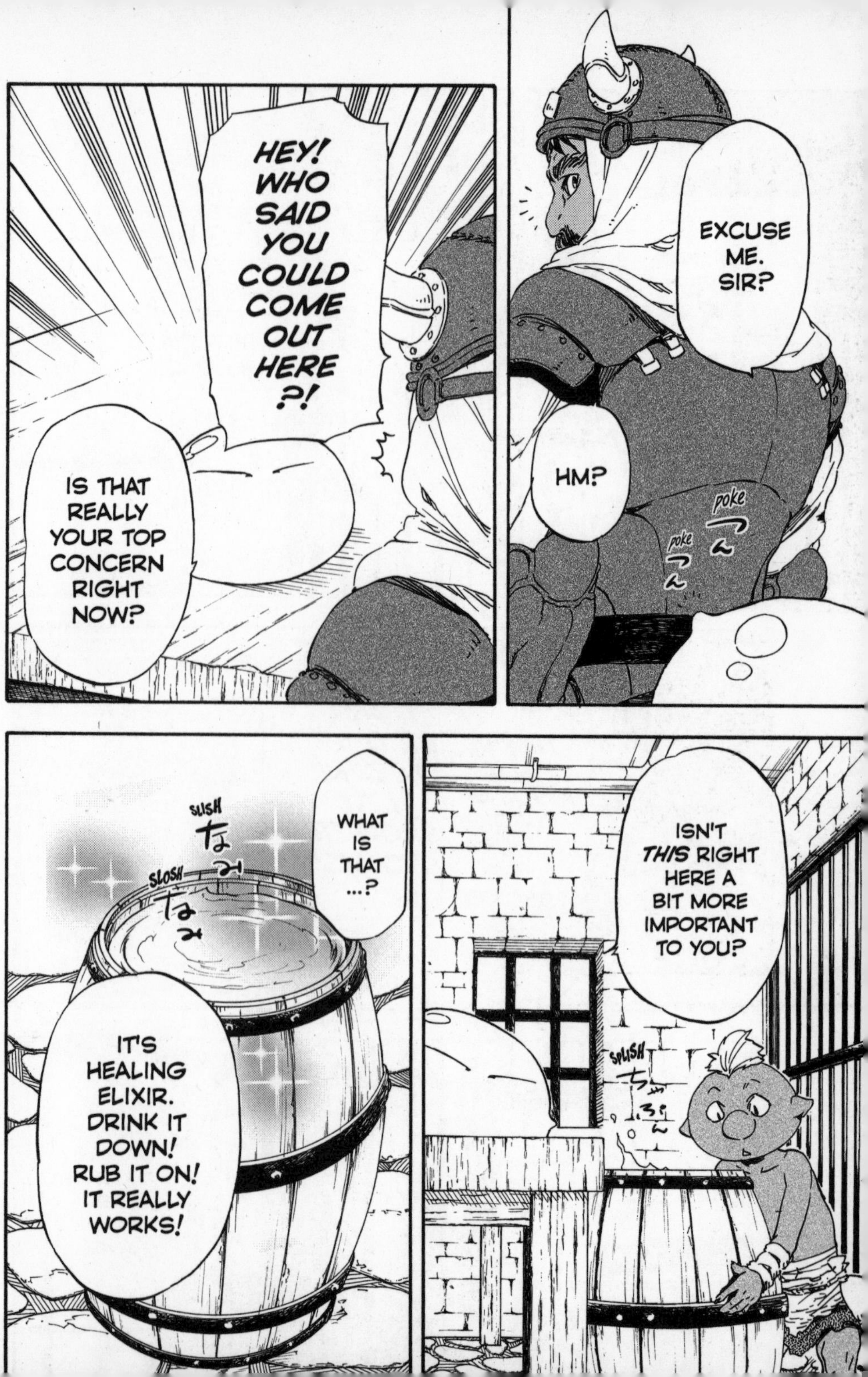
EXCUSE ME. SIR?
HM?
poke
poke
HEY! WHO SAID YOU COULD COME OUT HERE?!
IS THAT REALLY YOUR TOP CONCERN RIGHT NOW?
ISN'T *THIS* RIGHT HERE A BIT MORE IMPORTANT TO YOU?
SPLISH
WHAT IS THAT ...?
SLISH
SLOSH
IT'S HEALING ELIXIR. DRINK IT DOWN! RUB IT ON! IT REALLY WORKS!

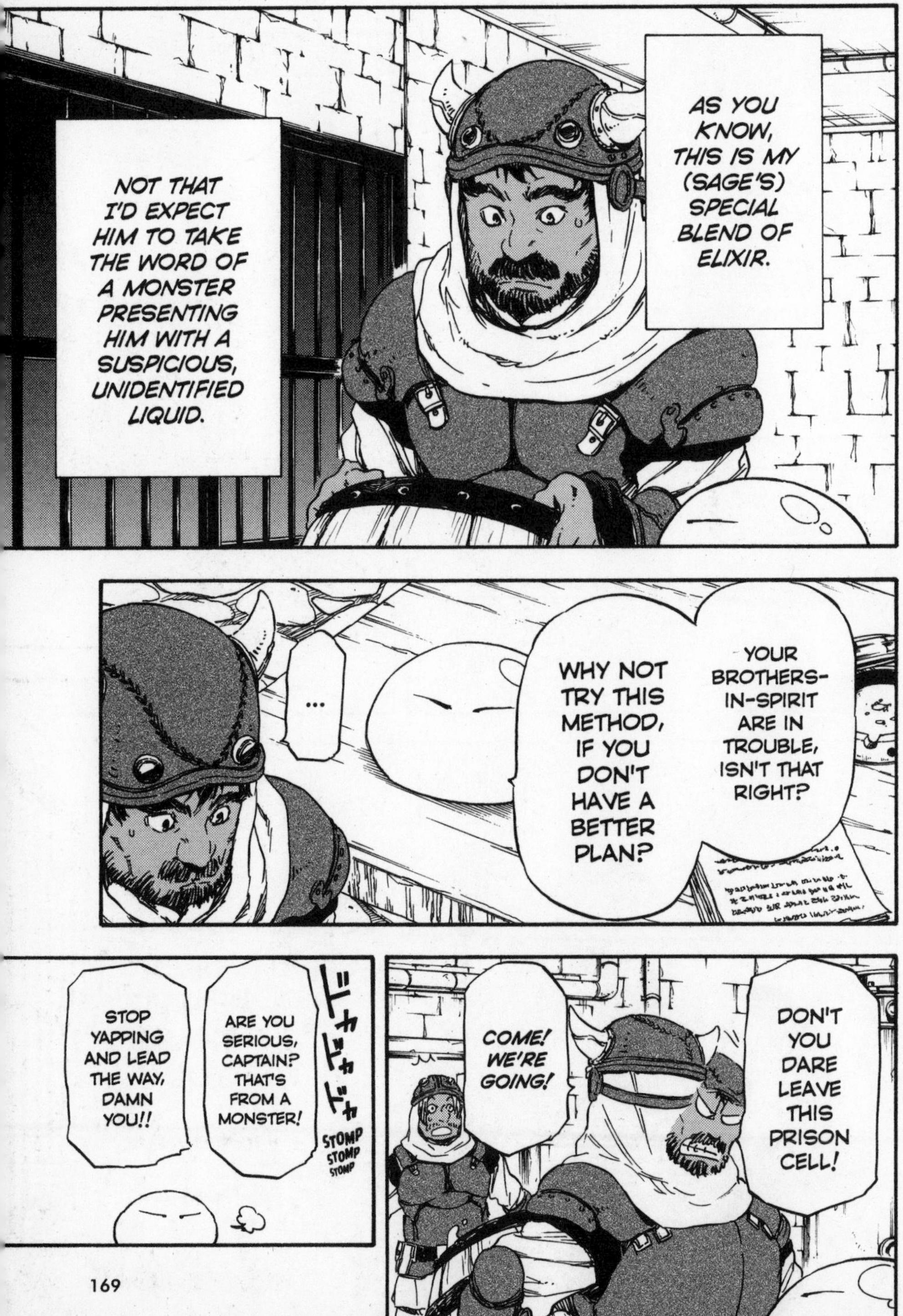

AS YOU KNOW, THIS IS MY (SAGE'S) SPECIAL BLEND OF ELIXIR.
NOT THAT I'D EXPECT HIM TO TAKE THE WORD OF A MONSTER PRESENTING HIM WITH A SUSPICIOUS, UNIDENTIFIED LIQUID.
YOUR BROTHERS-IN-SPIRIT ARE IN TROUBLE, ISN'T THAT RIGHT?
WHY NOT TRY THIS METHOD, IF YOU DON'T HAVE A BETTER PLAN?
...
DON'T YOU DARE LEAVE THIS PRISON CELL!
COME! WE'RE GOING!
ARE YOU SERIOUS, CAPTAIN? THAT'S FROM A MONSTER!
STOP YAPPING AND LEAD THE WAY, DAMN YOU!!
STOMP STOMP STOMP

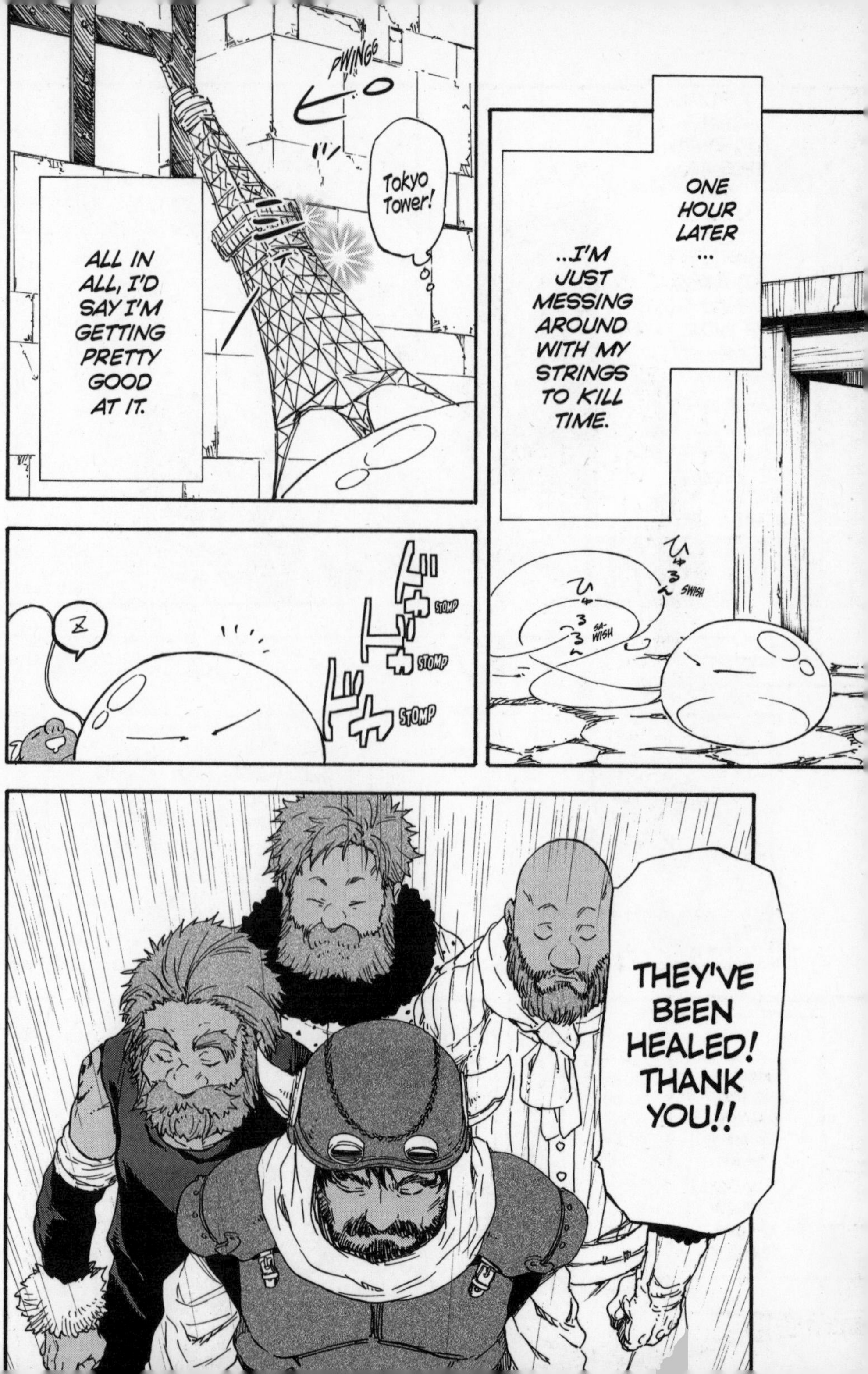
ONE HOUR LATER ...
...I'M JUST MESSING AROUND WITH MY STRINGS TO KILL TIME.
PWING
Tokyo Tower!
ALL IN ALL, I'D SAY I'M GETTING PRETTY GOOD AT IT.
SWISH
SA-WISH
STOMP
STOMP
STOMP
Z
THEY'VE BEEN HEALED! THANK YOU!!

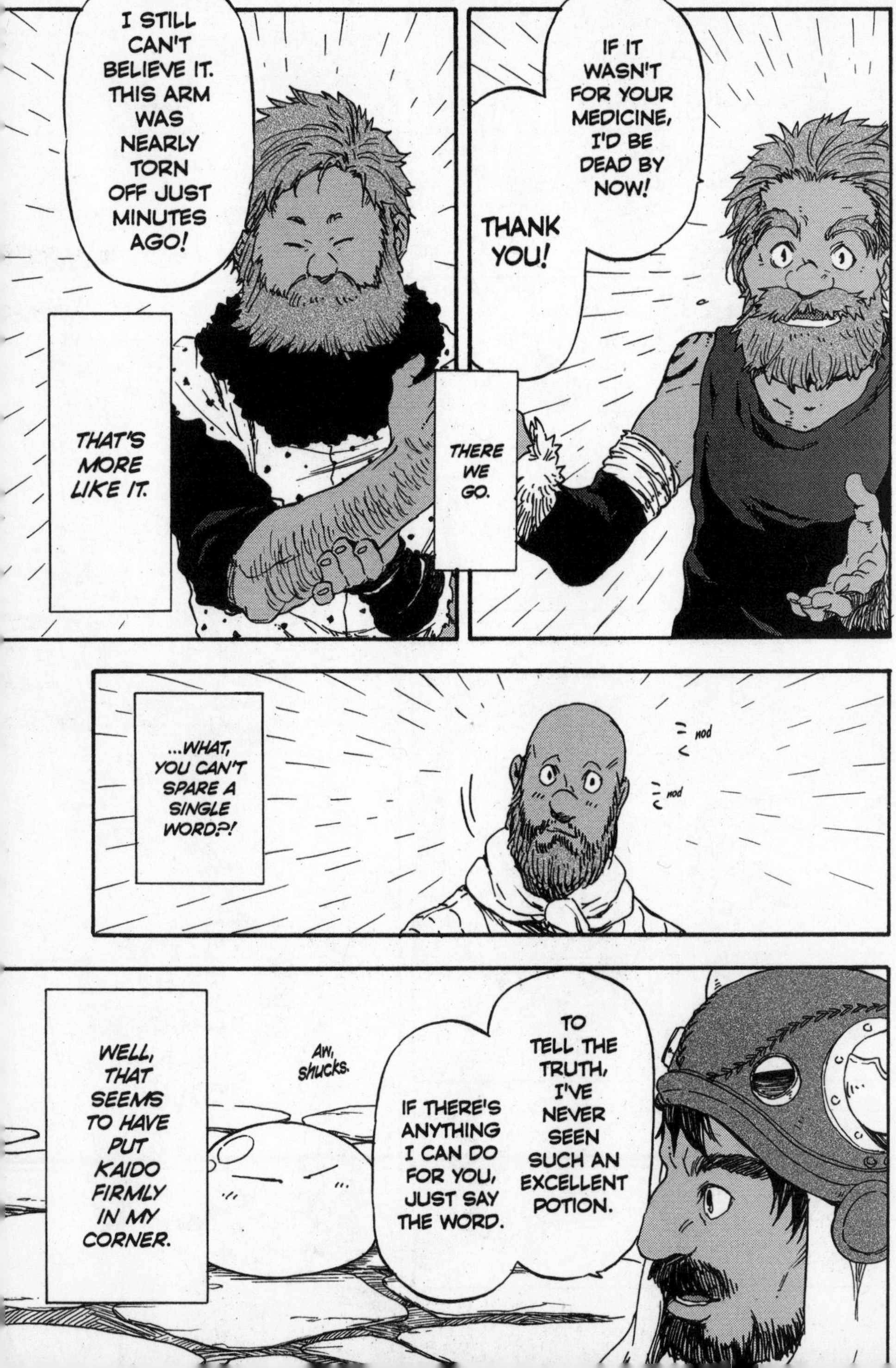
IF IT WASN'T FOR YOUR MEDICINE, I'D BE DEAD BY NOW!
THANK YOU!
THERE WE GO.
I STILL CAN'T BELIEVE IT. THIS ARM WAS NEARLY TORN OFF JUST MINUTES AGO!
THAT'S MORE LIKE IT.
nod
nod
...WHAT, YOU CAN'T SPARE A SINGLE WORD?!
TO TELL THE TRUTH, I'VE NEVER SEEN SUCH AN EXCELLENT POTION.
IF THERE'S ANYTHING I CAN DO FOR YOU, JUST SAY THE WORD.
Aw, shucks.
WELL, THAT SEEMS TO HAVE PUT KAIDO FIRMLY IN MY CORNER.

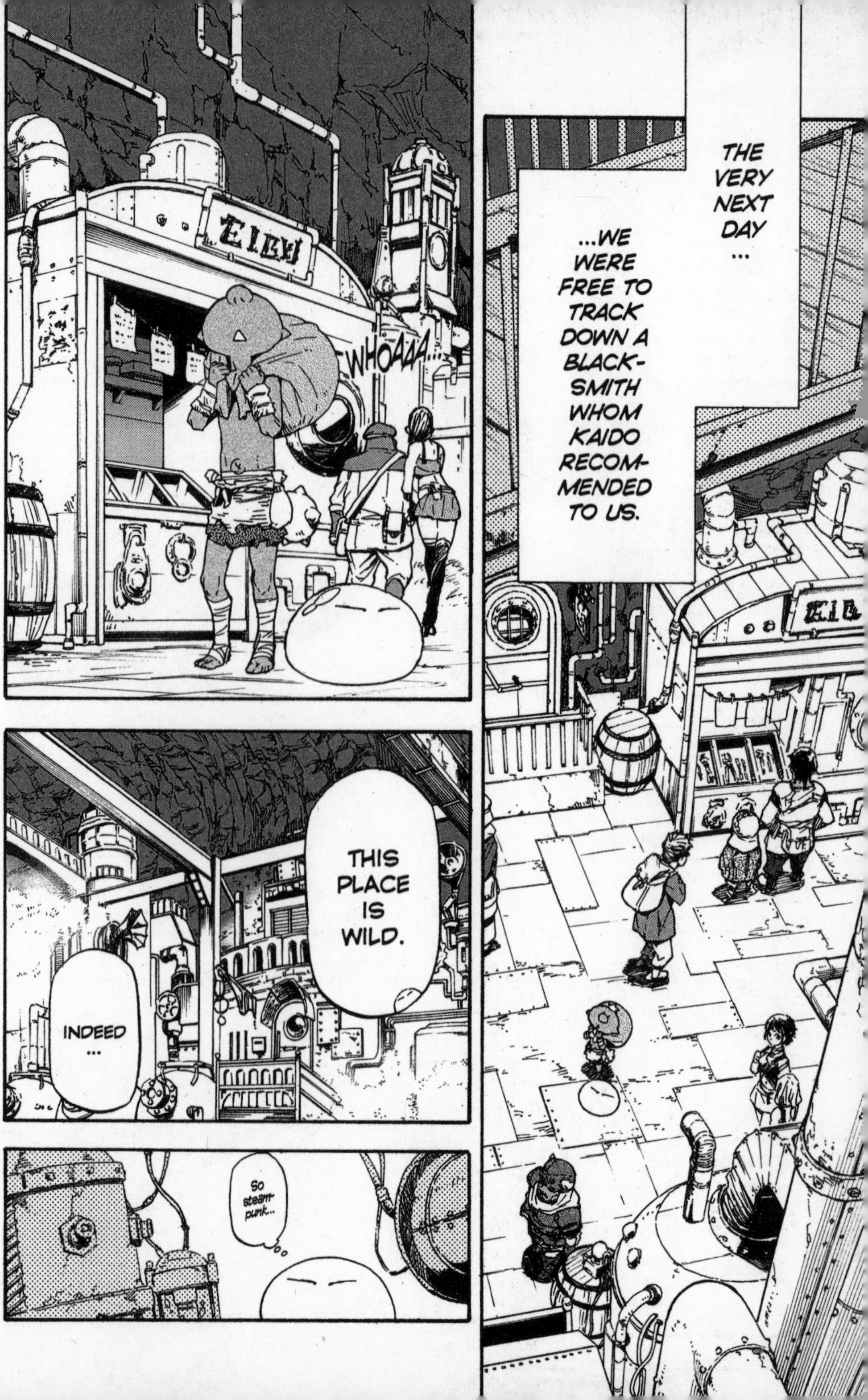
THE VERY NEXT DAY...
...WE WERE FREE TO TRACK DOWN A BLACKSMITH WHOM KAIDO RECOMMENDED TO US.
WHOAAA...
THIS PLACE IS WILD.
INDEED...
So steampunk...

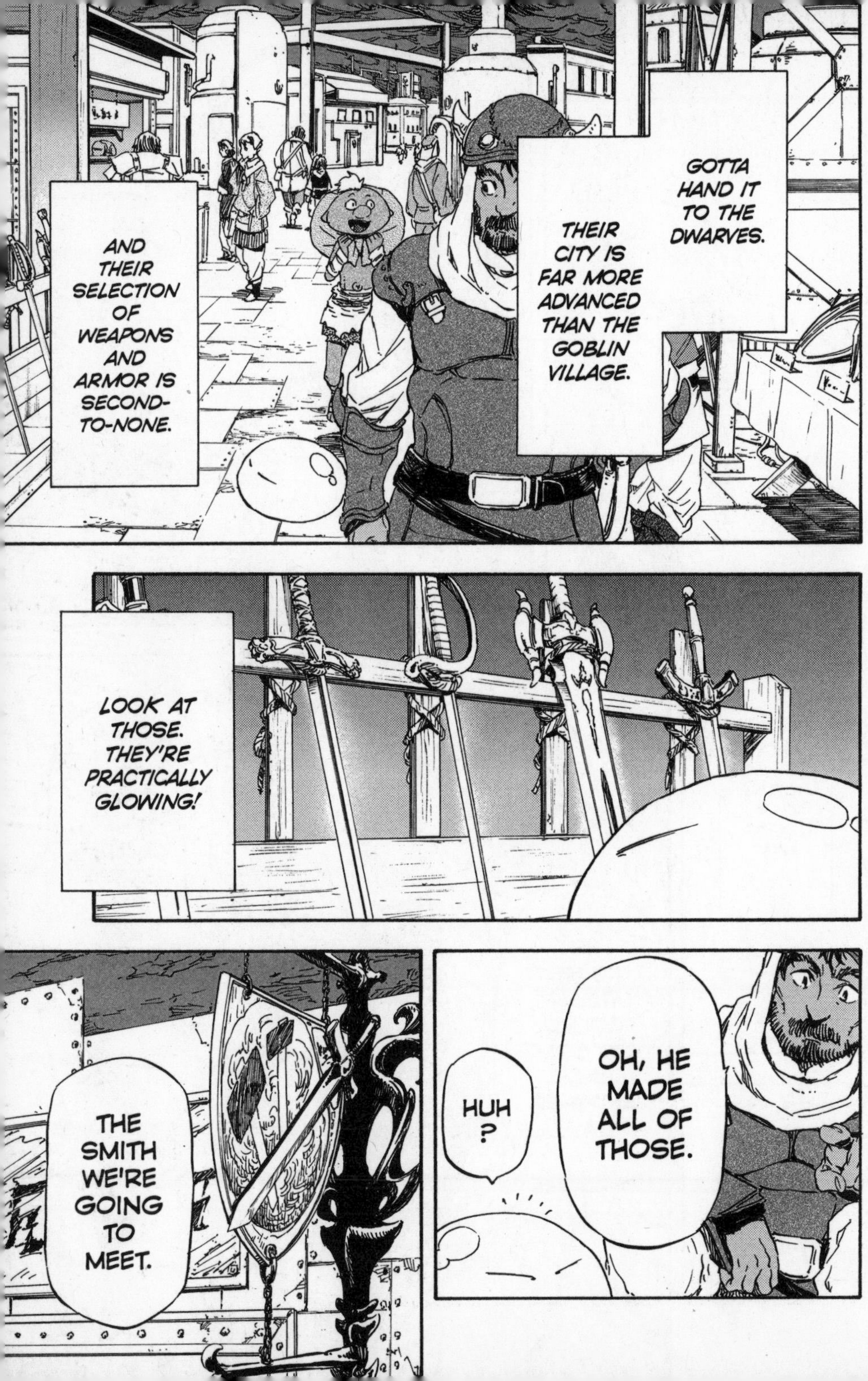
GOTTA HAND IT TO THE DWARVES.
THEIR CITY IS FAR MORE ADVANCED THAN THE GOBLIN VILLAGE.
AND THEIR SELECTION OF WEAPONS AND ARMOR IS SECOND-TO-NONE.
LOOK AT THOSE. THEY'RE PRACTICALLY GLOWING!
OH, HE MADE ALL OF THOSE.
HUH?
THE SMITH WE'RE GOING TO MEET.

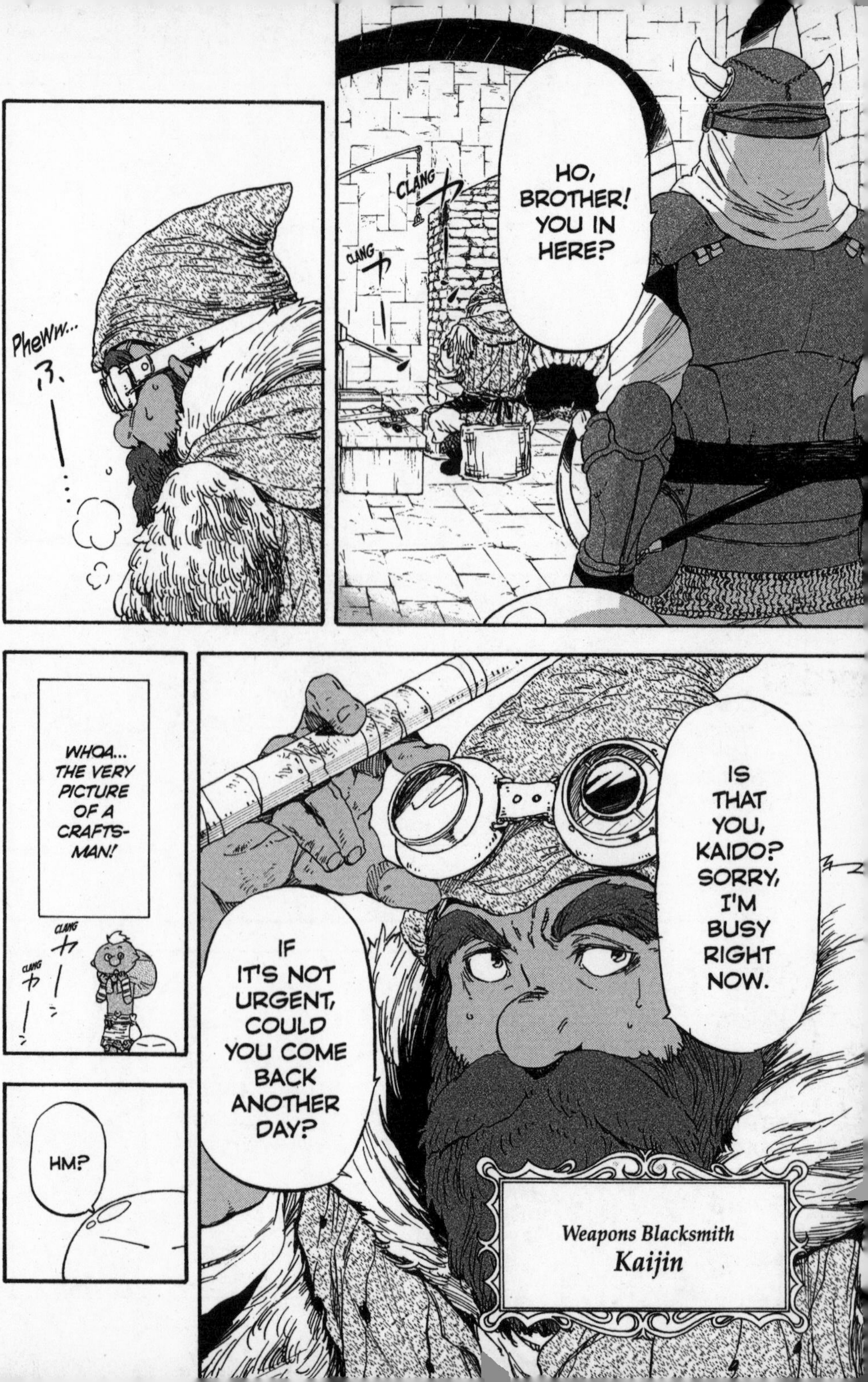
CLANG
CLANG
HO, BROTHER! YOU IN HERE?
Pheww...
IS THAT YOU, KAIDO? SORRY, I'M BUSY RIGHT NOW.
IF IT'S NOT URGENT, COULD YOU COME BACK ANOTHER DAY?
Weapons Blacksmith
Kaijin
WHOA... THE VERY PICTURE OF A CRAFTSMAN!
CLANG
CLANG
HM?

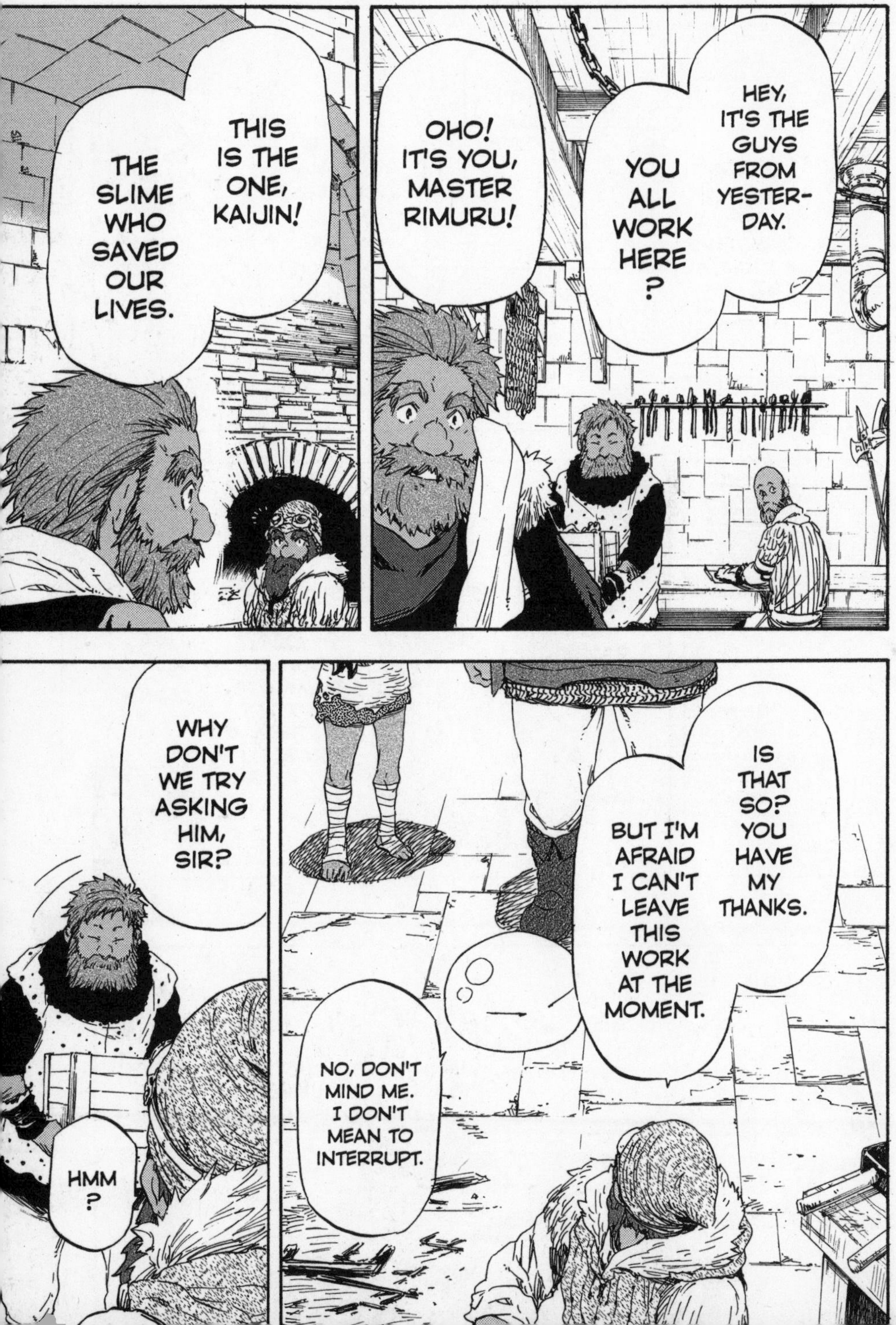
HEY, IT'S THE GUYS FROM YESTER-DAY.
YOU ALL WORK HERE?
OHO! IT'S YOU, MASTER RIMURU!
THIS IS THE ONE, KAIJIN!
THE SLIME WHO SAVED OUR LIVES.
IS THAT SO? YOU HAVE MY THANKS.
BUT I'M AFRAID I CAN'T LEAVE THIS WORK AT THE MOMENT.
NO, DON'T MIND ME. I DON'T MEAN TO INTERRUPT.
WHY DON'T WE TRY ASKING HIM, SIR?
HMM?

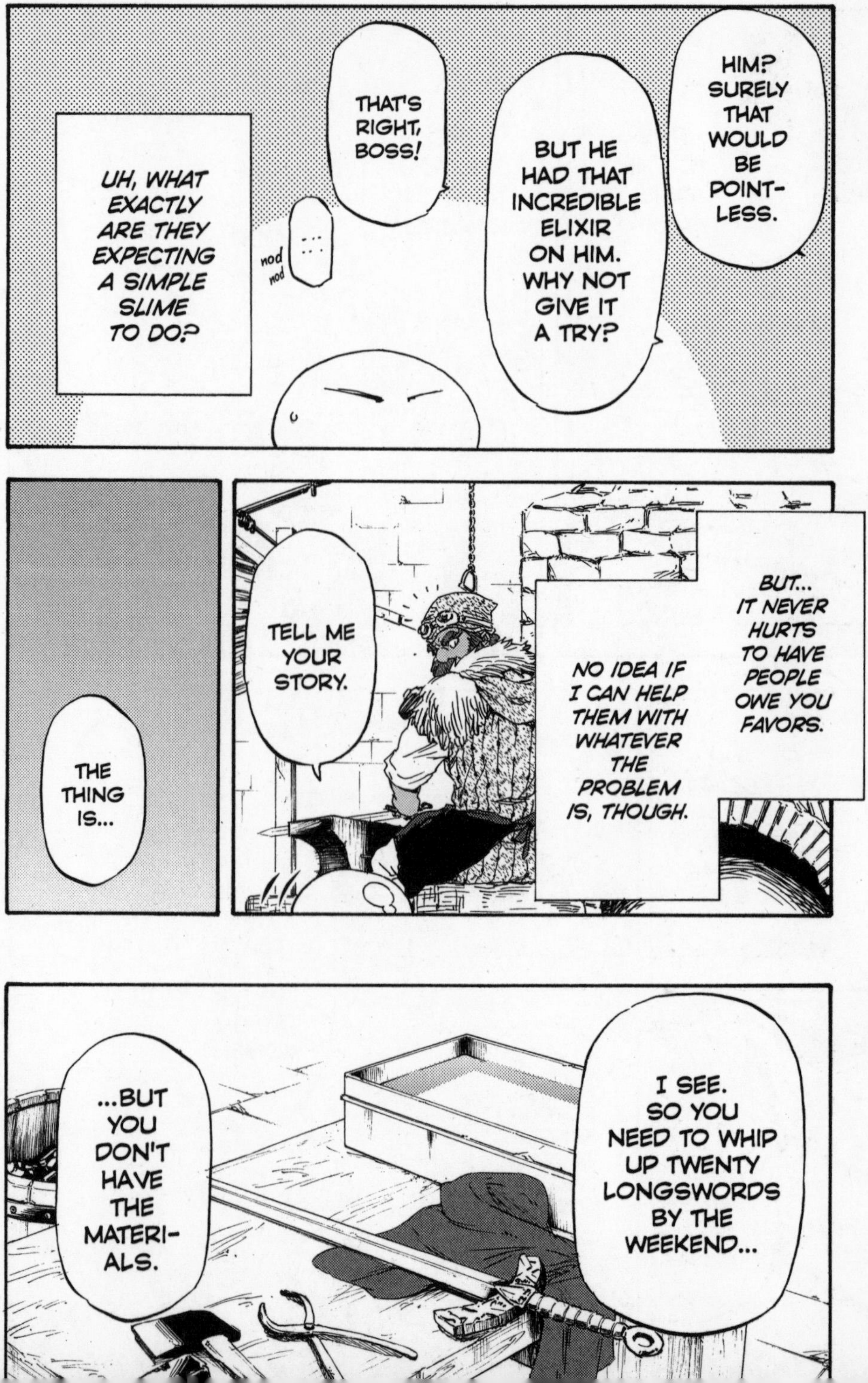
HIM? SURELY THAT WOULD BE POINTLESS.
BUT HE HAD THAT INCREDIBLE ELIXIR ON HIM. WHY NOT GIVE IT A TRY?
THAT'S RIGHT, BOSS!
...
nod nod
UH, WHAT EXACTLY ARE THEY EXPECTING A SIMPLE SLIME TO DO?
BUT... IT NEVER HURTS TO HAVE PEOPLE OWE YOU FAVORS.
NO IDEA IF I CAN HELP THEM WITH WHATEVER THE PROBLEM IS, THOUGH.
TELL ME YOUR STORY.
THE THING IS...
I SEE. SO YOU NEED TO WHIP UP TWENTY LONGSWORDS BY THE WEEKEND...
...BUT YOU DON'T HAVE THE MATERIALS.

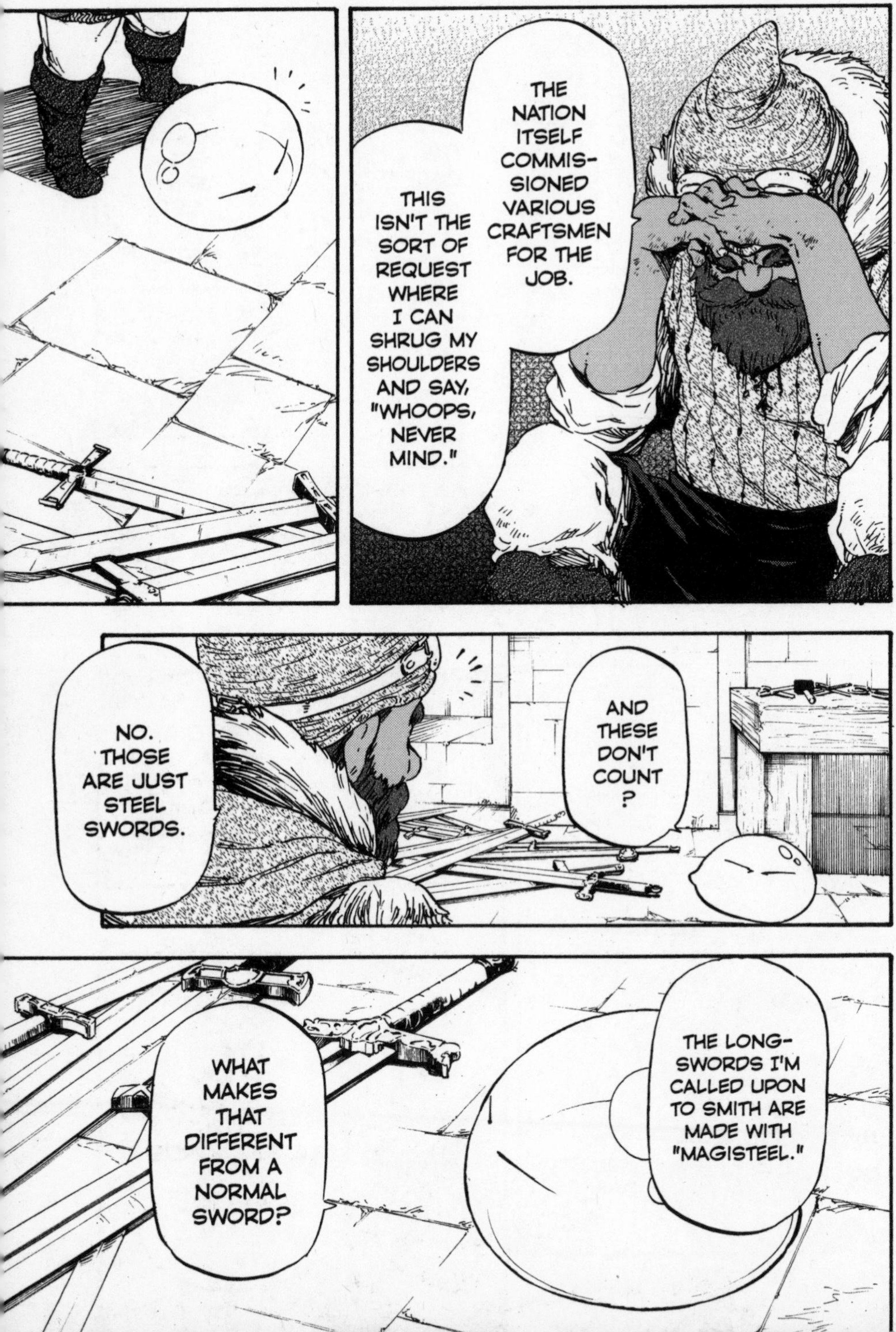
THE NATION ITSELF COMMIS-SIONED VARIOUS CRAFTSMEN FOR THE JOB.
THIS ISN'T THE SORT OF REQUEST WHERE I CAN SHRUG MY SHOULDERS AND SAY, "WHOOPS, NEVER MIND."
AND THESE DON'T COUNT ?
NO. THOSE ARE JUST STEEL SWORDS.
THE LONG-SWORDS I'M CALLED UPON TO SMITH ARE MADE WITH "MAGISTEEL."
WHAT MAKES THAT DIFFERENT FROM A NORMAL SWORD?

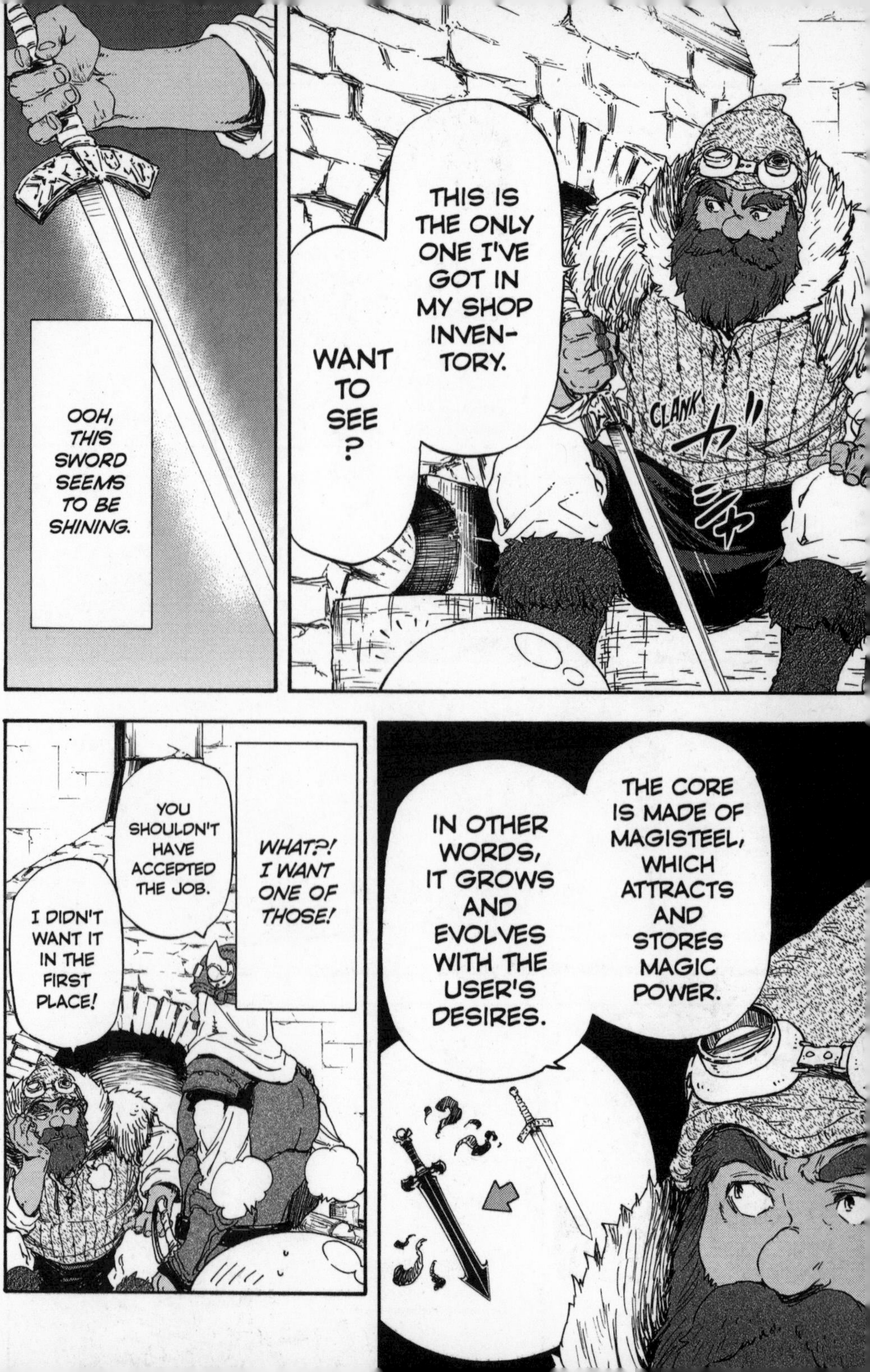
THIS IS THE ONLY ONE I'VE GOT IN MY SHOP INVENTORY.
WANT TO SEE?
CLANK
OOH, THIS SWORD SEEMS TO BE SHINING.
THE CORE IS MADE OF MAGISTEEL, WHICH ATTRACTS AND STORES MAGIC POWER.
IN OTHER WORDS, IT GROWS AND EVOLVES WITH THE USER'S DESIRES.
WHAT?! I WANT ONE OF THOSE!
YOU SHOULDN'T HAVE ACCEPTED THE JOB.
I DIDN'T WANT IT IN THE FIRST PLACE!

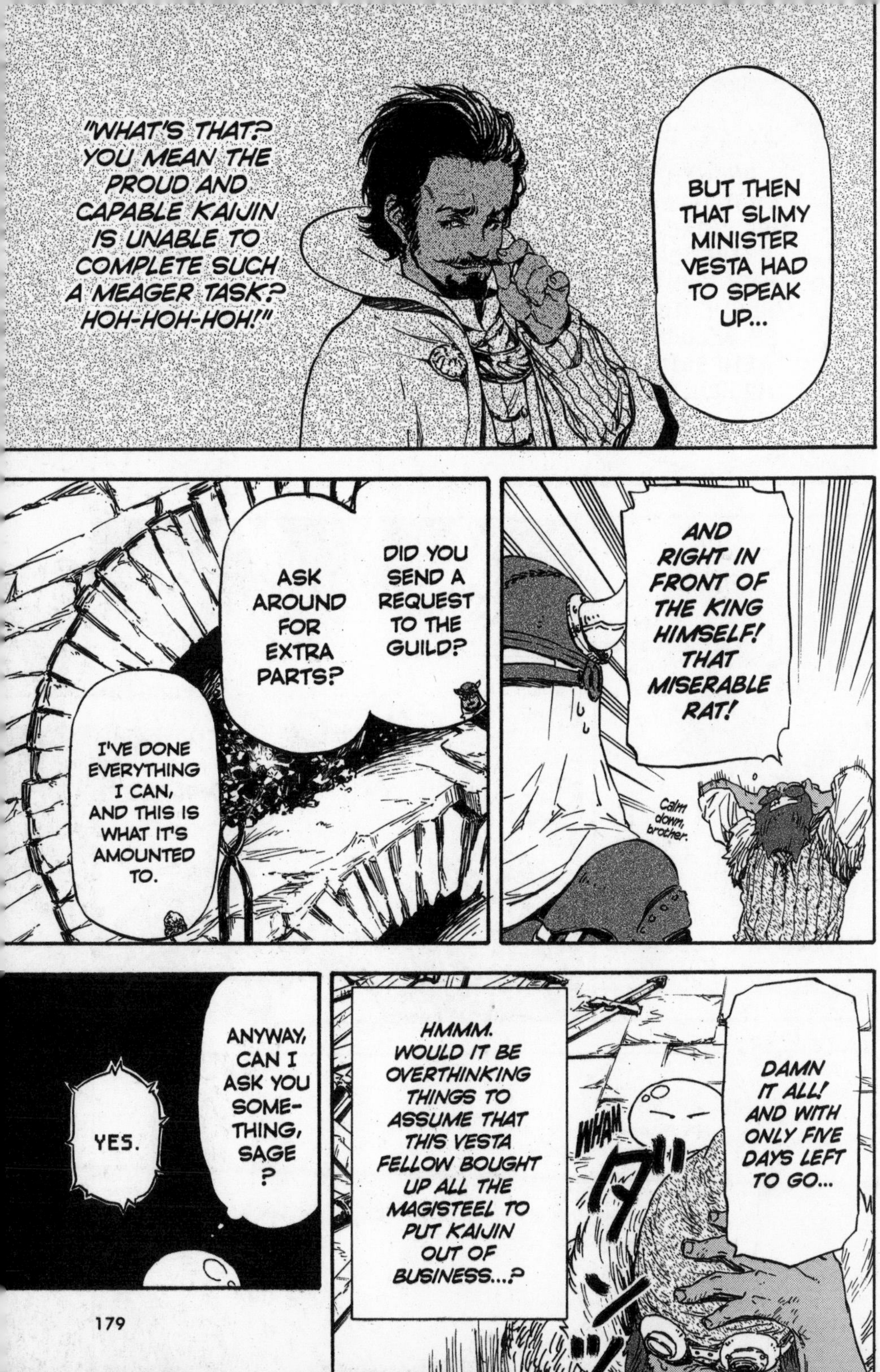
BUT THEN THAT SLIMY MINISTER VESTA HAD TO SPEAK UP...
"WHAT'S THAT? YOU MEAN THE PROUD AND CAPABLE KAIJIN IS UNABLE TO COMPLETE SUCH A MEAGER TASK? HOH-HOH-HOH!"
AND RIGHT IN FRONT OF THE KING HIMSELF! THAT MISERABLE RAT!
Calm down, brother.
DID YOU SEND A REQUEST TO THE GUILD?
ASK AROUND FOR EXTRA PARTS?
I'VE DONE EVERYTHING I CAN, AND THIS IS WHAT IT'S AMOUNTED TO.
DAMN IT ALL! AND WITH ONLY FIVE DAYS LEFT TO GO...
WHAM
HMMM. WOULD IT BE OVERTHINKING THINGS TO ASSUME THAT THIS VESTA FELLOW BOUGHT UP ALL THE MAGISTEEL TO PUT KAIJIN OUT OF BUSINESS...?
ANYWAY, CAN I ASK YOU SOME-THING, SAGE?
YES.

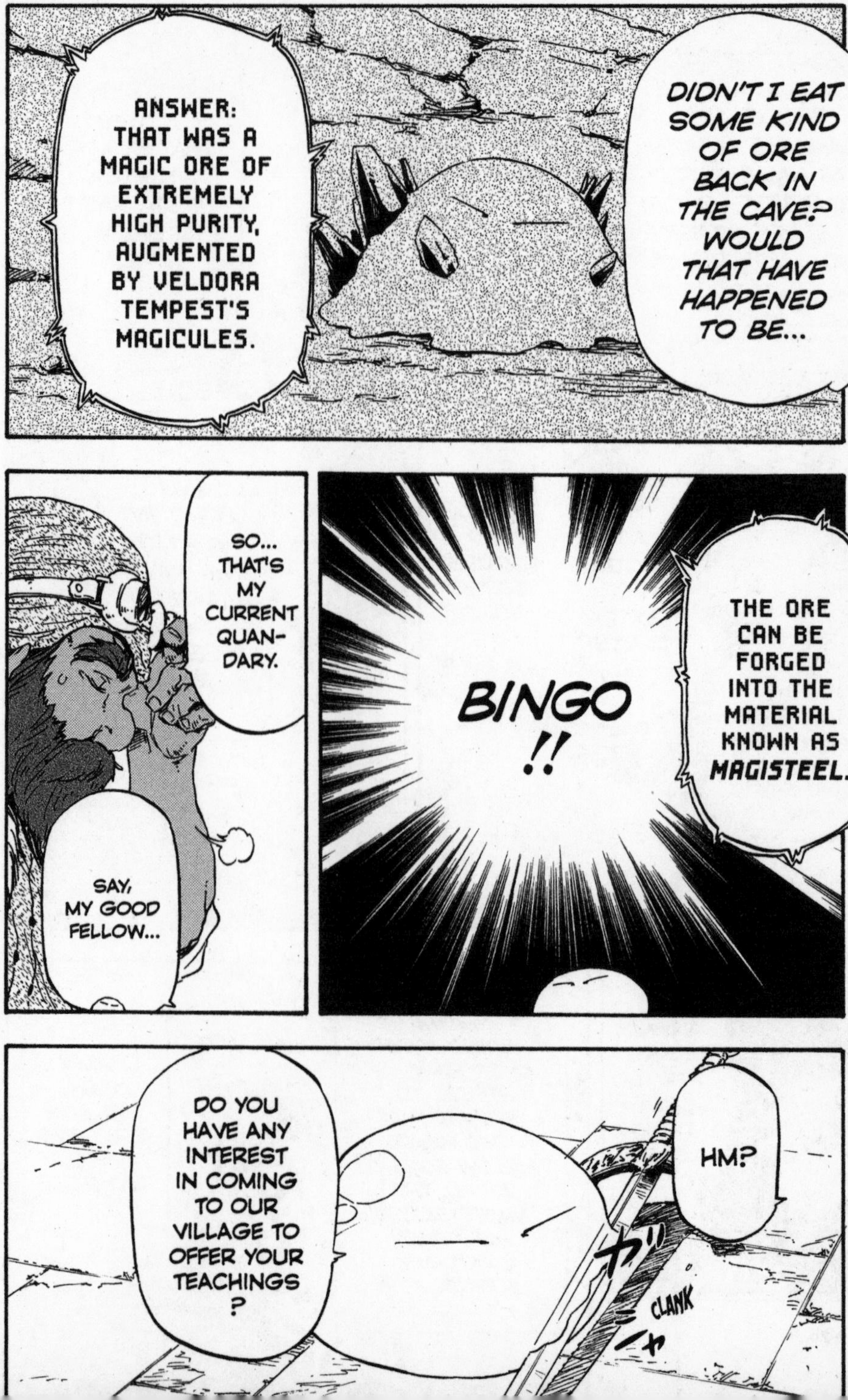
DIDN'T I EAT SOME KIND OF ORE BACK IN THE CAVE? WOULD THAT HAVE HAPPENED TO BE...
ANSWER: THAT WAS A MAGIC ORE OF EXTREMELY HIGH PURITY, AUGMENTED BY VELDORA TEMPEST'S MAGICULES.
THE ORE CAN BE FORGED INTO THE MATERIAL KNOWN AS MAGISTEEL.
BINGO !!
SO... THAT'S MY CURRENT QUAN-DARY.
SAY, MY GOOD FELLOW...
HM?
DO YOU HAVE ANY INTEREST IN COMING TO OUR VILLAGE TO OFFER YOUR TEACHINGS ?
CLANK

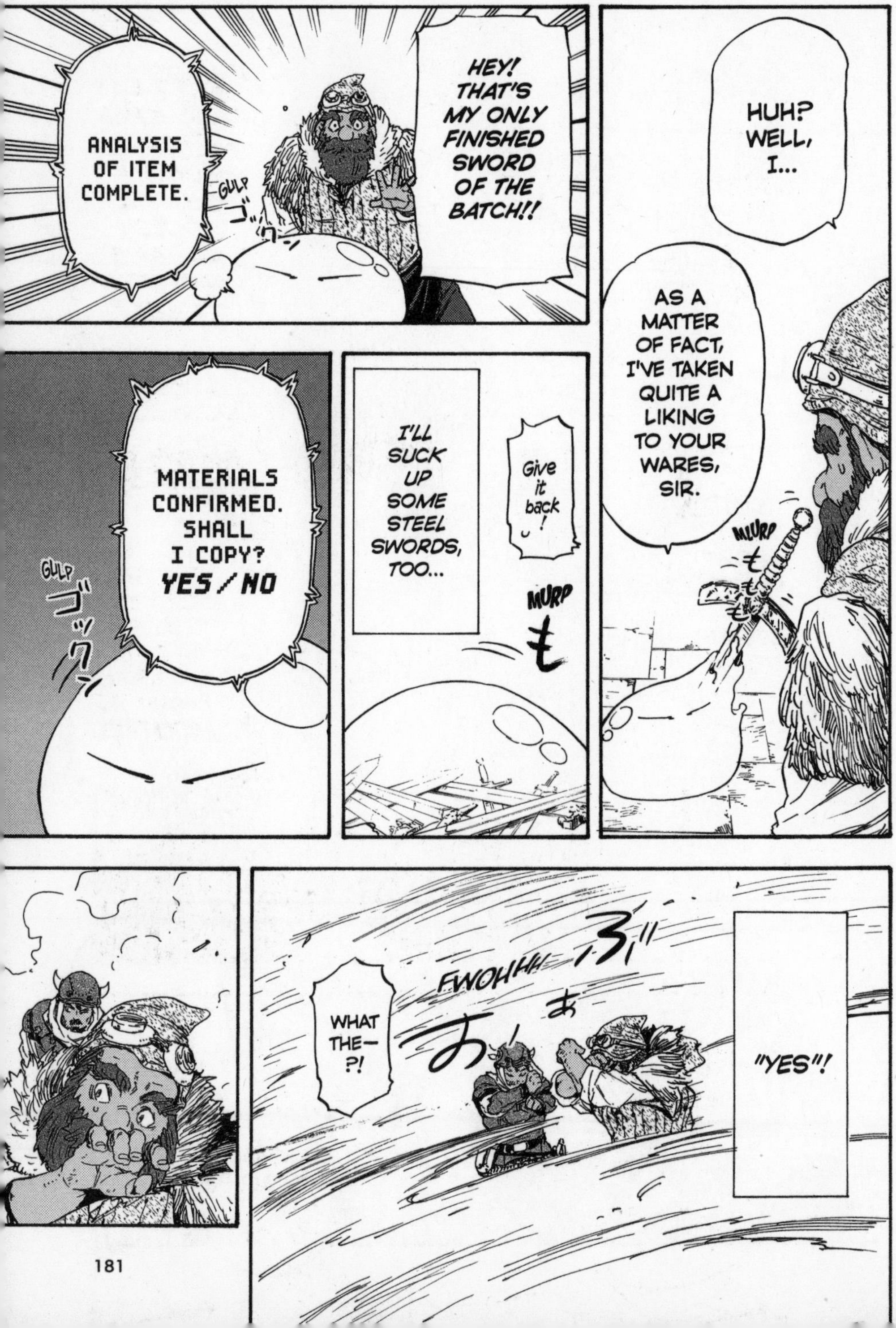
HUH? WELL, I...
AS A MATTER OF FACT, I'VE TAKEN QUITE A LIKING TO YOUR WARES, SIR.
MURP
HEY! THAT'S MY ONLY FINISHED SWORD OF THE BATCH!!
ANALYSIS OF ITEM COMPLETE.
GULP
Give it back!
I'LL SUCK UP SOME STEEL SWORDS, TOO...
MURP
MATERIALS CONFIRMED. SHALL I COPY? YES / NO
GULP
"YES"!
FWOHHH
WHAT THE—?!

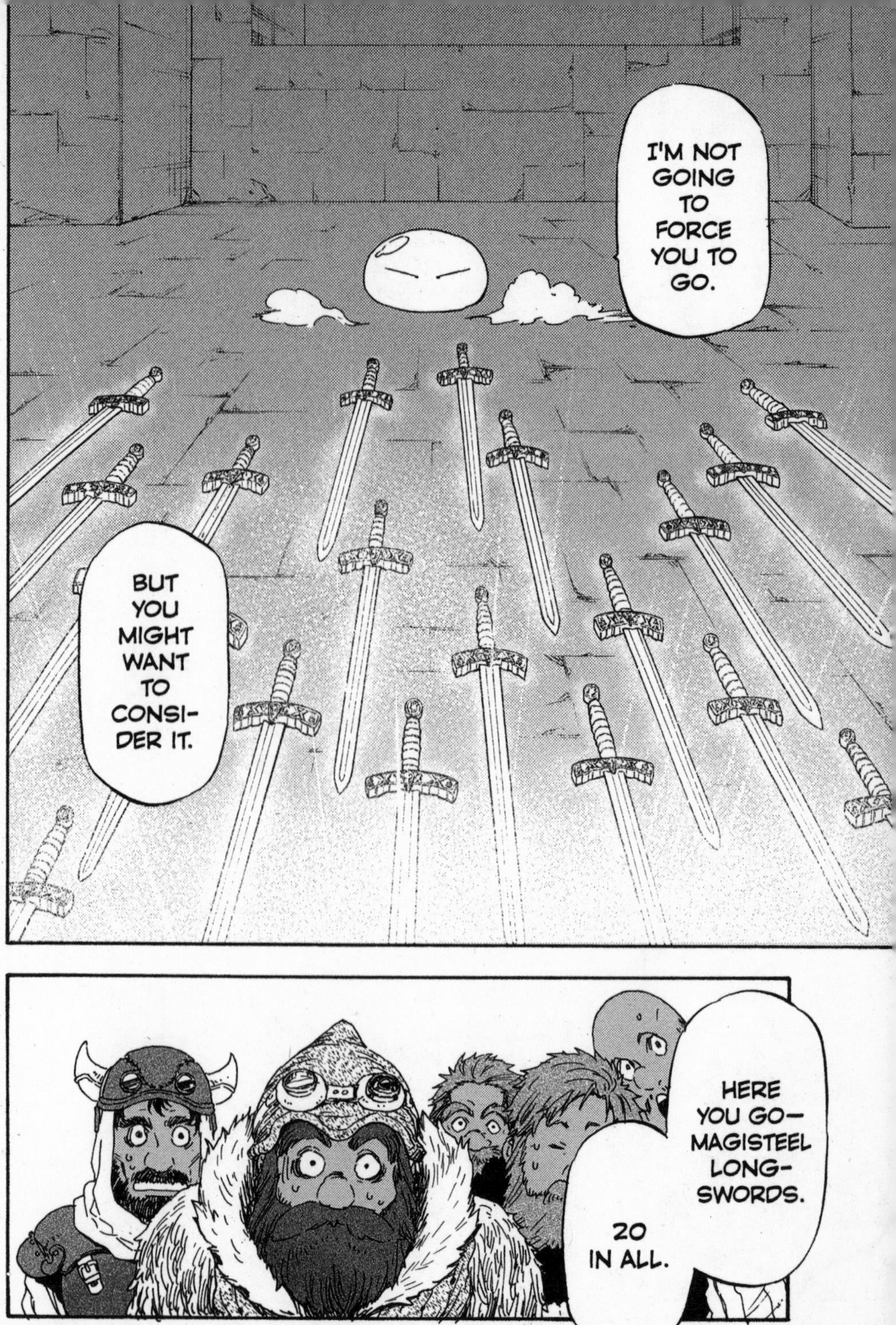
I'M NOT GOING TO FORCE YOU TO GO.
BUT YOU MIGHT WANT TO CONSIDER IT.
HERE YOU GO—MAGISTEEL LONGSWORDS.
20 IN ALL.

I
shall
protect
this
village
until
Lord
Rimuru
returns
!!

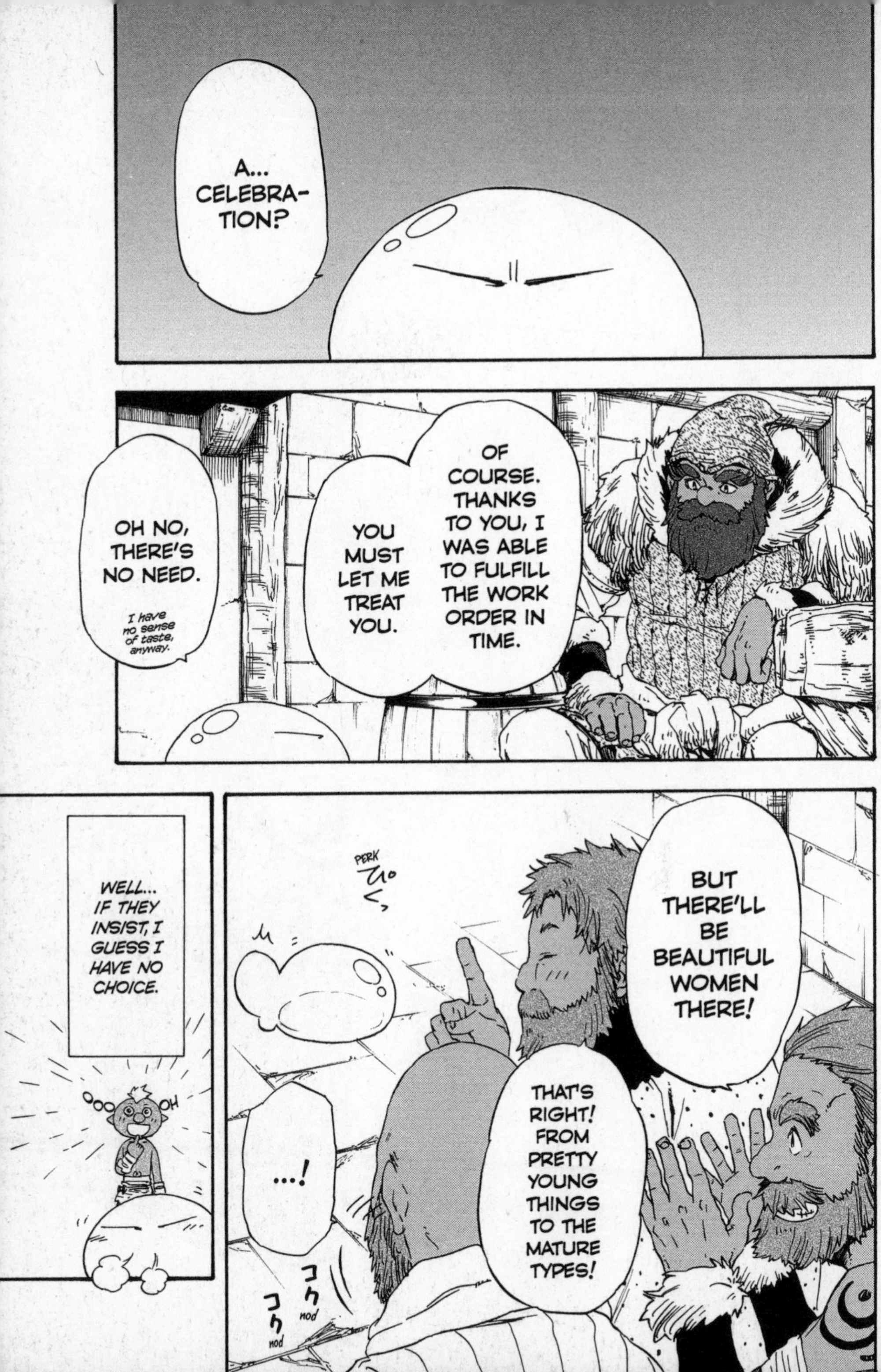
A... CELEBRATION?
OF COURSE. THANKS TO YOU, I WAS ABLE TO FULFILL THE WORK ORDER IN TIME.
YOU MUST LET ME TREAT YOU.
OH NO, THERE'S NO NEED.
I have no sense of taste, anyway.
PERK
BUT THERE'LL BE BEAUTIFUL WOMEN THERE!
THAT'S RIGHT! FROM PRETTY YOUNG THINGS TO THE MATURE TYPES!
...!
nod
nod
WELL... IF THEY INSIST, I GUESS I HAVE NO CHOICE.
OH

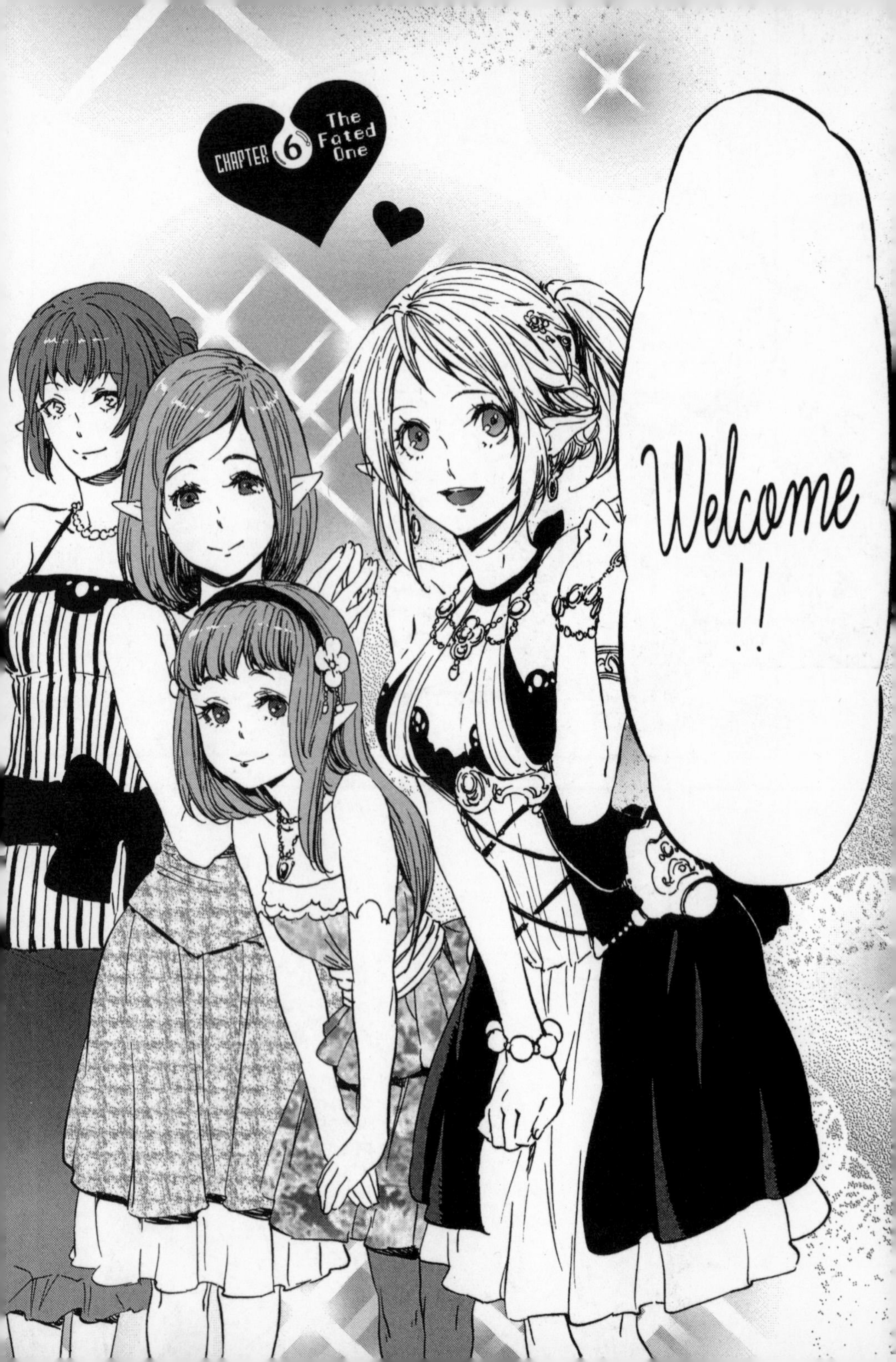
CHAPTER 6 The Fated One
Welcome!!

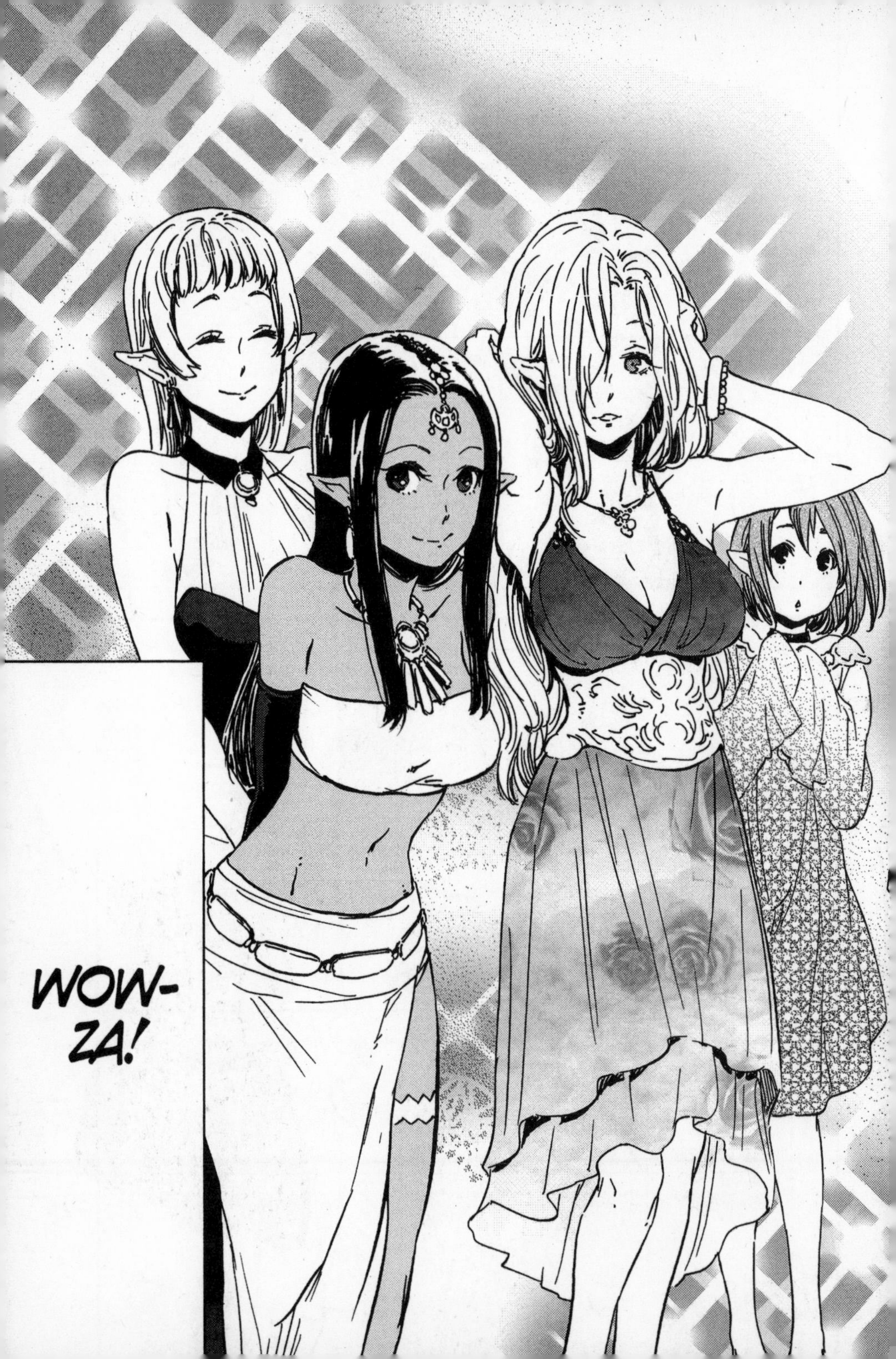
WOW-
ZA!

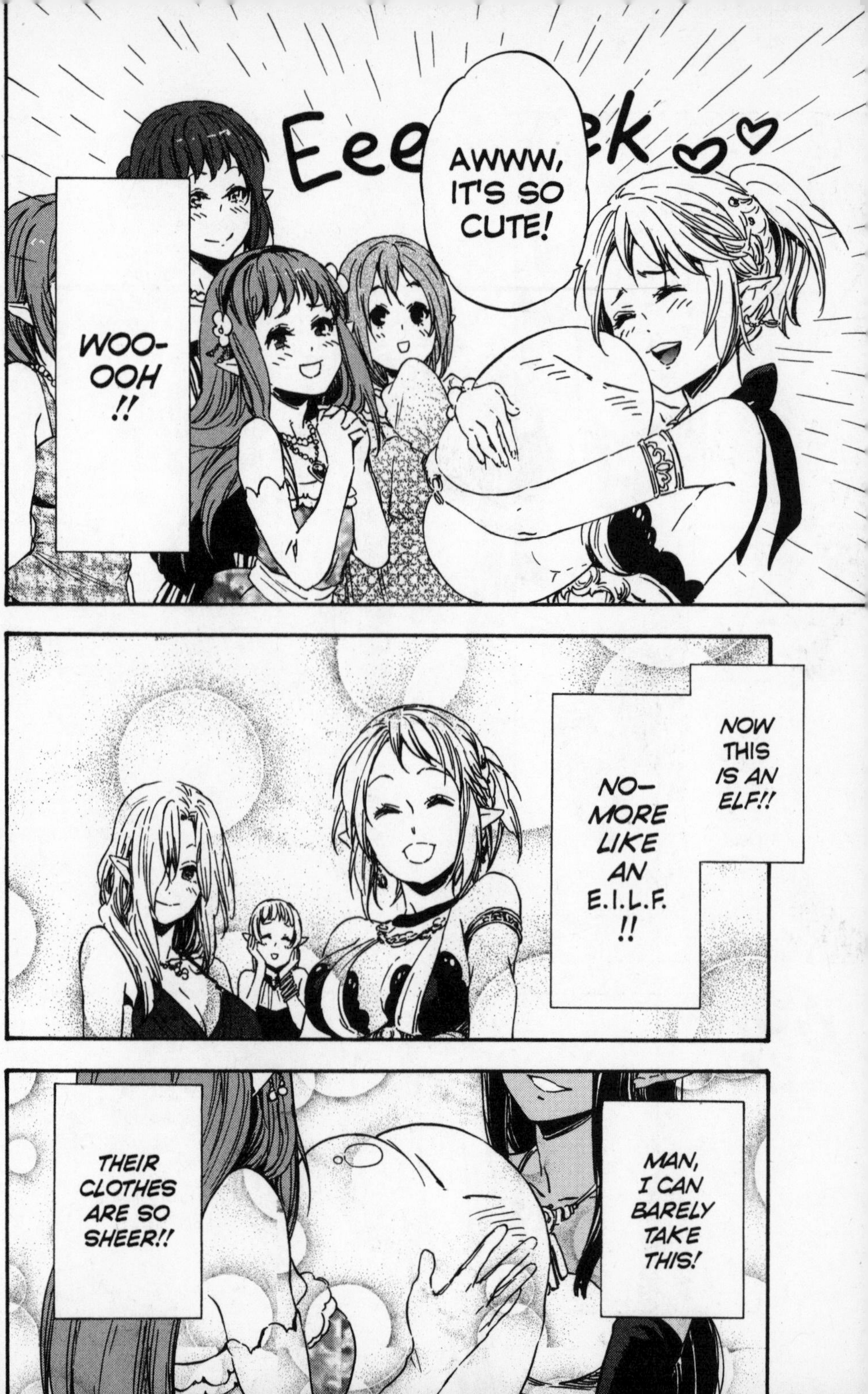
Eee
ek
AWWW, IT'S SO CUTE!
WOO-OOH!!
NOW THIS IS AN ELF!!
NO—MORE LIKE AN E.I.L.F.!!
MAN, I CAN BARELY TAKE THIS!
THEIR CLOTHES ARE SO SHEER!!

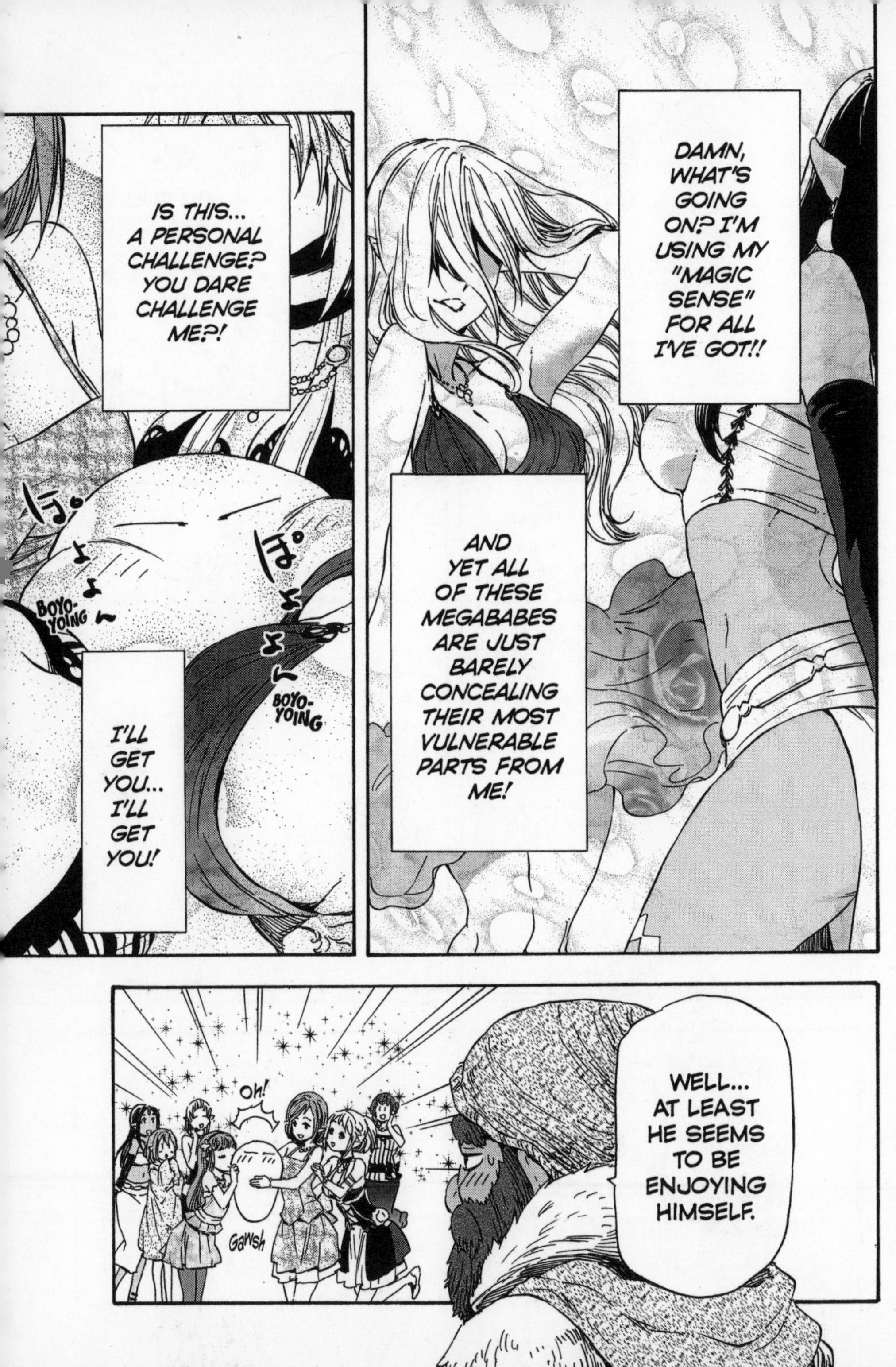
DAMN, WHAT'S GOING ON?! I'M USING MY "MAGIC SENSE" FOR ALL I'VE GOT!!
AND YET ALL OF THESE MEGABABES ARE JUST BARELY CONCEALING THEIR MOST VULNERABLE PARTS FROM ME!
IS THIS... A PERSONAL CHALLENGE? YOU DARE CHALLENGE ME?!
BOYO-YOING
BOYO-YOING
I'LL GET YOU... I'LL GET YOU!
WELL... AT LEAST HE SEEMS TO BE ENJOYING HIMSELF.
Oh!
Gawsh

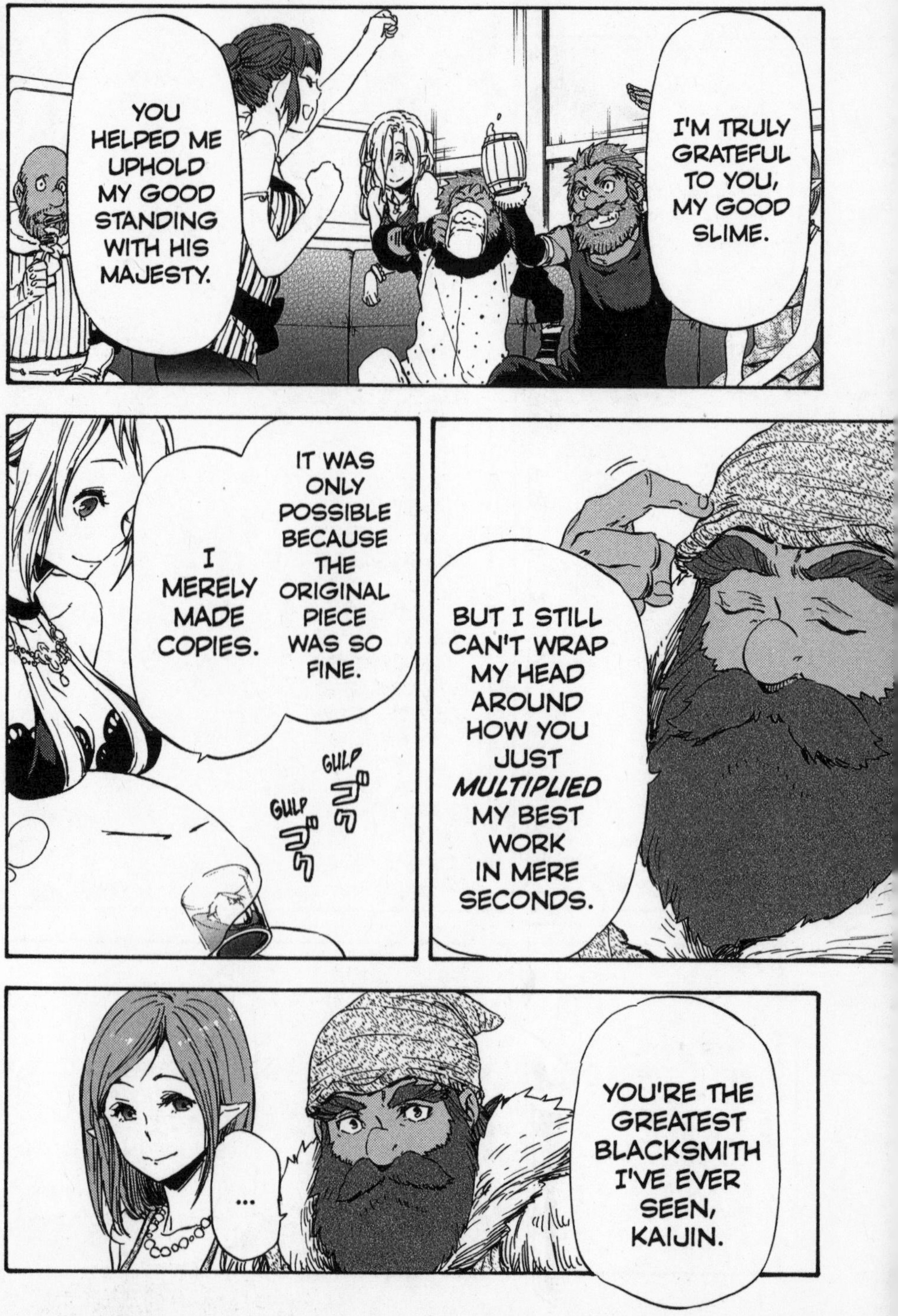
I'M TRULY GRATEFUL TO YOU, MY GOOD SLIME.
YOU HELPED ME UPHOLD MY GOOD STANDING WITH HIS MAJESTY.
BUT I STILL CAN'T WRAP MY HEAD AROUND HOW YOU JUST *MULTIPLIED* MY BEST WORK IN MERE SECONDS.
I MERELY MADE COPIES. IT WAS ONLY POSSIBLE BECAUSE THE ORIGINAL PIECE WAS SO FINE.
GULP
GULP
YOU'RE THE GREATEST BLACKSMITH I'VE EVER SEEN, KAIJIN.
...

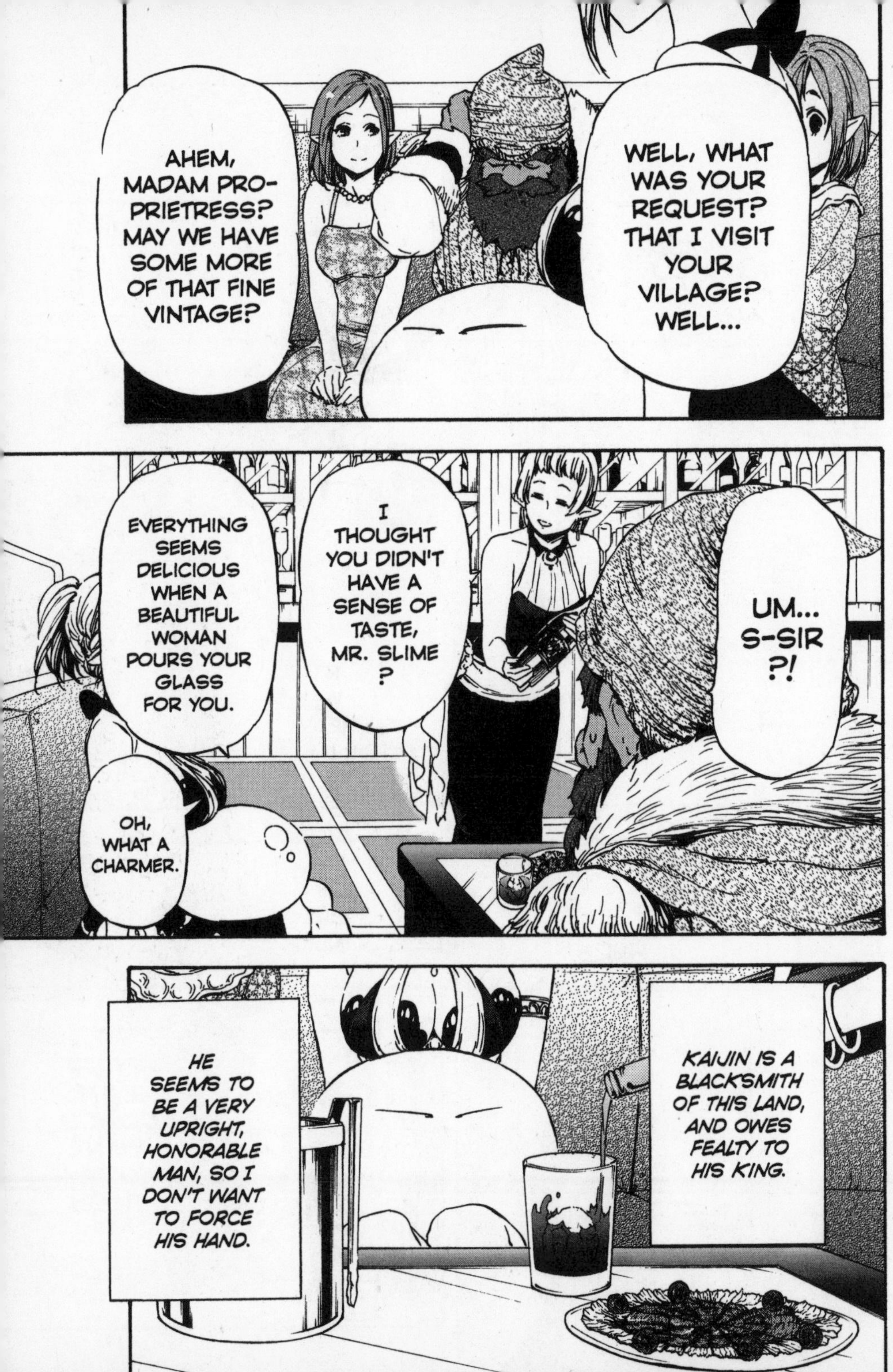
WELL, WHAT WAS YOUR REQUEST? THAT I VISIT YOUR VILLAGE? WELL...
AHEM, MADAM PRO-PRIETRESS? MAY WE HAVE SOME MORE OF THAT FINE VINTAGE?
UM... S-SIR ?!
I THOUGHT YOU DIDN'T HAVE A SENSE OF TASTE, MR. SLIME ?
EVERYTHING SEEMS DELICIOUS WHEN A BEAUTIFUL WOMAN POURS YOUR GLASS FOR YOU.
OH, WHAT A CHARMER.
KAIJIN IS A BLACKSMITH OF THIS LAND, AND OWES FEALTY TO HIS KING.
HE SEEMS TO BE A VERY UPRIGHT, HONORABLE MAN, SO I DON'T WANT TO FORCE HIS HAND.

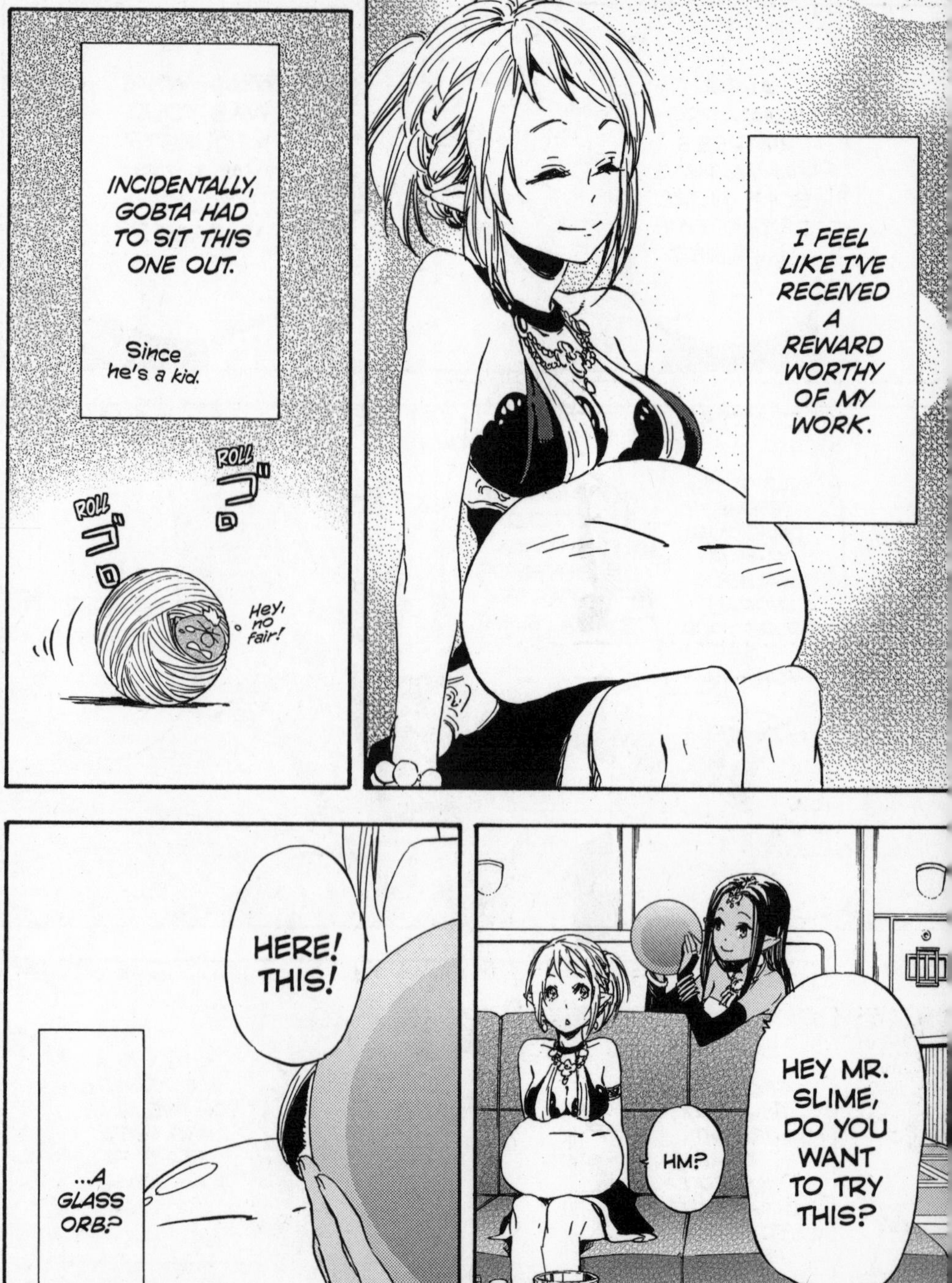
I FEEL LIKE I'VE RECEIVED A REWARD WORTHY OF MY WORK.
INCIDENTALLY, GOBTA HAD TO SIT THIS ONE OUT.
Since he's a kid.
ROLL
ゴロ
ROLL
ゴロ
Hey, no fair!
HEY MR. SLIME, DO YOU WANT TO TRY THIS?
HM?
HERE! THIS!
...A GLASS ORB?

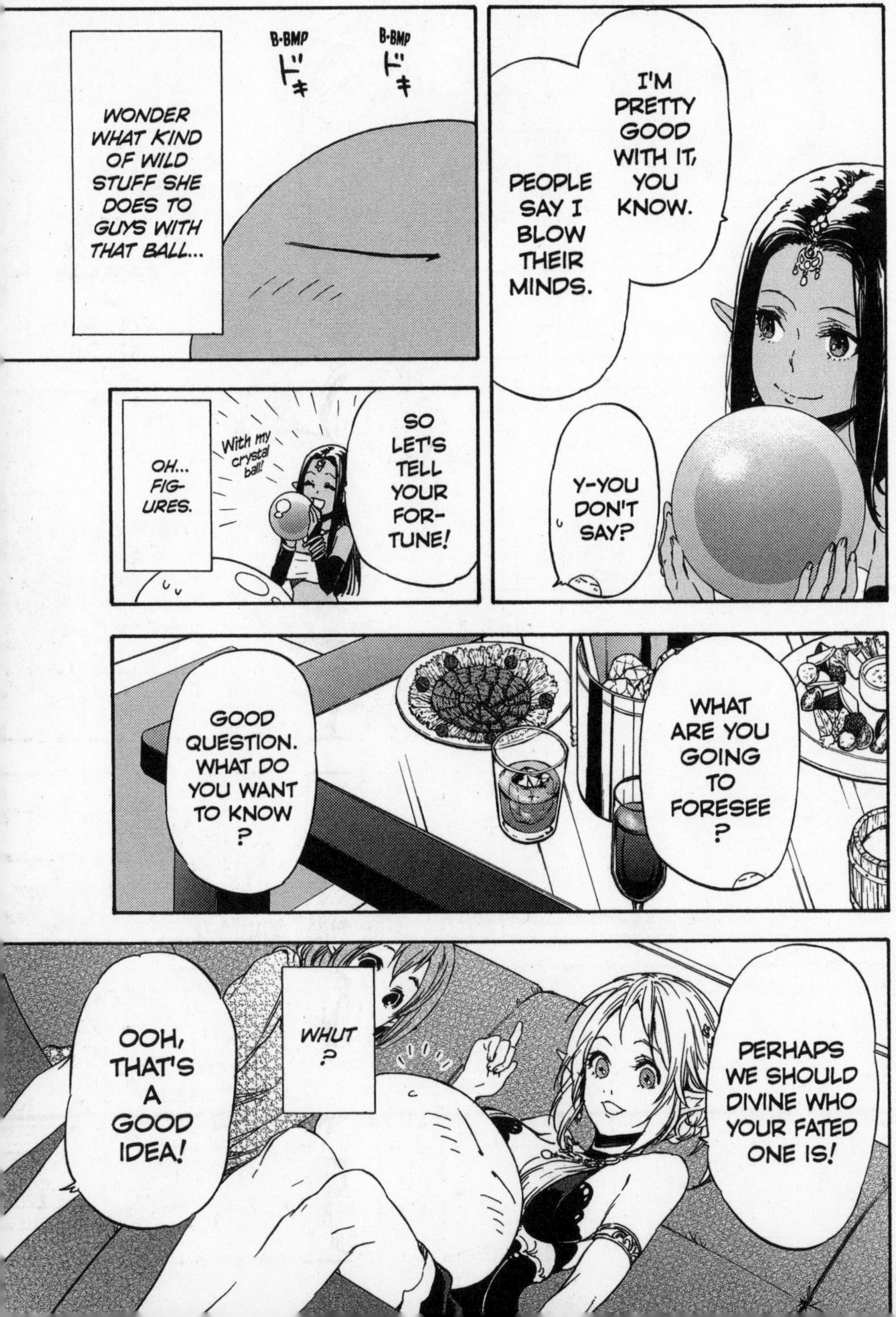
I'M PRETTY GOOD WITH IT, YOU KNOW.
PEOPLE SAY I BLOW THEIR MINDS.
Y-YOU DON'T SAY?
B-BMP ドキ
B-BMP ドキ
WONDER WHAT KIND OF WILD STUFF SHE DOES TO GUYS WITH THAT BALL...
SO LET'S TELL YOUR FOR-TUNE!
With my crystal ball!
OH... FIG-URES.
WHAT ARE YOU GOING TO FORESEE ?
GOOD QUESTION. WHAT DO YOU WANT TO KNOW ?
PERHAPS WE SHOULD DIVINE WHO YOUR FATED ONE IS!
WHUT ?
OOH, THAT'S A GOOD IDEA!

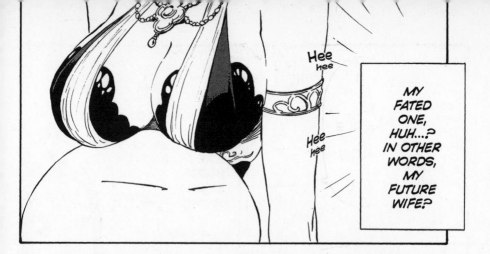

MY FATED ONE, HUH...? IN OTHER WORDS, MY FUTURE WIFE?
Hee hee
Hee hee
IS IT EVEN POSSIBLE FOR ME TO GET A WIFE IN THIS WORLD ?!
Satoru-san ♡
NO, WAIT... I'M A SLIME NOW, SO I GUESS...
...IT WOULD BE MORE LIKE THIS?
Rimuru-saan! ♡
All pink or whatever
ON THAT NOTE, DO SLIMES EVEN HAVE GENDERS?
NYORRRP
にょ――…
HOW DO THEY MULTIPLY? CELL DIVISION?

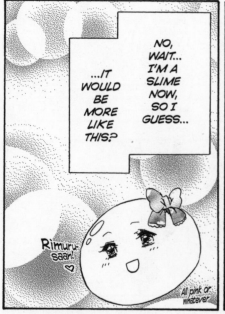

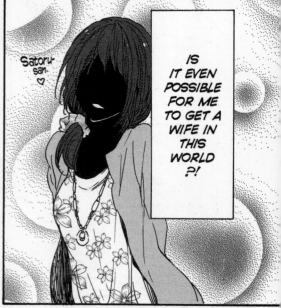

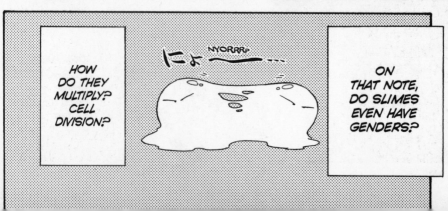

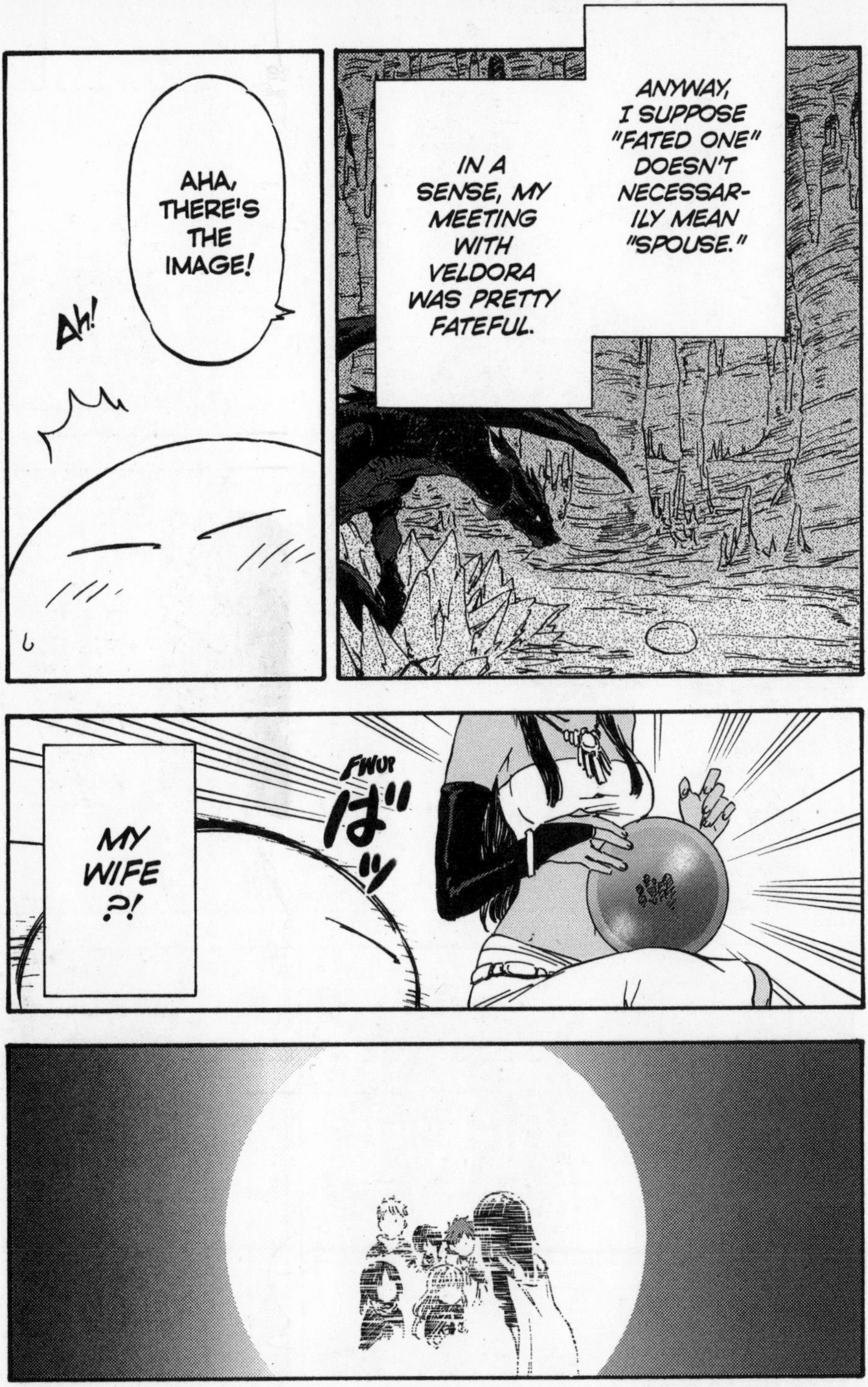
ANYWAY, I SUPPOSE "FATED ONE" DOESN'T NECESSARILY MEAN "SPOUSE."
IN A SENSE, MY MEETING WITH VELDORA WAS PRETTY FATEFUL.
AHA, THERE'S THE IMAGE!
Ah!
FWUP
ばッ
MY WIFE ?!

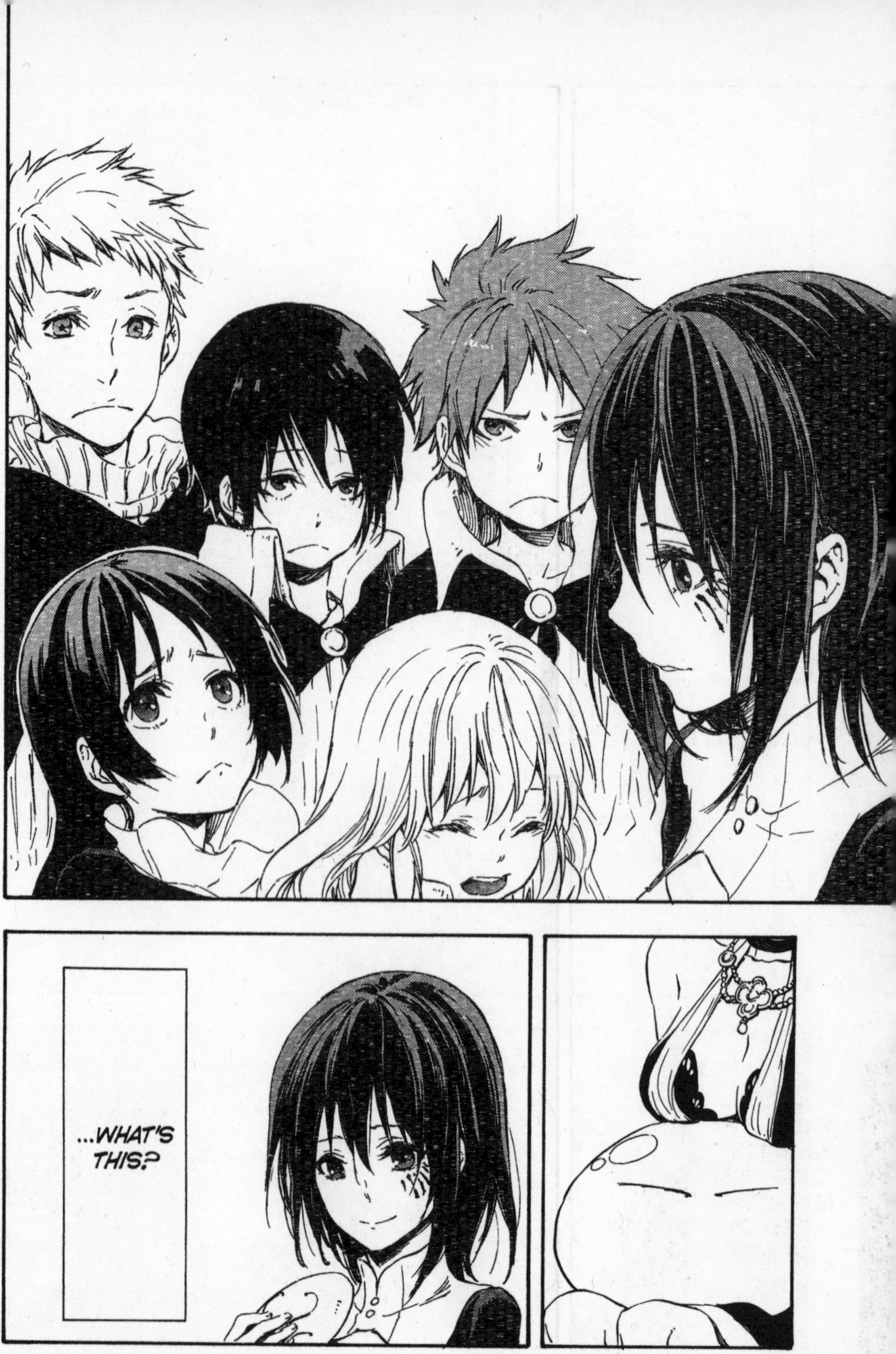
...WHAT'S THIS?

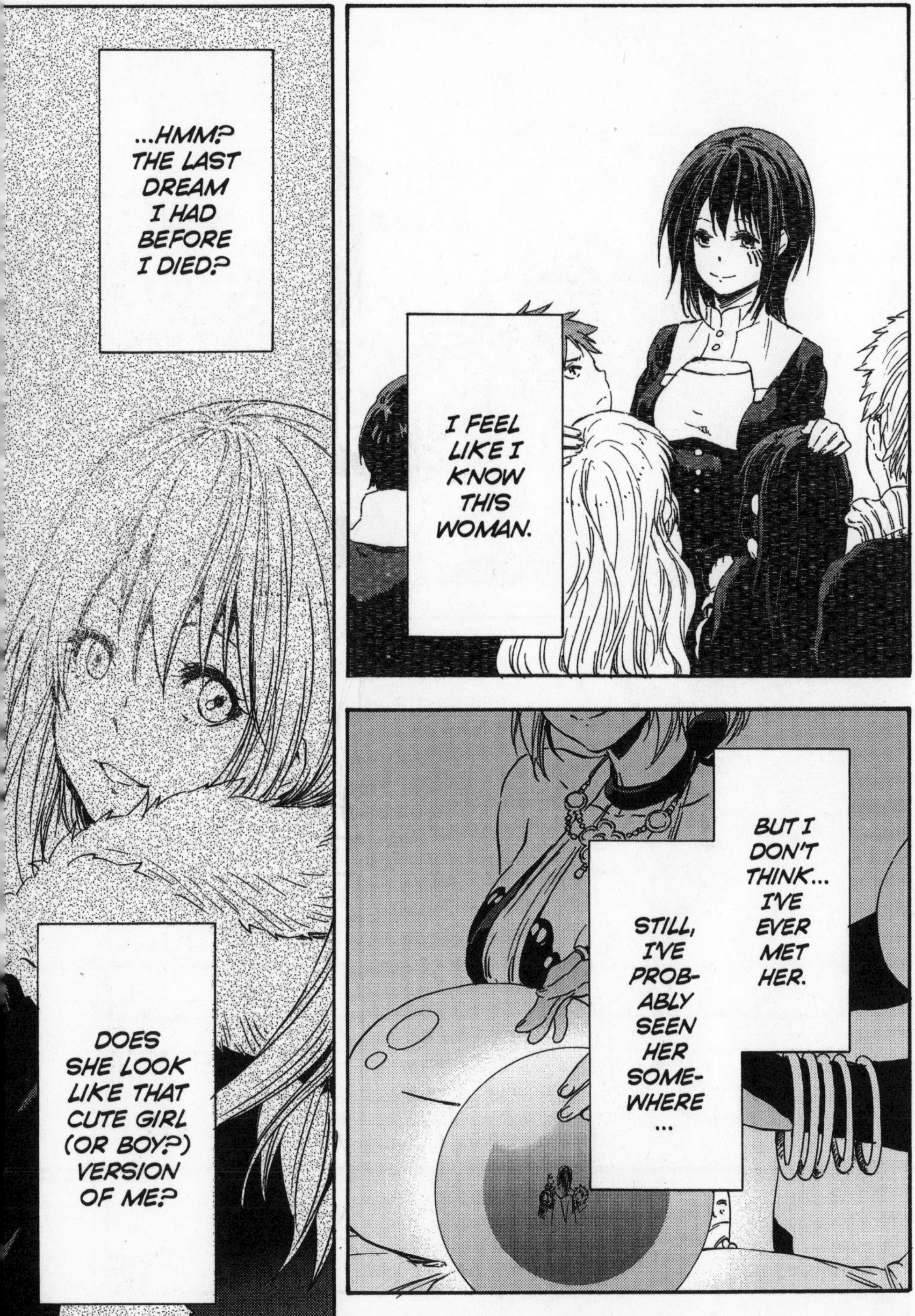
I FEEL LIKE I KNOW THIS WOMAN.
BUT I DON'T THINK... I'VE EVER MET HER.
STILL, I'VE PROB-ABLY SEEN HER SOME-WHERE ...
...HMM? THE LAST DREAM I HAD BEFORE I DIED?
DOES SHE LOOK LIKE THAT CUTE GIRL (OR BOY?) VERSION OF ME?

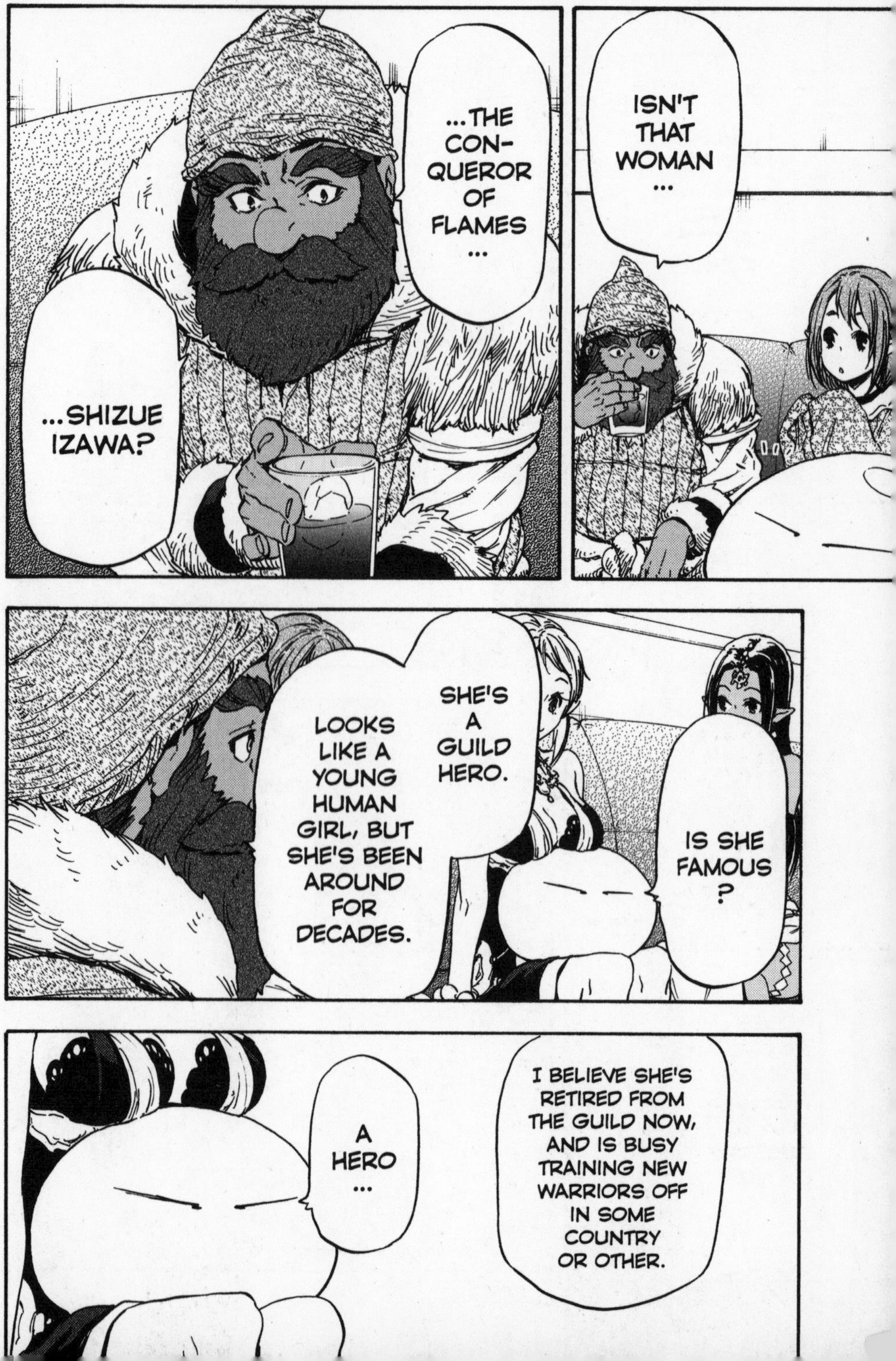
ISN'T THAT WOMAN ...
...THE CONQUEROR OF FLAMES ...
...SHIZUE IZAWA?
IS SHE FAMOUS?
SHE'S A GUILD HERO.
LOOKS LIKE A YOUNG HUMAN GIRL, BUT SHE'S BEEN AROUND FOR DECADES.
I BELIEVE SHE'S RETIRED FROM THE GUILD NOW, AND IS BUSY TRAINING NEW WARRIORS OFF IN SOME COUNTRY OR OTHER.
A HERO ...

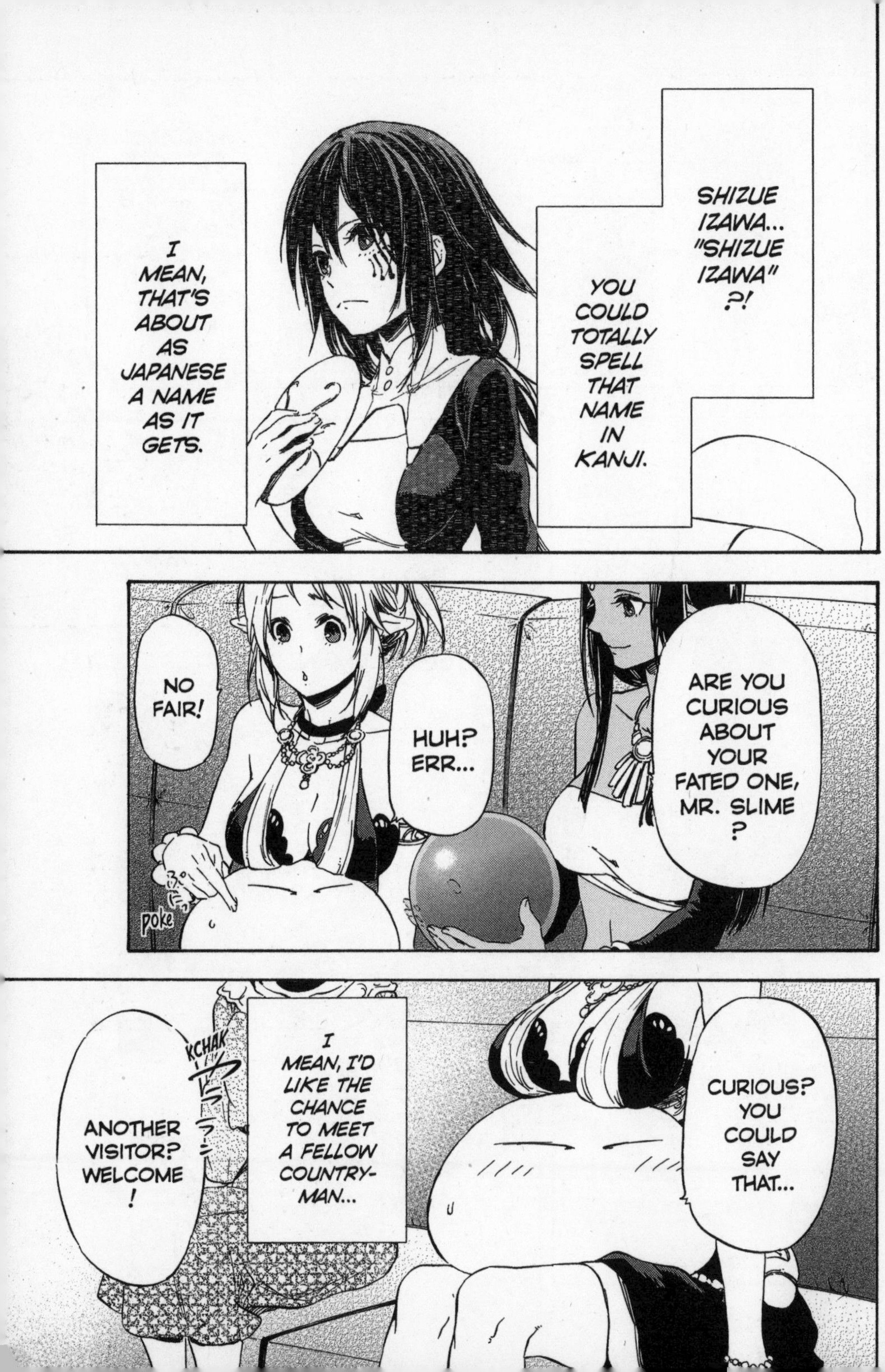
SHIZUE IZAWA... "SHIZUE IZAWA"?!
YOU COULD TOTALLY SPELL THAT NAME IN KANJI.
I MEAN, THAT'S ABOUT AS JAPANESE A NAME AS IT GETS.
ARE YOU CURIOUS ABOUT YOUR FATED ONE, MR. SLIME?
HUH? ERR...
NO FAIR!
poke
CURIOUS? YOU COULD SAY THAT...
I MEAN, I'D LIKE THE CHANCE TO MEET A FELLOW COUNTRY-MAN...
KCHAK
ANOTHER VISITOR? WELCOME!

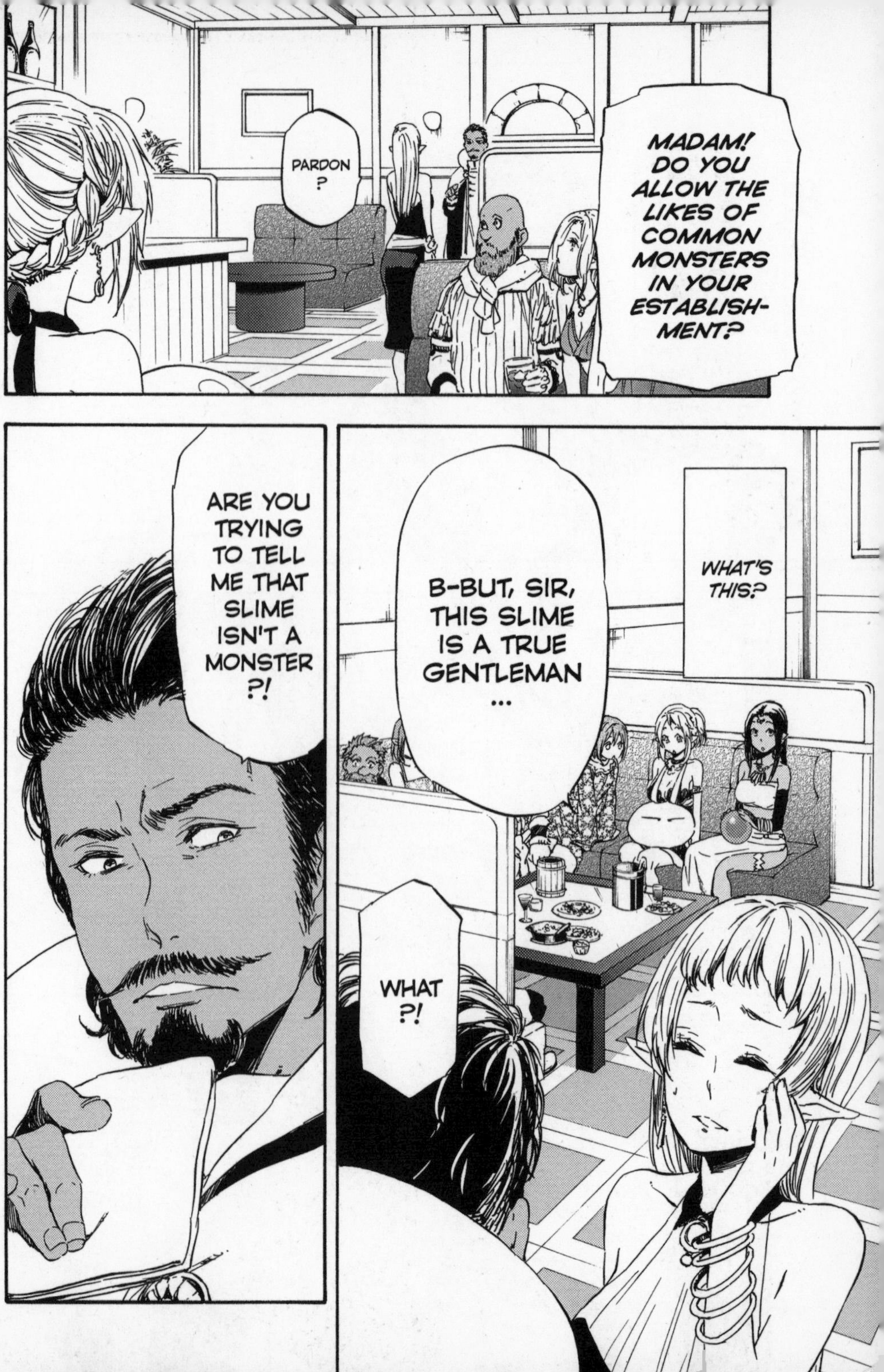
MADAM! DO YOU ALLOW THE LIKES OF COMMON MONSTERS IN YOUR ESTABLISH-MENT?
PARDON?
WHAT'S THIS?
B-BUT, SIR, THIS SLIME IS A TRUE GENTLEMAN...
WHAT?!
ARE YOU TRYING TO TELL ME THAT SLIME ISN'T A MONSTER?!

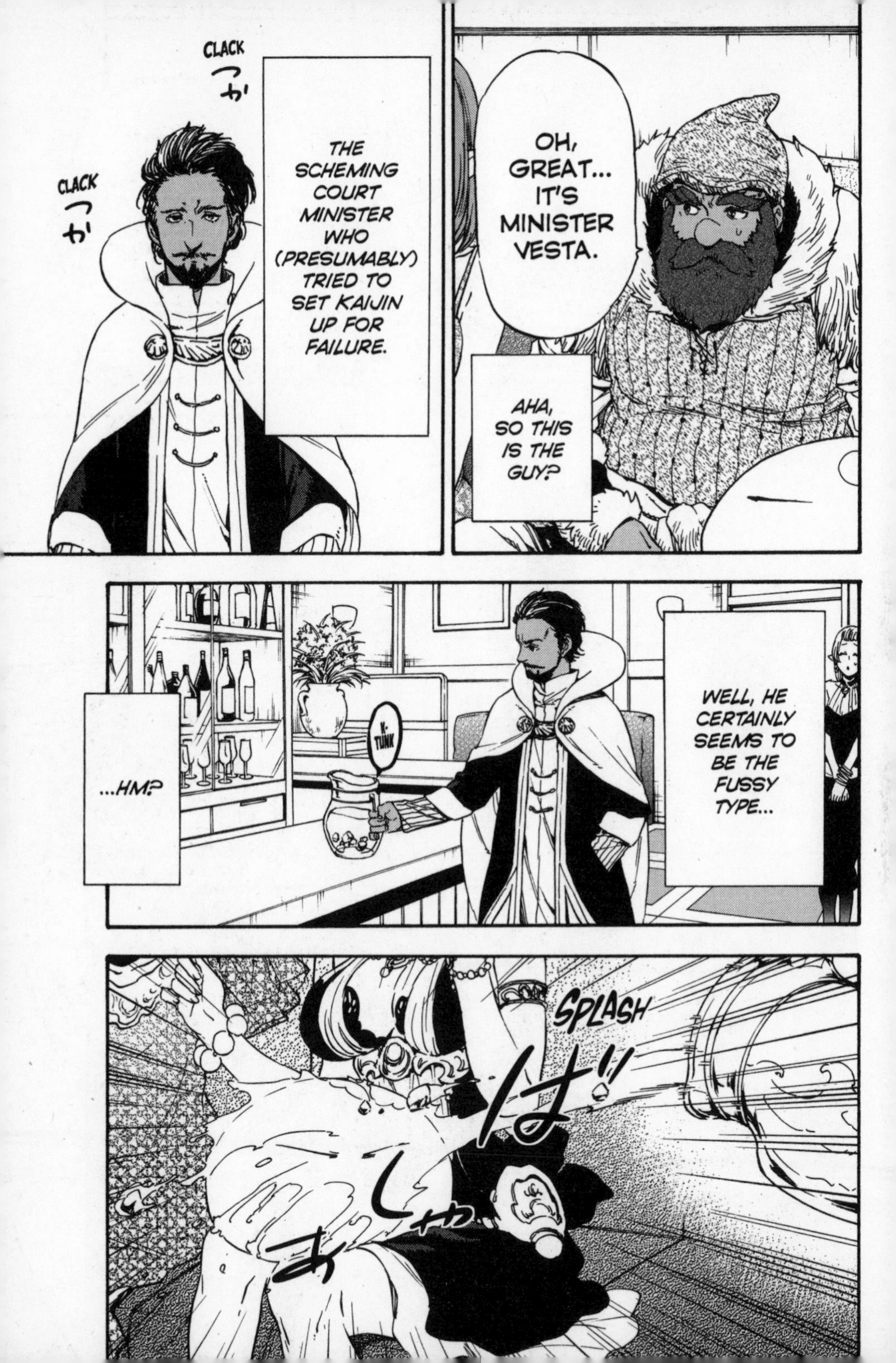
OH, GREAT... IT'S MINISTER VESTA.
AHA, SO THIS IS THE GUY?
THE SCHEMING COURT MINISTER WHO (PRESUMABLY) TRIED TO SET KAIJIN UP FOR FAILURE.
CLACK
つか
CLACK
つか
WELL, HE CERTAINLY SEEMS TO BE THE FUSSY TYPE...
K-TUNK
...HM?
SPLASH
は!!
しゃ
あ

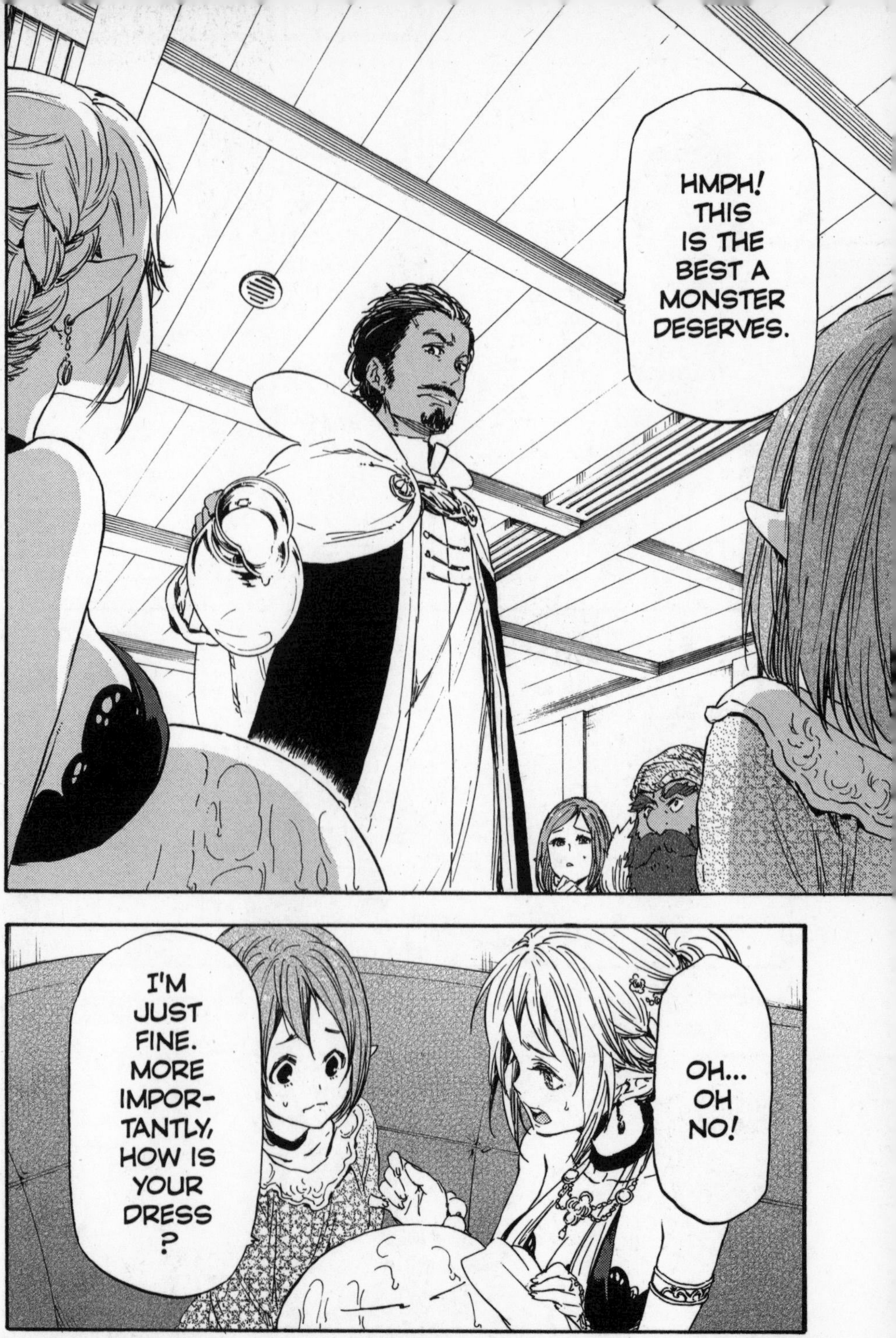
HMPH! THIS IS THE BEST A MONSTER DESERVES.
OH... OH NO!
I'M JUST FINE. MORE IMPORTANTLY, HOW IS YOUR DRESS?

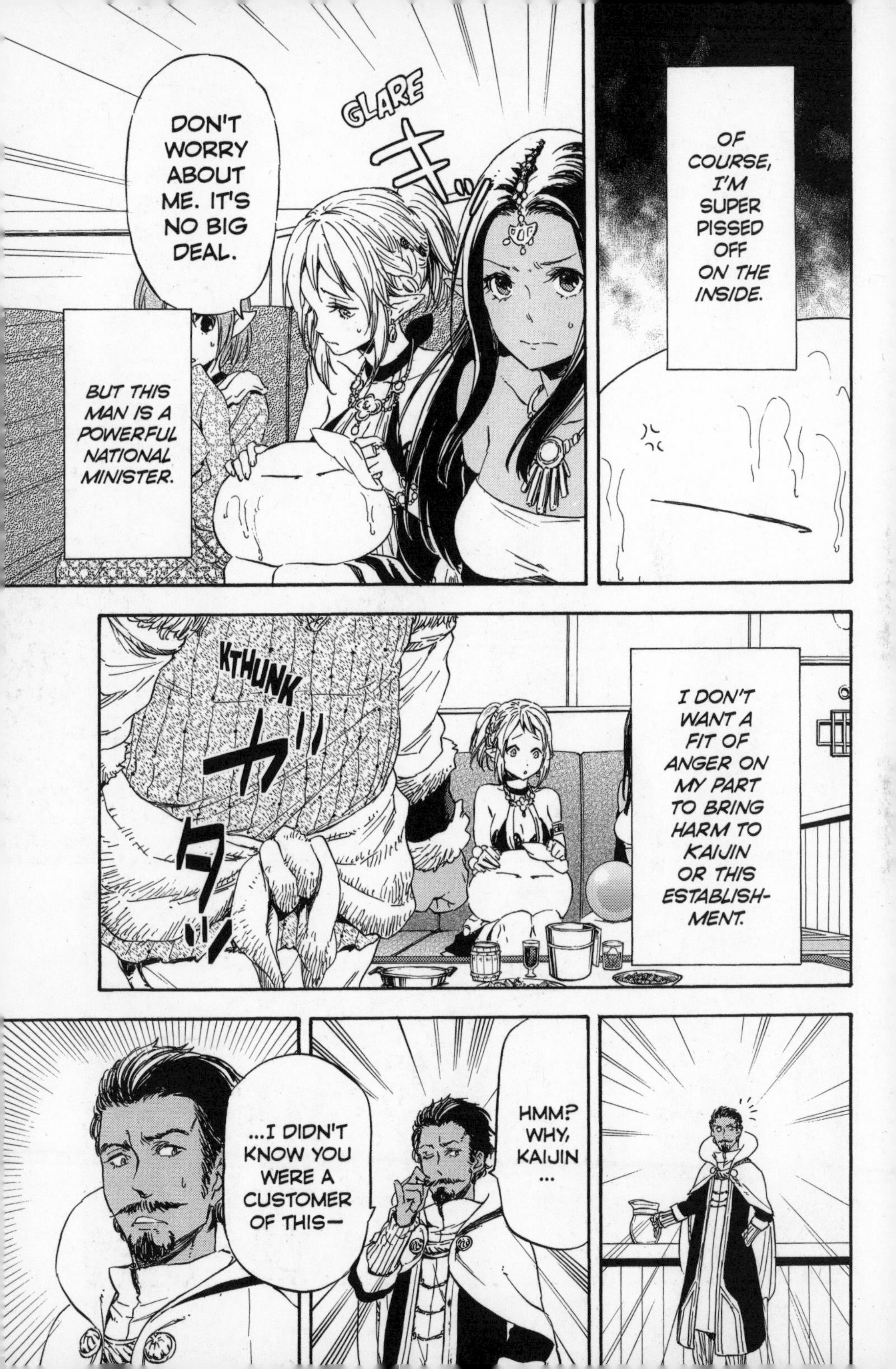
OF COURSE, I'M SUPER PISSED OFF ON THE INSIDE.
GLARE
DON'T WORRY ABOUT ME. IT'S NO BIG DEAL.
BUT THIS MAN IS A POWERFUL NATIONAL MINISTER.
I DON'T WANT A FIT OF ANGER ON MY PART TO BRING HARM TO KAIJIN OR THIS ESTABLISHMENT.
KTHUNK
HMM? WHY, KAIJIN ...
...I DIDN'T KNOW YOU WERE A CUSTOMER OF THIS—

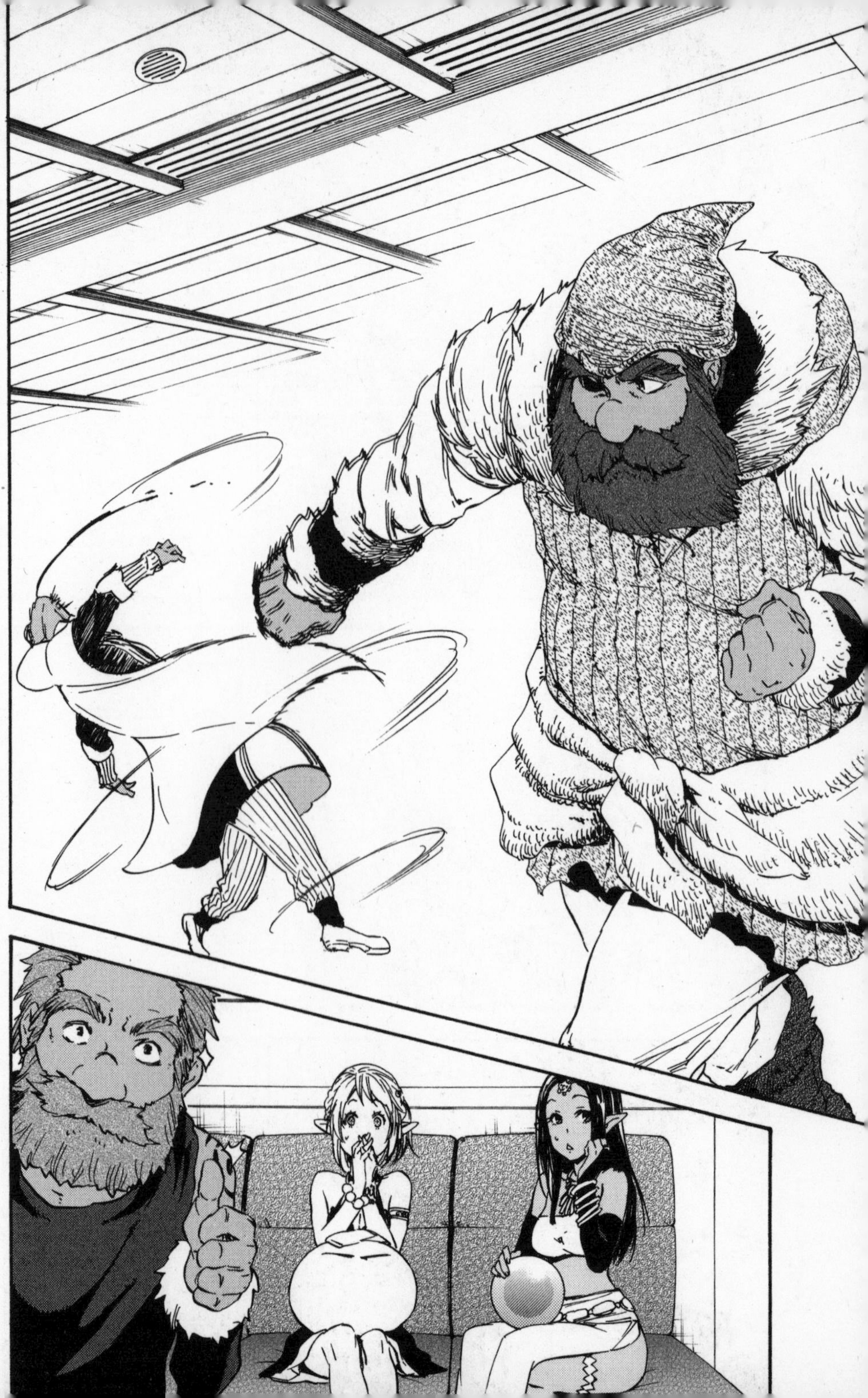

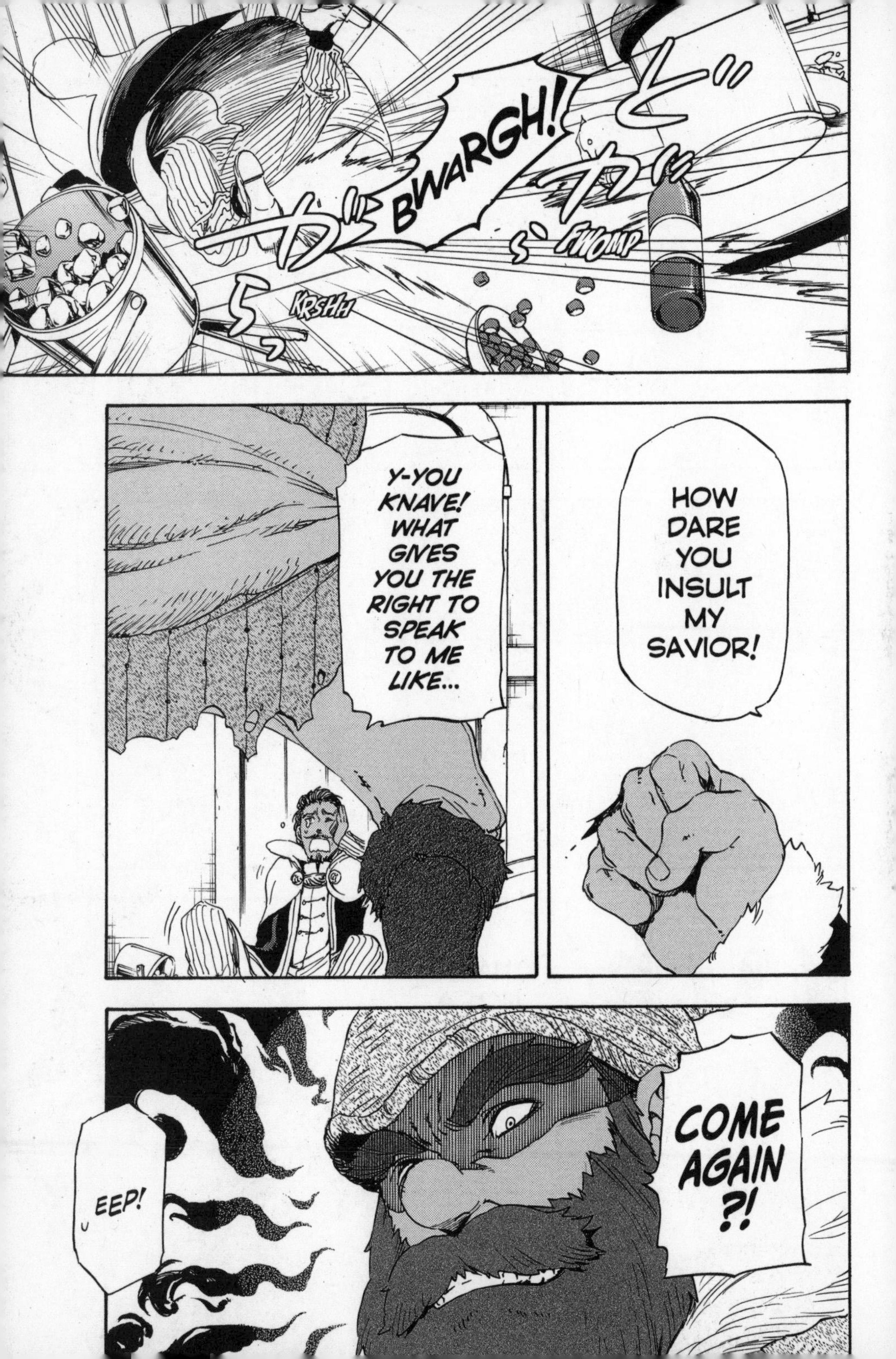
BWARGH!!
FWOMP
KRSHH
HOW DARE YOU INSULT MY SAVIOR!
Y-YOU KNAVE! WHAT GIVES YOU THE RIGHT TO SPEAK TO ME LIKE...
COME AGAIN?!
EEP!

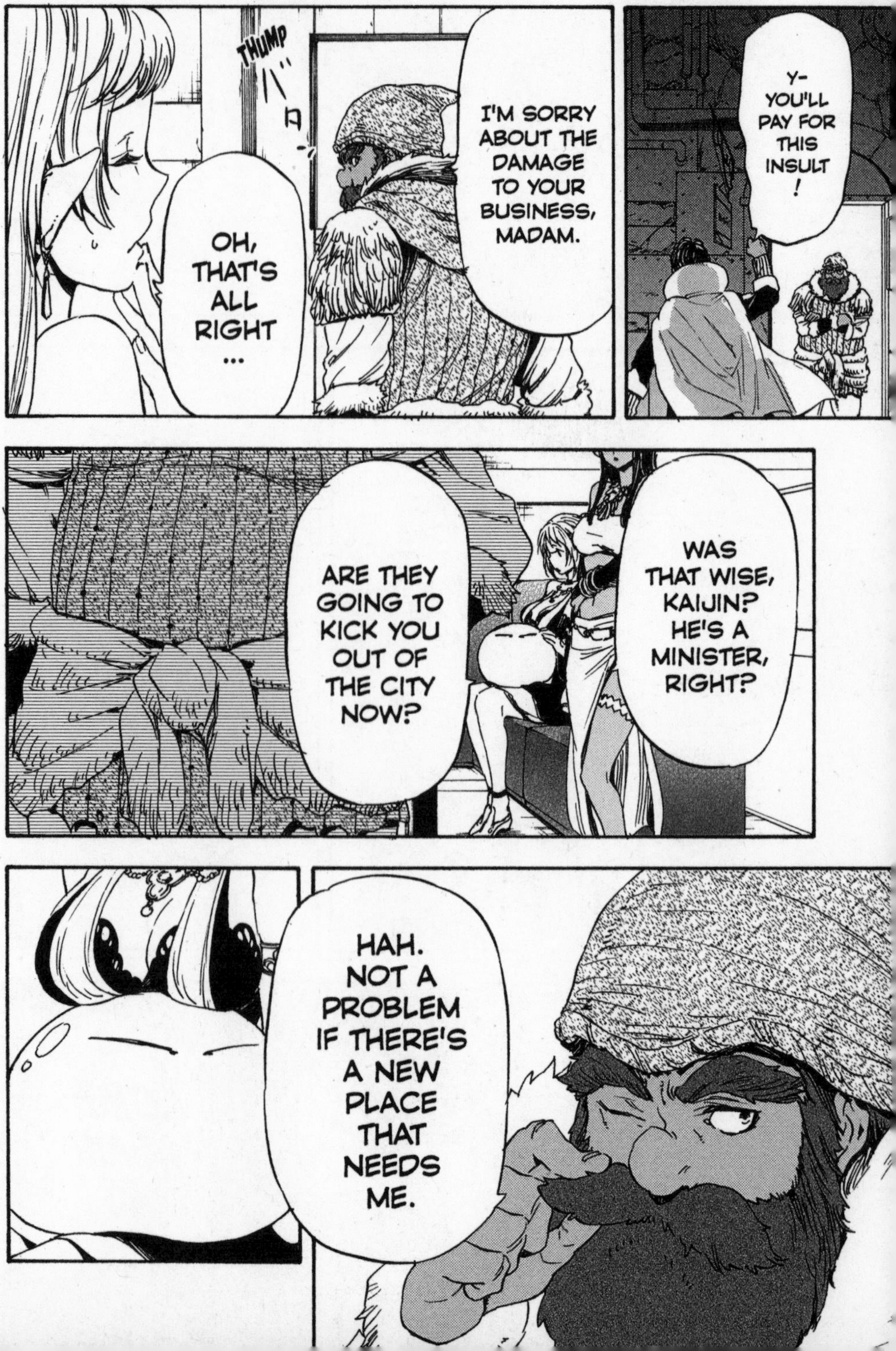
Y-YOU'LL PAY FOR THIS INSULT!
THUMP
I'M SORRY ABOUT THE DAMAGE TO YOUR BUSINESS, MADAM.
OH, THAT'S ALL RIGHT...
WAS THAT WISE, KAIJIN? HE'S A MINISTER, RIGHT?
ARE THEY GOING TO KICK YOU OUT OF THE CITY NOW?
HAH. NOT A PROBLEM IF THERE'S A NEW PLACE THAT NEEDS ME.

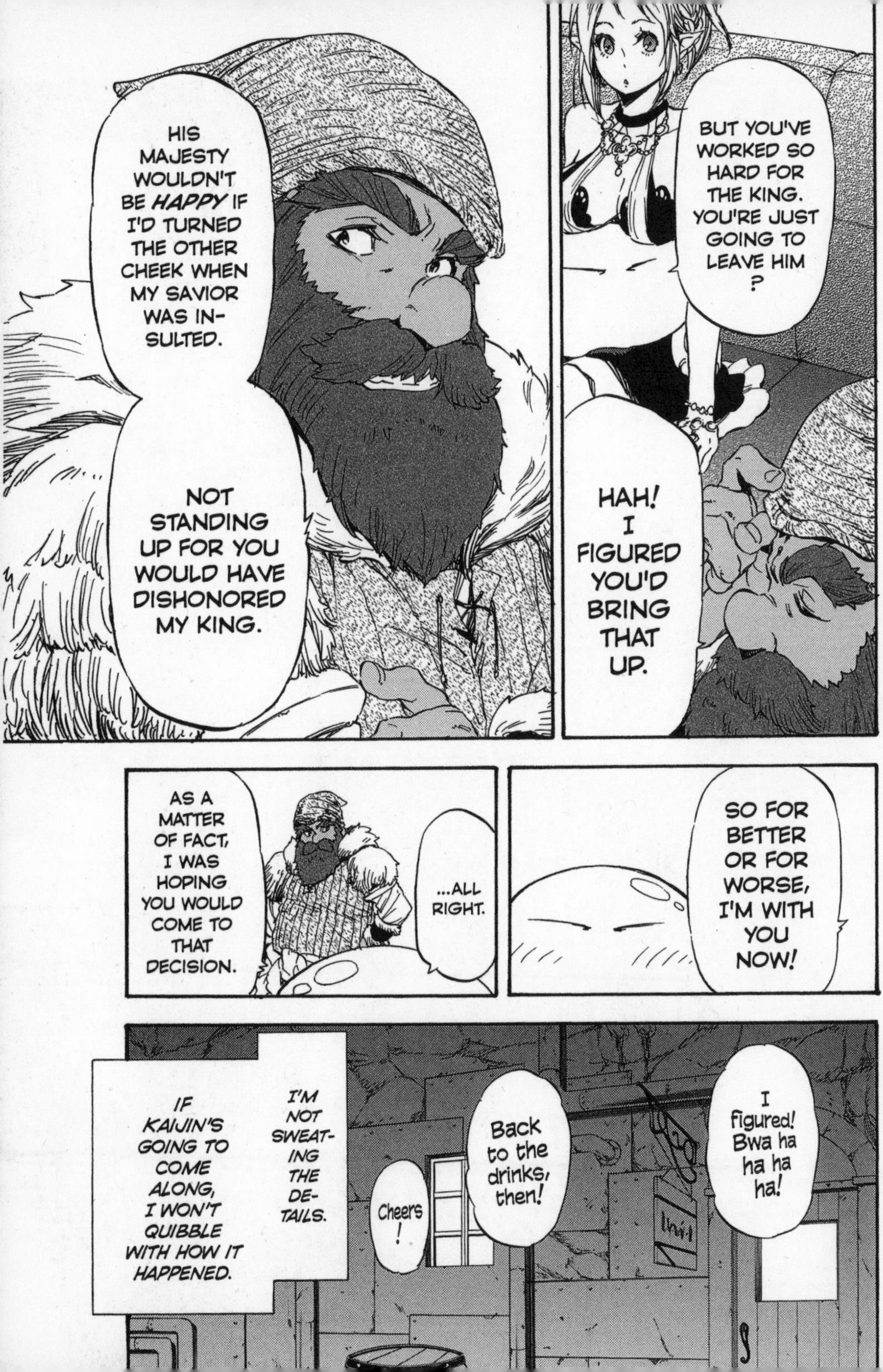
BUT YOU'VE WORKED SO HARD FOR THE KING. YOU'RE JUST GOING TO LEAVE HIM?
HAH! I FIGURED YOU'D BRING THAT UP.
HIS MAJESTY WOULDN'T BE *HAPPY* IF I'D TURNED THE OTHER CHEEK WHEN MY SAVIOR WAS INSULTED.
NOT STANDING UP FOR YOU WOULD HAVE DISHONORED MY KING.
SO FOR BETTER OR FOR WORSE, I'M WITH YOU NOW!
...ALL RIGHT.
AS A MATTER OF FACT, I WAS HOPING YOU WOULD COME TO THAT DECISION.
I figured! Bwa ha ha ha ha!
Back to the drinks, then!
Cheers!
I'M NOT SWEATING THE DETAILS.
IF KAIJIN'S GOING TO COME ALONG, I WON'T QUIBBLE WITH HOW IT HAPPENED.

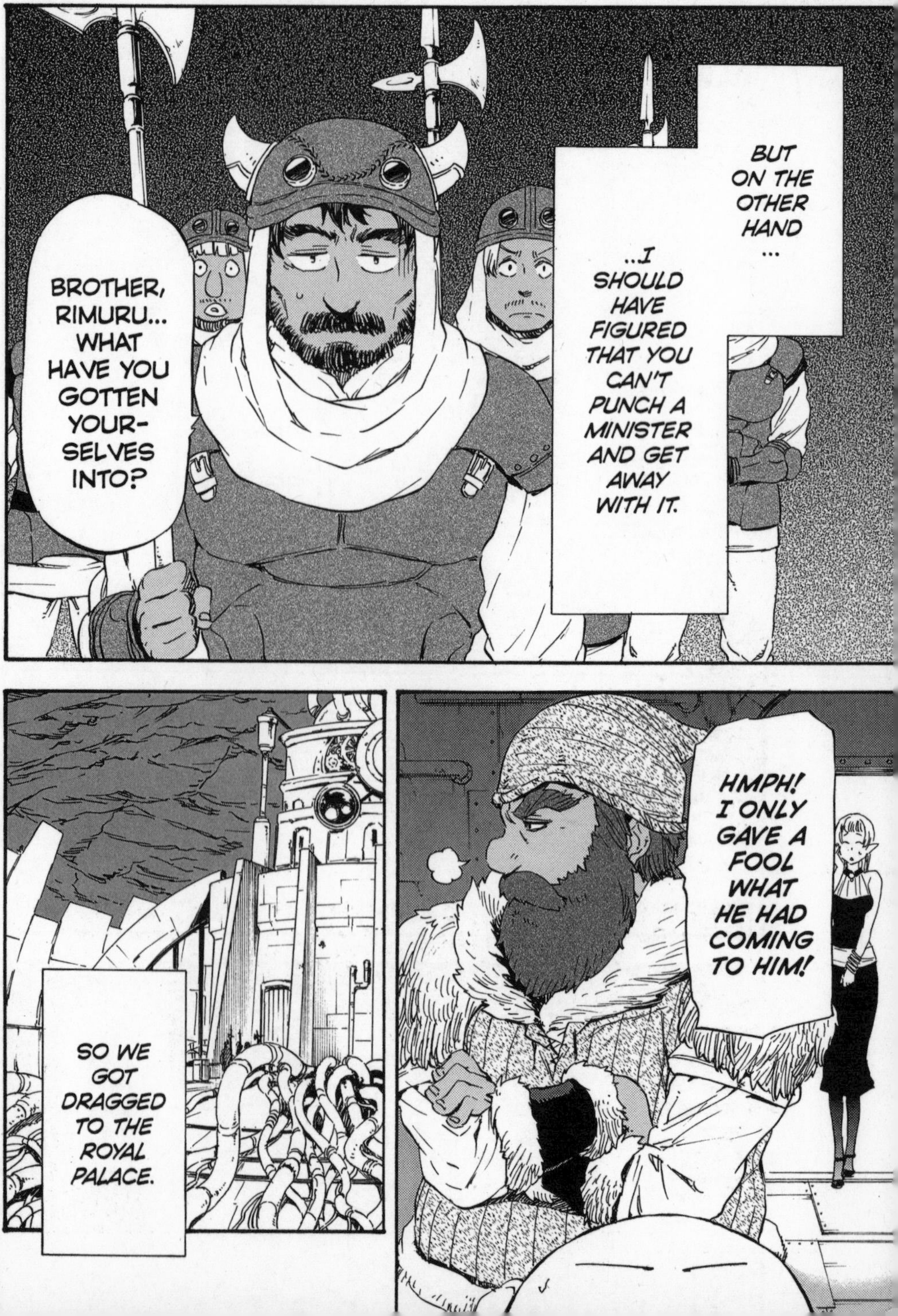
BUT ON THE OTHER HAND ...
...I SHOULD HAVE FIGURED THAT YOU CAN'T PUNCH A MINISTER AND GET AWAY WITH IT.
BROTHER, RIMURU... WHAT HAVE YOU GOTTEN YOUR-SELVES INTO?
HMPH! I ONLY GAVE A FOOL WHAT HE HAD COMING TO HIM!
SO WE GOT DRAGGED TO THE ROYAL PALACE.

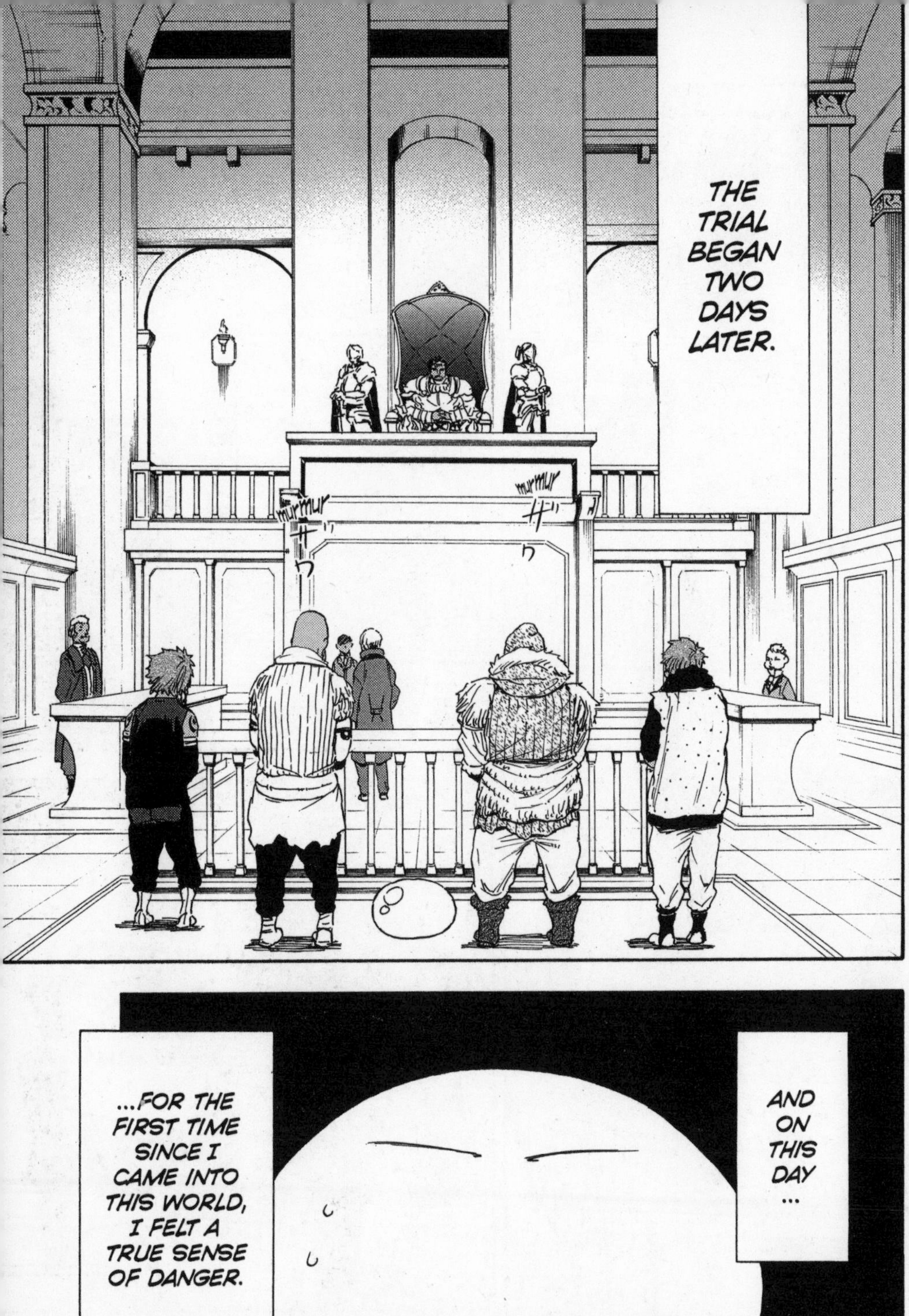
THE TRIAL BEGAN TWO DAYS LATER.
murmur
murmur
AND ON THIS DAY...
...FOR THE FIRST TIME SINCE I CAME INTO THIS WORLD, I FELT A TRUE SENSE OF DANGER.

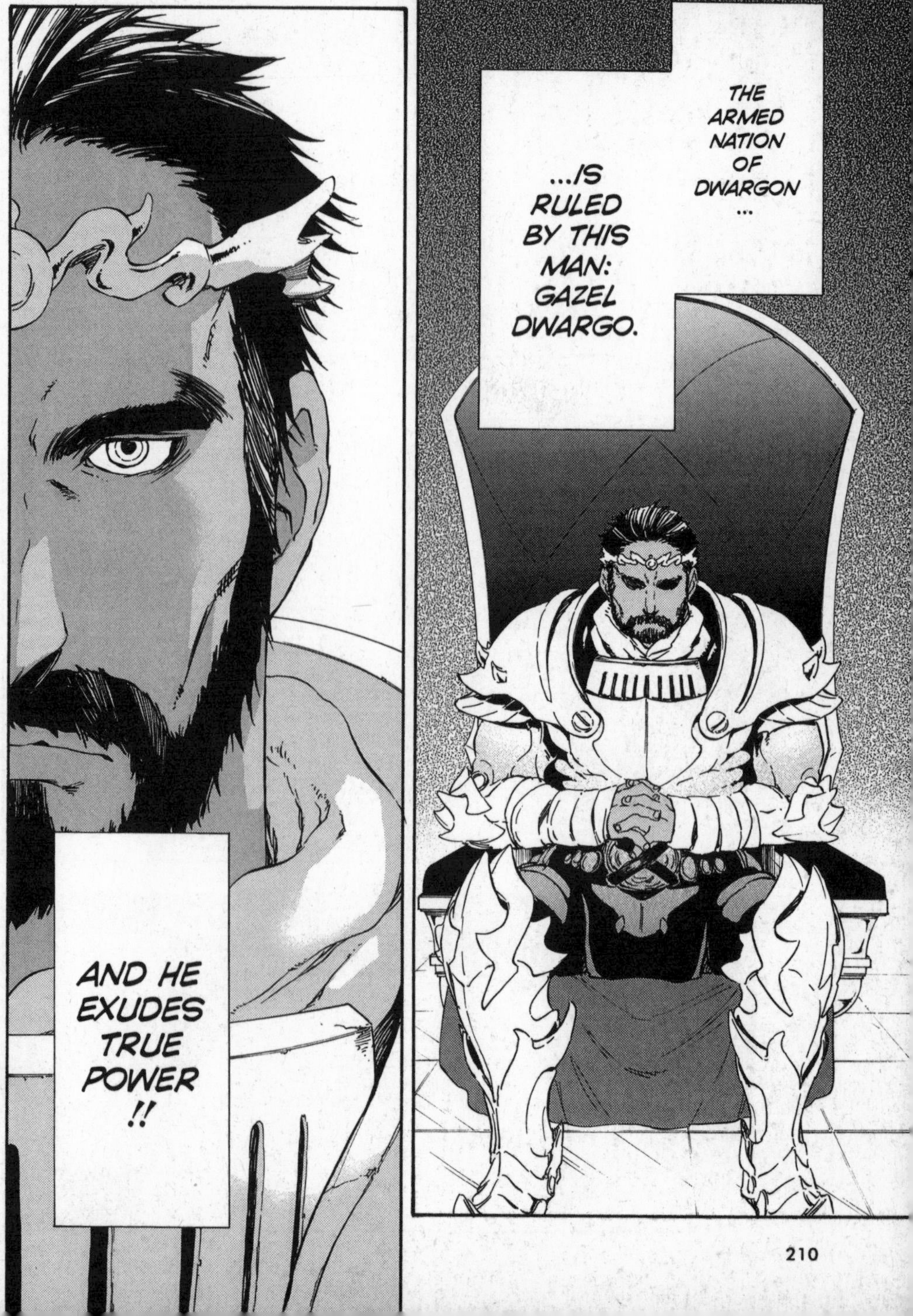
THE ARMED NATION OF DWARGON ...
...IS RULED BY THIS MAN: GAZEL DWARGO.
AND HE EXUDES TRUE POWER !!

Reincarnate
in Volume 2?

→YES

NO

Bonus
Short Story

Veldora's Slime Observation Journal
~THE FATEFUL MEETING~

Veldora's Slime Observation Journal
~THE FATEFUL MEETING~

◆DEATH AND REINCARNATION◆

Hello there. It's me, Veldora.

What? What do you mean, you don't know me?

Kwaaa ha ha hah! Your jokes are very amusing. Surely you are not ignorant of the great Storm Dragon, one of the most powerful beings in the entire world. On the other hand, I am currently nothing more than a prisoner. For eons I have been sealed away by this infernal "Unlimited Imprisonment," and am thus unable to escape. In fact, I recall a moment 300 years ago...

....

......

...

Porcelain skin. Dainty lips of deep crimson. Black-and-silver hair, tied into one tail. Not that tall, really. The petite stature and slender figure leads me to assume that the individual was female. Her eyes were hidden by a mask, but it could not hide their beauty.

A *hero*.

Her presence was so dazzling that my eyes could not help but follow her. Of course, it goes without saying that I was not charmed by this beauty. We fought one-on-one in fair contest, and I lost. It would be a lie to claim that I was not chagrined by my defeat. But strangely, I bore her no enmity. Was it because the girl was totally unafraid of me, and challenged me without any sign of emotion?

If anything, the presence of this hero has provoked within me not hatred, but an intense interest in people. How disappointing that she was indifferent to all but turning turned her blade upon me.

I wish that we could have spoken more. I fought as my spirit willed, and lived as my spirit willed. There were some who offered their opinions to me, but I did not offer them my ears in return. I had been invincible, and believed that I had the right to do as I pleased.

But then I lost. It was not my first defeat, but I cannot recall ever losing as thoroughly as I had in that moment. My arrogance in assuming that I was utterly unstoppable had been shattered, and came to a sudden, spectacular end at her hands. I was so impressed that I hoped to battle her again once I was freed from my prison.

But sadly, human lives are short. Assuming the hero was of human birth, my desire shall never come true, I fear. So as I sit in my prison, I have found a surprising, new side of myself—a self-reflective one.

....

......

...

However! 300 years is too long a time. Simply put, I am bored. Within a few more centuries, or perhaps not even that long, I would have been unable to maintain my existence, and would then reincarnate. When a dragon perishes, it always returns elsewhere. Had it happened, my identity would be lost, replaced with a different individual's...but I did not mourn this fact. On the contrary, I was looking forward to it. The unchanging boredom was so crushing that I welcomed my coming oblivion.

Such was my state until that clever little slime appeared before me.

Hurtling towards me with bursting energy, the slime brazenly slammed into me. I was stunned, to be honest. If I do say so myself, my aura is rich and powerful, with a tremendous magical density. It is for these reasons that very few can stand in my presence. Even in my imprisoned state, lower monsters are totally unable to approach me. Even a higher-level monster would find it difficult to touch a being of such pure energy as myself.

Intrigued, I decided I would speak to the creature. Perhaps it had no higher intelligence or will, or was too newly born to understand, but I was not concerned with these possibilities. All I wanted was something to stave off my boredom. But I had a feeling. A feeling that this encounter would bring something much greater. I knew that it had something in store for me. So with this unflinching, unerring premonition in hand, I decided to parlay with the slime.

"Can you hear me, little one?" I asked, directly into its mind.

To my delight, it reacted. The slime's mind was fiercely conflicted. That was enough to show that it had a will of its own. Next, I needed to converse.

"Hello? Answer me," I said, feeling excited.

Those who are as powerful as I am can learn to read the thoughts of beings in their presence, to an extent. Although limited to the surface level, it can be quite useful. As I had not spoken with another soul in a very long time, I decided to read the slime's thoughts without waiting for an answer, and...

"I'm trying to, asshole!!"

Why, I ought to crush that measly slime!!
Asshole! It dares call me an asshole?!

I was outraged. And let me tell you, it is no mean feat to anger one as patient as I. In fact, I was so taken aback that I almost felt admiration at the courage of this tiny creature to refer to a great dragon as—and I quote—an "asshole."

After this, I was able to successfully converse with the slime, and taught it the Extra Skill, "Magic Sense" as a means to make up for its lack of sight and hearing. The slime was a very quick learner, and it gained the skill for its own use in just minutes.

By my estimation, this slime was already an A-Rank monster, going by the scale often used by humans. As it had been likely birthed from the incredible magic field surrounding me, this is perhaps not such a surprise. And its quick mastery of the Magic Sense Skill is no mystery, either.

I thought that it would be overcome with gratitude when it saw me, but instead, it was terrified. The plucky little thing quickly overcame its fear, however.

That part was a little annoying, but I could overlook it. Speaking with the slime, I found it to be extraordinarily intelligent. This would be impossible for a freshly-born monster, so it must have been memory from its previous life.

Such things do happen on rare occasion, so on its own, this would not be a major shock. But I soon learned that there was more to this slime's story.

What an extraordinary twist! In fact, it was a human from another world that was reincarnated as a slime here. This was truly a re-markable combination of events. Even my Unique Skill, "Inquirer" —which allows me to consult a record of the world's events—was unable to find another example of this particular coincidence. This slime was clearly far more fascinating than I first realized. I was in-stantly intrigued.

Just then, it asked, "Ya wanna be friends with me?"

I couldn't believe my ears. A humble slime? And yet, I had never known a "friend" before this point. Plenty of enemies, however...

Not that it matters now. The slime looked like it was going to cry if I didn't agree to be friends with it. It was begging and pleading.

Naturally, with my generous and understanding nature, I granted its request. I didn't want it to start crying, of course. What a handful that little slime was.

And so, I gave the slime the name of Rimuru, and it became my closest, inseparable friend. This was the meeting of Veldora Tempest and Rimuru Tempest, and the beginning of our journey together.

◆ GUARDIAN OF THE GOBLIN VILLAGE ◆

Placing my full trust in Rimuru, I am now contained within his stomach. For the most part, he has rather ridiculous skills. To his good fortune, he was born with the Unique Skill, "Predator."

When traveling from another world to this one, one will die without the proper aptitude. Or in other words, with aptitude one gains tremendous magical energy and great strength. Most of these people use that energy to gain a power they desire—a Unique Skill. We call such individuals "Otherworlders." Like them, Rimuru gained his powers when he was reborn into this world.

I do not know what he wished for, but he clearly gained a most fortuitous skill, indeed. On the other hand, Rimuru is so lackadaisical that it seems he may not fathom what a rare power it is that he possesses. I find this situation to be quite humorous, and have thus chosen to hold my tongue. *Hah hah hah!*

But that will explain how it is that I am observing the world through Rimuru's eyes.

What do you mean, "That doesn't explain anything"?

I am a great and mighty dragon, you fool! Naturally, my Unique Skill, "Inquirer" interfaces with our shared name, gleaning the information for my sake—and other such details that I don't need to explain to you. Why would I waste my time with that, rather than just breaking my Unlimited Imprisonment?

You fool!! Boredom is a deadly affliction—it can easily kill those with no interest or joy in their lives. I am no different. Even with my invincible might, the span of 300 years was enough to drive me to despondence and resignation. But I will not make that mistake again.

I have found a fascinating figure, and we have become fast friends. Now I shall share my days with him, and enjoy this world to its fullest! My mind is made up. And thus this is not a waste of time, you buffoon. It is crucial!

Oh?! Rimuru just defeated the most powerful Tempest Serpent in the cave, has he? The beast had grown and transformed due to my mighty aura, until it was worthy of being called the guardian of this cave. The humans would classify it as A-Rank, meaning that it is quite strong...and yet, it fell in just one blow.

Rimuru is very mighty indeed, though he knows it not. Still, he is no more than a pitiful worm to me. *Kwaaaaah ha ha hah!*

And while I laugh, Rimuru continues his progress through the cave. Along the way, he preys upon monsters, stealing their skills. He shut off his Magic Sense to close his eyes as he ate, thanking his lucky stars that he does not have a sense of taste.

Actually, he is not using his Predator Skill properly. He doesn't need to literally eat the target, just touch and corrode it...but this is no matter to me. All I can do is watch, not speak, so there is no way for me to correct his behavior. And watching is certainly enjoyable enough on its own.

There he goes again. Right as he consumed a C+-Rank Giant Bat, something fascinating happened. I assumed that he would take its skills like usual, but this time, he also stole the monster's bodily functions. He found a most novel use for the hypnotic "Ultrasonic Wave" ability. Rimuru used the skill to re-create just the sound-emitting organ alone, and improved it to create a speaking voice. Truly a clever bit of insight. Surely, if he can come up with that, he could also re-create a monster's tongue and enjoy the sense of taste for his meals—but he hasn't come up with that idea yet. He's probably just forgotten about the concept, as he has no sense of hunger.
What a clever, yet forgetful little slime.

Apparently, he's done enough within the cave to satisfy his curiosity about his powers, as Rimuru has decided to leave now. Is he being cowardly, or just careful? I cannot determine the answer.

Rimuru seems to be very cautious in certain ways, and yet bold and fearless in others. Like just now. He is surrounded by pitiful little goblins, and unsure of what to do. I would have slaughtered them all by now, but Rimuru thinks differently.

After a brief conversation, he hides his own aura! There's just a bit leaking out now; only to the level of an ultra-low monster. I would have assumed that the goblins would take advantage of him...but then things took a startling turn.

❖

The goblins have sworn loyalty to him in exchange for his help. I have absolutely no idea why this is happening. I have no personal experience dealing with monsters so inferior to me. They would be unable to survive even my presence. And as a conqueror of this mortal plane, I certainly would never have considered it proper to lower myself to their standards... Yet Rimuru chose to do so without hesitation. And unlike me, he is no longer alone because of it.

Could I have been wrong? I do not regret any of my choices in life, but perhaps I could have chosen a different way for myself. Such was the sobering effect of Rimuru's actions.

◆MASTER OF THE DIREWOLVES◆

Well, Rimuru has taken on the duty of defending the village, and his first action was to heal the wounded. It seems he crafted a high-purity healing elixir from the Hipokute herbs that grew in abundance thanks to my aura. But he only just reincarnated into this world. How can he possess such acute knowledge already? Then again, he did seem to be conversing with someone else when I first met him. Perhaps it was...

Even with my Inquirer Skill, I cannot scry into the depths of Rimuru's mind. Perhaps Predator is not the only Unique Skill that he possesses. Predator is not a skill capable of performing an analysis on the Unlimited Imprisonment which holds me captive. I suppose I must assume that he holds some other, more secret ability. But wait...

When we first met, he was talking to his own skill then. And...what did he call it, again? It certainly wasn't Predator. Rimuru knew what that skill was, at the very least, but I couldn't hear it.

Was I being obstructed from hearing it? That would make sense. It is unheard of for a skill to act independently in order to sabotage another's senses. That Rimuru is a crafty one indeed to fool a dragon! Yes, I see now. I thought he was careless, but he is far more cautious than I ever dreamed. Endlessly fascinating, this Rimuru.

His bold plan for the goblins involved tearing down their worthless shanty huts and constructing a defensive fence of the sort humans build. Rimuru helped craft the fence using sticky thread he gained from a B-Rank Black Spider. With the help of steel thread, he strengthened the fence and set a trap.

It was a crafty trap, and an ingenious use of materials... When I tried to sense Rimuru's surface thoughts, it turned out the idea came from things that he called "manga" and "novels." He merely combined traps he had seen before, and "——" helped him optimize it. But what is this "——"? It seems that it sensed I was listening in, and prevented me from scrying. Just as I thought, Rimuru possesses some hidden skill I am not familiar with. I find it rather cruel of him to keep secrets from me, his closest confidant.

But setting that aside—manga and novels? These things are most curious. I also sensed the related terms "movies" and "anime." My curiosity is piqued mightily. This will require some investigation.

To that end, I spared some of my Inquirer resources that were busy trying to unlock my Unlimited Imprisonment and attempted to connect with Rimuru's surface memory. I found some resistance again, but I did my best in the service of my intellectual curiosity. To my delight, I succeeded in unlocking a portion of his surface memory. As a side effect, this made it a smoother process for Rimuru and I to share information, which suits my purposes anyway. As Rimuru would say, "I planned for that to happen."

What I found was a treasure trove of details. A wonderful mountain of information. The story was written in the language of another world, but studying and learning language is child's play to me. I treat it like solving a puzzle.

What's this? "And thus, the boy would become king"?

Simply fascinating. The protagonist enjoys the guidance of a tactician so brilliant, it is as if he can read the minds of the enemy forces. This story features a kind of sorcery, but not the vivid effects of magic spells. Therefore, there is no mass-slaughter through magic, and the main form of conflict is tactical battle. This is the ideal type of knowledge for our current situation.

Ah yes, I see. It is through knowledge from such writings that Rimuru is able to handle the wolves in the clever way he does. Based on the state of battle, I can see that the wolves fell into his trap, and are being soundly beaten by the inferior goblins.

If Rimuru himself bothered to fight, he could have easily destroyed the wolves on his own, but instead he chose to have the weaker goblins do the work—and the reason was clear. By forcing them to fight, he provides them with confidence and experience. That becomes trust in Rimuru, and binds them closer together.

So, this is all according to Rimuru's plan, is it? He seems to have some level of ability to see what magic or skills an opponent wields.

The ability to change his tactics depending on the foe makes him quite the expert tactician.

I cannot rest on my laurels. I must consume more of this information and gain greater wisdom.

Later, I was enjoying a fascinating story composed of a combination of images and text, when something unexpected occurred. I suddenly felt weak.

"What happened?" I wondered, focusing on Rimuru's senses, and found that he was speaking to the goblins and wolves, one by one.

What does he think he's...? I nearly doubted my own eyes, but the unthinkable was coming true. To my utter shock, Rimuru was foolish enough to give each and every individual a name. I screamed, "What are you doing?!" but of course, he could not hear me.

The naming of a monster is not at all like that of a human. The act is a kind of contract that binds the two parties closer than even a parent and child. This act is never undertaken without a deep trust. Unless the relationship between the two is one of shared power, such as the bond between Rimuru and I, the danger is too great to risk.

For one thing, the act of giving a name is the bestowing of one's power upon a trusted subordinate. It inevitably lowers one's own strength, so even the ultra-powerful such as I only attempt the act in extremely rare circumstances.

Now this fool Rimuru comes along and decides to use up not just his own magical energy, but my stockpile as well, merely to give the monsters names. Even my benevolence has its limits.

I hastily attempted to block his actions, but the smoothness of our information sharing made that quite difficult. Was this outcome part of his plan when he allowed me greater access to his mind?! I had thought I was getting the best of him, but ultimately I only fell into his trap. The devious slime.

Still, I will not be defeated. I did what I needed to in order to stop the outflow of magic energy. This continued until Rimuru eventually went into sleep mode.

◆ HEAD FOR THE DWARF KINGDOM ◆

When Rimuru awoke, the monsters had evolved.

That was no surprise. After all, he stole my own magical energy to name them. I suppose that it is pointless to complain at this stage, but it could mean that my freedom from Unlimited Imprisonment is delayed.

What did you say? "Stop reading manga and get back to my analysis"?

Kwaaaaa ha ha hah! Do not bother yourself with my affairs. Even if that should cause my efforts to be delayed, it makes little difference. But this train of thought does not further my own ends, thus I shall conclude it.

Back to observing Rimuru.

He claims that he will even find a way to co-exist peacefully with the humans. That is good. I have an interest in humans, and have wanted to visit one of their towns for myself. I could never do so as a dragon without inciting a battle, but through Rimuru, even I may have the chance to interact with humanity. Only once I am free of this infernal Unlimited Imprisonment, however.

It seems they had decided to rebuild the village they tore down in the first place. I read Rimuru's surface thoughts as usual, and found that he was planning to construct a home that he found pleasant and enjoyable.

This is, of course, a very self-centered line of thought, but I have no quarrel with it. One who cannot enjoy his own life cannot make others happy.

On the other hand, observing Rimuru has taught me that one must not only pursue one's own happiness, as I once did. In order for one to live happily, everyone must be happy. I never bothered with lesser beings, and it seems that was a mistake.

Now the goblins have evolved into hobgoblins, with greater intelligence and active wills. Perhaps Rimuru is correct, and they will develop culture and arts, bringing enjoyment to their lives.

The buds of possibility are to be cultivated, not plucked. Another fine lesson learned in the short time that I have been with Rimuru.

❖

It seems we are heading to the Dwarf Kingdom now. The wind is bracing from our position on the back of a racing wolf. I can fly through the air faster than sound, so I have never experienced what it means to run on the surface. I have now learned that because the ground is so close, it passes by very quickly.

The experience was more thrilling than I expected.

◆ THE DWARVEN CRAFTSMAN ◆

No sooner had we arrived at the Dwarf Kingdom than we ran into trouble. The humans are infamous for being unable to measure their foes' true strength, and some were foolish enough to interfere with us.

I have been similarly challenged by them in my time, and am well familiar with their lack of foresight. ...Then again, I suppose I cannot fault them for seeing a mere lowly slime and jumping to conclusions.

It seems the interlopers are adventurers, and no pushovers at that. Rimuru transformed into a Tempest Star Wolf hoping to scare them away, but they took his attempt as a bluff. This reveals the shallowness of their thinking.

An ordinary slime has no intelligence at all, much less the ability to transform. They ought to have been wary, yet the fools assumed no danger to themselves. I suppose that I was the only one who was undeceived by his appearance and could see through to his true nature.

Rimuru roared at the adventurers, and they received their just desserts, fleeing in terror. Some of the onlookers even voided their bodily waste, creating an embarrassing spectacle that was certain to bring them public shame.

Kwaaa ha ha ha! I bellowed—and no sooner had I started than our group was arrested. There is no end to the entertainment. Do you wish to kill me with laughter, Rimuru?

The group tried to play the fool to the authorities, but it did not work, of course. Rimuru attempted no further resistance, and they were tossed into a cell.

Naturally, being a slime, he could easily escape, but then what would become of his goblin companion? Rimuru seems unfazed by any of this, so I expect he has a plan to deal with it.

But does he really? I am not certain myself, but surely he must. He has an oddly powerful streak of luck, so as usual, some element or another will conspire to—

"Captain, big trouble! There was a huge accident in the mine!"

There, you see? While the guards panic, Rimuru busies himself with producing a healing draught for them. Clearly he intends to prove that he is no enemy to the dwarven people.

What a well-prepared slime he is! I must take notes on his ability to get by in the world.

So it came to pass that Rimuru was released from prison.

Not only that, but the captain of the guard has now promised to introduce us to a craftsman. Such good fortune that Rimuru is blessed with!

A grand view of the Dwarf Kingdom. It is my first visit, I will admit. I have viewed human settlements, but only from above. My dragon body was far too large to settle down among them for a proper visit. And the dwarves live in a natural fortress built into a massive cave within the Canaat Mountains. It is perfectly obvious why I could never fit into such a place.

To my surprise, the city was full of fascinating and entertaining sights and items. If I could use my unique Inquirer skill on these items to appraise them, I might learn how such things are meant to be used. Sadly, seeing and touching are two very different things.

Oh, how I curse my imprisoned body! Why could I not have found an interest in these things sooner? I am stunned at my own stupidity. During my reign as a Storm Dragon, I only found pleasure in conquest and terror. But as the saying goes, I was but a big frog in a small pond.

The world is vast. Experiencing the wonder of such novel sights has filled me with a powerful resolve—to gain my freedom and explore this world on my own two legs.

◆ THE FATED ONE ◆

Today, I experienced a "party" for the first time in my life. Rimuru's aid to the troubled dwarven craftsman was repaid with an invitation to celebrate.

Through some unknown means, likely another hidden skill, Rimuru managed to create copies of a mighty sword. I am unsure whether he truly means to keep his abilities a secret. Rimuru is so open about them that nobody is able to bring any accusations against him. I find myself in agreement with this tactic. When one considers that Rimuru can do anything, it all begins to make a kind of sense.

As for this "party," it is a bracing event. I have long had a curiosity about human food. Especially their spirits. I've heard of such things in stories, and always wanted the opportunity to sample them for myself. But with my enormous body, I could never have succeeded in drinking liquor, and thus the sensation is unknown to me. Now that the opportunity arises, I must certainly take it.

And now I realize that I had forgotten Rimuru possesses no sense of taste. Damn it all!

Meanwhile, Rimuru himself claims that "everything seems delicious when a beautiful woman pours your glass for you."

Easy to say when the women are fawning over you!

What good is a friend who forgets about you and only seeks his own enjoyment? So I warned him: grow yourself a tongue right this instant! A demand which never left the realm of mere thought, hurled into the void…

Envying Rimuru will earn me nothing. In a sense, he is unaware that I am watching at all, so sadly, I must abandon my hopes. But I will keep this place in mind. On the day of my revival, I shall return! Like Rimuru, I will glory in being fawned upon by these women.

I have been a fool until now. It feels much better to be revered than to be feared. I must exhibit my strength in an admirable manner, and gain the respect of all. The hobgoblins whom Rimuru named are the perfect start—he was quite clever and forward-thinking in this regard.

Rimuru is exceedingly skilled at blending among peoples. At this very moment, he has made himself the center of attention in this establishment, receiving some kind of divination.

Apparently, the figure that flashed across the crystal ball is Rimuru's "fated one." It seems to be a beautiful woman, albeit with a burn scar across her face. Something about her is vaguely reminiscent of the Hero. Perhaps they share some distant connection. But that is a discussion for another time.

What must one do to become well-liked? I wish to get along with others as Rimuru does.

This is all a waste of my time. I must read through more reference materials, and study dashing and attractive gestures and quotations.

Hmm? What's all the commotion about?

Just as I was readying myself for a good study session, some kind of scuffle arose. Is Rimuru accursed in some manner, that extraordinary events should follow him wherever he goes?

As soon as I take my attention away from him, something occurs. Of course, something occurs even when I *am* paying attention, so the cause surely does not lie with me.

In this latest bit of trouble, it seems a slender man threw water upon Rimuru, and claimed, most insultingly, "This is the best a monster deserves."

This man acts with purpose. He came to this place for the express purpose of causing trouble, and casting aspersions on Rimuru.

So what happens now?

I would turn the man into ash, of course, but how will Rimuru react? Out of curiosity, I read his surface thoughts, and found that he wishes to avoid conflict.

The man seemed to be a senior official of this nation, meaning that killing him would have significant consequences. This would not influence me in any way, of course. Why would he hesitate?

What's this? If such trouble arises, we will never be able to return to this place?! That is a dire consequence indeed!

What will happen, then? Shall we simply grin and bear it?

For the first time in ages, I am flustered. For one as mighty as I to feel such panic over so trivial a matter would have been unthinkable in the old days. No one who knows me would believe it possible. But now I am learning. When pleasures grow, sometimes patience is required in order to preserve them.

Such inconvenient and annoying rules society creates for us! But without these rules, I suppose such pleasures would be impossible. I feel as though I have learned another valuable lesson.

Just then, the dwarf who owed Rimuru his livelihood stood up. To my surprise, this dwarf named Kaijin walked over to the official and punched the hateful man.

I couldn't help but cheer. Yes, it was satisfying to watch. But more importantly, Kaijin struck that blow for my good friend Rimuru.

Surely, this is an act worthy of celebration. I've come to understand that it is more infuriating for one's friend to be insulted than to be the object of derision yourself. Life has become one surprise after another since I came to know Rimuru. I am satisfied that the choice I made on that day was the correct one.

Alas, it seems that Kaijin's actions did indeed cause trouble. Rimuru's group was once again arrested and locked in chains. This time, the stakes are more dire.

The dwarven king—Gazel Dwargo.

I can sense that Rimuru feels danger. But of course he does. This is no ordinary man he faces. Even Rimuru cannot get the better of him.

I must admit that I am eager to see how my slime friend reacts now.

To be reincarnated in Volume 2!

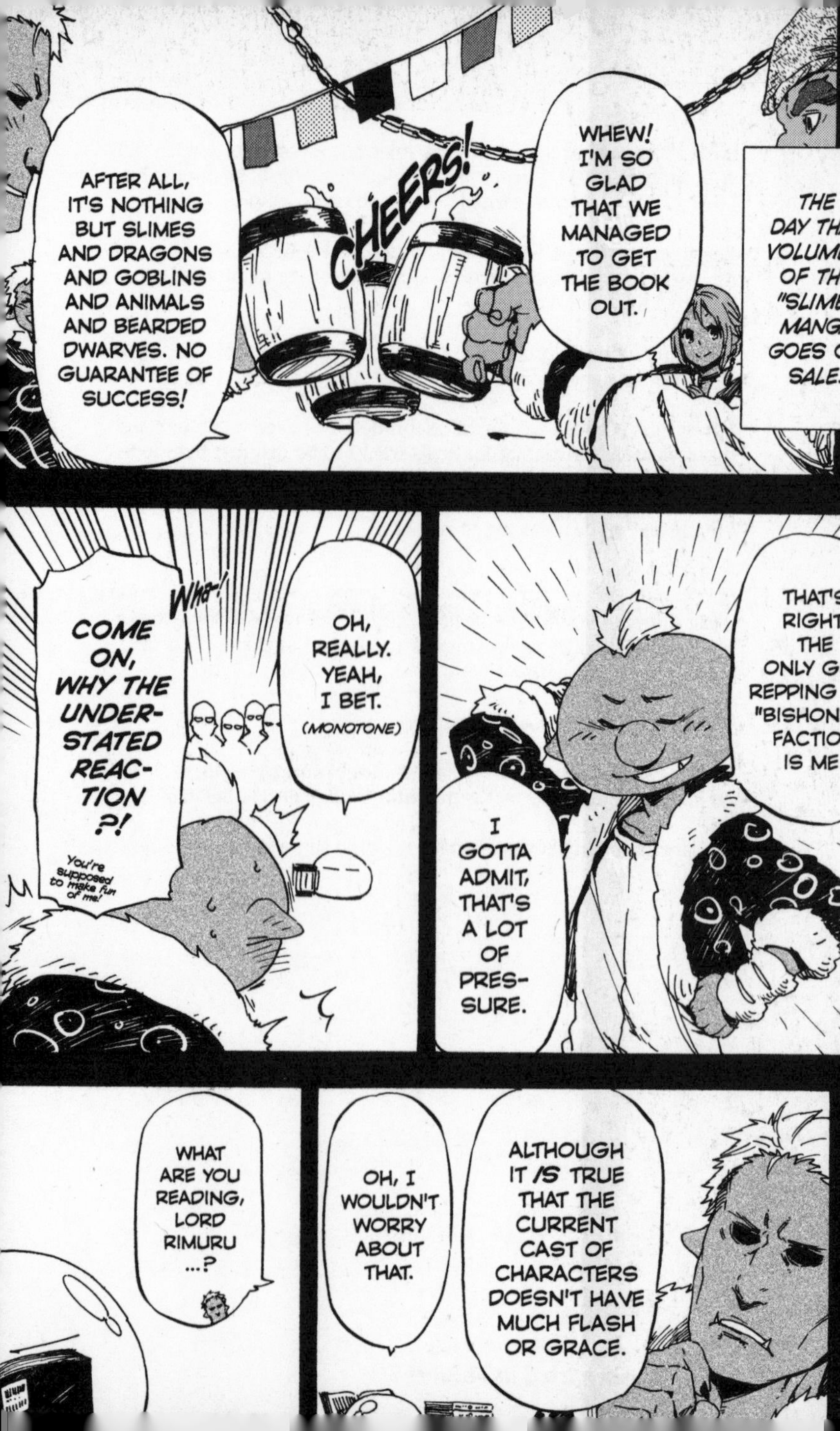
THE DAY THAT VOLUME 1 OF THE "SLIME" MANGA GOES ON SALE.
WHEW! I'M SO GLAD THAT WE MANAGED TO GET THE BOOK OUT.
CHEERS!
AFTER ALL, IT'S NOTHING BUT SLIMES AND DRAGONS AND GOBLINS AND ANIMALS AND BEARDED DWARVES. NO GUARANTEE OF SUCCESS!
THAT'S RIGHT. THE ONLY GUY REPPING THE "BISHONEN" FACTION IS ME.
I GOTTA ADMIT, THAT'S A LOT OF PRES-SURE.
OH, REALLY. YEAH, I BET. (MONOTONE)
Wha-!
COME ON, WHY THE UNDER-STATED REAC-TION ?!
You're supposed to make fun of me!
ALTHOUGH IT IS TRUE THAT THE CURRENT CAST OF CHARACTERS DOESN'T HAVE MUCH FLASH OR GRACE.
OH, I WOULDN'T WORRY ABOUT THAT.
WHAT ARE YOU READING, LORD RIMURU ...?

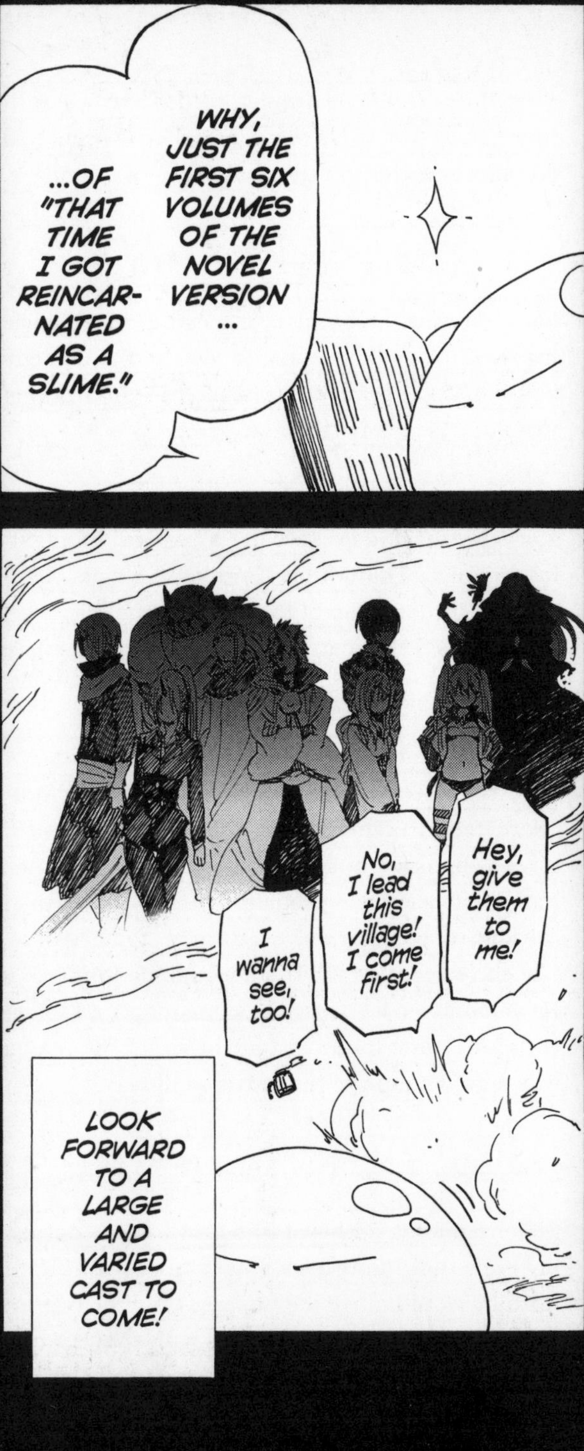
WHY, JUST THE FIRST SIX VOLUMES OF THE NOVEL VERSION ...
...OF "THAT TIME I GOT REINCARNATED AS A SLIME."
Hey, give them to me!
No, I lead this village! I come first!
I wanna see, too!
LOOK FORWARD TO A LARGE AND VARIED CAST TO COME!

LIST OF ACKNOWLEDGMENTS

AUTHOR:
Fuse-sensei

ASSISTANTS:
Taku Arao-san
Akoron-san
Takuya Nishida-san
Muraichi-san
Hino-san
Daiki Haraguchi-san
Shigemi Kudo-san
Akiko Takahashi-san

Everyone at the editorial department

And You!!

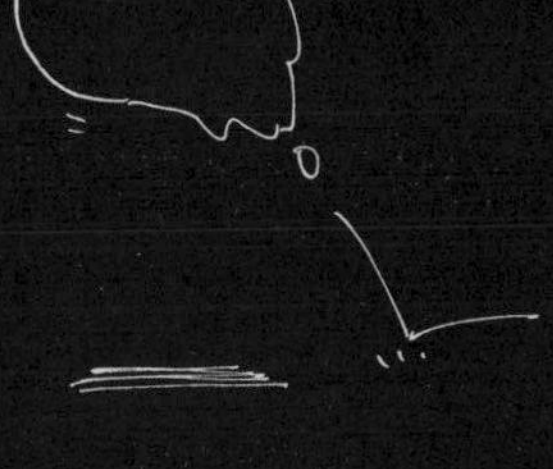

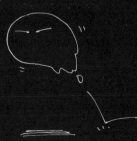

AFTERWORD

from the author, Fuse

That Time I Got Reincarnated as a Slime began its life as a novel on the Internet, and now it's actually got its own manga adaptation! So I thought I'd reflect on some of the challenges of turning it into a visual format...

◇◇◇

Late last year, I had my first meeting with Kawakami-sensei. At this meeting we did our planning, and also had to do signings for a giveaway, which was a difficult set of circumstances—not that I'm complaining.We settled on two main issues for the manga.

The first problem was the protagonist's sense of vision at the start of the story. Not having eyes wasn't a big deal in a text novel, but it's a major issue for a manga. Thankfully, Kawakami-sensei cleared that hurdle with flying colors! His depiction of the senses unfolding worked wonders. It's the exact sort of touch that can only be done in the manga format, and never in a novel.

The other problem was that the start of the story features very few characters. Yes, there are monsters, of course, but you just don't see any human characters. In other words, there's no female lead! It's quite possible not to have a "heroine" in the traditional sense, but not having any female characters whatsoever is a problem. There's no beauty in the manga. All we have are slimes, goblins, wolves, dwarves... I began to worry: is this story actually extremely unsuited to a visual medium?! Thankfully, the cute way that Kawakami-sensei drew our slime managed to assuage my fears a bit. I'm certain it won't take any time at all for the readers to forget that our hero was a grown man in his previous life...

◇◇◇

So for a manga for boys, this first volume hardly had any cute girls. It's my hope that Rimuru's slimy cuteness got us through that difficulty. Nothing would make me happier than for you to continue following along with Rimuru's adventures. And with that, my afterword is finished. Please check out the next volume of *That Time I Got Reincarnated as a Slime!!*

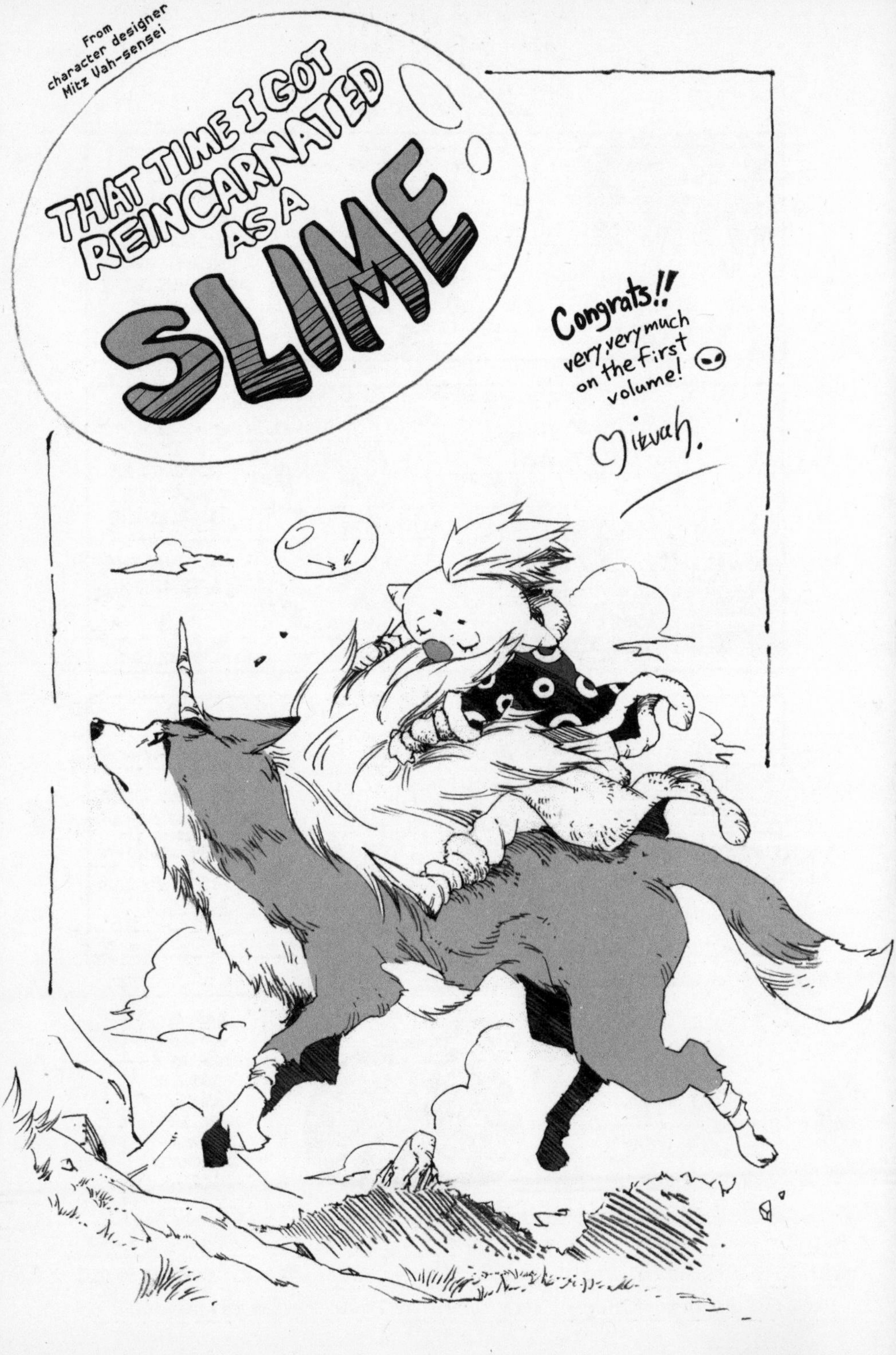
From
character designer
Mitz Vah-sensei
THAT TIME I GOT REINCARNATED AS A SLIME
Congrats!!
very, very much
on the first
volume!
Mitzvah.

Typical Conversation

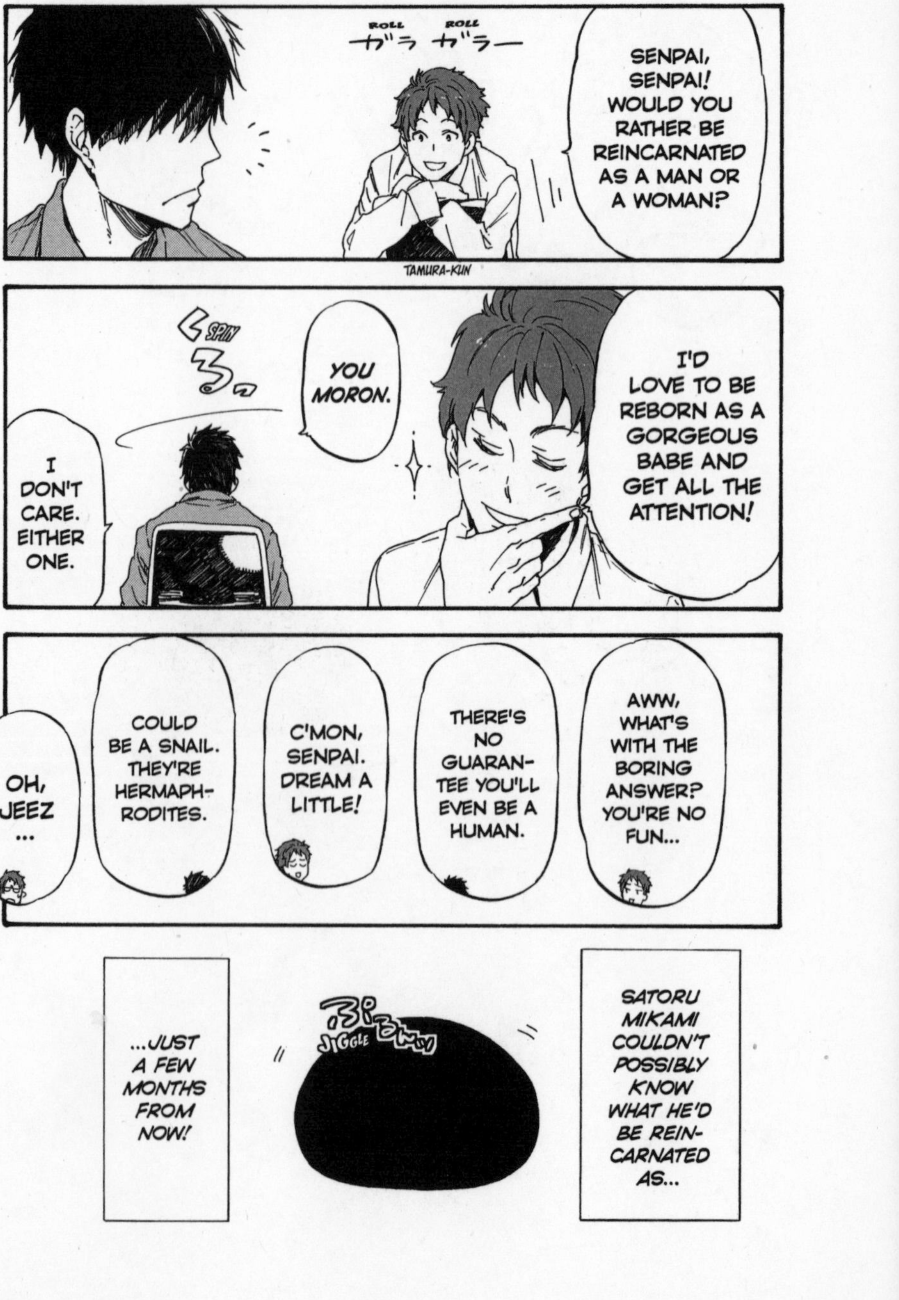
SENPAI, SENPAI! WOULD YOU RATHER BE REINCARNATED AS A MAN OR A WOMAN?
ROLL ROLL
ガラ ガラー
TAMURA-KUN
I'D LOVE TO BE REBORN AS A GORGEOUS BABE AND GET ALL THE ATTENTION!
YOU MORON.
SPIN
I DON'T CARE. EITHER ONE.
AWW, WHAT'S WITH THE BORING ANSWER? YOU'RE NO FUN...
THERE'S NO GUARANTEE YOU'LL EVEN BE A HUMAN.
C'MON, SENPAI. DREAM A LITTLE!
COULD BE A SNAIL. THEY'RE HERMAPHRODITES.
OH, JEEZ...
SATORU MIKAMI COULDN'T POSSIBLY KNOW WHAT HE'D BE REINCARNATED AS...
JIGGLE
...JUST A FEW MONTHS FROM NOW!

Hiding among the
sweet mochi

TRANSLATION NOTES

I sense an aura!
BING!
You do ?!
FLINCH
RECENT PROBLEM:
Nobody in this world gets references from my old world.

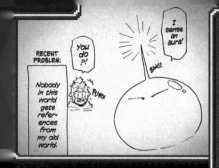

Rimuru is referring to the famous character Kitaro (of *GeGeGe no Kitaro* fame) developed by Shigeru Mizuki. Kitaro is a boy with both human and *yokai* heritage—*yokai* being the catch-all term for traditional folklore creatures of Japan. In his adventures to create peace between humans and *yokai*, Kitaro utilizes a number of special abilities, one of which is a "*yokai* sense" in which his hair acts as an antenna that picks up supernatural signals. When he senses *yokai*, Kitaro claims that he feels *yoki*, which could be translated as "*yokai* presence" or "otherworldly spirit." In this story, the term "aura" is written with the kanji characters for *yoki*, allowing Rimuru to make this Kitaro joke.

GOBLIN NAMES

page 116

Gobtsu.
Gobte.

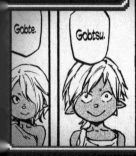

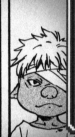

It's not just that these names all sound similar—it's that Rimuru is literally taking "gob" (from goblin) and running through the letters of the Japanese alphabet one after the other. Japanese characters (known as *kana*) are grouped together so that a consonant sound is then followed by a vowel, with each "row" having five kana for the five vowels. So the *ta* (or "t") row goes, in order: *ta, chi, tsu, te, to*. The other consonants (as we would call them) in the Japanese language follow a similar pattern: *ka, ki, ku, ke, ko; sa, shi, su, se, so*, etc.

"AND THUS, THE BOY WOULD BECOME KING"

page 220

would say, "I planned for that to happen."

What I found was a treasure trove of details. A wonderful of information. The story was written in the language world, but studying and learning language is child's pla treat it like solving a puzzle.

What's this? "And thus, the boy would become king"?

Simply fascinating. The protagonist enjoys the guidance cian so brilliant, it is as if he can read the minds of the e es. This story features a kind of sorcery, but not the vivid magic spells. Therefore, there is no mass-slaughter throu and the main form of conflict is tactical battle. This is the of knowledge for our current situation.

This and part of the text that follows in Veldora's musings are references to the *Heroic Legend of Arslan*, a series of novels by Yoshiki Tanaka that has also been adapted into manga and anime. The most current rendition of the series in manga form is currently being published by Kodansha and is illustrated by Hiromu Arakawa of *Fullmetal Alchemist* fame. The series follows the adventures of young prince Arslan of Pars, whose world is shattered when his country is defeated by a rival kingdom. He sets out on a journey to gather forces to reclaim his land, and along the way, picks up a crew of talented characters, including the brilliant tactician, Narsus. *The Heroic Legend of Arslan* is set in a fantasy world that appears to be inspired by the medieval Middle East. As Veldora points out, magic exists in Arslan's world, but it is limited, and not as powerful as it would be in an RPG-based world like that of *That Time I Got Reincarnated as a Slime*.

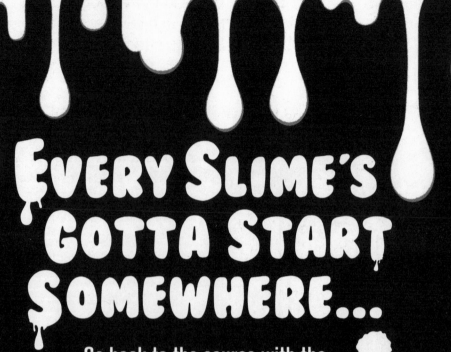

The award-winning manga about what happens inside you!

"Far more entertaining than it ought to be... what kid doesn't want to think that every time they sneeze a torpedo shoots out their nose?"
—Anime News Network

Strep throat! Hay fever! Influenza! The world is a dangerous place for a red blood cell just trying to get her deliveries finished. Fortunately, she's not alone…she's got a whole human body's worth of cells ready to help out! The mysterious white blood cells, the buff and brash killer T cells, even the cute little platelets— everyone's got to come together if they want to keep you healthy!

Cells at Work!

はたらく細胞

By Akane Shimizu

KC
KODANSHA
COMICS

A new series from the creator of *Soul Eater*, the megahit manga and anime seen on Toonami!

"Fun and lively... a great start!"
-Adventures in Poor Taste

FIRE FORCE

By Atsushi Ohkubo

The city of Tokyo is plagued by a deadly phenomenon: spontaneous human combustion! Luckily, a special team is there to quench the inferno: The Fire Force! The fire soldiers at Special Fire Cathedral 8 are about to get a unique addition. Enter Shinra, a boy who possesses the power to run at the speed of a rocket, leaving behind the famous "devil's footprints" (and destroying his shoes in the process). Can Shinra and his colleagues discover the source of this strange epidemic before the city burns to ashes?

Japan's most powerful spirit medium delves into the ghost world's greatest mysteries!

Story by Kyo Shirodaira, famed author of mystery fiction and creator of *Spiral*, *Blast of Tempest*, and *The Record of a Fallen Vampire*.

Both touched by spirits called yôkai, Kotoko and Kurô have gained unique superhuman powers. But to gain her powers Kotoko has given up an eye and a leg, and Kurô's personal life is in shambles. So when Kotoko suggests they team up to deal with renegades from the spirit world, Kurô doesn't have many other choices, but Kotoko might just have a few ulterior motives...

IN/SPECTRE

STORY BY **KYO SHIRODAIRA**
ART BY **CHASHIBA KATASE**

HAPPINESS

—ハピネス—

By Shuzo Oshimi

From the creator of *The Flowers of Evil*

Nothing interesting is happening in Makoto Ozaki's first year of high school. His life is a series of quiet humiliations: low-grade bullies, unreliable friends, and the constant frustration of his adolescent lust. But one night, a pale, thin girl knocks him to the ground in an alley and offers him a choice. Now everything is different. Daylight is searingly bright. Food tastes awful. And worse than anything is the terrible, consuming thirst...

Praise for Shuzo Oshimi's *The Flowers of Evil*

"A shockingly readable story that vividly—one might even say queasily—evokes the fear and confusion of discovering one's own sexuality. Recommended." —The Manga Critic

"A page-turning tale of sordid middle school blackmail." —Otaku USA Magazine

"A stunning new horror manga." —Third Eye Comics

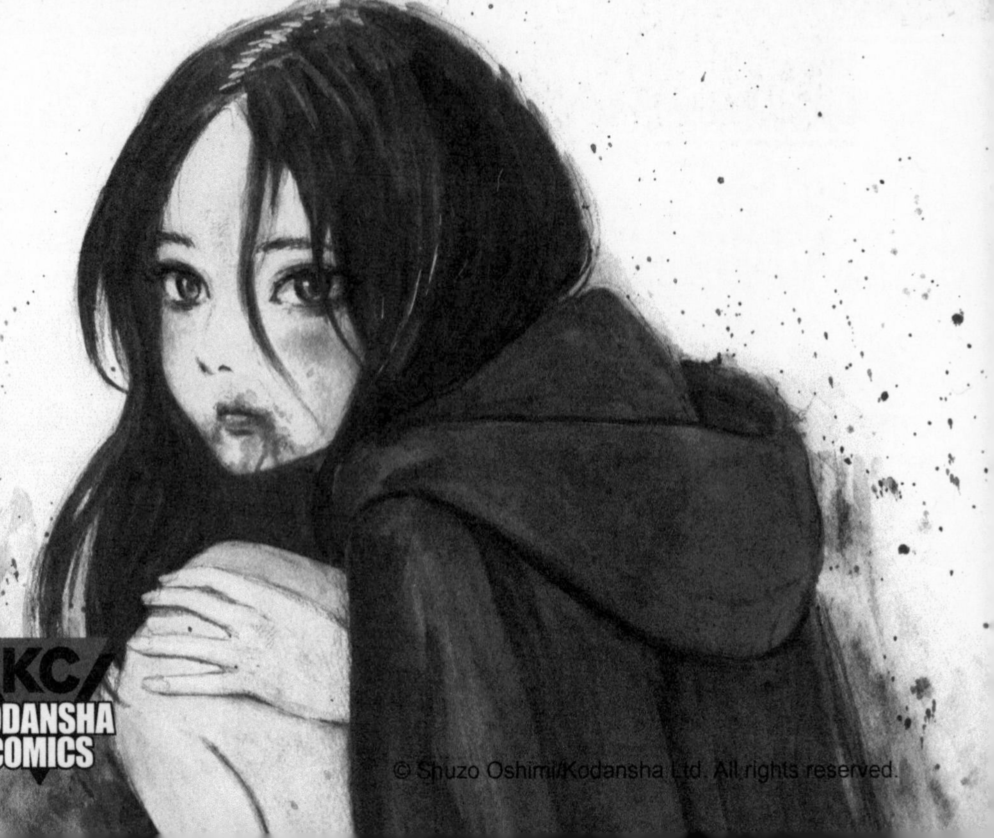

KC
KODANSHA
COMICS

The Black Museum The Ghost and the Lady

By Kazuhiro Fujita

Deep in Scotland Yard in London sits an evidence room dedicated to the greatest mysteries of British history. In this "Black Museum" sits a misshapen hunk of lead—two bullets fused together—the key to a wartime encounter between Florence Nightingale, the mother of modern nursing, and a supernatural Man in Grey. This story is unknown to most scholars of history, but a special guest of the museum will tell the tale of The Ghost and the Lady...

Praise for Kazuhiro Fujita's *Ushio and Tora*

"A charming revival that combines a classic look with modern depth and pacing... **Essential viewing both for curmudgeons and new fans alike.**" — Anime News Network

"**GREAT!** The first episode of Ushio and Tora captures the essence of '90s anime." — IGN

KODANSHA COMICS

New action series from Hiroyuki Takei, creator of the classic shonen franchise Shaman King!

In medieval Japan, a bell hanging on the collar is a sign that a cat has a master. Norachiyo's bell hangs from his katana sheath, but he is nonetheless a stray — a ronin. This one-eyed cat samurai travels across a dishonest world, cutting through pretense and deception with his blade.

NEKOGAHARA

STRAY CAT SAMURAI

By
Hiroyuki Takei

Based on the critically acclaimed classic horror manga

The first new *Parasyte* manga in over 20 years!

NEO Parasyte f

BY ASUMIKO NAKAMURA, EMA TOYAMA, MIKI RINNO, LALAKO KOJIMA, KAORI YUKI, BANKO KUZE, YUUKI OBATA, KASHIO, YUI KUROE, ASIA WATANABE, MIKIMAKI, HIKARU SURUGA, HAJIME SHINJO, RENJURO KINDAICHI, AND YURI NARUSHIMA

A collection of chilling new *Parasyte* stories from Japan's top shojo artists!

Parasites: shape-shifting aliens whose only purpose is to assimilate with and consume the human race... but do these monsters have a different side? A parasite becomes a prince to save his romance-obsessed female host from a dangerous stalker. Another hosts a cooking show, in which the real monsters are revealed. These and 13 more stories, from some of the greatest shojo manga artists alive today, together make up a chilling, funny, and entertaining tribute to one of manga's horror classics!

Having lost his wife, high school teacher Kōhei Inuzuka is doing his best to raise his young daughter Tsumugi as a single father. He's pretty bad at cooking and doesn't have a huge appetite to begin with, but chance brings his little family together with one of his students, the lonely Kotori. The three of them are anything but comfortable in the kitchen, but the healing power of home cooking might just work on their grieving hearts.

"This season's number-one feel-good anime!" —Anime News Network

"A beautifully-drawn story about comfort food and family and grief. Recommended." —Otaku USA Magazine

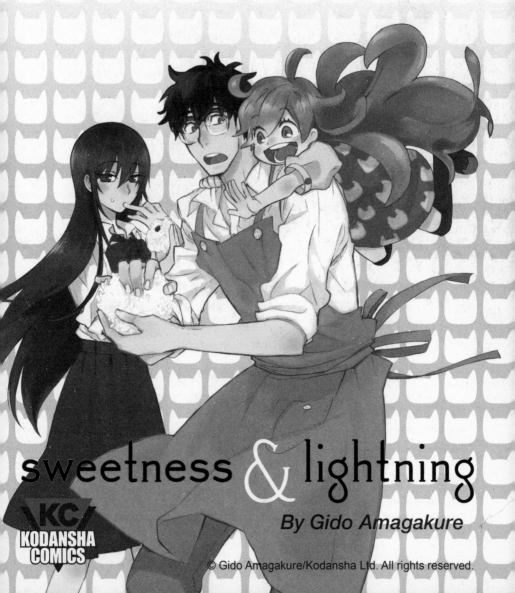

sweetness & lightning

By Gido Amagakure

KC
KODANSHA
COMICS